Long Distance Information

CHUCK BERRY'S RECORDED LEGACY

Fred Rothwell

MUSIC MENTOR BOOKS

York, England

British Library Cataloguing-in-Publication Data
A catalogue record for this book is available from the British Library.

ISBN 0 9519888 2 4

Published worldwide by Music Mentor Books *(Proprietor: G.R. Groom-White)*
69 Station Road, Upper Poppleton, York YO26 6PZ, North Yorkshire, England.
Telephone/Fax: +44 (0)1904 330308   *email:* musicmentor@bun.com

Technical support by PJP Information Systems, Bradford, West Yorkshire.

Cover by Raven Design, Ware, Hertfordshire.

Printed and bound in Great Britain by Antony Rowe Ltd, Chippenham, Wiltshire.

Contents

Acknowledgments

Writing a book such as *Long Distance Information*, which contains much armchair research, requires the assistance of many people and my thanks go to the following folks who very kindly provided information during the preparation of this book. Please forgive me if I have inadvertently missed anyone out: Gorgen Antonsson, Steve Armitage, Robert Baldori, Alan Balfour, Keith Briggs, Tony Burke, Steve Cairns, Trevor Cajiao, Robert Campbell, Marshall Chess, Nadine Cohodas, John Collier, Tony Collins, Norman Darwen, Scott Dirks, Maurice Dunn, Christoph Ebner, Simon Evans, Les Fancourt, Steve Fjeldsted, Byron Foulger, John Garodkin, Mike Gott, Fred Goulding, Bill Greensmith, Ray Harris, Johan Hasselberg, Tommy Holmström, Cilla Huggins, Ian Jones, Paula Kirby, Malte Koch, John Koenig, Adam Komorowski, Spencer Leigh, Dave Luxton, Michael Lydon, Tony Martin, Hugh McCallum, Seamus McGarvey, Andy McKaie, Jim Marsala, Bill Millar, George Moonoogian, Christian Nauwelaers, Bob Naylor, Crissi Newton, Pete Nickols, Pete O'Gorman, Victor Pearlin, Bill Pearson, Dave Penny, Bruce Pegg, Brian Plancke, Doug Price, Stefan Pingel, Robert Pruter, Jean-Pierre Ravelli, the late Bill Rowe, Dietmar Rudolph, Wayne Russell, Howard Rye, Steve Sher, Dick Shurman, Brian Smith, Chris Smith, Neil Slaven, Mike Stroot, Richard Tapp, Keith Tillman, Sandra B. Tooze, Billy Vera, Malcolm Vidrine, Tony Watson, Mike Wheeler, Phil Wight, Tony Wilkinson, Val Wilmer, Dave Williams and Tom Zimoski.

I would also like to thank the staff of the British Library Humanities Section and the British Film Institute for their assistance.

In particular, my thanks go out to Bill Millar for the loan of his extensive Chuck Berry files; to John Beecher, Trevor Cajiao, John Garodkin, Bill Millar and Showtime Archives (Toronto) for the loan of photographs from their collections, to Brian Smith and Paul Harris for use of their photographs; and to Steve Armitage, Dietmar Rudolph and Keith Tillman for many of the record label and cover shots which grace the pages of this book.

Special thanks go to my friend and publisher, George White, whose encouragement and attention to detail have improved the work no end.

Extra special thanks go to my good friend Morten Reff, without whom this work would not be half so detailed.

Last but not least, a big thank you to my wife Catherine — the queen of the apostrophe — for checking the grammar, spelling and punctuation and for her forbearance during the book's gestation.

Comments, corrections and brickbats to:

Fred Rothwell
4 Lower Farm Gate
Upton
AYLESBURY, Bucks
HP17 8UA

email: Fred@tesco.net

Introduction

I have seen Chuck Berry perform on numerous occasions but I have only met him face-to-face once. This memorable meeting (memorable to *me*, that is) was in March 1987 at a time when his profile was riding high following the publication of his autobiography and the release of his biographical film *Hail! Hail! Rock'n'Roll*.

Chuck was appearing at the Hammersmith Odeon, west London, and, as was my usual practice, I arrived in the early evening to pick up a ticket for the gig only to be faced with a large *'Sold Out'* sign on the illuminated board above the entrance. It was rumoured that Keith Richards was to guest with his hero, and this, together with Chuck's elevated profile, had brought the punters flocking. Rather dejected, I left the theatre and was retracing my steps back to the car park when, in the corner of my eye I spotted a long cherry red Mercedes hidden in the shadows of the flyover. The limo had dark glass but the side window was down and through it the familiar face of Chuck Berry could be seen busy videoing the façade, no doubt very pleased with the *'Sold Out'* sign.

Berry's legend abounds with tales of fans' approaches to the man being thwarted. After all, here was the dude who kicked Dr. John *and* Keith Richards off stage, who had slugged Richards and got away with it, who had snubbed the Stones, and who had held promoters to ransom in front of a baying crowd and humiliated them on stage for not providing the correctly specified equipment as per contract.

Dilemma No. 1: Should I approach my hero and risk the same treatment, or should it be a case of "I got my chance, I oughta take it"? With more than a little trepidation I approached the driver's side of the car, the grin on my face reflected in the blank darkened glass (Chuck was driving, naturally, and filming via the passenger side window).

Dilemma No. 2: What to do. Should I tap on the glass and disturb his concentration? Fortunately, the glass slid noiselessly down to reveal a smiling Mr. Berry. "How come you are in the right place at the right time?" he asked. I explained my lack of admission and muttered some banal and totally inadequate words of appreciation for the enjoyment his music had provided through the years, but all too soon the audience was over.

I turned to walk away, then realised I hadn't shaken my main man's hand. Without a second's thought to cause me to falter, I thrust my hand into the car's dark interior and wished him well. My hand was enveloped in a huge grip, by the hand that had written the lyrics of *Roll Over Beethoven,* by the fingers that had fashioned those immortal introductory notes to *Johnny B. Goode.* I drove the forty miles home with a smile on my face. I had met my hero, spoken with him and shaken his hand. Somehow missing the show didn't seem so bad anymore.

I recall this meeting here because it was at this moment that the germ of an idea to celebrate Chuck Berry's music was set, finally culminating in this publication.

Chuck Berry has been variously described as the 'Sheikh of Chicago', the 'Saint of St. Louis', the 'Poet Laureate of Rock' and the 'Shakespeare of Roll'. It has been said that, had he been white, he would have rivalled Elvis for his crown — but, had he been white, he wouldn't have been the same Berry.

By his own admission, he wasn't the greatest of vocalists; his nomination goes to Nat 'King' Cole. He possessed neither the pipes of Little Richard nor the soul of Sam Cooke, but he sang his songs clearly and with expression. He wouldn't even admit to a Chuck Berry guitar style, claiming modestly that his was a mixture of T-Bone Walker, Carl Hogan and Charlie Christian (to which should be added a dollop of Elmore James and a smattering of Muddy Waters).

His dynamic stage performance echoes the antics of an earlier generation of blues performers such as T-Bone (judging from the photographs) and Guitar Slim (judging from eye-witness reports) and was the equal of the wildest of rockers — Elvis, Jerry Lee Lewis, Jackie Wilson *et al*. The fun and *joie de vivre* exuded in a good Berry performance (take Coventry, 1972, for instance) recall the distant reverberations of his greatest hero, Louis Jordan.

Chuck's compositions and lyrics, firmly based in a tradition of swing, ballads and blues are second to none, the equal of the best efforts of the contemporary storytellers, Leiber & Stoller. Make no mistake about it, Chuck Berry — the singer, the guitarist, the performer, the composer — is a world-class artist.

Perhaps even more significant than all this is the influence Berry's music has had on the multitudes who followed his lead. Play rock music, play Chuck Berry. He represents a vital link between the past and the present. Even now, almost half a century later, his songs are constantly being recorded. Chuck is the conduit into which forties' jazz, swing, hillbilly and blues flowed to be processed by the Berry catalytic conversion and emerge as pure-bred rock and roll to inspire generations of musicians. He is the umbilical cord that links Nat 'King' Cole to the Rolling Stones, Big Joe Turner to the Dave Clark Five (now *there's* one to ponder!).

This publication concentrates on the recorded music of Chuck Berry on vinyl and CD and will hopefully be an antidote to the potted biographies that always seem to concentrate on Chuck Berry the jailbird, rather than Chuck Berry the musician. Of course, a lot has also been written about his music, but this is the first comprehensive overview of his entire recorded works. Each and every issued recording and some unissued masters have been listed with as much information as it has been possible to collate regarding the who, where and when of their creation. Careful listening to all the issued (and some unissued) songs has revealed interesting insights into the instrumentation and recording techniques.

This information is listed in the usual discographical format, divided into chronological sessions. Following each session is some narrative to put flesh on the factual bones and highlight the good, the bad and the indifferent.

More information follows the Sessionography: Chuck's singles, EPs and principal LPs, with all tracks cross-referenced to the sessions at which they were recorded. Compact discs are more comprehensively listed, but with weekly worldwide regurgitation of his back catalogue on all manner of cheapo labels, only the more noteworthy issues have been included.

Chuck wasn't the most prolific rocker when it came to chart entries — Elvis and Fats beat him by a mile. Nevertheless, he didn't fare too badly and was in fact Chess Records' biggest money-spinning artist, as is demonstrated by the section on the US and UK charts.

To show Chuck Berry's musical antecedents, details of influential songs referred to in the sessions are listed together with their current availability on CD.

Berry's celluloid performances contributed significantly to his early popularity and a survey of his film and video appearances, plus movies that have featured his music, is also included.

Finally, to demonstrate the tremendous influence his music has had on the world of popular music, an overview of cover versions is included (for a detailed survey of covers you must await the publication currently being compiled my good friend and fellow Berry fanatic, Morten Reff).

So, I hope you enjoy the book and that it tempts you, if nothing else, to dig out your Berry records and spin them again with a fresh insight into their creation and origins. If the prose gets up your nose, maybe you can relax with the facts. Before the music, to set the scene as it were, here is my version of the Chuck Berry story. I know it has been told a thousand times already, so a thousand and one won't hurt, will it?

1

Trials and Tribulations
The Chuck Berry Story

Chuck Berry was born 18th October 1926 at 2520 Goode Avenue, St. Louis (not in 1932, nor in San Jose, California as recorded in many biographies — this was a bit of misinformation spread by Chuck in an early press release which was, and still is, perpetuated). Goode Avenue has since been renamed Annie Malone Drive.

He was christened Charles Edward Anderson (the 'Anderson' being after Dr. Anderson Cheatem who delivered Martha and Henry Berry's fourth child) at the Antioch Baptist Church, where his parents had married and where his father was a deacon. Martha was a school teacher and Henry a contracting carpenter, and Chuck was brought up together with his three sisters, Lucy, Thelma and Martha, and brothers Henry Jr. (known as 'Hank') and Paul, with aspiring middle class values in 'The Ville', a respectable black neighbourhood just north of downtown St. Louis.

Chuck was educated at Cottage Avenue School, Simmons Grade School and finally Sumner High School. During his early teens, he developed a lifelong passion for photography which has latterly led to some rather nefarious uses. His musical interests were also beginning to rise: first it was gospel singing in the Antioch Church choir; then it was country and western music on the radio; then blues and boogie platters played on the sandwich shop jukebox across from Simmons (school days that were a clear influence on *School Day*). Chuck and his older brother Hank also joined the Jubilee Ensembles spiritual singing group and performed at various churches around St. Louis.

An undoubted influence on his musical development came from his grade school teacher, Miss Julia Davis, who provided much encouragement to his burgeoning talent. Even more significant was his appearance, aged just fourteen, at Sumner High's *'All Men's Review'* at which he sang the decidedly adult *Confessin' The Blues* accompanied on guitar by fellow student Tommy Stevens. Tommy's forceful playing was the catalyst to Chuck's determination to play guitar (thank you Tommy Stevens!) and he began laboriously to bang out the chords of *Going Down Slow* and *Worried Life Blues* on a beat-up old guitar borrowed from a friend, quickly realising that the blues stems from a common root. He also picked up tips from Nick Mannaloft's *Guitar Book Of Chords*, but his earliest guitar mentor was friend Ira Harris who provided important guidance to the chords of standards such as *Stardust* and *Heart And Soul*.

No doubt to the deep dismay of his family, aged just seventeen and before he had even graduated from high school, Chuck became unstuck. He and two buddies took a trip to Kansas City in an elderly Oldsmobile jalopy in which they had some "motor trouble that turned into a struggle". Stranded

252 miles from home, they took to a life of crime, robbing first a bakery (take=$62), then a barbershop ($32), then a clothes store ($51). Finally, on the way home, they hijacked and stole a car and were collared by the State Troopers. For his part in these crimes and misdemeanours, Berry took a ten-year fall in the Algoa Intermediate Reformatory for Young Men at Jefferson, Missouri. He was paroled three years later, but had spent his remaining teenage years in the can. Whilst inside, as well as trying his hand at a little pugilism, he continued his musical activities by singing in a gospel group.

On 18th October 1947 — his 21st birthday — Chuck regained his freedom. He returned to the family home at 4319 Labadie Avenue and became resigned to a steady routine of construction work, working with his dad and older brother Hank. He began dating Themetta Suggs, their romance blossomed and on 28th October 1948 they married. Chuck settled for a life of domesticity, setting up home in a bedsitter owned by his uncle (the same one who wrote the message on the wall?), working day jobs at the Fisher body plant and simultaneously as a janitor at the local radio station, WEW. Here he met Joe Sherman, a well-known St. Louis guitarist, from whom he bought his first electric guitar. He took to it like a duck to duckwalking and began to gig around at every opportunity. Around this time he also acquired a reel-to-reel magnetic wire recorder and commenced to concoct, construct and compose the little ditties that would one day lead him to fame and fortune.

In June 1952, he teamed up again with Tommy Stevens at Huff's Garden in East St. Louis for his first professional gig. By Christmas, the three-piece had built up such a reputation that, on New Year's Eve, pianoman Johnnie Johnson invited Chuck to gig big time with his Sir John's Combo at the Cosmopolitan Club on the corner of 17th and Bond Streets, East St. Louis.

It was with Johnnie at the Cosmo that Chuck's style — a potent mix of blues, boogie, hillbilly, swing and novelty numbers — was developed and he soon got noticed: "Who is that black hillbilly at the Cosmo?" went the cry. It wasn't too long before he took over as the leader of the group, signing a contract with the club's owner, Joe Lewis, as the 'Chuck Berryn *[sic]* Combo'. This engagement did not, however, stop our man playing other spots around St. Louis and East St. Louis with Tommy Stevens, such as the (appropriately-named) Moonlight Bar and the Crank Club, and in August 1954 he cut his first record as a member of a Latin-influenced outfit called the Cubans.

Berry had been to Chicago before with his friend Ralph Burris, but the trip they took in May 1955 would have momentous significance. It was on this visit that Chuck, eager to make a record of his own, met his hero, Muddy Waters, and asked where he should try. Muddy advised: "See Leonard Chess on 47th and Cottage."

Contrary to popular lore, that was it. There was no recommendation to Chess (Waters hadn't heard Chuck play), no introduction, and definitely no jam session. Chuck was in awe of the Chicago blues giant: in his eyes, Waters was the Don, the Godfather of the South Side, and you just didn't mess with the man.

Although he had only gone up for the weekend, Berry stayed on until Monday to meet Len Chess, who asked him if he had a demo tape. He didn't but said he did, and returned the following weekend to drop off four little tracks including an embryonic *Maybellene*, initially titled *Ida May*.

He then returned home to his family life, his manual labour, his Cosmo Club gig and a hairdressing course at Poro College of Cosmetology (yet more strings to his bow) and anxiously awaited the call to record. Eventually it came, and Chuck once again travelled up to Chicago, this time with Johnnie Johnson and drummer Ebby Hardy in tow, to record *Maybellene* at Chess.

Johnnie Johnson's contribution to Chuck Berry's music cannot be underestimated. Johnson, two years older and musically more experienced than Chuck, was Berry's musical mentor. However, like the unsuspecting bird that hatched the cuckoo's egg, he took Chuck under his wing only to be ousted as group leader by the young 'go-getter' (to use his own description of the ambitious Berry). It is true to say Johnson and Berry were collaborators on many of Chuck's songs, though not equal partners. True, Chuck took his lead from Johnnie's sparking left hand and emulated the sound on guitar, but like a musical magpie he also borrowed guitar licks from T-Bone Walker, Elmore James, Charlie Christian, Carl Hogan and others. By Johnson's own admission, Berry's guitar solos were his own, and I personally doubt if a single word of Chuck's lexicon of lyrics came from Johnnie. Had Johnson been more astute and forceful, he could maybe have claimed part-credit for some compositions, but ask yourself: would Johnnie Johnson be known today had it not been for his association with Chuck Berry? On the other hand, Berry would undoubtedly have succeeded without Johnnie.

By July 1955, *Maybellene* was being mercilessly plugged by Alan Freed on WINS in New York City prior to its release, in return for which the disc jockey received a 33⅓% writer's credit. The other third went to Russ Fratto, Chess's stationery supplier! The response was outstanding, and by the end of the month Chess 1604 had hit the streets. By the end of August, *Maybellene* was riding high on the R&B, country and popular charts. It was subsequently awarded a *Billboard* 'Triple Crown Award' for becoming the best-selling R&B record in stores, the most-played on the nation's radio stations and the most-played in jukeboxes. Not bad for a first attempt!

Chuck signed a contract with the Gale Booking Agency and the years of recordings, concerts, fame and fortune had begun. Although he claimed never to have lost the skills, his days as a carpenter, painter and decorator, and hairdresser were over. For Chuck Berry life would never be the same again.

During the first years of this rock and roll adventure, the Gale deal carried some heavy baggage in the form of a personal manager called Teddy Reig (or 'Roag' as Berry, in a subtle play on words, referred to him in his autobiography: Reig by name and rogue by nature) and it didn't take long for Chuck to check the percentages and to shake him loose along with the Frattos and Freeds. On the recording side, his second and third releases stiffed (in the popular charts at least), but his fourth, the immortal *Roll Over Beethoven*, made up for lost ground. From here on in, he chalked up twelve consecutive *Billboard* 'Top/Hot 100' entries.

The touring was incessant, but amongst the routine there were some memorable gigs: the Apollo and the Brooklyn Paramount in New York, the Regal in Chicago, and — unusually — the 1958 *Newport Jazz Festival*. During the late fifties, Johnny B. Goode went to Hollywood and was featured in three monochrome movies of debatable artistic merit. However, his performances were never less than terrific. He also toured overseas for the first time, visiting Honolulu and Australia in 1959 and Jamaica in 1960.

During this period, Johnnie Johnson, Ebby Hardy and sax-man Leroy Davis were regulars in his band, but he also started to gig as a single using pick-up bands.   As his reputation grew and his repertoire became more familiar, this developed into his chosen *modus operandi*: travelling light, the paladin of rock and roll — have guitar, will travel; hit and run to maximise the profits.

Possessed of a sound analytical and mathematical mind, Berry was as sharp a businessman as he was a guitarist and was quick to learn from his mistakes. For instance, at first he was frugal, sleeping in his car and living off sandwiches, but soon came to realise that travel, subsistence and other incidental expenses were tax-deductible, and from then it was a new Cadillac every other year and a new Gibson each year. With the help of his long-time secretary, Francine Gillium, he established a Chuck Berry Fan Club, Chuck Berry Music Inc. to publish his songs and Thee Investments Inc. for his burgeoning real estate portfolio. Amongst his property acquisitions were Club Bandstand in March 1958 (which he named after the *American Bandstand* television show) and thirty acres of yellow mud in Wentzville, west of St. Louis, which became Berry Park. During the late fifties and early sixties, he invested a great deal of time and money into the Berry Park development which included a one-acre lake, a guitar-shaped swimming pool, residential lodges and a clubhouse, and in 1960 he opened it to the paying public.

This incarnation of the American dream, all this fame and all this fortune, must have seemed too good to be true for a negro in the 1950s, and indeed it was. The comeuppance for Chuck came almost out of nowhere, from seemingly innocent incidents.

Firstly, he was arrested (ostensibly for having $19,000 and a concealed weapon to protect his cache in his peach-coloured Caddie). In truth, it was because he was a black man who also had a white female companion (French at that) in the car.

Secondly, he thought it would be a good idea to add a little colour to Club Bandstand by hiring an Apache girl he had met in El Paso as a little cutie to check your hat (and you can thank her, ma'am!). Little did he know she was practising the oldest profession in the world and was also under-age (fourteen was the unsubstantiated claim).

These two incidents resulted in almost two years of litigation and three trials of which he won one (the French lady) and lost the other (the Indian girl) but gained a replay as a result of the overt racism of the presiding judge. This retrial resulted in the original sentence of five years and $5,000 fine being commuted to three years and $5,000. Meanwhile, as a result of the adverse publicity, no-one wanted to touch Chuck Berry. His gigs began to dry up and his popularity waned.   By hook or by crook, the white city fathers were determined to tear his bandstand down. Little wonder then, that a rather large chip developed on the Berry shoulder, along with a strong determination never to be bitten by the same dog twice.

On 19th February 1962, Chuck began what eventually became a twenty-one month stay as the guest of Uncle Sam, briefly at Levenworth, Kansas, then at the Federal Medical Center at Springfield, Missouri. While in jail, he didn't waste his time: he completed his education, concentrating on business management, law and accountancy. He also wrote five stunning songs destined to provide the springboard for his sixties' renaissance. He was again released on his birthday — this time his 37th — 18th October 1963.

During Berry's incarceration, the soft-centred 'rockers' who had been insinuated on American record-buying teens by the music industry moguls had been usurped by the British beat boom boys: the Beatles, the Rolling Stones and a whole string of lesser lights. The significance for Chuck was that a large part of the style and substance of their sound was his music. Reinterpretations of his back catalogue flowed from these musical innocents; by this process, rock and roll metamorphosed first into white R&B and then rock music, but the Berry style flowed across the bounds with consummate ease. It wasn't just flowing in Europe either; in California the surf was up, and riding the crest were the Beach Boys with their own Berry beat hybrid.

In consequence, Chuck's star rose again in the firmament, and he got a second chart wind with new songs like *Promised Land* and *Nadine* and resurrected ones like *Memphis Tennessee* and *Let It Rock*, all of which charted on both sides of the Atlantic. In May 1964, he toured the UK for the very first time and set in train what was to become virtually an annual visit to Britain and Europe for the remainder of the sixties and throughout the seventies.

In June 1966, Berry's 'golden decade' at Chess Records ended when he defected to Mercury. The deal may well have been lucrative for him, but artistically the good stuff during this period was the exception rather than the rule. He had built a private recording studio at Berry Park, and during his Mercury spell spent many hours cutting demos and finished masters with his group of St. Louis irregulars which on occasion included Johnnie Johnson and multi-instrumentalist Billy Peek.

In the summer of 1967, at the height of flower power, Chuck cut a live album in the hub of hippiedom, San Francisco, with Steve Miller's band, which turned out to be the best thing he ever did for Mercury. He was greatly attracted to the hippie lifestyle (which was reflected in the psychedelic shirts he continued to wear way beyond their 'use by' date) and the 'free love' ethic, and starting in 1970, he staged three festivals in the grounds of Berry Park. This, almost inevitably, led to law trouble involving pot smoking and a minor shooting incident. Ironically, Chuck's apparent espousal of hippie values did not extend to free performances, and he passed up the opportunity to play Woodstock because the promoters didn't meet his price.

After three years in the Mercury wilderness, he returned to his natural home and re-signed with Chess. It wasn't, however, the same company that he had left in 1966. During his absence, Chess Records had changed from a paternalistic family record business that ostensibly cared for its artists and their music into an impersonal corporate conglomerate. Sadly, his music was never to be quite the same again.

Chuck toured incessantly throughout the seventies and became firmly ensconced on the 'oldies but goodies' treadmill, churning out his past glories for the punters often without much care or attention and developing little musically, if at all. Then, in 1972, the *Ding-A-Ling* phenomenon occurred. This silly novelty had been in his set for years, but his live performance at Coventry hit the spot (the audience contributing almost as much as Berry to the remarkable recording) and suddenly Chuck Berry was hot property yet again with a saucy hit topping the charts on both sides of the Pond. Ironically, the single and the *London Chuck Berry Sessions* album from which it was lifted became his all-time biggest-selling records (roll over Beethoven, tell Johnny B. Goode the news!).

In 1973, Chuck engaged in some shady under-the-table dealings with rock'n'roll revival concert promoter Richard Nader involving undeclared cash payments in brown paper envelopes ('malparamanopo' is how he put it). The long arm of the IRS finally felt his collar for the fraud which culminated six years later with 120 days in jail and 1,000 hours community service. His time was served at Lompoc prison, California, north of Santa Barbara on Route 1. As with his sixties' stretch, he didn't waste his time inside and began to write his autobiography longhand in little exercise books, which he sent to his faithful secretary, Francine Gillium, for typing.

By the time the eighties arrived, Chuck Berry was a made man — a dollar millionaire with a portfolio of real estate that gave him as much satisfaction as writing hit records. The music and showbusiness fraternity now suddenly also began to pick up on his achievements and awarded him a string of prestigious awards. In January 1981, he received a Special Merit Award at the eighth American Music Awards. In February 1985 came a Lifetime Achievement Award at the Grammys. January 1986 saw him inducted — as one of ten inaugural inductees — into the Rock And Roll Hall Of Fame. In March 1986, he was elected into the Songwriters' Hall Of Fame.

1986 also witnessed the capturing of his music and manner on film with the celebration of his 60th birthday in *Hail! Hail! Rock'n'Roll*. This in turn led to him receiving a star on the Hollywood Walk Of Fame in 1987. In 1988, thirty-three years after its conception, the song *Maybellene* won a Grammy, followed in 1990 by *Roll Over Beethoven*, while *Johnny B. Goode* became a true star, despatched via *Voyager 2* towards Neptune along with other items representative of our civilisation.

Almost inevitably — such is Chuck Berry's psyche — after the accolades comes the fall. In his autobiography (published in 1987) he reflected on his series of internments and speculated that it would be another seventeen years before his next spell in jail — which would have made it 1996. In the event, however, his time unfortunately arrived a little sooner.

Chuck's series of self-inflicted problems began in 1989 and ran well into the nineties. A former cook at his Southern Air Restaurant in Wentzville (the very same restaurant from which he had bought 'zoo-zoos' via the back window during his ill-fated Kansas City jaunt in 1944) brought a civil suit against him, alleging that he had installed video equipment in the female toilets to tape the ladies at their 'ablutions'. This led to a class action by two hundred other women. The authorities clearly had Berry in their sights and, in June 1990, agents seized drugs, cash, weapons and suspected pornographic videos from Berry Park. Chuck was charged with possession of drugs and child abuse. The abuse charges were unfounded but, after pleading guilty to the other charges, he received a six-month jail sentence and a $5,000 fine. A subsequent appeal on the grounds of a conspiracy to destroy him financially was rejected.

And so, at the start of the millennium, the seventy-something Mr. Berry continues rocking. His concert appearances have reduced, and he has developed a small paunch and lost a little hair. His duckwalks have diminished too, but he's still rocking, occasionally teaming up with other oldsters like Jerry Lee Lewis and Little Richard for *'Legends Of Rock'* shows. He clearly has no financial need to keep on playing, so maybe, despite the cynical view that he is only in it for the money, Chuck Berry really *does* love to rock and roll.

2

Sessionography

This sessionography follows the normal format of listing the artist as shown on the original release, the musicians involved, the date and location of the session, the matrix number, the song title, and labels and catalogue numbers of releases. Where known, the composer(s) are listed beneath each title. Alternative titles for songs are shown in square brackets alongside the usual title. Where session dates are disputed, alternative dated are shown in parentheses below.

For clarity (and sanity) only principal releases have been included. These are releases on which the song was first issued, albums which include new or unissued material, and significant reissues. A chronological listing of all these records appears in *Section 3* (pages 263-284), along with other notable releases and reissues.

Releases are listed in chronological order by format:

Singles and EPs are preceded by a **o** symbol.
'**a**' or '**b**' after a single release number denotes the play or flip side respectively.

LPs are preceded by a **■** symbol.
Catalogue numbers of Chess/Checker albums which were released in mono with an LP- prefix and stereo with an LPS- prefix are listed once with the prefix LP(S)-. Similarly, mono and stereo Marble Arch releases prefixed MAL- and MALS- are listed once with the prefix MAL(S)- .

CDs are preceded by a **◎** symbol.

GOLDEN DECADE
(1954-66)

From the mid-fifties to the mid-sixties,
Chuck Berry was at the cutting edge of rock and roll.
It was during this period that he wrote and recorded
most of his classic songs, establishing a reputation as one
of the finest lyricists of the Twentieth Century.

Billboard, September 1954

SESSION 1

JOE ALEXANDER AND THE CUBANS

Joe Alexander, vocal; 'Charles Berryn' *(Chuck Berry)*, guitar; 'Faith Douglas' *(Oscar Washington)*, guitar-1; Freddy Golden, bongos

Premier Studio
3033 Locust Street
St. Louis, Missouri   **13 August 1954**

M-5008	**Oh Maria**	● Ballad AA1008-X45**a**, Spindle
	(Oscar Washington, Joe Alexander)	SPN-2001**a** ◉ Mr. DJ 101
M-5009	**I Hope These Words Will Find You Well** -1	● Ballad AA1008-X45**b**, Spindle
	(Oscar Washington, Joe Alexander)	SPN-2001**b**

Nine months before he recorded for Chess, Chuck Berry teamed up with local St. Louis guitarist and record label owner, Oscar 'Fats' Washington, to cut these two Latin-influenced sides.

The AFM recording report for the session lists Douglas, Golden and one 'Charles Berryn' as the musicians employed, collectively called 'the Cubans'. The sheet is signed by Oscar Washington, who also recorded on this occasion under the pseudonym 'Faith Douglas'. Joe Alexander's name does not appear anywhere on the report, but it was normal practice at the time not to list vocalists, so his omission has no particular significance.

Washington had started his Ballad label in 1954, recording an early 'bird' group — the Swans — for whom he wrote lyrics to the melody of Jimmy Forrest's 1951 instrumental hit, *Night Train* (later a smash for James Brown in the sixties). *Oh Maria* was released around the same time, the mysterious Joe Alexander being promoted in the contemporary music press as a calypso act.

'Charles Berryn' is, of course, Chuck, who has said that he used this *nom de disque* to fool his dear dad that he was plucking eyebrows and not guitar strings. This is hardly tenable, as the Chuck Berryn name had already appeared on a Crank Club poster with a picture of the brown-eyed handsome man himself grinning at the world for all to see!

It has been suggested that it is Berry singing on *Oh Maria* and, while there is some similarity with the pseudo-West Indian patois Chuck used on later recordings such as *Havana Moon*, it is not our man. In fact, I hear only one guitar on this side, and I'm not even sure that this is Berry.

On the other hand, *I Hope These Words Will Find You Well* definitely has two guitars, and, as sure as there is a star to be born, the lead we hear is the embryonic Berry. The singing on both cuts is decidedly ropey, particularly on the latter, where the singer gasps for breath mid-line and cannot decide whether to sing in tenor or baritone.

While Chuck soon went on to greater things, Alexander didn't. After initially working various St. Louis clubs, he moved north to Chicago to try his luck but rapidly became disillusioned and gave up the music business to join a religious group.

It is rumoured that Berry cut two more tracks for Ballad. If he did, they are not listed on this session sheet and must be from a subsequent session. Washington, however, later stated that it was the biggest mistake of his life not to record Chuck and his group when later asked by Berry to do so, so the rumours of more recordings may well be just wishful thinking.

Yet another rumour has Berry recording in Memphis for David James Mattis of Duke Records. It is known that he did audition for Mattis in 1952 or 1953, but whether any demos were cut is open to speculation. Chuck himself denies any involvement in the recording studio before *Maybellene*.

The SPN-2001 single is a 1995 'limited edition' release from Spindle Records Inc. digitally remastered by Marc Bird; the Mr. DJ CD is a 1998 bootleg, probably emanating from the Netherlands.

Early publicity

21

SESSION 2

CHUCK BERRY & HIS COMBO (**CHUCK BERRY** on EP, LP and CD)

Chuck Berry, vocal/guitar; Johnnie Johnson, piano; Willie Dixon, double bass; Ebby Hardy, drums; *possibly* Jerome Green *or* Leonard Chess, maracas -1

Universal Studios
111 East Ontario Street
Chicago, Illinois   **21 May 1955**

U7844	**Maybellene** [Come Back Maybellene] -1 [Maybelline*] *(Chuck Berry)*	◉ Chess 1604**a** ■ Chess LP-1425, 1435, 1465, 1480*, 1485, LP(S)-1514D, CH2-8201, CH6-80001
U7845 (8382)	**Wee Wee Hours** [Wee Wee Hours Blues] *(Chuck Berry)*	◉ Chess 1604**b**, EP-5118 ■ Chess LP-1426, LP(S)-1514D, CH6-80001 ◉ Ace CDCH-397

Note: LP-1480 was overdubbed with audience noise.

During the early fifties, Chuck Berry was developing his distinctive style as a guitarist and singer in Tommy Stevens's band, and then later, after a fortuitous New Year's gig, as Johnnie Johnson's guitarist in the latter's Sir John's Trio. His dominant personality inevitably lead to him taking control of the trio as his confidence as a performer grew. The *Oh Maria* release hadn't done a thing for his career and Berry, desperate to make a record, started to peddle his wares around record labels in Chicago. Vee-Jay turned him down but, on the advice of Muddy Waters, he hustled up a session with Chess.

Chuck carried his two St. Louis musical compatriots, Johnnie Johnson and drummer Ebby Hardy to the recording session. (Jaspar Thomas has been suggested as an alternative drummer but this seems unlikely because he only joined Chuck's group when Hardy quit in 1956.) Whoever it is, he surely builds sheds on *Maybellene*. To fill out the sound, percussionist and Bo Diddley's alter ego, Jerome Green may have been present, or maybe it was Leonard Chess himself who shook maracas. Green was Diddley's longtime shaker, but around this time Bo and Co. were more or less constantly on tour, so Green on the beans is unlikely. On the other hand, Chuck recalls having to pay Len Chess session fees for percussion on an early date — perhaps it was for maracas on this one? Who knows? There is, however, no doubt about the rock-solid string bass playing from the nimble fingers of the big D: Willie Dixon, the backbone of a thousand blues.

With **Maybellene**, his very first Chess release, Chuck hit the ground running. It was released in July; by 6th August it had entered the *Billboard* R&B charts; by the 20th it had rocketed to the top, where it stayed for eleven weeks. More importantly, it broke through to the white mass market, rising to the dizzy heights of No. 5 on both the *Billboard* and *Cash Box* pop charts and rolling Mr. Berry right on up to fame.

Maybellene is a potent mix of hillbilly and blues (H&B?) which Berry had absorbed from the radio in his formative years in St. Louis. The style and lyrical content — a cautionary tale of fast cars and even faster women — was to set a formula which has served Chuck well throughout his career.

The song is said to have been born out of *Ida Red*, a Western Swing number recorded by Bob Wills & His Texas Playboys. However, *May's* daddy may equally well have been *Ida Red Blues* recorded in 1951 by Amos Easton alias Bumble Bee Slim, which sounds strangely familiar and may have slipped into Chuck's subconscious.

Lyrically, *Maybellene* must owe something to *Hot Rod Racer* by Arkie Shibley & His Mountain Dew Boys recorded in 1950 on the Gilt-Edge label out of Los Angeles. As the name suggests, Shibley's outfit was a hillbilly act. The song proved so popular that in 1951 both Red Foley and Ramblin' Jimmie Dolan recorded versions of this country boogie chase with the cars "rollin' side by side". Indeed, Foley's and Dolan's versions raced each other up the country charts. Yet another version, this time by rotund bandleader Tiny Hill, hit the pop charts.

Whatever the creative process, the finished *Maybellene* is pure, unadulterated Berry from the railroad air-horn guitar introduction to the point where he hits the top of the hill at 110. Chuck is a master wordsmith — this is, after all, the song that introduced "motorvatin' " into rock and roll vocabulary. His poetical prowess is clearly illustrated in his autobiography (no ghost writers for Chuck!), where he writes out a completely new set of lyrics that fit *Maybellene's* fine brown frame perfectly.

The original 78 and 45 rpm singles of *Maybellene* had the composer credited to Chuck Berry alone. However, very soon after, as the record began to break, the names 'Freed' and 'Fratto' strangely appeared. Freed was, of course, Alan Freed, the great rock and roll deejay and entrepreneur, and Fratto was Russ Fratto, the great Chess stationery supplier! Chuck's feelings on the matter can be clearly seen on the reproduction of the sheet music for the song in his autobiography, where the names Freed and Fratto have been scored through. It took all of thirty years before he wrested back the rights to *Maybellene.*

The issued take of *Maybellene* is said to have been the thirty-sixth. If this was due to studio inexperience on Chuck's part, or that of the young recording engineer, Malcolm Chisholm, it doesn't show as there is no loss of spontaneity.

Who christened *Maybellene*? When Chuck and Johnnie Johnson, Chuck's longtime pianist and musical collaborator, arrived at the studio the song was called *Ida May* and Len Chess suggested a name change. It has been variously suggested that *Maybellene* was named after an old school flame, or was the name of a storybook cow, or named after a range of cosmetics. Berry had been a trainee hairdresser at the Poro College of Cosmetology and perhaps, with his business acumen beginning to bud, he felt a little subtle product placement was in order. This is confirmed by Johnnie Johnson in the notes of his CD, *Johnnie B. Bad*, so it is probably safe to stick with cosmetics.

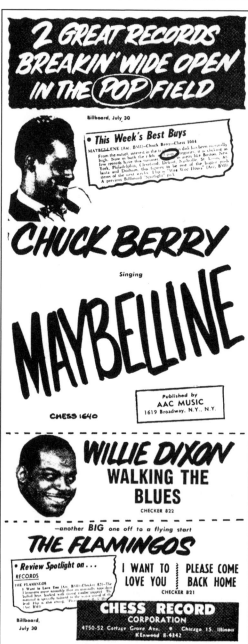

Billboard, August 1955

Maybellene has had a long and productive life. In its first year of existence, the song was covered by Elvis Presley (who featured it in his *Louisiana Hayride* concerts), by Marty Robbins and Jim Lowe for the country market, and Chicago bandleader Ralph Marterie for the popular market. *Maybellene* has spawned over one hundred cover versions from the sublime (Elvis) to the ridiculous (the Great Dames of Rock & Roll) and a handful of 'answer' songs including *Come Back Maybellene* by R&B saxman Big John Greer and bluesman Mercy Dee (Walton), both cut in 1955. That same year, Brownie McGhee also cut a thinly-disguised version called *Anna Mae* with pianist Ernest Hayes, who would later record with Chuck.

Maybellene had taken ages to record and another title was needed for a single release. Chuck and Johnnie put their heads together and within an hour a standard blues in G was hatched from their Cosmo Club back repertoire. **Wee Wee Hours**, a slow blues, is a total contrast to *Maybellene*. Johnson's rippling piano is featured prominently, which indicates perhaps that the number was more his creation than Chuck's. Chuck and Johnnie both originally considered it to be the stronger side (it did, in fact, chart in its own right, reaching No. 10 on the *Billboard* 'Most

Played In R&B Juke Boxes' listing, and No. 15 on the R&B Dee-Jay chart), but in the end Chess knew best!

Chuck says the song was inspired by Big Joe Turner's 1941 recording, *Wee Baby Blues*. However, apart from the similarity of the titles, the two have very little in common. (Berry later recorded Turner's song at the 1967 Fillmore gig with Steve Miller.) The plaintive tone of the song evokes the memory of Leroy Carr's *Midnight Hour Blues* cut in 1932. Carr and his guitarist, Scrapper Blackwell, had a significant and lasting influence on blues piano/guitar duos and some of it may have rubbed off on Chuck and Johnnie. Berry's vocal is akin to one of his declared idols, Charles Brown, whose laid-back 'after hours' tone he imitates successfully.

The song appears to have been remastered as *Wee Wee Hours Blues* (matrix 8382) at a later date, possibly for inclusion on an LP. The remastering is inferior to the original, but otherwise identical to matrix U7845.

Wee Wee Hours has not been covered by many artists. However, the song has had an enduring influence on the white blues fraternity — in Britain at least — probably because of its inclusion on the early Chess anthology, *The Blues (Volume 2)*. Eric Clapton, for instance, chose the song as his contribution in the *Hail! Hail! Rock'n'Roll* movie thirty-one years after its original release.

SESSION 3

CHUCK BERRY & HIS COMBO (CHUCK BERRY on LPs)
Chuck Berry, vocal/guitar; Johnnie Johnson, piano; Willie Dixon, double bass; Ebby Hardy, drums; *possibly* Jerome Green *or* Leonard Chess, maracas -1; band chorus-2.

Universal Studios
111 East Ontario Street
Chicago, Illinois   **September 1955**

U7898	**Thirty Days (To Come Back Home)** -1-2 *(Chuck Berry)*	◉ Chess 1610a ■ Chess LP-1425, 1465, 1485, LP(S)-1514D, CH2-8201, CH6-80001
U7899	**Together (We Will Always Be)** *(Chuck Berry)*	◉ Chess 1610b ■ Chess LP-1426, 2CH-60023

During the summer of 1955, Chuck, Johnnie and Ebby hit the road, riding the success of *Maybellene* in a series of one night stands. Chess knew, however, that the record would soon start to cool and it was time to cut a follow-up to keep up the momentum. U7898 and U7899 formed Chuck Berry's second Chess single and followed the same pattern as his first: a rocking top deck and a bluesy flip. The same questions about the drummer and percussionist personnel arise here also and the previous comments apply.

Thirty Days is, in fact, *Maybellene* Part 2 from its opening guitar figure on down, and that's probably why it fared relatively poorly saleswise. With *Maybellene* still occupying the top spot, *Thirty Days* peaked at No. 8 on the R&B 'Best Seller' listings and never made the pop charts at all.

It seems Chuck never did catch old *Maybellene*, and here he resorts to the judiciary to get her back. The law (cops, judges and courts) is a recurring theme in Berry's repertoire — no doubt reflecting his own brushes with the same. His guitar is a tone heavier than on *Maybellene* and Johnnie gets to fly a bit higher too, while the band bawl out "Thirty days!" in unison in the background.

Ronnie Hawkins made a classic cover of the song but was more lenient with his girl, allowing her *Forty Days* to get back home. Hawkins's waxing (which misguidedly also credited him as composer) made the *Billboard* 'Hot 100' in the spring of 1959. Needless to say, writs soon began to fly from Chess's New York publishing house, Arc Music, to correct the 'error'. In France meanwhile, Johnny Hallyday's French language version, *Rien Que Huit Jours* only gave his dame eight days. Johnny 'nice guitar, shame about the voice' Winter also cut a notable version in 1974, Ernest Tubb had a country hit with it in 1956, and, as recently as 1998, John Lee Hooker rambled on for a full *90 Days*. As Mick Jagger tells it, Keith Richards also got the title of the Stones' *(I Can't Get No) Satisfaction* from Berry's ungrammatical line: "If I can't get no satisfaction from the judge".

The best thing about **Together (We Will Always Be)** is the power-chording at the beginning. From then on in, the performance is pretty bland. Chuck sings the song straight, *à la* Nat Cole — one of his professed heroes — but his voice is very thin and at one point cracks up. The convoluted lyrics don't help matters, but note the pronunciation of "especially" — which is straight from the Georgia woods!

SESSION 4

CHUCK BERRY & HIS COMBO (CHUCK BERRY on LPs and CD)
Chuck Berry, vocal/guitar; Johnnie Johnson *or* Otis Spann, piano (except -1); Willie Dixon, double bass; Ebby Hardy, drums; unknown, maracas -2

Universal Studios
111 East Ontario Street
Chicago, Illinois   **20 December 1955**

U7951	**You Can't Catch Me** *(Chuck Berry)*	● Chess 1645**a** ■ Chess LP-1425, LP(S)-1514D, CH2-8201, CH6-80001
U7952	**Rolli Polli** [Roly Poly] *[instrumental]* *(Chuck Berry)*	■ Chess LP-1426, 2CH-60028
U7953	**Berry Pickin'** *[instrumental]* -2 *(Chuck Berry)*	■ Chess LP-1426
U7954	(The) **Down Bound Train** -1 *(Chuck Berry)*	● Chess 1615**b** ■ Chess LP-1426, 2CH-60028, CH6-80001
U7955	**No Money Down** *(Chuck Berry)*	● Chess 1615**a** ■ Chess LP-1426, 2CH-60023, CH6-80001 ◎ Ace CDCH-397
	I've Changed *(Chuck Berry)*	■ Reelin' 001, Chess CXMP-2011, Checkmate LP-1955, Chess CH6-80001

It is not certain who played piano on this session, Johnnie Johnson or that stalwart of the Muddy Waters band, Otis Spann. Johnnie is sure he was there, although this recollection is through the haze of a lifetime of drinking. It does, however, seem strange that Chuck's usual drummer Ebby Hardy would have been there but not his piano-man. On the other hand, previous discographies all list Spann, so who knows? Waters was one of Chuck's main men and it must have been quite something for the young Berry to have Spann — if it is indeed he — on the session, knowing that he was such an integral part of Muddy's sound.

The session kicked off at a blinding pace with **You Can't Catch Me**, with its speeded-up *Good Morning Little Schoolgirl* riff and tremendous slapped bass from Willie Dixon. Chuck has always claimed it was cut at his first Chess session, and he is certainly on familiar ground with this little ditty about 'motorvating' down the New Jersey Turnpike in the wee wee hours. He allows his imagination full rein with the fanciful "airmobile named Maybellene". In his autobiography he relates with obvious pleasure the incident that inspired the song where, overtaken by two flat-tops in a souped-up jitney, he quite naturally

drops back to plan his revenge for such an affront, puts his foot in the tank and zooms ahead only to be hassled by the law. He finally escapes "like a cool breeze from a camel's ass", as he later put it.

You Can't Catch Me was featured in *Rock, Rock, Rock*, Chuck's first movie. Dressed in a white suit, white suede shoes, and holding a Gretch 'Chet Atkins' solid-bodied guitar loaned to him for the filming, Berry became the first rock and roll guitarslinger, rubberlegging and duckwalking as he mimed (badly) to the disc. Made in the fall of 1956 and taking all of two weeks to shoot, the picture is pretty dire, saved only by some of the musical interludes (Chuck's being the best) which make up a good proportion of the proceedings.

To cash in on the film's pending release in November 1956, Chess released a soundtrack album — coincidentally their very first LP release. Four Berry tracks were included although only one, *You Can't Catch Me*, was actually featured in the final cut. The song was, of course, also released as a single, but to no avail as it did zilch on the charts, even missing the R&B listings.

The Rolling Stones built their career on Berry's solid rock. *You Can't Catch Me* is one of sixteen songs written by or closely associated with Chuck Berry that they have covered. Thirteen of these were officially released (three as singles), the others on bootlegs. In fact, there have been an amazing 72 separate recordings of Berry songs by the group and the count is still rising. This excludes Berry songs cut by individual Stones and their own Berryesque outings such as *Star Star*, and indicates the strength of influence of Chuck's music on the so-called 'greatest rock and roll band in the world'. *You Can't Catch Me* is included on their second LP, whilst their fourth contains the song *Flight 505*, the title of which I'm convinced is derived from a reference in *You Can't Catch Me*. This connection might be considered tenuous, but remember that Keith Richards is an obsessive Berry fan — obsessed to such an extent that he named his son 'Jo Jo' after Berry's meddlesome monkey!

John Lennon, another stone Berry fan, also included the song on his *Rock'n'Roll* tribute album. *Come Together*, a Lennon composition from his Beatle days, opens with the line "Here come old flat-top" lifted from the Berry original, no doubt in tribute to his hero. This fact was not overlooked by the owner of the publishing rights of *You Can't Catch Me*, Morris Levy, who sued Lennon and settled when the latter agreed to include a couple of his copyrights on his tribute album. Levy, incidentally, was a well-connected 'wise guy' with numerous sticky fingers in the music industry pie (he was owner of New York's Birdland dancehall, Roulette Records and a number of music publishing companies, as well as being Alan Freed's manager). He was not above taking 'direct action' and was under indictment on a charge of extortion when he died in 1991.

The instrumentals **Rolli Polli** and **Berry Pickin'** were, according to Chuck, warm-ups at the session which Chess recorded, mastered, and — much to his chagrin — independently named.

For a warm-up, *Rolli Polli* is pretty hot, if a little lacking in form. Berry lets rip with his own bag of guitar licks, most of which recur in later, greater recordings. There is also an undermiked piano solo with Chuck chugging in the background. The track ends with Hardy taking a dive off the drum kit.

Berry Pickin' has the kind of Latin rhumba rhythm much loved by Chuck, complete with maracas, percussive piano and a dollop of cowbells. A yell of encouragement and the middle eight changes to a mid-tempo boogie beat, then returns to the Latin melody that would reappear as *La Jaunda* in 1957. *Berry Pickin'* was mistakenly substituted for *Deep Feeling* as the 'B' side of some light blue 1960's reissue singles of *School Day* [Chess 1653] although the label still said '*Deep Feeling*'. A real rarity for all vinyl junkies to seek out!

While Johnson/Spann nipped out for a swift half, Chuck took the opportunity to cut **Down Bound Train**, a cautionary tale about the demon drink. The song is like nothing else he had recorded before or since and is the nearest he has come to cutting gospel. In fact, it is clearly descended from *Death's Black Train Is Coming*, a solid seller in 1926 for Rev. J.M. Gates (subsequently reworked in 1962 by Rev. Robert Ballinger as *The Little Black Train*). Berry's song has a distinct country feel with echoes of the Sons of the Pioneers' *Ghost Riders In The Sky*, particularly in the way he drags out sections of the lyrics. His rapidly-strummed guitar fades in, and together with Dixon's bass sets the rhythm of the train as it careers downward at a barely-controllable "terrible pace". The flickering guitar licks add an eerie tension to the piece, which intensifies as the song and the train speed on to their devilish final destination.

Berry's lyrics so vividly describe the train with its boiler filled with "lager beer" and the "motley crew" of "rich men in broadcloth and beggars in rags" that one wonders if he himself, an avowed abstainer, isn't the "stranger on the bar-room floor".

No Money Down puts Chuck back on *terra firma* with this stop-time blues typical of the Chicago school. The piano player takes the lead with consummate ease which, if it *is* Spann, isn't surprising as he had hit the same groove on Muddy Waters's *Hoochie Coochie Man* twelve months earlier in

January 1954, Bo Diddley's *I'm A Man* in March 1955, and latterly Waters's *Manish Boy* in May 1955. Of course, Willie Dixon also knew more than a little about this style of blues!

Once again, Chuck is on a favourite subject: cars. Here, he turns the tables on the high-pressure salesman and specifies exactly what he wants in a car "that'll eat up the road". His requirements rival those in that other great paean to consumerism, *Shoppin' For Clothes*, originally written as *Clothesline* by Kent Harris and recorded by him in 1956 under the pseudonym 'Boogaloo & His Gallant Crew'.

Clothesline was issued shortly after *No Money Down* and may well have been influenced by Berry's composition. As things turned out, Harris's song remained unnoticed until redrafted by Leiber & Stoller and remade as *Shoppin' For Clothes* by the Coasters. Where Chuck wants a "fo'-do' DeVille with a continental spare and wire chrome wheels", the Coasters' Will 'Dub' Jones (as the clothes salesman) offers Carl Gardner a "two-buttoned box back, Western style, in pure, pure herringbone". Eventually, however, Chuck wins out because, despite having a good job "sweepin' up everyday" Carl's credit doesn't come through, while all Chuck needs to do is "sign on the dotted line" and drive the Caddie off the lot. Berry has always taken pride in the clear articulation of lyrics, and lyrics as good as these deserve to be heard.

Released at the start of 1956, *No Money Down* made No. 8 on *Billboard's* 'Most Played by R&B Dee-Jays' chart and No. 11 on the R&B Best-Sellers listing, but — perhaps unsurprisingly — this 'blackest' of Berry releases saw no pop chart action at all. Interestingly, a comment in the contemporary press suggested that this may have been due to a lack of radio airplay because of the references to Cadillac and Ford cars.

I've Changed is hard to place, primarily because it has no matrix number allocated to it. Some sources list this as an alternative take of *How You've Changed [see Session 10]*, but this is incorrect because it is a completely different song, and the piano and drums sound much more like Johnson/Spann and Hardy than Lafayette Leake and Fred Below.

The track was first issued on *America's Hottest Wax* [Reelin' 001], a bootleg LP that was later officially released by UK Chess [Chess CXMP-2011]. The song is a blues ballad with some wonderfully expressive lines like: "When I cared so much for you, I was love-blind and couldn't see" and "I waited for you in the morning, right behind a sleepless night". It also contains a rare R&B reference to golf: "let's tee off together". Blues for the middle classes!

Chess #1615

"NO MONEY DOWN"

b/w

"DOWN BOUND TRAIN"

by

CHUCK BERRY

CHESS RECORD CO.
4750 S. Cottage Grove Ave
Chicago 15, Ill.
Phone Kenwood 8-4342

ANOTHER BIG ONE FROM-
Chuck Berry

"TOO MUCH MONKEY BUSINESS"
b/w
"BROWN EYED HANDSOME MAN"

CHESS # 1635

Billboard, September 1956

SESSION 5

CHUCK BERRY & HIS COMBO (CHUCK BERRY on LPs, EP and CD)

Chuck Berry, vocal/guitar; Johnnie Johnson, piano; Willie Dixon, double bass; Leroy C. Davis, tenor saxophone (except -1); *possibly* unknown trumpet (except -1); Fred Below, drums

Chess Records studio
4750-2 South Cottage Grove Avenue
Chicago, Illinois   **16 April 1956**

8108	**Drifting Heart** *(Chuck Berry)*	◐ Chess 1626**b** ■ Chess LP-1426, 2CH-60028, CH6-80001 ◉ Beat Goes On BGOCD-428
8109	**Brown Eyed Handsome Man** -1 *(Chuck Berry)*	◐ Chess 1635**b**, EP-5118 ■ Chess LP-1426, 1485, LP(S)-1514D, CH2-8201, CH6-80001
8110	**Roll Over Beethoven** *(Chuck Berry)*	◐ Chess 1626**a** ■ Chess LP-1425, 1435, 1465, 1485, LP(S)-1514D, CH2-8201, CH6-80001
8111	**Too Much Monkey Business** *(Chuck Berry)*	◐ Chess 1635**a**, EP-5118 ■ Chess LP-1426, 1485, LP(S)-1514D, CH2-8201, CH6-80001

Chuck Berry once said about his music and his influences: "I identify myself with Louis Jordan more than any other artist. If I had only one artist to listen to through eternity it would be Nat Cole. And, if I had to work through eternity it would be Louis Jordan." This shows where Berry is coming from and the four songs in this session illustrate this perfectly.

His guitar licks are based on Jordan's guitarists, Bill Jennings and particularly, Carl Hogan. He uses his guitar to reinterpret Jordan's horn riffs, and his lyrical style is firmly based on the latter's sharply-observed and witty repertoire. However, try as he may, he never quite cuts it vocally when he tries to emulate his other idol, Nat 'King' Cole. Ably assisted by Dixon, Johnson and 'ace' drummer Fred Below, with this session Mr. Berry comes of age.

Drifting Heart is about the closest Chuck ever got to sing like Cole. The song is a Latin-influenced ballad in which he takes extra care to pronounce the words clearly. Pity, therefore, that like his earlier attempt at balladry, the words are so unmemorable. Johnnie Johnson's piano has a percussive oriental tinge while saxophonist Leroy Davis moods along in the background together with an unknown trumpeter... maybe. What do you think?

Brown Eyed Handsome Man is, on the other hand, a classic Berry composition, each of its seven verses a tasty vignette extolling the virtues of the good-looking brown-eyed male. Berry himself could be that self-same brown-skinned hunk and the song is his own subtle and sophisticated version of braggart blues like Muddy Water's *Hoochie Coochie Man* or Howlin' Wolf's *Back Door Man*.

His wit shines through with lyrics that are the measure of Louis Jordan's finest. Compare, for instance, Berry's gag about the Venus de Milo losing both her arms in a wrestling match with the Marie Antoinette "let them eat cake" quip in Jordan's *Ain't That Just Like A Woman*.

Chuck's guitar break, played on his trusty Gibson ES-350T, is as sharp as his Gilbert Roland moustache and melds perfectly with Johnnie Johnson's rippling piano. The opening guitar figure was lifted note-for-note by Johnny Winter on his recording debut, *School Day Blues*, cut in 1959, and his guitar break on the track is also straight-ahead Berry. So is Duane Eddy's on his first hit, 1958's *Movin' & Groovin'*.

Brown Eyed Handsome Man has been recorded by all and sundry. Original rockers Holly, Perkins, Presley and Lewis cut it, as did retro-rockers Mitch Ryder and Johnny Rivers. Even one of those damn Bobbys (Vee, to be precise) had a crack at it! It is intriguing to eavesdrop on the Million Dollar Quartet as they marvel at Berry's wit and skilful wordplay while struggling to recall his couplets. As late as 1999, Paul McCartney paid tribute to Chuck — via Buddy Holly — with a truly excellent cover of the song laced with a button-accordion sound to give it a Southern Louisiana Cajun flavour.

Almost a decade before Bob Dylan made an art form of the protest song, Chuck Berry was in there having a go in his own sweet way on *Too Much Monkey Business*. Chuck's protestations, however, are not about senators and congressmen and other matters that exercised middle class minds, but about the everyday hassles of the average working stiff. In this sense, *Too Much Monkey Business* echoes the sentiments expressed in Louis Jordan's classic, *Choo Choo Ch' Boogie,* where "the only job open needs a man with a knack, so put that paper right back in the rack, Jack." Who but Chuck Berry would consider writing about such an everyday irritant as losing change in a payphone, and who else would do it so succinctly: "Payphone, something wrong, dime gone, will mail/ I oughta sue the operator [for] telling me a tale!"

Bob Dylan's *Subterranean Homesick Blues* is said to have been influenced by *Too Much Monkey Business*. Certainly the staccato delivery is similar, and there's even a 'Johnny' in the basement. However, the pissed-off sentiments expressed by the Stones in *Satisfaction* seem nearer the mark to me. Berry has salesman trouble: "Go on, try it, go on, buy it, you can pay me

London, 4 February 1990.

Johnnie Johnson, backbone of the Chuck Berry sound.

next week" while Jagger has the man telling him how white his shirt should be. Chuck's lady wants him to settle down and write a book, while Mick gets the ultimate put down from his "stupid girl"! Chuck's frustration builds with each verse — even his guitar solo winds itself up — until at the end of the song he utters in desperation: "Don't want your botheration! Go away, leave me be."

Too Much Monkey Business was a firm favourite with the beat boom boys: the Kinks, the Hollies, the Downliners Sect and the Animals all had a go at it. First generation rockers Presley and Charlie Gracie cut it. The Beatles (with John Lennon on vocals) recorded it at the BBC in the sixties. Clapton cut it with the Yardbirds, as did that other slow-hand, the late, great Lightnin' Slim.

Released in September 1956, *Brown Eyed Handsome Man* b/w *Too Much Monkey Business* was a cracker of a single, which, in spite of its quality failed to dent the pop charts. It did, however, become a double-sided R&B hit, *Brown Eyed Handsome Man* peaking at No. 5 in *Billboard's* 'Most Played By R&B Dee-Jays' chart, and *Monkey Business* at No. 4 in the 'R&B Juke Boxes' listing.

If *Brown Eyed Handsome Man* and *Too Much Monkey Business* are icons of rock and roll, then **Roll Over Beethoven** is a goddamn masterpiece! The all-consuming energy level in the glorious guitar intro has no equal in rock and roll, although interested parties are invited to compare and contrast the opening bars of bluesman Goree Carter's 1949 waxing, *Rock Awhile*. In rock though, even the similar-sounding intro to *Johnny B. Goode* isn't this BAD. This is truly a Berry showcase with the band content to lay down a solid beat for Chuck to ride. Only Dixon strays from the ensemble with his subtle change of rhythm pattern before the guitar break.

In his biography, *Father Of Rock & Roll*, Johnnie Johnson relates how the music for this Berry classic was created. He describes in detail his favourite left-hand "choppin' bass" figure which can be played at any tempo from slow blues to rocking boogie — the basis of *Johnnie's Boogie*, a tune he and Chuck played for years at the Cosmo and elsewhere. After a solo, Chuck would drop back in with Johnnie's bassline rhythm, and this pattern became so familiar as to become second nature to both musicians: "We got comfortable with each other. Chuck could just start out with a solo and fall right into the rhythm, and then it was just blendin' and playin' off each other." It was only natural, therefore, that they would rework *Johnnie's Boogie*.

When he was playing on stage, Chuck required a steady rhythm so that he could sing and duckwalk and use his hands without worrying about the music stopping. Speeded up a little to give it more drive than bounce, *Johnnie's Boogie* proved to be the perfect accompaniment for his latest composition, *Roll Over Beethoven*.

Such was the creative process behind many of Berry's recordings. As in this instance, songs would often start off with an idea for a theme such as going to school or a car chase, from which Chuck would develop the lyrics. He and Johnnie would then set them to music, trying out fast and slow tempos to suit the words. Sometimes, Chuck would come up with the tune; sometimes Johnnie would hit on it (*Maybellene*, for instance, was Berry's tune, while *Wee Wee Hours* had been in Johnson's repertoire for some time as an instrumental before Chuck added the words) — in other words, a true creative partnership: "Songs like *Roll Over Beethoven*, those were things we did together from the start. The words were all his, but can't one of us say we did the music all by ourself. We did the music together."

Curiously enough, Johnson appears to underplay Berry's knowledge and love of boogie woogie — despite the fact that both men borrowed from this musical genre, as they have both freely admitted. Regarding his guitar solos, however, Johnnie concedes: "Chuck's solos was all his. I gave him some change-ups, turnarounds, and of course I gave him that boogie rhythm style. But I never taught Chuck any solos. That *Johnny B. Goode* solo, how he started the song, how he started *Roll Over Beethoven*, Chuck did all those on his own. 'Cause he was listenin' to a lot of jazz guitarists like Carl Hogan and Charlie Christian and T-Bone Walker. Chuck had his own guitar style that was different from everyone else. I didn't teach him how to play the guitar, I just gave him some ideas and a rhythm style to lay his guitar over."

What Johnson describes here is a musical collaboration that has happened many times, before and since, when musicians gel and musical magic is made. Whether it was a collaboration of equals, you must decide, although he surely deserves some measure of recognition for his contribution to Berry's recorded legacy.

Roll Over Beethoven was released in the middle of May 1956, hit the *Billboard* R&B charts in June, and by early July had entered the 'Top 100' pop chart. After missing the pop charts with his last two releases, Chuck was back where he belonged: a nine week stay, peaking at No. 29 in the popular listings and No. 2 in the black charts. The record became an instant anthem of the emerging teenage youth culture and gave him an inkling of an untapped market for which he was increasingly to cater, or as he later put it: "the dollar dictates what is written".

Billboard, May 1958

The song itself appears to have been the product of Chuck's fertile mind, although he may have got a germ of an idea from a 1947 song by Red Mack called *Disc Jockey Blues* which likewise refers to one Peter Ilich Tchaikovsky. Only Berry would have the audacity to compare the classics to rhythm and blues and get away with it, and in the process produce something as durable as anything from Beethoven or Tchaikovsky themselves. Note also that Chuck was asking Beethoven to "dig these rhythm and blues" and not, as yet, rock and roll.

The lyrical imagery in *Roll Over Beethoven* is stunning. In the length of one line: "I got the rocking pneumonia, I need a shot of rhythm and blues", Berry provides the titles of two future R&B hits for Huey 'Piano' Smith and Arthur Alexander. He is not, however, averse to borrowing from a one-time travelling partner, Carl Perkins, and at one point in the song quotes from the latter's *Blue Suede Shoes*.

As Recorded by CHUCK BERRY on CHESS Record No. 1626

ROLL OVER, BEETHOVEN

Words and Music by CHUCK BERRY   75¢

ARC MUSIC CORP.
Sole Selling Agent:
KEYS-HANSEN, INC.
119 West 57th Street   New York 19, N.Y.
02674

Roll Over Beethoven is one of Chuck Berry's most-covered songs. Helene Dixon rushed out a cover version on the Vik label almost immediately in an attempt to garner sales before the original became established. The most famous cover, however, was that by the Beatles, who used it for the opening track of their second LP. George Harrison plays lead guitar note-for-note as per the original, but the tone of his Rickenbacker cannot match Berry's mellow Gibson. The song became so synonymous with the group that Berry took to introducing it at his gigs — not without heavy irony — as a Beatles number.

It wasn't only the Fab Four who implored Beethoven to roll. Carl Perkins and Gene Vincent did it, and Jerry Lee Lewis cut it on three separate occasions. Those wooden beat boys, the Dave Clark Five, covered it, as did the Electric Light Orchestra, who gave the world a 'Chuckovsky Berrythoven' version! Mike Harding, the 'Rochdale Cowboy', gave us *Roll Over Cecil Sharpe,* and folky joker Richard Thompson cut in with *Roll Over Vaughan Williams*. There have been French, German, Danish, Norwegian and Swedish versions. It seems that only the Chinese have missed out on the action because, when pop music was finally permitted in China in 1988, *Roll Over Beethoven* was banned because it was considered to be disrespectful to old Ludwig van B.

SESSION 6
CHUCK BERRY
Chuck Berry, vocal/guitar; Jimmy Rogers, guitar; Willie Dixon, double bass

Chess Records studio
4750-2 South Cottage Grove Avenue
Chicago, Illinois   **29 October 1956**

8303   **Havana Moon**   ◉ Chess 1645**b**, 1963**b** ■ Chess
              (Chuck Berry)   LP-1426, LP(S)-1514D, CH2-8201,
                                                    CH6-80001

Havana Moon is firmly based on Nat 'King' Cole's *Calypso Blues*, recorded in 1949 and featured in the Apollo jukebox shorts made in the 1950s, shown a while back on television, with Nat in a nautical striped T-shirt accompanied by a bongo player. In Berry's song, the bongo sound is replicated by the repeated playing of his bass strings in unison with Willie Dixon's firm bass figures.

Chuck has also mentioned Harry Belafonte's *Banana Boat (Day-O)* and *Jamaica Farewell* as influences. Certainly the melancholy theme of *Jamaica Farewell* (which Berry was later also to record) is echoed in *Havana Moon*'s storyline: a sad little tale of apparently unrequited love caused by the demon drink — rum in this instance.

Chuck adopts a Caribbean patois to express the feelings of an islander waiting for his American lover to arrive and take him to the promised land. He can hardly contain his feelings as he daydreams about the girl and their plans to live in a New York skyscraper apartment. But all is not well, and as the rum takes effect, the doubts begin to grow: "She say 'till then', she mean 'goodbye'." Eventually, the daydreams blend with real dreams and Chuck literally misses the boat. Like Romeo and Juliet, they part, each unaware of the other's true feelings.

The sparse backing and single-song session makes one wonder if the recording was intended to be cut as a master or if it was a rehearsal for a future date. The presence of Jimmy Rogers is debatable but one thing's for sure, two guitars can be heard — which could be the start of Berry's overdubbing days. Rogers himself has stated that he was on the session and, as he was in the studio on the very same day, his claim has a deal of credence. He cut two songs that same day — matrices 8304 and 8305 coming directly after *Havana Moon*'s 8303.

Jimmy Rogers was, of course, a founding member of Muddy Water's dynamic fifties' 'headcutting' band and recorded some wonderful archetypal Chicago blues in his own right. Matrix 8305, *Walking By Myself*, with its pounding beat and tremendous Big Walter Horton harp, is one of these. One also wonders if there aren't other songs from this dynamic trio lying dormant in the can?

In late 1956, a young Turk out on the West Coast recorded a song that went on to be recorded by at least three hundred other people and sell in excess of 100 million copies. That song was *Louie Louie* by Richard Berry & The Pharaohs. It was based on a Latin number called *El Loco Cha Cha* which provided the distinctive beat, and Chuck Berry's *Havana Moon* which provided the lyrical content. In Richard Berry's own words: "Chuck Berry had a song out then called *Havana Moon*, and that influenced me too. He sang it with a calypso beat, using a Jamaican accent. I guess those two songs were my main inspiration when I started writing *Louie Louie* in late '55." *[As 'Havana Moon' was cut in 1956, Berry must have meant late '56.]*

Originally coupled with *You Can't Catch Me* [Chess 1645], *Havana Moon* was reissued in 1966 as the flip of *Ramona, Say Yes* [Chess 1963] and unexpectedly went to No. 7 on the *Cash Box* R&B chart, perhaps benefitting indirectly from the popularity of *Louie Louie* with the mid-sixties US punk contingent.

SESSION 7
CHUCK BERRY

Chuck Berry, vocal/guitar; *possibly* Count Basie, piano; *possibly* Eddie Jones, double bass; *possibly* Sonny Payne, drums; *possibly* Wendall Culley *or* Reunald Jones *or* Thad Jones *or* Joe Newman, trumpet; Alan Freed, master of ceremonies

LIVE RECORDINGS
Camel Rock'n'Roll Dance Party (WINS/CBS)
New York City   **May/June 1956**

Maybeline *[sic]* (Chuck Berry)	■ WINS 1010, Radiola MR-1087, Deja Vu DVLP-2130 ◎ Magnum Force CDMF-075, Wolf 2010CD
Roll Over Beethoven (Chuck Berry)	■ WINS 1010, Radiola MR-1087, Deja Vu DVLP-2130 ◎ Magnum Force CDMF-075, Wolf 2010CD

"And here's the guy that is just the greatest" is Alan Freed's introduction to these two tracks. Recorded live for Freed's *Camel Rock'n'Roll Dance Party* radio show from WINS in New York City, sponsored by Camel cigarettes and syndicated coast-to-coast by CBS, they are a unique glimpse at a pre-*Johnny B. Goode*, still merry Mr. Berry. Except for his brief appearance in the 1958 *Newport Jazz Festival* film, *Jazz On A Summer's Day*, this is the only record of the live sound of Chuck Berry until his 1964 UK tour. More's the pity then, that the sound is so untogether, due mainly to the unsympathetic backing of the Basie band and Berry hitting some rather dubious notes. (Basie's aggregation was used as Freed's house band for a few months in the late spring and early summer of 1956 and backed other guests such as LaVern Baker, Etta James and Ivory Joe Hunter. The sound on these recordings is similar to that on Berry's cuts and this, together with the clearly-heard trumpet on both tracks, leads me to conclude it must be Basie's outfit backing our man.)

One of Chuck's professed ambitions was to play rhythm guitar in a big band and it must have been quite something for him to play with the Count — a hero of his from way back — to whom he later paid tribute by cutting his theme, *One O'Clock Jump*.

Despite being voted top rock and roll band in the country by *Cash Box*'s jukebox operators, Bill Basie admits in his autobiography that rock and roll was not their thing and, quite frankly, it shows here. However, what the tracks lack in musicianship, the audience make up for with their enthusiasm. The kids go apeshit during **Roll Over Beethoven**, no doubt when Chuck is practising his crazy legs routine or perfecting his duckwalk. During the guitar break they commence to chant: "Go, go, go..." Now, where have I heard that since?

Maybeline *[sic]* is a shortened reading consisting of only two verses. One is the "...top of the hill/ ...medicine pill/ ...Cadillac grille" verse that Chuck later said he added to *Maybellene* "after about five years". Well, here's proof that he had come up with the lyric within twelve months of the record's appearance — most likely to break the monotony of singing his two hits verbatim night after night.

These two tracks, and the others on the WINS LP, were recovered from a collection of twenty-three broadcasts that were preserved by the Armed Forces Radio & Television Service which provided entertainment for US forces overseas, and were discovered in Frankfurt, Germany. One wonders if there is more Berry material amongst these archives.

SESSION 8
CHUCK BERRY
Chuck Berry, vocal/guitar; Johnnie Johnson, piano; Willie Dixon, double bass; Fred Below, drums

Chess Records studio
4750-2 South Cottage Grove Avenue
Chicago, Illinois   **15 December 1956**

Rock And Roll Music *[demo]* *(Chuck Berry)*	■ Reelin' 001, Chess CXMP-2011, Chess CH-9190, Checkmate LP-1955
Untitled Instrumental *(Chuck Berry)*	■ Chess CH-9318 ◎ Chess CHD-9318

This session was never intended for release but was a demo date to try out two new tunes, both of which were destined to become enduring Berry titles.

Rock And Roll Music is an unashamed attempt by Chuck to cater for the mass white teenage market. The success of *Roll Over Beethoven* highlighted to him that there was a lucrative audience out there — one that he was to increasingly supply with the product he believed they wanted. *Rock And Roll Music* was a tentative start.

The demo of *Rock And Roll Music* is less relentlessly rhythmic and lacks the polish of the later released master, but it is nevertheless a robust cut. Clearly at an embryonic stage, the song at this point consists of just two verses sandwiched between choruses. Chuck sings "I never liked a Latin mambo, until I heard it on piano" and Johnnie Johnson shows us exactly what he means with a short piano break, followed closely by Berry's own guitar break. The demo finally fades out on the chorus rather than the definite stop of the issued version.

Untitled Instrumental could easily have been titled '*Jazz At The Philharmonic*' because it is a rough and ready precursor of *Rock At The Philharmonic*, recorded twelve months later. The tune is played at a slower, jazzier tempo than *Rock At The Phil*, and is one of those warm-up pieces Berry cites as unworthy of release. While it is no classic, neither did it deserve to languish in the vaults for thirty-four years until its release on the 1990 US album, *Missing Berries: Rarities (Volume 3)*. It was also one of five tracks unfortunately missed off Charly's otherwise comprehensive 1991 UK 9-CD box set, *The Chess Years*.

SESSION 9
CHUCK BERRY

Chuck Berry, vocal/guitar, steel guitar -1, vocal (double-tracked) -2; Johnnie Johnson, piano; Hubert Sumlin, guitar -3; Willie Dixon, double bass; Fred Below, drums; omit double bass and drums, add bongos -4

Chess Records studio
2120 South Michigan Avenue
Chicago, Illinois   **21 January 1957**

8378	**Deep Feeling** *[instrumental]* -1 -3 (Chuck Berry)	● Chess 1653**b** ■ Chess LP-1426, Pye International NPL-28031, Chess LP(S)-1514D ◉ Ace CDCH-397, Beat Goes On BGOCD-428
8379	**School Day** (Ring! Ring! Goes The Bell) (Chuck Berry)	● Chess 1653**a**, EP-5118 ■ Chess LP-1426, 1465, 1485, LP(S)-1514D, CH2-8201, CH6-80001
8380	**Lajaunda** (Español) -2 -4 (Chuck Berry)	● Chess 1664**b**
	La Jaunda (Español) *[alt. take]* -2-4 (Chuck Berry)	● Chess EP-5119 ■ Chess LP-1432, CH2-60023
8381	**Blue Feeling** *[instrumental]* (Chuck Berry)	● Chess 1671**b**, EP-5119 ■ Chess LP-1432 ◉ Ace CDCH-397
	Low Feeling *[instrumental]* (Chuck Berry)	■ Chess LP-1432

Up to this point, Chuck's Chess recordings had been made with his trusty blond Gibson ES-350T guitar (the 'T' stands for the two and a quarter inch 'Thin' body, as opposed to the fatter Byrdland model). On **Deep Feeling**, he shifts to a five hundred buck Gibson Electraharp pedal steel guitar to get the 'electra slide in blue' effect he so admired in the blues of Elmore James and Muddy Waters. Berry's *Deep Feeling*, however, has more than a tinge of country slide in it. He rides atop of a flowing rhythmical beat set by the Dixon–Below–Johnson ensemble, augmented by Howlin' Wolf's dynamic guitarist, Hubert Sumlin on rhythm guitar.

Deep Feeling is closely based on *Floyd's Guitar Blues*, recorded in 1939 by Andy Kirk & His Clouds of Joy featuring Floyd Smith on pedal steel guitar. The tune has been very influential on a number of blues and rhythm and blues combos — the best known probably being the hit version cut by Bill Doggett in 1958.

Berry's tune, in turn, has also inspired covers, notably *Stealing* by Jeff Beck and — to a lesser degree — *Snake Drive* by Eric Clapton & Jimmy Page. The most successful cover, however, was *Albatross* by Fleetwood Mac which replicates *Deep Feeling's* loping beat exactly. *Albatross* was a worldwide hit in 1968, and it's strange that Chuck's lawyers didn't hang it round the Mac's neck! Maybe the spirit of Floyd Smith was just too powerful for them to try.

At the close of the film *Hail! Hail! Rock'n'Roll*, there is a magical sequence where the camera glides through the grounds of Berry Park to the dreamy sounds of a steel guitar. It travels past the dilapidated guitar-shaped pool, along a path and through a doorway, passing from bright sunlight into the darkened interior of the clubhouse, finally settling on the concentrating figure of Chuck Berry hunched over his Gibson Electraharp, playing a version of *Deep Feeling*, totally absorbed in the beautiful sounds he is making.

The main song of the session was **School Day** (note the singular, and not the frequently misused '*Schooldays*'). The parenthesised subtitle was added to avoid confusion with similarly-named songs such as Louis Jordan's *School Days*.

Released in March 1957, the record was another smash hit for Chuck. It stormed up the *Billboard* R&B charts in April, hitting No. 1 on all three in August *[see page 285]* and shaking Elvis's *All Shook Up* from the top of the tree. More significantly, *School Day* made No. 3 and No. 5 respectively on the *Cash Box and Billboard* pop charts and even breached the British singles chart at No. 20 (a rare occurrence indeed in the fifties).

School Day was the song that finally put Chuck Berry on the popular music map. From here on in until the end of the decade he scored no fewer than twelve consecutive *Billboard* 'Top/Hot 100' entries with his single releases. It was also the lead song on his first LP, the aptly-named *After School Session*, whose title may itself have been inspired by the 1940 Louis Jordan waxing, *After School Swing Session*.

School Day, which Chuck composed towards the end of 1956 in a room at the Street Hotel, St. Louis, is a day in the life of an idealised middle class high school student and is squarely aimed at the white teenagers of the day... written and sung by a thirty-something year old black man. Berry recognised this dichotomy in his autobiography, wherein he explained that he was writing about his own high school days and not current schooldays. This is demonstrated by his reference to a 'juke joint' in the song... not the usual place to find the *Happy Days* crowd!

Whilst working on the music for the song, Chuck and Johnnie struggled to find an opening refrain. Eventually, Johnson suggested the intro from *Honky Tonk Train Blues* by Meade Lux Lewis, which he had used for years in his theme, *Johnnie's Boogie,* while working at the Cosmopolitan Club. When transferred from piano to guitar it sounded like a ringing school bell and provided the perfect opening.

The song, set to a rumbling bass and bouncy drumming, has each line echoed by a staccato guitar refrain, intended — in Berry's words — "to illustrate the frenetic timetable of school life". When the kids finally do "lay their burdens down", they still have the energy to chant *the* teenage anthem of the rock and roll decade: "Hail, hail, rock and roll/ Deliver me from the days of old!"

There is no doubt that *School Day* is a major Berry composition, but, as it was so deliberately tailored for the white teenage market, it doesn't quite ring true. Compare it to *No Particular Place To Go*, for instance, and feel the difference.

Upon its release, *School Day* was quickly covered by Big Tiny Little (an exile from Lawrence Welk's band) on Brunswick and has subsequently been covered by more than sixty others. It was particularly popular with the 1960s surfing fraternity, being cut by both the Beach Boys and Jan & Dean. Other less notable artists to cover it were Los Teen Toppers from Mexico, the Sleepy Sleepers from Finland and the Simpsons from Springfield, USA.

La Jaunda finds Chuck back south of the border, not in Cuba this time, but in Tijuana, Baja California. Willie Dixon takes five and Below swaps his drumkit for a pair of bongos whilst Berry adopts a very Spanish-sounding style on his Gibson.

Chuck once said he preferred the sweet harmonies of the Everly Brothers to those of the Beatles, and on *La Jaunda* he double-tracks his voice to emulate this feel. The second voice on the Chess 1664 single is a multi-tracked single vocal track, whilst the LP release includes an alternative cut with a true second vocal that is not multi-tracked. The LP version is more appealing because the voices are not perfectly synchronised.

Some cynical critic wrote that the song is a tale about a prostitute propositioning Berry who, being 'Mr. Too-Tight', pretends not to understand the lingo! This is an altogether jaundiced view based more on Berry's reputation and a personal incident rather than an analysis of the song. In essence, the story is a sweet come-on from a dusky Mexican beauty, so obvious that no language barrier could disguise it — and if you think Chuck misses the point, then so have you!

It is interesting to note that, on the original single release the title is written as one word (*Lajaunda*), while on subsequent releases it is in its more familiar form, sometimes being mis-spelled *La Juanda*. The song was earmarked to feature in the rock and roll exploitation movie, *Mister Rock And Roll* along with *Oh Baby Doll* — the other side of the single on which it was first released. Unfortunately, Chuck's celluloid performance hit the cutting room floor along with wildman Screamin' Jay Hawkins's contribution. Maybe, somewhere in some ageing film can, these gems await resurrection!

Blue Feeling really does sound like its title: a low-life, laid back, wee small hours blues. This time maybe it was a warm-up groove for the gang before they got down to the serious record making. The tune is notable for a tremendous staccato piano solo from Johnnie Johnson and the metronomic brushwork of Fred Below. Berry's playing is reminiscent of Johnny Moore's work with Charles Brown, whom he is known to have admired and with whom he was to tour on Irvin Feld's *Greatest Show Of 1957* extravaganza just a month after this master was cut.

Blue Feeling is not a remarkable cut, but what *is* remarkable is the audacity of the Chess brothers in foisting **Low Feeling** on their listening public. *Low Feeling* is, in fact, *Blue Feeling* slowed to half speed with twelve bars removed to fit a three-minute space on Chuck's second LP, *One Dozen Berrys*. This wasn't the first time that the Chess engineers had made 'house mixes'. The same fate befell John Lee Hooker's *Walkin' The Boogie* with a speeded-up guitar part grafted onto the original 1952 master. As Chuck was later to comment wryly: "I really loved the steel guitar, and the tunes would mysteriously emerge on the albums: *Deep Feeling*. *Blue Feeling*, which would be slowed down to *Low Feeling*. I was wondering if there'd be a '*No Feeling*' coming!"

SESSION 10
CHUCK BERRY
Chuck Berry, vocal/guitar, overdubbed guitar -1, vocal (double tracked) -2; Ellis 'Lafayette' Leake, piano; Willie Dixon, double bass; Fred Below, drums

Chess Records studio
2120 South Michigan Avenue   **6 May 1957**
Chicago, Illinois   **(15 May 1957)**

8498	**How You've Changed** -1 *(Chuck Berry)*	■ Chess LP-1432 ◉ Wolf 2010CD
8499	**Rock And Roll Music** *(Chuck Berry)*	◉ Chess 1671**a**, EP-5119 ■ Chess LP-1432, 1465, 1485, LP(S)-1514D, CH2-8201, CH6-80001
	Rock And Roll Music *[alt. take]* -2 *(Chuck Berry)*	■ Chess CH2-92521

8500	**Oh Baby Doll** *(Chuck Berry)*	● Chess 1664**a**, EP-5119 ■ Chess LP-1432, 1465, 1485, LPS(S)-1514D, Mercury 6463 044, Chess CH2-8201, CH6-80001
8501	**13 Question Method** *(Chuck Berry)*	■ Reelin' 001, Chess CXMP-2011, Checkmate LP-1955
12495	**Cranberries** *[instrumental]* *(Chuck Berry)*	unissued
12496	**How High The Moon** *[instrumental]* *(Nancy Hamilton, Morgan Lewis)*	■ Chess LP-1480, Reelin' 001, Chess CXMP-2011

Note: Chess LP-1480 was overdubbed with audience noise.

On this and the following three sessions — at which Berry cut some of his most famous tracks — Lafayette Leake replaced Johnnie Johnson on piano. In the film *Hail! Hail! Rock'n'Roll*, Keith Richards propounds the theory that Chuck Berry got his musical ideas by ripping off Johnnie Johnson and points to the fact that Chuck plays in keys more suited to piano than guitar. Berry has refuted this contention by pointing out that both his and Johnnie's influences came from a forties' jazz background, not a sixties' rock background. To infer that E♭ or B♭ are unusual keys for guitar players is to overlook a whole jazz guitar generation: Charlie Christian, T-Bone Walker and Carl Hogan all played in these keys.

The theory is perpetuated and expanded to an extraordinary degree in Travis Fitzpatrick's biography of Johnnie Johnson, *The Father Of Rock & Roll*. There is no doubt that Johnson was an important contributor to Berry's music, and Chuck would be the first to admit that there is nothing new under the sun, but if he *did* rely on Johnnie as much as is claimed, how do we square this with the fact that, during probably his most productive period when he recorded *Rock And Roll Music*, *Sweet Little Sixteen*, *Reelin' And Rockin'* and *Johnny B. Goode*, Johnson didn't even play on the tracks. Of course, the answer to this dilemma by the pro-Johnson camp is that Johnnie played on all of Chuck's sessions except the *Johnny B. Goode* session. During this period, however, Johnson was not a full-time musician and maintained a day job back home at the American Steel Foundry. Could he really have found the time to make these sessions in Chicago?

Ellis 'Lafayette' Leake had previously played in a number of West Side Chicago blues bands and recorded for Cobra with his friend and mentor Willie Dixon on the classic Otis Rush cuts. His powerful rhythmic playing — if it is indeed he — contributed enormously to the music and, with Dixon and Below also in tow, Chuck could hardly fail.

How You've Changed is a sad little song about fading love. Chuck laments that his girl has "changed our romance to a playful game" over a slow blues backing similar in tone to *Blue Feeling*, especially the brush-work by Fred Below. It's possible that the inspiration for the song came from the 1941 Dick Haymes recording with the Harry James Band, *You've Changed*. It isn't the same song, but the sentiments are very similar and Berry has mentioned James as a bandleader he liked. The track was also issued on *One Dozen*

Berrys, and it's here that the Animals heard it and cut it for *their* second LP, *Animal Tracks*, in the mid-sixties.

Rock And Roll Music encapsulates the feelings of the fifties' teenage generation, fired with enthusiasm for the brand new genre of music, rock and roll. Chuck expresses their desires and frustrations as he alternately samples and rejects the musical tastes of the older generation (which — ironically — is his generation). Out with the old, in with the new-fangled rock and roll music. Modern jazz, mambo, tango and congo (congo?!?!) all get the old heave-ho.

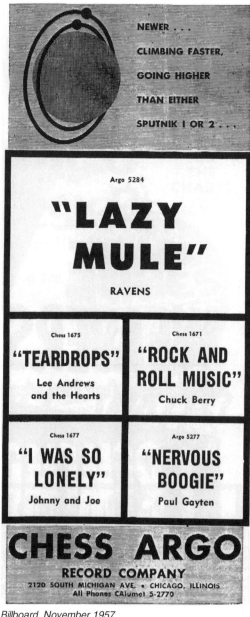

NEWER . . .

CLIMBING FASTER,

GOING HIGHER

THAN EITHER

SPUTNIK I OR 2 . . .

Argo 5284

"LAZY MULE"

RAVENS

Chess 1675

"TEARDROPS"

Lee Andrews and the Hearts

Chess 1671

"ROCK AND ROLL MUSIC"

Chuck Berry

Chess 1677

"I WAS SO LONELY"

Johnny and Joe

Argo 5277

"NERVOUS BOOGIE"

Paul Gayten

CHESS ARGO

RECORD COMPANY

2120 SOUTH MICHIGAN AVE. • CHICAGO, ILLINOIS
All Phones CAlumet 5-2770

Billboard, November 1957

What began as a two-verse demo five months earlier had by now been developed into an out-and-out Berry classic. Chuck says the song was all his own invention, and you'd better believe it. Part of the song's success must, however, lie with the rambunctious virtuoso performance by Lafayette Leake on piano. Boy, could he ride the rhythm! At one point Chuck instructs him to "keep on rockin' that piano", and rock he certainly does. Berry doesn't even get space to solo. Below throws in everything from his kit including cowbells, and Dixon's bass is, of course, as solid as ever.

Between the recording of the demo and master versions of *Rock And Roll Music*, Elvis Presley had released *All Shook Up*. Not missing a trick, Berry slips the phrase into the new 'jubilee' verse: "They're drinkin' homebrew from a wooden cup/ The folks dancin' got all shook up". Also, the "If you want to *rock* with me" from the demo is now toned down to the less salacious "If you want to *dance* with me" on the master.

On the alternative take of *Rock And Roll Music* we find a twin vocal from the 'Berry brothers'. Here, the song is taken at a slightly faster tempo and is more rhythmic, but apart from this there is little variation from the master.

44

Rock And Roll Music was released at the end of September 1957. On Friday, 8th November, Chuck performed the number on his debut appearance on *American Bandstand*, the top-rated national TV music show. Three days later, the record jumped into the charts — such is the power of television. It went on to become a massive hit, peaking at No. 8 on the *Billboard* 'Top 100', No. 14 on the *Cash Box* pop chart and No. 6 on the *Billboard* 'R&B Best-Sellers' chart.

Since then, the song has inspired well over one hundred cover versions, the most famous being by the Beatles (included on their 1964 *Beatles For Sale* album) and the Beach Boys (which reached No. 5 in the *Billboard* 'Hot 100' in 1976). It has also been recorded several times as an instrumental — including versions by James Last and one Otto Weiss on his upright organ! But then, there's no accounting for taste!

In 1956, Elia Kazan made the film *Baby Doll* — a steamy, sexy, Southern saga that spawned a craze in shortie baby doll lingerie. In 1957, Chuck Berry made the song **Oh Baby Doll**. Coincidence? I think not.

The number was itself featured in another Alan Freed film spectacular, *Mister Rock And Roll*. This time, dressed in a white suit, black suede shoes and holding his famous blond Gibson ES-350T, Chuck mimes a little better than in his first silver screen appearance and demonstrates how he got his 'crazy legs' moniker. The film was released in September 1957, a couple of months behind the single — by which time sales were fading and Chess had already put out the follow-up, *Rock And Roll Music*. This failure to synchronise film and record undoubtedly contributed to its relatively low sales.

Oh Baby Doll was Chuck Berry's seventh single release and the first not to make a major impression on the *Billboard* R&B charts, only making the twelve spot on the Dee-Jay listings for one week in July 1957. This is probably because the average R&B fan didn't care diddley-squat for the old alma mater. It did, however, sell well enough to reach No. 57 in the *Billboard* 'Top 100' and No. 45 in the *Cash Box* 'Top 60' — which was far more important to both Chuck and Chess.

The song is a classic tale of teenage insecurity: "Baby doll, when bells ring out, the summer free/ Oh baby doll, will it end for you and me?" and is really a sequel to *School Day*. The music, however, is anything but juvenile. The group set up a tremendous boogie rhythm, the piano and guitar chopping away in unison until Berry breaks loose with a surging solo. Despite the quality of the composition, it has not been popular in the cover version stakes, chalking up a mere half-dozen in its forty-something lifespan. The latest, cut in 1997 by the British group the Stargazers in true fifties doo-wop style, is probably the best.

13 Question Method remained unissued for twenty-three years until it was included on the 1980 bootleg LP, *America's Hottest Wax* [Reelin' 001]. This is strange because it is a neat little song, the equal of other Berry classics issued at the time. It is based around the simple idea of counting from one to thirteen (Berry would later use a similar plan to greater effect in *Reelin' And Rockin'*) and builds in tension as the questions are posed: "Will she or won't she?" — or to put it another way: "She said she don't, but I know she do!" The song ends in a big question mark from Chuck's guitar, so I guess we'll never know.

Ry Cooderised the song on his album, *Get Rhythm*, Steve Hooker cut it in the UK and Norwegian duo Bjørn Berge & Rita Eriksen covered it as recently as 1999, but otherwise it remains entirely Berry's.

How High The Moon was written by Nancy Hamilton *(words)* and Morgan Lewis *(music)* in 1940 for the musical *Two For The Show* and quickly became a jazz standard, recorded amongst many others by Count Basie, Stephane Grappelli, Lionel Hampton, Stan Kenton, Django Reinhardt and, of course, Nat 'King' Cole. In 1950, Les Paul & Mary Ford had a huge hit with the tune (it stayed at the No. 1 slot in the pop charts for ten weeks) and Chuck's version is most likely based on this reading.

The number is taken at a frenetic pace and has all the hallmarks of a studio jam, with each instrument taking a verse in true jazz fashion. First piano, then guitar, then a tremendous run from Dixon that hits all the bases. When he isn't soloing, Chuck sets up a frantic rhythm strumming his guitar 'til it comes.

Berry's recording first came to light on the so-called *Chuck Berry On Stage* LP as a one-minute forty-second uncredited run-out track complete with a fake overdubbed MC and audience. The full three-minute version was finally issued on the Reelin' bootleg and subsequently on several legitimate reissues. The cut was mastered on 1st August 1963 together with the still unreleased **Cranberries** (most probably another instrumental), possibly also for use on the *On Stage* album.

Matrixes 8502 (*Someday Baby)* and 8503 (*Oh Baby)* have previously been attributed to Berry, but I am assured that they are actually the Lowell Fulson tracks *Don't Drive Me Baby* and *You're Gonna Miss Me* (the latter also known as *'Oh Baby'* and *'Someday Baby'*).

SESSION 11

CHUCK BERRY

Chuck Berry, vocal/guitar; Ellis 'Lafayette' Leake, piano; Willie Dixon, double bass; Fred Below, drums

Chess Records studio
2120 South Michigan Avenue
Chicago, Illinois   **December 1957**

Sweet Little Sixteen *[demo]* *(Chuck Berry)*	■ Chess CXMP-2011, Checkmate LP-1955, Chess CH-9190

The recording engineer's sound level check introduces this demo of **Sweet Little Sixteen**, later to become one of Chuck Berry's greatest (in terms of sales) and most enduring (in terms of cover versions) compositions. The recording is relatively unpolished and Chuck fluffs his lines a couple of times, but otherwise the song's all there as regards structure and content.

Musically, it owes a great deal to Clarence 'Bon Ton' Garlow's 1954 recording, *Route 90*, which employs a very similar melody. Chuck must surely have heard this disc and used it as a basis for his composition. (Garlow, incidentally, got his nickname from his influential 1950 hit, *Bon Ton Roula* — Creole French for "[Let the] good times roll".)

The lyrics themselves are, however, pure Berry and are based on a backstage incident at a gig in Ottawa where Chuck saw an eight year old girl chasing autographs. Here, she is transmuted into a sweet little sixteen year old, her enthusiasm perfectly captured in the lyrics and the exciting rhythms. Note the consummate ease with which he slips from third person to first person to highlight the young girl's desire to see "somebody steal the show".

This plot is supported on Berry's patented chugging guitar boogie pattern which allows the piano to float on top: He confines his guitar to the rhythm and lets his pianoman take the sweet little solo. When he blows the lyrics just before the break, you can almost hear him smile. Realising the take is doomed, the band wing it with sweet abandon.

SESSION 12
CHUCK BERRY
Chuck Berry, vocal/guitar; Ellis 'Lafayette' Leake, piano; Willie Dixon, double bass; Fred Below, drums

Chess Records studio
2120 South Michigan Avenue   29 December 1957
Chicago, Illinois   (6 January 1958)

8627 (12551)	**Sweet Little Sixteen** *(Chuck Berry)*	○ Chess 1683**a**, 1866**a**, EP-5121 ■ Chess LP-1432, 1465, 1480, 1485, LP(S)-1514D, CH2-8201, A&M SP-6500, Chess CH6-80001
	Sweet Little Sixteen *[alt. take]* *(Chuck Berry)*	■ Reelin' 001, Chess CH2-92521
8628	**Rock**(in') **At The Philharmonic** *[instrumental]* *(Chuck Berry)*	○ Chess EP-5121 ■ Chess LP-1432 2CH-60023, CH6-80001
8629	**Guitar Boogie** *[instrumental]* *(Chuck Berry)*	○ Chess EP-5121 ■ Chess LP-1432 Pye International NPL-28031, Chess 2CH-60023 ◎ Beat Goes On BGOCD-428
8630	**Night Beat** *[instrumental]* *(Chuck Berry)*	■ Chess LP(S)-1488, 1495 ◎ Wolf 2010CD, Official 4012-FS
8631	**Time Was** *[slow version]* *(Gabriel Luna, Miguel Prado,* *Sidney Keith Russell)*	■ Chess CH6-80001
8632	**Reelin' And Rockin'** *(Chuck Berry)*	○ Chess 1683**b**, EP-5121 ■ Chess-1432, 1465, Pye Int'l. NPL-28039, Chess LP(S)-1514D, Marble Arch MAL(S)-702, Chess CH2-8201, CH6-80001 ◎ Beat Goes On BGOCD-428
	Reelin' And Rockin' *[take 1]* *(Chuck Berry)*	■ Reelin' 001, Chess CXMP-2011, Checkmate LP-1955, Chess CH2-92521
	Chuckwalk *[instrumental]* *(Chuck Berry)*	◎ Chess CHD-9170

Note: Chess 1866 and LP-1480 were overdubbed with audience noise.

Back in the studio less than a month after they cut the demo, the same gang are ready to cut two classics of rock and roll and a bunch of instrumentals.

So far, two takes of **Sweet Little Sixteen** have surfaced from the session with very little to choose between them. Berry again restricts himself to playing rhythm while Leake produces a nail-blackening *tour de force* solo — particularly on the alternative take — that would bring a wry smile to Jerry Lee's face. (It should be noted that Johnnie Johnson is adamant that it was he and not Leake who played on this session, and his recollection that Leonard Chess insisted he rip up the keys does add some credence to his claim.)

The alternative take, which is immediately recognisable by its false starts, runs at a slightly faster tempo than the master and in my view has the edge on the better-known version. The Chess brothers must have felt the same, because they cranked up the master tape a few ips's for the single release and subsequent EP and LP releases. The cut was finally issued at its proper speed in 1988 on *The Chess Box* [Chess CH6-80001], adding a sweet little sixteen seconds to the epic.

I remember first hearing the 45 while standing at the side of the waltzer when the travelling funfair visited our town, and thought it was terrific. However, listening to it again in the cold light of digital day, the guitar sounds tinny and Berry seems to have overdosed on helium. Nostalgia just ain't what it used to be.

The reference to "*Bandstand*, Philadelphia, PA" (which occurs twice on the master but only once on the alternative take) was probably aimed at securing an appearance on Dick Clark's influential TV show. If it was, the ploy worked, and in the early weeks of 1958 Chuck found himself back in the WFIL-TV studios in Philly lined up for another major promo.

The story goes that he wouldn't lip-sync to his record on the show which lead to an altercation with its presenter. As Berry tells it: "I said: 'Chuck Berry is not going to open his mouth and have nothing come out'."

This is mighty strange because he was merrily lip-syncing along to his songs in the films he made at this time. However, a phone call to Leonard Chess apparently quickly set Chuck wise to the power and ways of the broadcast media and, with the dollar signs buzzing in his mind, he made it up with Clark and, as he put it, 'pantomimed' to the song.

Released at the beginning of February 1958 with *Reelin' And Rockin'* on the flip, *Sweet Little Sixteen* was an immediate hit. Within a couple of weeks it was rattling up the *Billboard*

Billboard, February 1958

48

'Top 100' and *Cash Box* 'Top 60', eventually coming to rest at No. 2 on both, pipped by the Silhouettes' *Get A Job*. Indeed, sales were so swift that it made the pop charts ahead of the R&B listings, which it eventually topped. Even in the UK, *Sweet Little Sixteen* managed to breach the bastion known as the 'Top Twenty', peaking at a very reasonable No. 11.

It was reissued in July 1963 coupled with *Memphis Tennessee* — only this time both cuts were taken from the *Chuck Berry On Stage* LP and were therefore marred by the fake audience which disgraced this album. Needless to say, this single met with no chart success whatsoever.

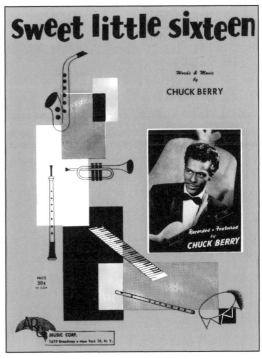

Sweet Little Sixteen has been extensively covered by rockers (Lewis and Cochran), rock stars (notably Springsteen), beat groups (Searchers and Hollies) and, most famously, the Beach Boys. Brian Wilson was so taken by the tune that he rewrote it as *Surfin' USA* and subsequently bequeathed 50% of the song to Berry at the insistence of Chuck's lawyers, thereby "adding glory to his name" as well as zeroes to his bank balance. And, lest we forget, the subject of Bobby Darin's 1958 Atlantic smash, *Queen Of The Hop*, was also a "sweet little sixteen".

The song was a particular favourite of John Lennon, who recorded it with the Beatles and also chose it as one of the two Berry songs for his *Rock'n'Roll* album. This was apparently another legal settlement: Lennon had agreed to record two Berry compositions on his album as a result of a legal action over the plagiarism of *You Can't Catch Me* on the Beatles' *Come Together*. I would guess the only problem this presented to him was which two Berry tunes to choose.

Sweet Little Sixteen was also recorded by Eddie Clearwater, one of a relatively small number of black bluesmen who were influenced by Berry. Clearwater (who at one point was promoted as 'the left handed Chuck Berry') began his recording career with a Berry soundalike called *Hillbilly Blues*, based on *Roll Over Beethoven*. His stage act was also full of Berryisms, and he may well have been one of the bunch of Berry imitators playing the chitlin' circuit in the '50s. His best shot at Berry is *I Wouldn't Lay My Guitar Down* on his 1979 Rooster LP, *The Chief*. Supported by none other than Lafayette Leake on piano, he damn near out-boogies Chuck and plays the way Berry should have been doing at the time.

In 1944, jazz impresario Norman Granz started a series of jazz concerts at the San Francisco Philharmonic Hall under the generic title *Jazz At The Philharmonic*. The series was a great success and developed into worldwide touring jazz concerts that ran into the sixties. Top jazz musicians were employed, including many who influenced Chuck Berry, such as Nat Cole and Illinois Jacquet, and it's no surprise that Chuck named one of his most enduring instrumentals, **Rock At The Philharmonic**, in acknowledgement (not *Rockin' At The Philharmonic* as it has frequently been mis-titled). He also had the opportunity to experience the talents of Illinois Jacquet directly when they toured together in 1956 and jammed with Johnnie Johnson at some 'after school sessions'.

In the late 1930s, two colossi of the electric guitar arose from Texas, both of whom were have a profound influence on Chuck Berry. One, Aaron 'T-Bone' Walker, moved into blues and became a founding father of the smooth post-war 'West Coast' style; the other, Charlie Christian, turned to jazz to become the man who moved the jazz guitar out of the rhythm section and into the spotlight as a solo instrument. Christian died aged twenty-three, and only recorded for three years between '39 and '41 with Benny Goodman's band, but his single-string runs on sides such as *Air Mail Special* and *Flyin' Home* clicked with Berry, who recycled them via outings such as *Rock At The Philharmonic*. As Chuck himself said about Christian's playing on Goodman's *Solo Flight*: "It's so great man, it's a sonofabitch! I got the first sixteen bars down — took me thirty years."

Rock At The Philharmonic is really a slowed-down version of *Big Three Stomp* recorded in 1949 by the Big Three Trio, which features some tremendous guitar from Ollie Crawford and — surprise, surprise — big Willie Dixon on bass. It's no coincidence that Dixon is on both tunes, but what *is* surprising is that he didn't claim authorship.

The tune leads off with a simple chord progression from Berry before he hits with an extended single-string solo. The baton is then passed to Leake at the piano for his spicy interlude. Underlying these pyrotechnics are the solid bass and drums of Dixon and Below, the former also getting to solo in a style very reminiscent of his work with the Big Three.

Guitar Boogie is a simple, stop-time twelve bar blues instrumental played at a medium-paced shuffle beat. After eight bars, the band abruptly stop to allow Chuck to solo for four bars before they cut back in. The solos are typical Berry guitar figures except where he wittily slips a phrase from *London Bridge Is Falling Down* into one of the breaks.

Over the years, there have been umpteen *Guitar Boogies* recorded, but none I've come across is a precursor of Berry's tune. There is, however, the case of rock guitar hero Jeff Beck, who, whilst with the Yardbirds, cut a note-for-note version of Chuck's number disguised as *Jeff's Boogie* and laid title to it! C'est la vie in rock and roll!

Night Beat is a perfectly-titled blues instrumental featuring prominent walking basses from Lafayette Leake, who also contributes a beautifully understated solo. The tune has a similar feel to *Deep Feeling* except that the sliding guitar notes are played by Chuck on his Gibson without using a slide.

It also bears a passing resemblance to the 1940 recording *After Hours* by Erskine Hawkins & His Orchestra, which included within its ranks the composer of the tune, pianist Avery Parrish. This subsequently became *Blues*

After Hours in the hands of the Texan blues guitarist Pee Wee Crayton, who hit with his version in 1948. Crayton's guitar influences were much the same as Berry's: Charlie Christian and T-Bone Walker, from whom Crayton received guitar lessons. It's quite feasible, therefore, that Chuck might have picked up on the tune from the Crayton hit.

Night Beat was probably one of those infamous warm-up tracks of which Berry has been so critical. In any event, it lay dormant for nigh-on seven years until released in quick succession as a filler track on the LPs *St. Louis To Liverpool* (November 1964) and *Chuck Berry In London* (April 1965).

Time Was — Chuck Berry's first cover song — was written in 1936 by two Mexicans, Gabriel Luna *(music)* and Miguel Prado *(words)*, and was originally entitled *Duerme*. In 1941, Sidney Keith Russell substituted English words and the song was a big seller on Decca for Jimmy Dorsey & His Orchestra with Bob Eberley on vocals. (Later on in the forties, Russell worked as a performer, recording artist and composer under the name 'Bob Russell' and wrote *You Came A Long Way From St. Louis*, which Berry would later record.)

The song is a twee romantic ballad, full of nostalgic yearnings for a rose-coloured past. Chuck obviously liked the tune as he recorded two versions, slow and fast. This is the slow version, which only escaped the Chess vault in 1988 on the *Chess Box* collection. He also used the song's idyllic/nostalgic theme in later compositions such as *Vacation Time* and *Lonely School Days*.

In 1942, Big Joe Turner played the Rhumboogie Club at 55th and South Parkway on Chicago's South Side. One of the songs he sang was *Around The Clock Blues*, and watching the fun through a ventilator window was a young, impressionable Mr. Berry. Chuck never forgot the experience, and fifteen years later reinterpreted the song as **Reelin' And Rockin'**.

Around The Clock Blues (Parts 1 & 2) was first recorded in 1945 by Wynonie Harris on the Philo label, and by Joe Turner himself (under the guise of Big Vernon) in 1947 on Stag, likewise in two parts; Apollo Theatre MC Willie Bryant cut it three months after Harris, appropriately for the Apollo label; there was even a Latin-American version cut as late as 1958 by Esther Sutherland called *Clock Mambo*. Berry's song, however, is an amalgam of the Harris and Turner cuts, but with the tempo definitely taken from the Big Vernon platter.

Turner's song rocks at a terrific pace, spurred on by tremendous piano accompaniment from his long-time associate Pete Johnson. His version leaves nothing to the imagination as he sings: "Lookin' at the clock and the clock struck three/ She said: 'Just a minute baby, I got to wee, wee, wee!' " and "Lookin' at the clock and the clock struck four/ Bed broke down and we got down on the floor!"

Harris's version is taken at a far more relaxed pace but is just as explicit with such memorable lines as: "Well the clock struck seven, she said: 'Please don't stop'/ 'It's like Maxwell House coffee, good to the last drop'!" (The song also begins with the couplet: "Sometimes I think I will, sometimes I think I won't/ Sometimes I believe I do, then again I believe I don't". Sound familiar?)

In late 1949, blues pianist Jimmy McCracklin cut a song called *Rockin' All Day*, which was later retitled *Reelin' And Rockin'*. Although it is not the same song as Chuck's, it does contain the refrain "I started reelin', I started rockin', and we rolled till the break of dawn". It also contains some tasty guitar licks, very reminiscent of Chuck's style, played by either Robert Kelton or a young Lafayette Thomas under the influence of the master himself, T-Bone Walker.

Berry's song is a combination of these recordings, taking the best from each. Chuck developed the number for his teenage audience, bowdlerising it to a song about dancing rather than copulating. He would, of course, revert to a much raunchier version in the liberated seventies.

Reelin' And Rockin' is the equal of its illustrious predecessors: from the wonderfully tense guitar intro to the time the bandleader says he "ain't playin' no more", the song rocks to its bobby socks. Harris's and Turner's songs set their rhyming couplets on the hour, every hour. By introducing minutes into the couplets, Chuck establishes an infinitely variable rhyming scheme which he utilises to the full. The pattern is set, but just when you think you have it sussed, he slips in the surreal line: "I looked at my watch, and to my surprise, I was dancing with a woman that was twice my size." The number is a rare instance of a Berry rocker without a guitar break, probably because it is packed with no fewer than a dozen verses.

It's difficult to comprehend in this day and age of dub mixes, house mixes and deejay mixes that crowd the 'B' sides of modern singles (or their CD equivalents) that *Reelin' And Rockin'*, an absolute classic of rock and roll, would be relegated to the flip side of a 45, albeit that of *Sweet Little Sixteen*. But this is how it was at Chess back in '58.

The alternative take of *Reelin' And Rockin'* is arguably even better than the issued master: it opens with a more conventional Berry guitar lick, followed by a spirited "Oh yeah!" from Chuck, obviously enjoying himself. He skips the "Sometimes I do..." bit and ploughs straight into the body of the song. Five of the first six couplets are similar to the master, but at 10:37 things start to get a little funky: "She made a boogie woogie bow and stretched out straight". By midnight, they are "rocking like an old steam shovel", which leaves little doubt about what's going down. This may be why the other version was selected for release, although the engineer seemed to think it was okay, as he comments: "That's just right! You wanna hear it Chuck?" Berry's quizzical "Yeah?" gives the impression that maybe he knew it was too hot to trot!

Reelin' And Rockin' has become one of a dozen or so songs that have formed the backbone of Chuck Berry's concert repertoire for the past thirty years. However, despite achieving such prominence and becoming a rock and roll standard, it has been recorded by relatively few other artists (if almost fifty can be called 'few' — but remember we are talking *Chuck Berry* covers here!). The Scandinavians in particular seem to have a soft spot for the song, as do quite a few blues-based artists and bands. Probably the most successful cover, in terms of sales at least, has been by the Dave Clark Five, who took it into the UK charts in 1965.

SESSION 13
CHUCK BERRY
Chuck Berry, vocal/guitar, overdubbed guitar -1; Ellis 'Lafayette' Leake, piano; Willie Dixon, double bass; Fred Below, drums.

Chess Records studio
2120 South Michigan Avenue   30 December 1957
Chicago, Illinois   (6 January 1958)

8633   **Johnny B. Goode** -1   ◉ Chess 1691**a**, EP-5126 ■ Chess
              (Chuck Berry)   LP-1435, 1465, 1485, LP(S)-1514D,
                                                   CH2-8201, CH6-80001

              Johnny B. Goode *[alt. takes 2/3]*   ■ Chess CH2-92521
              (Chuck Berry)

Quote: *'On August 20th, 1977, as part of the US bicentennial celebrations, a Voyager spacecraft left Cape Canaveral with a message to other life forms in our universe and beyond. On board was a recording of the 5th Movement from Beethoven's String Quartet in B Flat Number 13, Opus 130; also, a piece of rock and roll music called Johnny B. Goode by Chuck Berry'.* Hail, hail, rock and roll, roll over Beethoven, tell the Martians the news, the true quasar of rock and roll is born!

If *Too Much Monkey Business* and *Brown Eyed Handsome Man* are icons of rock and roll and *Roll Over Beethoven* a masterpiece, then **Johnny B. Goode** is the whole National Gallery! If not, why choose it out of a million songs to let the little green men know where it's at?

This is the song that launched a thousand anonymous groups who wouldn't know a gunny sack if they were trussed up in one and dropped in the Bridgewater Canal, in a thousand equally anonymous clubs across the world. It is the song recorded by the rich and famous, the not-so-famous and the infamous. The song that has closed more supergroup jam sessions than any other, simply because anybody who is anybody in rock knows *Johnny* (or at least think they do).

Not only did it influence a whole generation of white sixties' rockers, it also became a staple of black rollers such as Ray Sharpe and Eddie Clearwater who played the chitlin' circuit across the States. There are numerous interviews with black journeymen blues singers who refer to *Johnny B. Goode* and other Berry material as featuring in their repertoire of the late '50s and early '60s.

One of Chuck's musical rivals in his St. Louis days was the recently much-maligned Ike Turner. Not being one to miss a trick, shrewd Ike was quickly on the Goode trail with a manic song called *Jack Rabbit*, sung by one of his crew, Jimmy Thomas, and released under the quasi-anagrammatical pseudonym 'Icky Renrut'.

But where did the song originate? Disregarding the Michael J. Fox/ Cousin Marvin *Back To The Future* theory, Chuck says that *Johnny B. Goode* was written over a two-week period and was originally about Johnnie Johnson's wayward ways. He intensely disliked his partner's excessive drinking and the song started as a plea: Johnnie be good. However, his mother's conviction that someday he would be a star also inspired him to write

53

the opus and it is undoubtedly semi-autobiographical. Of course, Chuck never lived "way back in the woods in a cabin made of earth and wood" but his grand-daddy did, and he knew it too. He wasn't even a "little country boy", but sure as you're born he was a "little colored boy" — the way it was first written before he had second thoughts.

And what of the world's most famous guitar introduction? Berry has acknowledged the influence of Carl Hogan, Louis Jordan's guitarist from 1945 to 1949, but couldn't recall exactly where the intro came from. One listen to Jordan's 1946 recording, *Ain't That Just Like A Woman*, will solve the mystery. Hogan plays the famous intro note-for-note, but without the power that is behind Berry's version. To his powerhouse opening, Berry arc-welds a T-Bone Walker double-string figure that has the notes ping-ponging off the strings like balls in a pinball machine. This T-Bone device, which became as much a Berry trademark as his duckwalk is repeated in the lengthy guitar break later on in the song.

Len Chess was very keen on the number and supervised the session throughout. He can be heard doing just this on takes 2 and 3 when he stops the group in full flight, and in response to Berry's query: "What you want, Jack?" tells them that Leake is making *Roll Over Beethoven* and should "stay away from that". At the end of this attempt, Chuck states: "That's alright," and it is just that, nothing more.

You couldn't slide a cigarette paper between the difference in the lyrics of this take and the master, but there is a world of difference in the instrumentation: Take 3 has none of the famous Berry guitar 'ringing like a bell', and Lafayette Leake solos in the break. This might seem strange on a song about a guitar hero, but the *modus operandi* at this time on many of his recordings was to lay down a strong guitar introduction and a powerful rhythm track over which Chuck would then dub his wonderful guitar fills. This is certainly the case with the *Johnny B. Goode* master.

The 'rags-to-riches' theme of the song was one dear to Berry's heart and he continued the saga of Johnny in later songs such as *Bye Bye Johnny* and *Go Go Go* right on through to 1970's *Tulane*.

The title *Johnny B. Goode* is typical of Berry's witty play on words, but why the 'e' on 'Goode'? Many musical encyclopaedias give Berry's birthplace as San Jose, California; however, Chuck is quite precise in his autobiography that he was born at 6:59 am on 18th October 1926 at 2520 Goode Avenue, St. Louis... and therein lies the explanation.

Johnny B. Goode was released to an unsuspecting world on 7th April 1958. Compared to *Sweet Little Sixteen* (which was still in the charts at the time of the release), the record was initially only moderately successful. It reached a respectable No. 11 in the *Cash Box* 'Top 60' and an even more respectable No. 8 in the *Billboard* 'Top 100', No. 2 on the *Billboard* R&B Dee-Jay chart and No. 17 in the British charts — one of only three hits for Berry in the UK in the fifties (the others being *Sweet Little Sixteen* and *School Day*).

In the long term, however, *Johnny B. Goode* has been very good for Mr. Berry. I wish I was thrupence behind the royalties he must have earned from the extraordinary 340+ (and rising) cover versions of the song. Notables who have been touched by the 'Johnny' bug include the Beatles, Elvis, Hendrix, the Beach Boys, Johnny Winter and Wailer Peter Tosh, who cut a reggae version in 1983. Untouchables who have got into the '*Johnny*' bag include Liverpool comedian Jimmy Tarbuck, Freddie & The Dreamers and Elton John.

Even the nihilistic Sex Pistols, who professed to no musical influences, recorded it. There has been a *Johnny B. Bad*, *Johnny B. Cool* and *Johnny B. Goode's Good*, but none — repeat *none* — comes close to the original.

Billboard, April 1958

SESSION 14
CHUCK BERRY
Chuck Berry, vocal/guitar, overdubbed second guitar, steel guitar -1, piano, drums

Chess Records studio
2120 South Michigan Avenue
Chicago, Illinois   **28 February 1958**

8693	**Around And Around** ['Round And 'Round] *(Chuck Berry)*	⦿ Chess 1691**b**, EP-5126 ■ Chess LP-1435, 1465, Pye Int'l. NPL-28039, Chess LP(S)-1514D, CH2-8201, CH6-80001 ◉ Beat Goes On BGOCD-428
	Around And Around *[alt. take]* *(Chuck Berry)*	■ Marble Arch MALS-702
8694	**Ingo** [In-Go] *[instrumental]* *(Chuck Berry)*	■ Chess LP-1432, 2CH-60028
8695	**It Don't Take But A Few Minutes** *(Chuck Berry)*	■ Chess LP-1432, 2CH-60023
8696	**Blues For Hawaiians** *[instrumental]* -1 *(Chuck Berry)*	■ Chess LP-1435, 2CH-60028 ◉ Ace CDCH-397
	Do You Love Me *(Chuck Berry)*	unissued

The consensus view is that this session was the work of Chuck Berry alone, produced by overdubbing all the instruments and vocals himself. I have no doubt that this is so. The whole session has the ambience of an unfinished demo set and, except for the guitars, the other instrumentation is rudimentary. The piano is content to vamp along, the drums laying down a basic beat, while the bass part (played on the bass strings of the guitar) plays in unison with the rhythm guitar.

In earlier sessions, Chuck had frequently overdubbed his incisive lead guitar over the top of rhythm tracks. That this was also the case with *Around And Around* is clear when the two versions of the song are compared: they are identical in all respects except for the lead guitar — the final layer on the musical cake.

Around And Around is really *Reelin' And Rockin'* Part 2, a simple song based on a great riff about an after hours joint "rockin' 'til the moon went down" despite the intrusion of a police raid (shades of Brother Louis Jordan's *Saturday Night Fish Fry* here).

In its undeveloped state, *Around And Around* is only a minor classic and perhaps that's why it was relegated to the 'B' side of *Johnny B. Goode*. Had Chuck chosen to work up the song with Dixon, Below and Johnson, it would surely have ranked higher in the classics stakes.

The alternative version of *Around And Around* is so rare as to be practically raw. It is only available on the twelve-track stereophonic pressing of the UK Marble Arch LP, *You Never Can Tell*, and even on this disc it's not actually listed on the sleeve or the label. No wonder Charly missed it off their

Chess Years box set!

The alternative version doesn't improve on the regular version. As noted above, the only variation between the two is the lead guitar, and on the latter cut — despite it being a spirited effort full of the Berryisms we all know and love — it just doesn't gel so well with the rhythm.

As Chuck tells it, the song was born out of a pre-concert jam session (remember these were the early days) and is most definitely *not* autobiographical as far as the po-lice raid goes!

Around And Around has been well-covered down the years and has proved equally popular on both sides of the Atlantic: the Animals, Hollies and Pretty Things Britside; the Flamin' Groovies, Grateful Dead and Bruce Springsteen Stateside. None can compare, however, with the Rolling Stones' version of the song, on which the disciples out-rock the master. *Around And Around* was the very first song a spotty-faced Mick Jagger sang in public, accompanied by Keith Richards and Alexis Korner's Blues Incorporated in a funky basement club in Ealing. The song was also on a demo tape the boys were touting at the time, so by the time they reached 2120 South Michigan Avenue in 1964, they had it down pat.

The Stones had a wonderful knack of recognising the potential in Chuck's bluesy songs, emphasising their surging rhythms and milking them for all they were worth — and more. It is the combination of Ian Stewart's powerful piano and Richards's slashing guitar that makes the Stones cut *the* version to reckon with. Note the tremendous head of steam they generate at the end of the track. Berry himself was mightily impressed when, upon visiting the Chess studio during their recording session, he heard the playback. Not surprisingly *Around And Around* has remained in the band's repertoire for years. It was featured in their concerts in the late 1970s and Jagger sang it in an impromptu jam with another Berry disciple, George Thorogood, in the '80s.

Ingo is a pleasantly-relaxed jazzy instrumental with some fine interplay between Chuck's two overdubbed guitars, the rhythm guitar chords sounding almost like a saxophone. The piano break is pretty basic stuff: a percussive phrase followed by a repeated figure, then back to the staccato phrase. More proof, if proof be needed, that this is a lone Berry concoction.

One query remains: the title '*Ingo*' (which, incidentally, is spelt '*Ingo*' on the LP label and '*In-Go*' on the sleeve). What does it mean, if anything at all? Does it relate to Chuck's then seven year old daughter Ingrid (or to use her given name, Darlin Ingrid), or is it just another Chess invention?

Sounding very demo-like (it starts with a fade and ends abruptly), **It Don't Take But A Few Minutes** is about as country as Chuck Berry gets. The song consists of five verses, the last being a repeat of the first, each separated by a few bars of very countrified guitar played over a polka beat. The third verse introduces a recurring theme in Berry's repertoire, that of geographical distance and travel: "If I was in San Diego and you were in Portland, Maine" — about as far apart as you can get in mainland USA, and an idea repeated later in *Promised Land*, *Memphis Tennessee* and, of course, *Route 66*.

Chuck recounts the genesis of the song in his autobiography. Its inspiration was a white groupie girl down in Jackson, Mississippi who would make it with him irrespective of the time, the place or the consequences of a black man and white girl in physical congress. Little wonder that it "took but a few minutes" for Chuck to settle the case!

Blues For Hawaiians finds Berry seated at his Gibson Electaharp again for another crack at the *Deep Feeling* theme, only this time not so well executed. The recording is very primitive and even has some feedback at one point. Again, the backing is rudimentary, indicating this is a tune 'built up from the ground'. *Blues For Hawaiians* is sometimes confused with *Crying Steel*, but the latter is an altogether more professional cut dating from 1960.

Believe it or not, there is a cover version of this tune by Cub Koda, formerly of the Del-Tinos and Brownsville Station, one time Chess LP sleevenote-writer and Berry nut extraordinaire. Koda, who sadly recently died at the age of 51, was a member of that elite group of souls who have recorded a whole album of Berry songs (the others being Bill Black's Combo, Jim & Jesse, the Routers and the mysterious Sir Albert Douglas). His *Cub Digs Chuck* [Garageland LP-625 — note the number] is something else. The cover is almost identical to the *One Dozen Berrys* cover, with Cub striking Chuck's poses from his album (wrong Gibson though!). The song selection isn't exactly the same, but then, even Koda wouldn't have chosen to cut *Low Feeling*.

Berry is also rumoured to have cut a version of **Do You Love Me** at this session. If it does exist, it remains unissued. The cut on *Missing Berries: Rarities (Volume 3)* [Chess CHD-9318] which purports to be this item in fact dates from 1959.

SESSION 15
CHUCK BERRY

Chuck Berry, vocal/guitar, overdubbed guitar -1; Johnnie Johnson *or* Ellis 'Lafayette' Leake, piano; G. Smith, double bass (except -2); Willie Dixon, double bass -2; Ebby Hardy *or* Jaspar Thomas, drums

Chess Records studio
2120 South Michigan Avenue
Chicago, Illinois   **20 April 1958**

8848	**Beautiful Delilah** *(Chuck Berry)*	⏺ Chess 1697**b**, EP-5124 ◼ Chess 2CH-60028, CH2-8201, CH6-80001
	Beautiful Delilah *[alt. takes 15/16]* *(Chuck Berry)*	◼ Chess CH2-92521
8849	**Vacation Time** -1 *(Chuck Berry)*	⏺ Chess 1697**a**, EP-5124 ◼ Checkmate LP-1955, Chess CH-9318 ◉ Chess CHD-9318
	21 Blues -2 *(Chuck Berry)*	◼ Reelin' 001, Chess CXMP-2011, Checkmate LP-1955, Chess CH-9318 ◉ Chess CHD-9318
	21 -2 *(Chuck Berry)*	◼ Reelin' 001, Chess CXMP-2011

Something is flawed with **Beautiful Delilah**. Is it Chuck's guitar up-stroke on the beat, is it in the wrong key, or is the guitar out of tune?

Whatever it is, it spoils a great song with great lyrics about a great gal who's got it, knows it, and sure enough uses it. Beautiful Delilah who's so "tantalising" she "just can't be true"; beautiful Delilah who is so enticing that the "local Casanova let her steal his heart away and break it just for fun"; beautiful Delilah who is ogled by an "audience of seventeen" and is so cool as to "notice not a one"; beautiful Delilah, "swinging

BREAKING OUT!!
Chuck Berry
"VACATION TIME"
b/w
"BEAUTIFUL DELILAH"
Chess 1697

like a pendulum, walkin' down the aisle" (like the opening scene from *The Girl Can't Help It*). Poor Chuck can only observe from a distance because "Rebecca don't 'low me to fool around with you". (The choice of the name Rebecca as the steadying influence is another biblical reference, Rebecca being the faithful wife of Isaac and mother to Jacob and Esau.)

Alternative takes 15/16 first surfaced in 1986 on the *Rock'n'Roll Rarities* album [Chess CH2-92521]. The sum total of Take 15 goes:

— Guitar chord —

Chuck:	"Ready."
Engineer:	"Take 15."
Chuck:	"Sure-nuff?"

— Plunk —

Engineer:	"Eh?"
Chuck:	"Sure-nuff?"
Engineer:	"It's 16 now!"

Take 16 lacks the menacing guitar introduction of the released version, but benefits from a more prominent string bass played by one 'G. Smith', whoever he was. The cut is also taken at a faster pace than the single and features a spirited *Little Schoolgirl* based guitar break and enthusiastic piano. All in all probably the better cut of the two.

Vacation Time, **21** and **21 Blues** are versions of the same composition. A sickly-sweet song that'll have your teeth aching if you don't brush after every listening, I'm afraid this is a lapse into the nauseous moon/June, romantic/nostalgic mode to which Berry was occasionally prone. It seems they struggled with the song, because the three versions are very different, suggesting that they couldn't decide on a suitable treatment: *Vacation Time* is a ballad, *21* a rocker, and *21 Blues* a boogie.

21 Blues is the best of the bunch on account of its rumbling boogie beat and the embryonic *No Particular Place To Go* style 'ringing guitar'. *21* is the least accomplished: kicking off with the *Maybellene* intro, it drifts and almost loses its direction mid-way. It ends with Chuck, realising it's gone, not even bothering to finish the last line.

There is doubt about the piano-player on this session: Chess files list Leake, whilst Willie Dixon recalled that it was Johnson (who from aural evidence does seem the favourite). I would also question Ebby Hardy as the drummer on this and the following session considering he seemed to have quit the scene in 1956. Perhaps Berry's occasional road band drummer, Jaspar Thomas was in the seat?

The session produced one of Chuck's weakest single releases, *Vacation Time* backed by the flawed but *Beautiful Delilah*. The coupling was released at the beginning of July 1958 to tie in with the school summer recess but failed to attract attention, only making No. 81 in the *Billboard* 'Top 100' and not managing to scrape into the R&B chart at all.

It is a reflection of the quality of the two songs that *Vacation Time* has only been covered once (an obscure waxing by the Finnish group, Teenage Kicks), whilst *Beautiful Delilah* has so far only tempted a score of performers to succumb to her charms — including the Kinks, the Downliners Sect and the Rolling Stones in the sixties, and pub rockers Dr. Feelgood and the Count Bishops a decade later .

SESSION 16

CHUCK BERRY

Chuck Berry, vocal/guitar, overdubbed guitar -2; Johnnie Johnson, piano -1; G. Smith, double bass; Ebby Hardy *or* Jaspar Thomas, drums/percussion-3

Chess Records studio
2120 South Michigan Avenue
Chicago, Illinois

12 June 1958
(2 May 1958)

8864	**Oh Yeah** -1 *(Chuck Berry)*	■ Chess 2CH-60028, CH2-92521
8865	**Hey Pedro** -2-3 *(Chuck Berry)*	○ Chess 1700**b**, EP-5124 ■ Chess LP-1435, 2CH-60028
	Hey Pedro *[alt. take]* -2-3 *(Chuck Berry)*	unissued
8866	**Time Was** *[fast version]* -1 *(Gabriel Luna, Miguel Prado, Sidney Keith Russell)*	■ Chess 2CH-60028, CH2-92521
8867	**House Of Blue Lights** -1 *(Don Raye, Freddie Slack)*	■ Chess 2CH-60028, CH-9190, CH6-80001
8868	**Carol** -1-2 *(Chuck Berry)*	○ Chess 1700**a**, EP-5124 ■ Chess LP-1435, 2CH-60023, CH2-8201, CH6-80001

Oh Yeah is nothing but a list of Chuck's song titles strung together to a fast boogie beat — a veritable celebration of his wonderful music. In just three short years he had accumulated a catalogue of copper-bottomed rock and roll durables that lesser mortals would have died for. In all, twenty-one titles are mentioned (twenty-two if you count *Oh Yeah* itself), most of which are classics. No wonder he felt it was time to celebrate.

Over the years, record company errors have resulted in *Oh Yeah* being credited to Bo Diddley (who cut a completely different song called *Oh Yea)* and Chuck being credited with authorship of Muddy Waters's *Oh Yea* (again an entirely different composition from Berry's and Diddley's). "C'est la vie," say the old folks!

Hey Pedro, the 'B' side of *Carol*, is another excursion south of the border down Mexico way. A pretty daft little novelty ditty half-sung, half-spoken by Chuck in his pseudo-Spanish patois. The instrumentation consists of string bass, guitar, overdubbed guitar, claves and cymbals. The latter is usually listed as 'unknown', but surely it must be either Ebby Hardy or Jaspar Thomas sitting at the drumkit?

The alternative take of this song is almost a minute longer and contains different lyrics ("Hey Pedro, I see New York, the big city, let's go Pedro") but is equally unrevealing as to why Pedro was so idle. The song is alternatively titled *Lazy Pedro* by its publisher, Arc Music, but as far as I'm aware it has never been released under this title.

Six months after his first crack at **Time Was**, Chuck gives it another go. This cut is sometimes referred to as the 'fast version', but would more appropriately be called the 'swinging version' thanks to Hardy's prominent drumming, which really does oscillate. This *Time Was* has an instrumental passage and a repeated final verse, making it the better version of the two, all told.

House Of Blue Lights first saw the light on 12th February 1946. Written and played by boogie woogie man Freddie Slack with Don *'Down The Road Apiece'* Raye, and sung by Ella Mae Morse ('The Cow Cow Girl'), then vocalist in Slack's band. The original opens with some very hip jive talk between Ms. Morse and Raye before cutting into the boogie proper.

The record was only a modest R&B hit, but proved more influential with acts working in different musical styles. Not only did Chuck dig it, but earlier in the fifties another white boogie master, Merrill E. Moore (a pupil of Slack) cut it. The Andrews Sisters softened it up for Jerry Lee to maul later on down the line. Later still, country band Asleep At The Wheel cut it in a Western Swing mode, in contrast to George Thorogood, whose rendition was resolutely executed in Berry's style.

Chuck's version, which remained unissued until the release of *Chuck Berry's Golden Decade (Volume 3)* [Chess 2CH-60028] in 1974, skips the jive and hits the beat straight off with a *Johnny B. Goode* guitar intro which sounds like it might have been spliced into the track. Although the song rolls along nicely, it doesn't hit the top of the rhythm Richter scale. My guess is that this is because Chuck didn't overdub the lead, as on many of his best boogies, but covers vocal, lead and rhythm bases on the same take. Nevertheless, his *House Of Blue Lights* still has some great moments: love the jazzy bass, for instance, and dig his scat singing (*à la* Ella) as the song plays out.

Clearly the star of the session, **Carol** (named after Chuck's niece) is a rock and roll thoroughbred from the Berry stable of fillies, second only to *Maybellene* in the popularity stakes. The distinctive intro from Chuck hails one of his best rocking songs, a jumping little record expressing his fear of losing his girl, Carol, to a body who can dance better than he can. "Oh Carol, don't let him steal your heart away/ I've *got* to learn to dance if it takes all night and day," he sings... and boy does he mean it too!

If the band in the joint is as hot as Chuck's little combo, then Carol's bound to get her kicks. The bass, drums and guitar set up an awesome rhythm. Listen to the bass strings slap the neck of the bass fiddle and hear the

Billboard, September 1958

hammer-blow drumming in the stop-time breaks. Above this well-oiled machine, Berry's patented lead guitar rips and runs. Damn fine!

Keith Richards once said: "There was a time in my life where the only thing I wanted to do was to play guitar like Chuck Berry." On the Rolling Stones' cut of *Carol* he gets as close as it gets. The song was one of the highlights on the group's first epoch-making album and remained a mainstay of their gigs for decades, racking up eight different recorded versions courtesy of the bootleggers. The Beatles, with Johnny B. Lennon on vocal, also had their *Carol* bootlegged. Last and least, *Carol* also suffered the indignity of being recorded by the tedious boogie band Status Quo who built their whole career on the back of Berry's beat.

Carol was released as Chess 1700 at the beginning of August 1958, and by the end of September had peaked at No. 18 in the recently-renamed *Billboard* 'Hot 100', No. 31 in the *Cash Box* 'Top 75' and No. 9 in the *Billboard* R&B Dee-Jay chart.

SESSION 17
CHUCK BERRY WITH THE BLUES BAND

Chuck Berry, vocal/guitar, speech -1; Buck Clayton, trumpet; Jack Teagarden, trombone; Tony Scott, clarinet, George 'Buddy' Tate, tenor saxophone; Elman 'Rudy' Rutherford, baritone saxophone; George Auld, alto saxophone; Ray Bryant, piano; Kenny Burrell, guitar; Tommy Bryant, double bass; Jo Jones, drums; George Wein, master of ceremonies -1

LIVE RECORDINGS
Newport Jazz Festival
Freebody Park
Newport, Rhode Island   **5 July 1958**

Introduction -1	◎ Phontastic PHONT NCD-8815
Schooldays [School Day] (*Chuck Berry*)	◎ Phontastic PHONT NCD-8815
No Money Down (*Chuck Berry*)	◎ Phontastic PHONT NCD-8815
Sweet Little Sixteen (*Chuck Berry*)	◎ Phontastic PHONT NCD-8815, Wolf 2010CD
Johnny Be Goode [sic] (*Chuck Berry*)	◎ Phontastic PHONT NCD-8815

In 1954, Louis and Elaine Lorrilard launched the *Newport Jazz Festival* with the assistance of John Hammond Sr, who helped and advised with the musical content of the concerts. Hammond was a major supporter of African American music and in the vanguard of the Civil Rights movement from the thirties on. He had a hand in the recording careers of many jazz and blues greats: Bessie Smith, Billie Holiday, Benny Goodman, Charlie Christian, Joe Turner, Meade Lux Lewis, Pete Johnson and Albert Ammons all benefited from his largesse. It was Hammond who persuaded the Lorrilards to book Chuck Berry for the 1958 event — much against the wishes of many a hardened jazz buff, who considered Berry and his upstart rock and roll too vulgar, too commercial and not authentic enough for the show.

By most accounts, Saturday evening's *Blues In The Night* segment of the festival wasn't received too well. A contemporary *Billboard* report of the concert states: *'Let it be said here and now that all of the performers involved here, Ray Charles, Joe Turner, Big Maybelle and Chuck Berry, performed splendidly. The failure of rapport between them and the audience (except in the case of Chuck Berry, who did get a reaction) was not wholly the fault of the artists... Chuck Berry received the biggest response from the crowd, the younger set, especially. But he also received the worst response from the older set, the critics and the introspective jazz fans. Chuck sang his record hits, 'Sweet Little Sixteen', 'Johnny B. Goode', etc, and did a fine job. But a straight rock & roll singer like Chuck was out of place on a blues or jazz show.'*

Berry's set at Newport is preceded by a straight-laced and ponderous introduction by the master of ceremonies, George Wein, who, together with the Lorrilards, had started the whole *Newport Jazz* scene. As though to justify his presence, Wein introduces Chuck as "One of the originals of the blues," quickly realises his *faux pas* and adds: "Not one of the *original* blues singers." Through him we learn that Chuck Berry's first influence was Joe Turner and he has been profoundly influenced by Big Bill Broonzy; that at 31 years old he's only been a professional performer for three years, but began singing in fourth grade and for a couple of years led a gospel quartet. We hear that Chuck feels there's room for all kinds of music — blues, jazz, dance music and rock and roll — and that you can get the same intensity of soul from all categories of music. We're told that most of his songs are his own compositions and, like calypso music, they are a social commentary. The introduction finally ends: "From St. Louis, with three records which to date have sold more than a million copies apiece, even by record company report, Chuck Berry."

Chuck steps up to the microphone and adds to the introduction in a more flowing manner: "I must say I think it's an honor to be here, believe me, amongst such great musicians and such fine people. I might say that I'm comparatively new in the music world as of three years ago. As of the day before yesterday I made my first recording and since then have recorded a number of twelve records, of which three or four of these might have reached your ears."

If this is correct, *Maybellene* would have been recorded on 3rd July 1955 and not on 21st May. Berry probably confused the recording date with the release date which must have been far more memorable to the young star. Surely everyone remembers the date on which their very first record came out?

Chuck really must have considered it an honour to be playing on the same bill as Big Joe Turner, one of his seminal influences and the guy he had watched through a Chicago club fanlight like a one-eyed cat in his teenaged years. He must also have got a kick out of playing with the 'Blues Band', a scratch outfit put together for the day to back the blues artists: Joe Turner and Big Maybelle Smith. Buck Clayton, Buddy Tate and Jo Jones had all played in Count Basie's band, and George Auld had played on the Benny Goodman/ Charlie Christian sides — all very influential on the young Mr. Berry.

Although these guys are listed above, they don't all play on Berry's songs. It's difficult to determine who plays when with ensemble playing, as here. I cannot hear any second guitar or piano, for instance, and if the saxes are indeed there, they are pretty low in the mix.

Chuck wows 'em at the Apollo, 1959.

The fifth *Newport Jazz Festival* was filmed in colour by the renowned fashion photographer Bert Stern and the edited highlights were released a year later as *Jazz On A Summer's Day*. Sandwiched incongruously amongst the jazzers is our man singing **Sweet Little Sixteen**, which he introduces as "*Sweet Sixteen*". Trombonist Jack Teagarden doesn't play but stands grinning in a rather self-conscious way as Chuck demonstrates his duckwalk to the jazz cognoscenti. Only clarinettist Tony Scott seems to enter into the spirit as he joins Chuck during the instrumental break. The crowd, however, seem to like it (maybe they got no kicks from modern jazz!) and the boogie is certainly appreciated by one old-timer in a baggy suit, buck-dancing in the twilight. This is a rare — possibly unique — filmed glimpse of Berry in the '50s actually performing rather than miming, and it would be great to see his complete performance out on video.

"Another song that came along in my repertoire is a song about a car I'd always wanted," is how Chuck introduces **No Money Down**. This is the cream of the set, with strong guitar and a Dixieland backing that works surprisingly well.

Chuck likewise produces some mighty tough sounds from his trusty blond ES-350T on **Schooldays** and **Johnny Be Goode**, and sings it as though he means it. The band appear to start rather tentatively, but by the end of the set they are won over by the young pretender. A battle royal rages between Berry and the band, as he slices through the backing with his sabre-sharp licks, at times sounding like you're tuned into two radio stations simultaneously.

The Phontastic CD is a good quality product, but the track on the Wolf release is poor, probably dubbed from the video or film soundtrack.

SESSION 18

CHUCK BERRY

Chuck Berry, vocal/multi-tracked guitar, overdubbed bass and drums; omit multi-tracked guitar and bass -1

Chuck Berry's office
4221 West Easton Avenue
St. Louis, Missouri   **July 1958**

9071	**Jo Jo Gunne** [Joe Joe Gun] -1	⦿ Chess 1709**b**, EP-5126 ∎ Chess
	(Chuck Berry)	LP-1435, 2CH-60023, CH6-80001

9073	**Memphis Tennessee**	⦿ Chess 1729**b**, 1866**b** ∎ Chess
(12552)	*(Chuck Berry)*	LP-1480, 1485, LP(S)-1514D,
		CH2-8201, CH6-80001

Note: Chess 1866 and LP-1480 were overdubbed with audience noise.

July 1958, the weather is hot and so is Chuck Berry. The Chess brothers need more Berry material and Chuck resorts to home produce made in his newly-formed offices in St. Louis. Out of this necessity comes beauty: **Memphis Tennessee**.

Recorded on a $79 Sears Roebuck reel-to-reel recorder on a muggy July afternoon, what *Memphis* lacks in production values is more than compensated for by its home-grown, apple pie charm. Chuck layered the tracks, guitars, bass and vocals over the 'ticky-tick' drums that sound so good to him and so good to a million other ears too. It's been claimed that the drums were overdubbed at Chess later when they received the tape from Berry, but don't you believe it!

Memphis is a sad story of long-distance love, with an unexpected twist at the tail end of the tale. Right up until the last verse it seems the party that the caller is trying to contact is a girlfriend, wife, lover... an adult female, anyway. The last verse, however, reveals all and 'Marie' turns out to be his six year old daughter with "hurry home drops on her cheek", from whom he is torn apart by marital strife. An altogether more adult theme than Berry's usual fare and ultimately more satisfying as a result. (Muddy Waters's *Long Distance Call* is quoted by Chuck as the inspiration for his telephone epic, but other than this there are no other points of reference to this original Berry composition.)

Memphis features in the 1958 rocksploitation flick *Go, Johnny, Go!* in which we see Chuck (white tux, black slacks and his big blond Gibson) miming the song in front of a huge camera which transmits the images of him grinning, bobbing and duckwalking like some demented Egyptian hieroglyphic to the children of Middle America watching the show on enormous TV sets with tiny, almost circular screens.

Despite its obvious charms, *Memphis* had to wait twelve months for a release, and only then as the 'B' side of *Back In The USA*. Although the song never meant much chartwise in the USA, scraping into the *Cash Box* 'Top 100' pop chart at No. 87 and never making *Billboard*'s listings at all, it rose again five years later and six thousand miles to the east to become a British beat boom anthem. Premier League groups like the Animals, Beatles, Stones and Hollies all cut it along with numerous other lesser-known and lesser-talented bands. Dave Grundy (who changed his surname to 'Berry' in deference to his idol) covered it as 'Dave Berry & The Cruisers'. Ironically, in October 1963, D. Berry found himself in direct competition with C. Berry for chart honours when Chuck's original recording (coupled with *Let It Rock*) was issued in the UK on the Pye International label. In the event, Chuck won the tussle, reaching No. 6 against Dave Berry's No. 19.

Back in the USA, the airwaves reverberated to Johnny Rivers's summer '64 hit version of the song. That same year, Carole Coby cut an 'answer' record called *Memphis Calling New York City* in which daughter Marie makes a return call to her dear dad. The song is credited to 'C. Berry', but I doubt if Chuck wrote the new lyrics. Unusually for Berry material, three great soul brothers — Messrs. Pickett, Covay and Green — also picked up on the number. *Memphis* also turned out to be a popular instrumental theme and notables who recorded it in this mode were: Bill Black (who cut a whole album

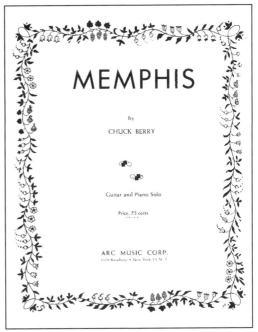

of Berry tunes), Bill Doggett (the great *Honky Tonk* man), Travis Wammack (the 'scratchy' Memphis guitar man) and Chuck's old musical sparring partner, Bo Diddley. It must have been particularly gratifying for Berry to find out that one of his big band idols, Count Basie, cut a version in 1967. The best and most inventive instrumental version, however, is the 1963 hit by Lonnie Mack, a tremendous *tour de force*, as many a returning rocker will testify.

Jo Jo Gunne (or *Joe Joe Gun*, as it was mis-spelt on some early pressings) is Berry's version of the old folk 'toast', *The Signifying Monkey*, which he heard whilst in the Algoa Intermediate Reformatory for Young Men. Chuck was highly amused by its ribald content and, if you want a flavour of the original, try to hear the two unexpurgated versions on Rounder LP-2014, *Get Your Ass In The Water And Swim Like Me*. These performances were recorded in 1968 and 1970, but the rhyme goes way back (albeit not quite to "ancient history" as Chuck would have it) and is related to *The Dirty Dozens*, *Monkey And The Baboon*, *Dirty Mother Fuyer*, *Shave 'Em Dry* and many other bawdy blues and pre-blues songs.

The Signifying Monkey was also recorded in less explicit terms in 1946 and again in 1947 by Berry's bosom bass man, Willie Dixon, early on in his career with the Big Three Trio. Bandleader Cab Calloway cut Willie's version of the song in 1947 under the title of *The Jungle King*. Later, in 1955, Smokey Joe Baugh, an early Sun rockabilly artist, recorded *The Signifying Monkey*. Later still, in 1972, West Coast R&B guru Johnny Otis cut his own raunchy interpretation.

Nat Cole's recording of *Straighten Up And Fly Right* also had resonance with Chuck in his early days, and echoes of this song can likewise be detected in *Jo Jo Gunne*.

Berry's composition is no carbon copy of the old tunes, however, though it does follow the traditional storyline about a "meddlesome monkey" who creates bad vibes between the lion and the elephant, gets cornered for his mischief by the lion, but finally outwits the jungle king. There is a clear parallel to be drawn here with the Br'er Rabbit tales where the crafty underdog is an allegory for the black man who outwits the dominant white man.

Musically, the song is full of Berryisms, each verse punctuated by snatches of *Carmen*, *Dragnet*, *London Bridge Is Falling Down* and the *Gillette Razor Theme*. Berry acquits himself well with some energetic drumming and yelling in the background, although I do detect a splice in the cut.

The then-popular *Peter Gunn* television show, with its even more popular theme, may have given Chuck the idea for the title. Don & Dewey's *Ko Ko Joe*, another rock and roll monkey tale, may also have been an influence. Whatever, Berry's song title certainly influenced others. Apart from Keith Richards naming his son Jo Jo, it was also the name of two sixties' rock bands — an obscure British group and a more famous US outfit. And, lest we forget, the character in the Beatles' *Get Back* was also a 'Jo Jo'.

Surprisingly, only three artists have recorded the *Jo Jo* saga, one of these being Dave Edmunds who knows a thing or two about the Berry canon.

SESSION 19
CHUCK BERRY
Chuck Berry, vocal/guitar, overdubbed guitar; Johnnie Johnson, piano; Willie Dixon, double bass; Fred Below, drums; band vocal -1

Chess Records studio
2120 South Michigan Avenue
Chicago, Illinois   **28 September 1958**

9070	**Anthony Boy** -1 *(Chuck Berry)*	⦿ Chess 1716**a** ■ Chess LP-1435 LP(S)-1514D, CH6-80001
9072	**Sweet Little Rock And Roll**(er) *(Chuck Berry)*	⦿ Chess 1709**a**, EP-5126 ■ Chess LP-1435, 2CH-60023, CH2-8201, CH6-80001
	Sweet Little Rock And Roller *[alt. take]* *(Chuck Berry)*	■ Chess CH-9190

Back at Chess with his full band after his sojourn in St. Louis, Chuck Berry's next session produced only two masters, neither of them worth emailing home about.

Anthony Boy is a pretty naff cut by Berry standards. It was produced to order at Phil Chess's behest supposedly to catch the Italian contingent. Chuck gets a chance to practise another foreign accent and the band get to shout, but all in all this is a pretty sub-standard effort.

Strange, then, that it ended up as the 'A' side of Chess 1716 (released

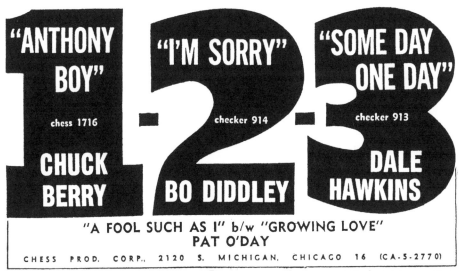

"ANTHONY BOY"
chess 1716
CHUCK BERRY

"I'M SORRY"
checker 914
BO DIDDLEY

"SOME DAY ONE DAY"
checker 913
DALE HAWKINS

"A FOOL SUCH AS I" b/w "GROWING LOVE"
PAT O'DAY

CHESS PROD. CORP., 2120 S. MICHIGAN, CHICAGO 16 (CA-5-2770)

Billboard, February 1959

in the middle of January 1959) and stranger still that it got to No. 60 and No. 76 on the *Billboard* and *Cash Box* pop charts! Perhaps Chuck's appearance on *American Bandstand* on 5th March 1959 had something to do with it.

Sweet Little Rock And Roller is better, but still only minor league Berry. The song, a sort-of sequel to *Sweet Little Sixteen*, contains some interesting lyrics, particularly the home-spun philosophy included in the alternative take: "Her daddy must be proud, 'cause there's so many places young folk aren't allowed" and "It must be good, 'cause bad things don't draw crowds." The description of the "famous performer" comes straight from direct experience: "10,000 eyes, 5,000 tongues and 1,500 waiting outside the door."

Comparison of the two versions confirms the production methods of some of Chuck's records. The alternative has only a lead intro and then a rumbling boogie rhythm guitar. The 'chicken cluck' lead guitar chops and the guitar solo as heard on the finished master were overdubbed on a separate track. The rhythm of the alternative track is stronger than the issued master, with Johnnie Johnson's wonderful rippling piano to the fore and, together with the additional lyrics, this is actually the more interesting of the two versions.

Despite these reservations, *Sweet Little Rock And Roller* has proved quite popular with other artists over the years. The most famous cover is by Rod Stewart who loved Berry's rhythmic drive so much that in 1976 he poached his guitar-player, Billy Peek, for his own band. Peek, who had played with Chuck for several years and recorded with him in Wentzville, can be seen duckwalking along a railway track, in true master's fashion, in Stewart's *Hot Legs* video. However on Rod's *Sweet Little Rock And Roller* it is Stone-in-waiting Ron Wood who plays the blistering boogie guitar.

Sweet Little Rock And Roller (mistitled *Sweet Little Rock And Roll* on some early pressings) was issued with *Jo Jo Gunne* on the back, but was flipped on many local charts and both sides breached the US hit parade. *Sweet Little Rock And Roller* climbed to No. 47 and No. 52 on the *Billboard* and *Cash Box* pop charts in December 1958, while *Jo Jo Gunne* peaked at No. 83

and No. 74 respectively. Additionally, the top deck also made No. 13 on the *Billboard* R&B chart.

SESSION 20
CHUCK BERRY

Chuck Berry, vocal/guitar, overdubbed guitar except -1; Johnnie Johnson, piano; Willie Dixon, double bass; Fred Below, drums; unknown tambourine -2

Chess Records studio
2120 South Michigan Avenue
Chicago, Illinois   **19 November 1958**

9166	**Merry Christmas Baby** *(Johnny Moore, Lou Baxter)*	❍ Chess 1714**b** ◼ Chess 2CH-60023, CH6-80001 ◎ Ace CDCH-397
	Merry Christmas Baby *[alt. take]* -1 *(Johnny Moore, Lou Baxter)*	◼ Chess LP(S)-1488
9167	**Run Rudolph Run** *(Chuck Berry.-Marvin Brodie)*	❍ Chess 1714**a** ◼ Chess 2CH-60023, CH2-92521, CH6-80001
9206	**Little Queenie** *(Chuck Berry)*	❍ Chess 1722**b** ◼ Chess LP-1435, 2CH-60023, CH2-8201, CH6-80001
	Little Queenie *[alt. take 8]* *(Chuck Berry)*	◼ Chess CH2-92521
9207	**That's My Desire** -1-2 *(Carroll Loveday, Helmy Kresa)*	❍ Chess 1716**b** ◼ Checkmate LP-1955 ◎ Chess CHD-9318

Previous discographies have divided this session into two with alternative dates of 9th September for the first two titles and 21st October for the last two. The date used here is that from Chuck's own records, reproduced in his autobiography, which lists all four titles as being cut at one session. This also ties in with the Chess convention of cutting four songs per session. Finally, the tune, the groove and the general ambience of the two principal songs, *Run Rudolph Run* and *Little Queenie*, are so close as to be inseparable.

As *the* rock and roll chronicler of all-American life, it was inevitable that Berry would record a Christmas disc. This said, it was just as inevitable that it would be **Merry Christmas Baby**, first recorded by Chuck's main cool dude of the blues, Charles Brown, for the Los Angeles-based Exclusive label in 1947. It was a seasonal hit for him and led to him cutting a further twenty or so cool Yule tunes — including *Merry Christmas Baby* six times over.

Brown came to fame as singer and pianist with Johnny Moore's Three Blazers, and, just as Chuck was to do with Johnnie Johnson's Sir John's Trio, he came to dominate the group. Moore, the guitarist in the group, had a younger brother, Oscar, who was also a guitarist with the more famous King Cole Trio. Both brothers played very jazzy blues in the T-Bone mould and the original *Merry Christmas Baby* featured both of them. No wonder Chuck dug the vibes!

"BABY, BABY" LARRY WILLIAMS chess 1745

"BREAK IT UP" LITTLE WALTER checker 938

"JUST FOR YOUR LOVE" the FALCONS chess 1743

"IT TOOK A LONG TIME" LOWELL FULSON checker 937

"SAY MAN, BACK AGAIN" BO DIDDLEY checker 936

"MERRY CHRISTMAS, BABY" CHUCK BERRY chess 1714

"HERE 'TIS" RAMSEY LEWIS argo 5352

Billboard, December 1959

His version of the song follows the original closely, taking it real cool and allowing plenty of room for Johnnie Johnson's rippling piano. Fred Below's subtle drumming is also a treat not to be overlooked. One significant variation does occur at the end of the song where Chuck, no doubt with his teenage audience in mind, censors Brown's line: "I haven't had a drink this morning, but I'm all lit up like a Christmas tree" and substitutes the rather lame "I'll always love you baby, I'm as happy as can be." And, whereas Brown only hints at *Jingle Bells* during his instrumental break, Berry develops the idea and blatantly interjects a passage from *White Christmas* into his version.

The alternative version is almost identical to the released cut, with just the odd word change between the two. It is taken at a marginally faster tempo, and the presence of the *'White Christmas'* guitar interlude suggests that it was laid down on the base track. On the single version it is overdubbed and this may well be the reason it was originally chosen for release, as it is the better version of the two. There has been much confusion about which version is which and, although it is commonly held that the song on *Chuck Berry's Golden Decade (Volume 2)* is the alternative cut, this isn't so. The *Golden Decade* track is the single version; the alternative appears on the 1964 *St. Louis To Liverpool* album and has only been infrequently issued since.

The other side of Chuck's 1958 Christmas single was **Run Rudolph Run**, and herein lies a mystery wrapped in an enigma! The title is almost always credited to Marvin Brodie and Johnny Marks — the two guys who wrote the multi-million selling *Rudolph The Red Nosed Reindeer* for singing cowboy Gene Autry in 1949. Try as I might, I have been unable to unearth an earlier version of *Run Rudolph Run* than Berry's. It is also hard to believe that lines such as "All I want for Christmas is a rock and roll electric guitar" or "A little

Still from 'Go, Johnny, Go!' with Alan Freed on the skins.

baby doll that can cry, sleep, drink and wet" did not emanate from Berry's pen. The original release credits the song to 'Chuck Berry Music Inc.– M. Brodie', and it would therefore appear that Brodie had some kind of copyright that protected his interest in any reindeer called Rudolph. Christmas comes but once a year, but boy is it lucrative!

The song is a heartfelt plea on behalf of all believing kids, a sort of musical equivalent of Clement C. Moore's seasonal epic, *'Twas The Night Before Christmas,* urging Rudolph to run and get the goodies delivered on time: "Santa make him hurry, tell him he can take the freeway down!" (Incidentally, Chuck never sings "Run Rudolph run" but always "Run, run Rudolph".) The song is performed to a relentless boogie guitar lick, so good it just had to be used again (as the basis for *Little Queenie*). Notables who have covered it are Bryan Adams, Keith Richards (on his first waxing outside of the Stones) and Welsh guitar wizard Dave Edmunds.

1958 had been a great year for Chuck Berry record sales-wise. *Sweet Little Sixteen* was the 29th overall best-selling single of the year, and with *Merry Christmas Baby* and *Run Rudolph Run*, he notched up his seventh and eighth entries into the *Billboard* 'Hot 100' that year. The coupling was released pretty late to catch the Christmas market, but both sides charted. *Rudolph* won the race by a short head, racking up a position 69 (if you'll pardon the expression) to *Merry Christmas Baby's* 71, though neither figured in the R&B chart. The following winter, Chess reissued the single and tried again, this time without chart success. In 1963, however, a belated release in the UK went to No. 36.

Recognising a great groove when he created it, and not wanting to squander it on a mere Christmas disc, the loose-limbed, relentless boogie riff of *Run Rudolph Run* reappears for the second time this session as the backbone of **Little Queenie**. The number has since become a staple in his repertoire, often performed in conjunction with *Carol* in an entirely logical medley.

Berry's intro winds up the band before he spins his tale of *Little Queenie* — the untouchable, the unapproachable, the unbelievable; *Little Queenie*, "too cute to be a minute over seventeen" but "looking like a million-dollar model in a magazine". Chuck, still the wallflower from his *Carol* days, mulls over the situation in his mind: "Meanwhile, I's thinking" he half-speaks, half-sings. "She's in the mood, no need'n break it/ I got my chance, I oughta take it" — but he doesn't, because meanwhile... "I's *still* thinking". This 'meanwhile' idea may stem from the "Meanwhile, back in the States/back in the jungle" quotes from the 1956 Jayhawks'/Cadets' hit, *Stranded In The Jungle*.

Little Queenie is a tremendous track which I don't believe Chess recognised as such. All four songs from this session were used on singles, but *Little Queenie* was the last to be issued and even then only as the 'B' side of the inferior *Almost Grown*. However, you can't keep a good song down, and, despite the fact that it was relegated to the flip, *Queenie* broke into the pop charts in its own right in April 1959, making No. 80 in the *Billboard* 'Hot 100' and No. 91 in the *Cash Box* pop listing.

The alternative take only surfaced in 1986 on the *Rock'n'Roll Rarities* double album and, apart from a few extra "go, go, gos" in the chorus, is virtually identical to the previously released version. There is a spoken introduction in which we learn the cut is Take 8. The engineer asks: "Alright Chuck. You ready baby?" to which Berry replies: "Right-ho" in his best Cary Grant English accent.

Little Queenie also turns up in the film *Go, Johnny, Go!* Berry (black suit, white shoes this time) lip-syncs the tune in the Krazy Koffee Kup Cafe — one of those all-American, gingham-tableclothed establishments that only existed in the psyche of 1950s film producers. He's backed by an all-white band which includes Alan Freed on drums (well, *drum* actually). Still, it's good to see Chuck move in a restricted space, shoulders bobbing and guitar swinging. The audience consists of only five people, but one of these is Richie Valens, so I guess it's quality not quantity that counts. To be fair, the film is better than the other rocksploitation quickies Berry appeared in. He also gets to do a little acting and comes across as a pretty cool cat despite having to sing the praises of a no-talent Johnny Melody (played by Jimmy Clanton) throughout the film. One interesting scene has Chuck knocking out a *Down The Road Apiece*-type boogie on piano, his huge hands dwarfing the keys, but like everything else in the film it's dubbed, so may not really be him playing after all.

The opening titles of *Go, Johnny, Go!* are accompanied by a heavily-doctored version of *Johnny B. Goode* which is overdubbed by a brass section and was retitled *Go Johnny Go* in the publicity blurb issued when the film was released. *Little Queenie*, *Go Johnny Go* (which is in fact the unadulterated *Johnny B. Goode*) and *Memphis Tennessee* were included on a rare-as-hen's-teeth soundtrack LP issued free to disc jockeys and movie theatre owners by the Hal Roach Advertising Department as a tie-in with the film's release in 1959. The remaining sixteen tracks on the album are by the other featured acts. The press release exhorts theatre proprietors to play the platter in the lobbies of their establishments.

During the late '50s, Chuck embarked on a series of 'big beat' package tours across the States. The first of these was called *The Biggest Show Of Stars For 1957*. Starting in Pittsburgh on 6th September, the tour cut a swathe across the length and breadth of the USA during the months of September, October and November. The other 'stars' were Buddy Holly and the Crickets, Fats Domino, the Drifters, Paul Anka, the Everly Brothers, Frankie Lymon, LaVern Baker, Clyde McPhatter, Johnnie & Joe, the Spaniels and the Bobbettes.

Barely four months later, Chuck was out on the road again, this time for forty-four days (and nights) with Holly and the Crickets and Frankie Lymon again, plus Danny & The Juniors, Screamin' Jay Hawkins, Larry Williams, the Diamonds, the Chantels, Jo-Ann Campbell, the Pastels, Billie & Lillie, Ed Townsend and Jerry Lee Lewis. Instrumental backing was provided by the Alan Freed Orchestra and 'Mr. Rock and Roll' was, of course, the MC.

The whole shebang was called *Alan Freed's Big Beat Show* and has gone down in rock and roll infamy for two incidents, one being a riot on 6th May 1958 in Boston, caused by racist zealots objecting to white and black artists appearing on the same show — which in turn led to a complete overreaction by the establishment, FBI Director J. Edgar Hoover declaring that rock and roll was a communist plot, and the beginning of the end for Freed. The other was a hard-to-believe incident on the opening night of the tour, 28th March, at New York's Brooklyn Paramount: Chuck's arch-rival for top billing was the 'Ferriday Fireball', the 'Louisiana Lip', Mr. Jerry Lee Lewis, at the time riding high on his *Great Balls Of Fire*. Legends abound about the rivalry on these tours and it was more than egos that got bruised at times. The tale goes, that having been thwarted for top billing, Lewis set fire to his piano with lighter fluid to make his act impossible for Berry to better.

Great story, but hard to believe even with a character as volatile as Lewis. Imagine his feelings, then, when his mother, Mamie, took a shine to Chuck's *Little Queenie* and played it incessantly. Jerry Lee's response was to cut the song himself so that his momma would junk the original. As if fired by the rivalry, Lewis takes the song for his own, pumping up a storm on a rendition that is the equal of Berry's.

Also at the Brooklyn Paramount Theatre during one of these tours, Chuck discovered the wider appeal of the crouching movement that became universally known as his 'duckwalk'. He used to perform the manoeuvre as a four year old to amuse his family and friends, bobbing beneath the table, but here he chose to do it to hide the creases in his $66 rayon suit. It was an instant hit with the fans and Chuck developed the movement together with other tricks, such as the one-legged scoot and the splits, into an integral part of his stage act.

This was all back in the fifties. Ten years down the line, in New York's Madison Square Garden, the Rolling Stones cut their great version of *Little Queenie* for their best-ever live LP, *Get Yer Ya Ya's Out*. The song is slowed to a powerful, sinewy grind topped by Jagger's leering vocals and went down so well that it remained in the Stones set throughout the seventies and was bootlegged *ad infinitum*.

Little Queenie has been covered by a fair few others, including the bootlegged Fab Four with John Lennon on vocals. The famous boogie riff has also formed the backbone of other hits, most obviously Humble Pie's *Natural Born Bugie* and T. Rex's *Get It On* (at the end of which Marc Bolan quotes Berry directly: "Meanwhile, I's *still* thinking..."). My favourite cover of all has got to be the driving instrumental version from Elvis's erstwhile bassist, Bill Black, which was a single hit for him in 1964 when lifted from his LP of Berry covers.

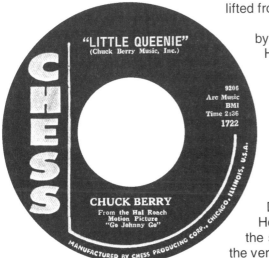

That's My Desire was written by Carroll Loveday *(words)* and Helmy Kresa *(music)* in 1931 and introduced to the unsuspecting listening public via radio by one Lanny Ross. In 1947, Frankie Laine scored his first hit with the song and it has since become something of a standard, being recorded by artists as diverse as Louis Armstrong, the Flamingos, Dion & The Belmonts and Buddy Holly. Where Chuck picked up on the song is unclear because none of the versions I've heard are remotely like the cod tango rhythms he uses in his rendition (his penchant for Latin rhythms surfacing yet again).

The track is not without its own peculiar charm, mainly due to the rippling piano and corny percussion including an enthusiastic unknown tambourine player. It's a pity, therefore, that it remained hidden on the 'B' side of the feeble *Anthony Boy* single until its first official reissue over thirty years later on the *Missing Berries: Rarities (Volume 3)* CD.

SESSION 21

CHUCK BERRY

Chuck Berry, vocal/guitar; Johnnie Johnson, piano; Willie Dixon, double bass; Fred Below, drums; Harvey & The Moonglows (Harvey Fuqua, Marvin Gaye, James Nolan, Reese Palmer, Chuck Barksdale, Chester Simmons) and Etta James, vocal group

Chess Records studio
2120 South Michigan Avenue
Chicago, Illinois   **17 February 1959**

9235	**Do You Love Me** *(Chuck Berry)*	■ Chess 6641 177
	Do You Love Me *[alt. take]* *(Chuck Berry)*	■ Reelin' 001, Chess CXMP-2011, Checkmate LP-1955, Chess CH-9318 ◎ Chess CHD-9318
9236	**Almost Grown** *(Chuck Berry)*	○ Chess 1722**a** ■ Chess LP-1435, 1465, LP(S)-1514D, CH2-8201, CH6-80001

9237	**Back In The USA**	⊙ Chess 1729**a** ■ Chess LP-1465,
	(Chuck Berry)	Pye Int. NPL-28039, Chess
		LP(S)-1514D, Marble Arch
		MAL(S)-702, Chess CH2-8201,
		CH6-80001 ◎ Beat Goes On
		BGOCD-428
9238	**Blue On Blue** *[instrumental]*	■ Chess 2CH-60028 ◎ Chess
	(Chuck Berry)	CHD-9318, Ace CDCH-397

For his first session of 1959, Chess rang the changes for Berry by introducing a vocal backing group... and what a group! The Moonglows were an established, big-selling act on the Chess roster with a string of hits behind them like 1955's sublime *Sincerely*, featuring their trademark 'blow harmonies', and 1958's ludicrously kitsch *Ten Commandments Of Love*, on which they were billed as 'Harvey & The Moonglows' ('Harvey' being Harvey Fuqua, the group's leader and lead tenor).

However, by the time they came to record with Chuck, only Fuqua remained of the original line-up: he had fired the original Moonglows in November 1958 and recruited the Marquees from Washington, DC (including a nineteen year old Marvin Gaye) as their replacements. Fuqua and Gaye were of course to go on to much greater fame at Motown — and greater fortune too — by both marrying into the Gordy dynasty.

Fuqua and the original Moonglows had also sung backing on Bo Diddley's *Diddley Daddy* and *Diddy Wah Diddy*, and Bo had produced the Marquees' only single *Wyatt Earp* b/w *Hey Little School Girl* on OKeh. With that kind of pedigree, it isn't surprising that Chess set their top vocal group behind their current brown-eyed boy.

Added to the usual line-up was Fuqua's current girlfriend, Jamesetta Hawkins alias 'Little Miss Peaches' — the great Etta James. Etta of course also went on to greater things, making many fine sides for Chess including probably their greatest soul pairing ever, *I'd Rather Go Blind* b/w *Tell Mama*.

In addition to Fuqua, Gaye and James, the bass of Chuck Barksdale is also present. Except for a nine-month stint in the new Moonglows, Barksdale spent thirty years plus in the Dells — another magnificent vocal group who likewise recorded extensively for Chess and who reached their peak on their subsidiary, Cadet, in 1968 with the phenomenal *Stay In My Corner*. (Incidentally, the Dells later cut a song called *Nadine* — a completely different song to Chuck's 1963 opus, 'written' by Alan Freed and originally recorded in 1954 on Chess by the Coronets.)

Truly then, a backing group not to be messed with.

The first song of the session, **Do You Love Me**, is also something of a departure in that it contains no lead guitar but allows Johnnie Johnson full rein on the keys. It is his piano intro — copied directly from Fats Domino's intro to Lloyd Price's *Lawdy Miss Clawdy* — that kicks off the tune. Chuck sings the song straight, whilst the Moonglows 'bill and coo' in the background. I can't honestly say I recognise the distinctive tenor of Marvin Gaye, but certainly Etta James is prominent in the mix, almost duetting with Berry at times, and Chuck Barksdale's deep bass bobs up in true doo-wop fashion throughout the song.

The song first appeared on the UK version of *Chuck Berry's Golden Decade (Volume 3)* [Chess 6641 177] in 1974, and later in a shorter, slightly different version on the classy 1980 bootleg, *America's Hottest Wax* bootleg [Reelin' 001]. Rumour has it that a tape of these Chess out-takes was given by Marshall Chess to Keith Richards, and that the bootleggers somehow got hold of it via him. Whatever, the album proved so popular that it inspired an identical legitimate British release, *Chess Masters* [Chess CXMP-2011] in 1983. Chuck's fellow Americans finally got to hear the track in 1990 on *Missing Berries: Rarities (Volume 3)* [Chess CH-9318].

On the British release, the song is credited to 'Overbea' — that is, Danny Overbea, an early Chess artist who in 1955 recorded a completely different song of the same name. Hope he got the royalties! (Incidentally, the *Do You Love Me* on the *Missing Berries* album is said to be an earlier version, possibly that recorded in 1958 *[Session 14]*, but I'm afraid it's not.)

In contrast to *Do You Love Me*, Chuck pulls out most if not all of the stops with his singing on **Almost Grown**, which captures him at his insinuating best.

Moonglows:	"Whoa-whooa!"
Chuck:	"You know I'm almost grown!
Moonglows:	"Whoa-whooa!"

goes the introduction before the band cuts in and Chuck and the 'glows are off and running. "I don't run around with no mob/ Got myself a little job"... "Don't bother us, leave us alone/ Anyway, we almost grown" whines Chuck while the gang chant "Rat-tak-tak-tak-tak-ta" in the background.

Instrumentally, Johnnie gets the lion's share. As he glides up and down the keyboard, Chuck yells: "Ow!" as though he has touched the keys and got his fingers burned. If anything, Chuck's solo tends to slow the thing down, but not a note is wasted from the start to the abrupt stop.

Almost Grown was the second Berry release of 1959, following hard on the heels of *Anthony Boy*. It reached No. 32 in the *Billboard* 'Hot 100', went one better in the *Cash Box* 'Top 100', and made a very respectable No. 3 on the *Billboard* R&B chart in April/May of that year following a promotional appearance on *American Bandstand* in March.

"Oh well, oh well, I feel so good today," sings Chuck at the beginning of **Back In The USA**, echoing his teen-years hero Joe Turner's 1956 waxing *Feelin' Happy,* or maybe Helen Humes's 1945 hit, *Be-Baba-Leba*. But then, from here on in, he upgrades from Club Class rhythm and blues to Executive Class rock and roll.

It's been suggested that Berry's *Back In The USA* is an ironic statement of the black man's burden in the States, a satirical lament on the lot of the mid-century African American race. For instance, "Looking *hard* for a drive-in, searching for a corner cafe" has been cited as a coded message to illustrate the racism that was only too real in the Southern states at the time, where blacks had to eat from the back doors of diners.

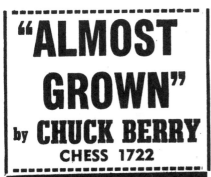

"ALMOST GROWN"
by CHUCK BERRY
CHESS 1722

CHESS PRODUCING CO.
2120 Michigan Avenue
Chicago 16, Illinois

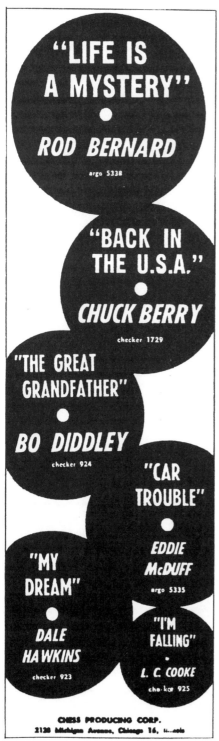

"LIFE IS A MYSTERY"
•
ROD BERNARD
argo 5338

"BACK IN THE U.S.A."
•
CHUCK BERRY
checker 1729

"THE GREAT GRANDFATHER"
•
BO DIDDLEY
checker 924

"CAR TROUBLE"
•
EDDIE McDUFF
argo 5335

"MY DREAM"
•
DALE HAWKINS
checker 923

"I'M FALLING"
•
L. C. COOKE
che·kœ 925

CHESS PRODUCING CORP.
2120 Michigan Avenue, Chicago 16, Illinois

Billboard, June 1959

Attractive as this notion seems, I'm afraid I don't subscribe. Chuck's *Back In The USA* quite simply celebrates the good things to be had in America towards the end of the fifties, much as his hero Louis Jordan had done a decade before in *Reconversion Blues*, which celebrated the return of goods at the end of the war. This was a favourite song of the twenty year old Berry when it was released in 1946 and was itself an answer song to *Ration Blues* cut by Jordan at the height of the conflict in 1943. Both Jordan's and Berry's songs describe in exquisite detail the material things in life. Louis sings of automobiles and two-tone shoes, and there's likewise no irony in Chuck's voice as he glories in the materialism of the Union, the skyscrapers, the long freeways: "anything you want, they got it right here in the USA". Berry's feelings are clear and, as we know, he is a pretty materialistic guy. The song is a straightforward celebration of the good ol' US of A, the land of dreams, by a guy returning home from his first overseas trip (Chuck had toured Hawaii and Australia a month earlier).

Chess 1729 was released at the beginning of June 1959 and by midsummer had become a popular favourite, reaching No. 37 on *Billboard's* 'Hot 100' listing and No. 16 on their R&B chart.

Back In The USA has had a fair number of covers. Linda Ronstadt turned it into a hit all over again in 1978, securing her appearance in Berry's celebratory *Hail! Hail! Rock'n'Roll* film. The Boss cut it too (maybe to complement his own *Born In The USA*?). The Beatles took the theme, combined it with the Beach Boys' *California Girls* and produced a memorable pastiche called *Back In The USSR*. The song, however, took on a whole new dimension when the 1970

version by proto-punk band the MC5 became an anthem for GI's returning from Vietnam.
The last cut of this session, the instrumental **Blue On Blue**, may well have been the first cut because, with its *Lawdy Miss Clawdy* piano figure, it sounds like a warm-up for *Do You Love Me*. Like *Wee Wee Hours*, it's an informal jam that features Johnnie Johnson's piano more than Chuck's guitar and is typical of those instrumentals Berry criticised Chess for releasing . This tune, however, stayed in the can until its inclusion on the 1974 retrospective album, *Chuck Berry's Golden Decade (Volume 3)*.

SESSION 22
CHUCK BERRY / ECUADORS -1
Chuck Berry, vocal/guitar, overdubbed guitar -2; Leroy C. Davis, tenor saxophone -3; Johnnie Johnson, piano (except -4); Willie Dixon, double bass; Fred Below, drums; Ecuadors, vocal group (except -5)

Chess Records studio
2120 South Michigan Avenue
Chicago, Illinois   **27 and 29 July 1959**

9626	**Betty Jean** *(Chuck Berry)*	■ Chess LP-1448, CH6-80001
	Betty Jean *[alt. take]* *(Chuck Berry)*	■ Chess 2CH-60023, CH2-92521
9627	**County Line** *(Chuck Berry)*	■ Chess 2CH-60028, CH2-92521
9628	**Childhood Sweetheart** *(E. Anderson)*	○ Chess 1737**b** ■ Chess LP-1448 2CH-60028, CH6-80001
	Childhood Sweetheart *[alt. take]* *(E. Anderson)*	■ Reelin' 001, Chess CXMP-2011, Checkmate LP-1955, Chess CH-9318 ◎ Chess CHD-9318
9629	**One O'Clock Jump** *[instrumental]* -3-5 *(Count Basie)*	■ Reelin' 001, Chess CXMP-2011, Checkmate LP-1955, Chess CH-9318 ◎ Chess CHD-9318
9630	**I Just Want To Make Love To You** *(Willie Dixon)*	■ Chess LP-1480 ◎ Ace CDCH-397
9631	**Broken Arrow** -3-4 *(Chuck Berry)*	○ Chess 1737**a** ■ Chess LP-1448, 2CH-60028
9632	**Let It Rock** -2-5 [Rocking On The Railroad*] *(E. Anderson)*	○ Chess 1747**b** ■ Chess LP-1448, 1465, 1480*, CH2-8201, CH6-80001
	Let It Rock *[alt. mix]* -5 *(E. Anderson)*	■Chess 2CH-60023, Checkmate LP-1955
9633	**Too Pooped To Pop** [Casey] -3 *(Roquel Davis, Alonzo Mitchell)*	○ Chess 1747**a** ■ Chess LP-1448, LP(S)-1514D, CH6-80001

9634	**Say You'll Be Mine** -1 (*R. Butler*)	⊙ Argo 5353**a** ■ Reelin' 001, Chess CXMP-2011
9635	**Let Me Sleep Woman** -1 (*R. Butler*)	⊙ Argo 5353**b** ■ Reelin' 001, Chess CXMP-2011, CH-9318 ◎ Chess CHD-9318
9636	**Up There** -1 (*Chuck Berry? R. Butler?*)	unissued

Note: LP-1480 was overdubbed with audience noise.

No doubt chuffed with the outcome of the Moonglows session, Chuck used another backing group for this mammoth two-day set — this time the totally anonymous Ecuadors. Despite extensive enquiries, the personnel of the Ecuadors remains unknown, lost in the mists of doo-wop. Could they have been a more famous group moonlighting at Chess? The only possible clue is that both of the Ecuadors songs are credited to one 'R. Butler', who may also have been a group member (though they are actually copyrighted to Chuck Berry Music Inc.).

There are, in fact, three known sessions by groups rejoicing in the name 'Equadors' or the more geographically correct 'Ecuadors'. The original 'Equadors' recorded four tracks in February 1958 for the RCA–Victor label. *I'll Be The One* and *A Vision* are in a soft doo-wop style; *Sputnik Dance* and *Stay A Little Longer* are rockers more akin to the Ecuadors that Berry recorded with, and on aural evidence they possibly could be the same group, though this of course is pure conjecture. The third 'Ecuadors' group recorded *Someone To Call My Own* and *You're My Desire* for the Motown subsidiary Miracle in August 1961. These sides have a more modern 'sixties' feel to them and are definitely not Berry's group.

Apart from his very first recording, the two tracks issued by the Ecuadors on Chess's Argo subsidiary are the only instances in his recording career where Chuck Berry played second fiddle to anyone, and my guess is that he 'discovered' the group and fancied his chances at producing them.

The session kicks into gear with a pair of 'Jeans' Mr. Strauss never envisaged. Another Berry female fantasy, **Betty Jean** ("I love the way you walk/ Looks like you're dancin' but you're not") follows on from *Maybellene* and *Carol*, with *Brenda Lee* and *Ramona* yet to come.

The Ecuadors are prominent throughout, gasping: "Oh yeah Betty Jean" as Chuck extols the virtues of his "livin' end" girl. He never in fact refers to Betty Jean by name but leaves this to his backing crew. In alternate stanzas, the guys switch their attention from Betty to urge Chuck on to "sing the song, Chucky boy" — and he a thirty-two year old big daddy! Yet, despite all the enthusiasm, the song is only a second-tier rocker on Berry's rock and roll cake.

There is precious little to choose between the two versions of *Betty Jean*. If anything, Chuck's vocals on the alternative take are a little hesitant, but it must have been a coin-toss that decided which was to be released on the *Rockin' At The Hops* album. The alternative cut finally emerged in 1974 — probably unintentionally — on *Chuck Berry's Golden Decade (Volume 2)*.

County Line is archetypal Berry: a succinct cartoon tale featuring two of Chuck's favourite themes: cars and cops. The first line: "It was a ten-mile stretch on a Pennsylvania road/ A sky blue Jaguar and Thunderbird Ford" sets the scene for an exciting race between the Jag, the 'bird and the sheriff (car unspecified, but without synchromeshed gears) who, tipped off by a stool pigeon, lays "half hid in the weeds" waiting for the speed kings. Strange thing is, no matter how many times you play the record, the sheriff doing more than "one hundred in the shade" never catches the culprits before "bumper to bumper" they cross that county line!

Incredibly, *County Line* remained unissued for almost fifteen years before eventually being included on 1974's *Golden Decade (Volume 3)*, though a later, inferior reworking of the theme entitled *Jaguar And Thunderbird* was released in 1960 and became a minor hit.

Chuck's two **Childhood Sweethearts** are twelve-bar blues based on Elmore James's famous *Dust My Broom* guitar figure, which is more prominent on the alternative take. Aside from this, there is little to choose between the two cuts and, whilst the guitar is better on the alternative, its tempo drags and consequently lacks the bounce of the issued version. The alternative also suffers from excessive use of cymbal by Fred Below which sounds like someone frying bacon in the studio.

There is nothing particularly outstanding about the lyrics, although it's interesting to note that Berry borrows the "walking home from school/ broke my mother's (teacher's) rule" couplet that was almost public domain amongst blues singers around this time (check out Elmore's *Early One Morning*; Junior Wells's *You Sure Look Good To Me* and Little Richard's *Early One Morning Blues*). Chuck most likely picked up the phrase from Big Joe Turner's 1941 *Wee Baby Blues* or maybe Willie Dixon's Big Three's 1947 recording of *You Sure Look Good To Me*. There is also an echo of Turner's *TV Mama* in the first verse of *Childhood Sweetheart* (which incidentally — or maybe not so incidentally — featured the famous Elmore James riff played by Elmore himself).

The alternative *Childhood Sweetheart* first appeared on the *America's Hottest Wax* bootleg [Reelin' 001], then on its UK legitimised progeny, *Chess Masters* [Chess CXMP-2011], before finally being issued in the USA in 1990 on *Missing Berries: Rarities (Volume 3)* [Chess CHD-9318].

As late as the year 2000, a cover of *Childhood Sweetheart* appeared on an album by the Swedish rock and roll trio, Hank T. Morris & The Amazing Buffalo Brothers, alongside seven other Berry compositions and two other songs closely associated with Chuck.

Berry's (and Johnson's) love of big band swing rise to the surface once again with the choice of Count Basie's theme song, **One O'Clock Jump**, first cut by Basie in 1937. Berry's version is an energetic *tour de force*, not so much because of his own contribution, but on account of Leroy C. Davis, who contributes a beautifully fluid tenor solo that drops neatly into Johnnie's piano break — straight from the Basie book of jazz dynamics. Davis was the sax-man in Berry's road band from 1956 until Chuck's second stay with Uncle Sam in 1962 and, as far as can be determined, apart from the four sessions he cut with Chuck, he didn't make any other recordings. Beneath all this musical fun, Fred Below's crisp, swinging beat really makes the number jump. The cut deserves to be better known because it is one of Berry's more accomplished instrumentals. Its release history is identical to that of the alternative *Childhood*

Sweetheart above.

Muddy Waters was without doubt Chuck Berry's main man of the blues. The Godfather of Chicago blues from the 1950s until his death in 1983, his bands contained a veritable who's who of blues legends: Little Walter, Otis Spann, Jimmy Rogers, Junior Wells and James Cotton. His music influenced a legion of musicians from Lightnin' Slim to Slim Harpo, from Jimmy Reed to Johnny Winter, not to mention the hordes of non-Americans who picked up the blues baton in the sixties when it slipped in the States.

Chuck sang Muddy's songs in 1952 on his first professional gigs as a member of the Tommy Stevens Trio at Huff's Garden, St. Louis and they remained in his set when he became the major third of Johnnie Johnson's Sir John's Trio later that year. Shortly afterwards, he got to meet his idol at the Palladium Club in Chicago and asked him for advice as to how to get into the recording business. Muddy advised him to seek out Leonard Chess over on 47th and Cottage and the rest, as they say, is geography.

Waters's influence and advice led Berry to later write of him: *'He was perhaps the greatest inspiration in the launching of my career. I was a disciple in worship of a lord who had granted me a lead that led to a never-ending love of music. May his music live forever, he will always be in first place at the academy of blues, my man, McKinley Morganfield, Muddy Waters.'* Amen, brother, amen!

It is no surprise, then, that Chuck would cut a Muddy tune or two in the course of his career, and *I Just Want To Make Love To You* was the first. Unfortunately, his version — which is by no means bad — pales in comparison with the master's magnificent original, containing as it does one of the most electrifying harp solos in the history of blues recording from Little Walter Jacobs. In Berry's hands, Muddy's slow, menacing blues is lightened and given a Latin feel with the assistance of the Ecuadors. The tempo is doubled from the original, but is still only about half the speed of the frenetic, supercharged 1964 Rolling Stones version. My guess is that the Berry treatment gave the Strolling Ones the idea to pep it up still further, and I'm afraid Chuck looses out on both counts.

Until it was finally issued by UK's Ace Records in 1993 in its unadulterated state, *I Just Want To Make Love To You* was only available on *Chuck Berry On Stage* — an extremely doctored piece of vinyl. Released in August 1963 whilst Chuck was otherwise indisposed at his government's displeasure, the album contained a mixture of old hits (*Memphis*, *Maybellene* and *Sweet Little Sixteen*) and more recently recorded material all quite expertly overlaid with a false audience and a master of ceremonies to give the impression that it is a live recording.

"BROKEN ARROW"

CHUCK BERRY

CHESS 1737

Chuck Berry On Stage is introduced thus: "Ladies and gentlemen, this is Rodney Jones welcoming you to the beautiful Tivoli Theatre here in Chicago, where it's showtime once again. And this evening we proudly present the young man who made very, very popular,

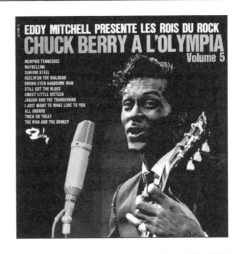

Maybellene (surge of fake applause), *Memphis* (surge again), *Surfin' USA* (surge) and some new favourites, ladies and gentlemen, you haven't heard before. Let's give a nice Chicago welcome, ladies and gentlemen, to the one, the only, Chuck 'crazy legs' Berry!" (almighty surge).

Deejay E. Rodney Jones was one of the 'good guys' at WVON, 1450 on the dial, a Chicago black radio station purchased by the Chess organisation in 1963. I don't doubt that Chuck had played the 'beautiful Tivoli Theatre' on occasion, but the intro is a studio sham.

The LP was released in the UK on Pye International, in West Germany on the Bellaphon label, and the French got it as *Eddy Mitchell Présente les Rois du Rock (Volume 5: Chuck Berry à l'Olympia)* on Barclay 80258. Here, a French compère (Mitchell?) replaces Rodney Jones and makes like the gig is at the Olympia in Paris (the French introduction *was* actually recorded there). Between tracks, Chuck practises his second-grade French on an appreciative audience. "Let me hear you say: Olé! Olé!" (French?) he urges. "Aah, Paree," he extols. "Viva la musica! Viva la rock and roll!" he yells, hinting at songs yet to be written. All completely false. The great rock and roll swindle is born when the Sex Pistols were just a twinkle in Malcolm McLaren's middle class eye.

Broken Arrow is a silly little song set to the tune of the nursery rhyme, *Old Macdonald,* and incorporating that old hambone/*Bo Diddley* beat. Punctuated by a guitar and sax break, the number is three verses long, each telling a cautionary tale with the Ecuadors chanting: "I'll never do that again" at suitable intervals.

It's hard to comprehend why this song became the 'A' side of a single release. Maybe the idea was to latch on to the late fifties/early sixties western craze: *Bonanza* and *Rawhide* on TV, *The Magnificent Seven* on the silver screen, and on the jukeboxes, Link Wray's *Rawhide*, Bo Diddley's *Gunslinger* and the Coasters' *Along Came Jones* among others. Needless to say, *Broken Arrow* didn't break into the charts, though it bubbled under the *Billboard* 'Hot 100' for a while at No. 108. Even so, two groups later cut versions of the song — both in 1964: the Underbeats from Minneapolis and Kingsize Taylor & The Dominoes from Liverpool, who that same year backed the merry Mr. Berry on his first UK tour. They'll never do that again either!

Let It Rock is one minute forty-three seconds of tremendous rocking, rolling boogie with nary a second wasted. Like a sexual climax, however, it's exquisite but doesn't last nearly long enough. In fact, the *only* thing wrong with the song is that it is about three minutes too short.

A brief snatch of Berry guitar introduces the powerhouse vocal: "In the heat of the day down in Mobile, Alabama/ Working on the railroad with a steel-driving hammer," setting the scene for a tale of panic, with the foreman trying to get the workers out of the way of "an off-schedule train coming two miles out." Rhythm guitar, piano, bass and drums coalesce in one mighty rhythmic pulse atop of which Chuck's whining overdubbed lead guitar imitates the engine's steam whistle. We never find out if they get the teepee out of the way, nor do we once hear the phrase "let it rock" used in the song. The cut was, in fact, retitled *Rocking On The Railroad* on the *Chuck Berry On Stage* album, no doubt to add to the subterfuge of this phoney LP. It is one of a very small number of Berry songs pseudonymously credited to 'E. Anderson' — after Chuck's middle names — possibly to confuse the IRS.

It's hard to believe, but here we have another stone Berry classic which only made a flipside (that of *Too Pooped To Pop*, of all things) when first released. Despite this, it made No. 64 and No. 60 respectively on the *Billboard* and *Cash Box* pop charts and No. 22 on the newly-launched *Cash Box* R&B chart in 1960. It was later released in Britain backed with *Memphis Tennessee* and hit No. 6 in the UK 'Top Twenty' in 1963.

The 'alternative mix' is the same base track with a slightly shortened guitar introduction and no lead guitar, which once again illustrates the *modus operandi* of Berry's sessions.

Let It Rock has been quite influential in the rock world. It became the title of a short-lived but highly respected magazine and the phrase has become *de rigour* with good-time rock'n'rollers. Some major American rock heavies including the Flamin' Groovies, the Stray Cats, the late Jerry Garcia (Grateful Dead), Bob Seger, and George Thorogood aided and abetted by Mick Jagger have had a go at covering it. The Brits had a field-day, too: the Animals, the Big Three, Dave Edmunds (alone, and with Rockpile in tandem with the other Glimmer Twin), the Nashville Teens, the Pirates, Savoy Brown and the Yardbirds all cut the song, but the best cover of all is by — who else? — the Rolling Stones.

To date fourteen separate Stones versions of *Let It Rock* have appeared thanks mainly to the Under Assistant West Coast Bootleg Man, but the version from a live gig at Leeds University in 1971, released on the 'B' side of *Brown Sugar*, is the best. Here they slow the tempo, thicken the mix with a little sax, and their downbound train becomes a surging juggernaut to Berry's smokestack lightning.

From the sublime to the ludicrous, the next cut of the session is perhaps most kindly described as a novelty number. **Too Pooped To Pop** isn't a Berry song but a composition by Roquel 'Billy' Davis' and Alonzo Mitchell.

Davis, Chess's talent scout in Detroit, boyfriend of Gwen Gordy and (as 'Tyran Carlo') co-writer with Gwen's brother Berry Jr. of Jackie Wilson's early hits, *Reet Petite, Lonely Teardrops* and *I'll Be Satisfied*. He subsequently became A&R man at Chess for all non-jazz recordings and produced — among

"LET IT ROCK"

Billboard Best Buys
February 15, 1960

"TOO POOPED TO POP"
CHUCK BERRY CHESS NO. 1747

"MY STORY"
BO DIDDLEY CHECKER NO. 942

"BLUE SKIES"
HARVEY CHESS NO. 1749

AN
OLDIE
SOARS
AGAIN

Breaking!

"LITTLE GIRL, LITTLE GIRL" | THE FAIRLANES

ARGO
NO. 5357

CHESS PROD. CORP.
2120 S. Michigan, Chicago 16, Ill.
Phone: CAlumet 5-2770

Billboard, February 1960

85

many other hits — Fontella Bass's 1965 chart-topper, *Rescue Me*. Davis later moved into advertising and made a packet with the tune *I'd Like To Teach The World To Sing* when Coca-Cola picked up on it.

Chuck was initially reluctant to cut *Too Pooped,* but was persuaded to do so by Len Chess who wanted to reward Davis and maybe entice him into the A&R job with a hit by one of his star performers. The irony of an oldster trying to stay hip beyond his time might also have appealed to Berry's sense of humour. After all, he was penning teenage laments such as *Dear Dad* when he was in his forties. On some releases, Casey (the name of the old man in the song) was used as an alternative title. The number itself is the type of stuff at which the Coasters excelled. They were very big at this time, so maybe it was also an attempt to emulate their success? In fact, the saxophone — which is by far the best thing on the recording — is reminiscent of King Curtis, whose presence graced most of the Coasters' classics.

Too Pooped To Pop was released early in 1960 backed with *Let It Rock*, and by February the 'B' side had made its mark in the *Billboard* 'Hot 100'. Quite inexplicably, however, the facile *Pooped* rose beyond this, peaking at No. 42 and No. 56 in the *Billboard* and *Cash Box* pop charts, and also featuring in their R&B charts at No. 18 and No. 20 respectively. The tune was covered for the UK market in 1960 by Dudley Heslop (alias Cuddly Dudley), and he got what he probably deserved: obscurity. There really is no accounting for taste.

For backing Berry on six numbers, the Ecuadors were rewarded with two songs under their own name. **Say You'll Be Mine** and **Let Me Sleep Woman** were issued in late 1959 on the Chess pop and jazz subsidiary, Argo.

Say You'll Be Mine is in the very popular doo-wop style of the time with plenty of 'shooby-doobys', 'ahh-ahhs' and 'wup-wups' emanating from the gang while the lead singer praises his girl ("You know I love you, goodness cheese!") and begs her to marry him. In *Let Me Sleep Woman*, he appears to have got his wish, but subsequently wishes he hadn't because, after busting his nuts down in the coal yard, he returns home to a lady who nags him constantly and won't let him rest. This amusing tale of marital stress is clearly from Coasters territory.

Chuck's contribution is a pair of fiery guitar solos which are very similar, both accompanied by syncopated handclaps from the group. Argo 5353 is a pretty good disc and deserves to be better known. More's the pity then, that *Up There* remains to this day unissued and unheard.

SESSION 23
CHUCK BERRY
Chuck Berry, vocal/guitar, steel guitar -1; Leroy C. Davis, tenor saxophone -2; unknown tenor saxophone -2; Johnnie Johnson, piano; Matt Murphy, guitar; Willie Dixon, double bass; Ebby Hardy *or* Jaspar Thomas, drums; unknown vocal group -3

Chess Records studio
2120 South Michigan Avenue   **12 February 1960**
Chicago, Illinois   **(29 March 1960)**

10075   **Drifting Blues** -2 -3   ◐ Pye International NEP-44033
       (Charles Brown, Johnny Moore,   ■ Chess LP-1448, Pye International
         Eddie Williams)   NPL-28031, 2CH-60023 ◉ Ace
                                 CDCH-397

10076	**I Got To Find My Baby** -2	○ Chess 1763**a** ■ Chess LP-1448,
	(Walter Jacobs)	2CH-60028
	I Got To Find My Baby -2 *[stereo remix]*	■ Chess CH-9190 ◎ Ace CDCH-397
	(Walter Jacobs)	
10077	**Don't You Lie To Me** -2	■ Chess LP-1456, Pye International
	(Hudson Whittaker)	NPL-28031, Chess 2CH-60023
		◎ Ace CDCH-397, Beat Goes On
		BGOCD-428
10078	**Worried Life Blues**	○ Chess 1754**b** ■ Chess LP-1448
	(Maceo Merriweather)	2CH-60028 ◎ Ace CDCH-397
10079	**Our Little Rendezvous**	○ Chess 1767**b** ■ Chess LP(S)-
	(Chuck Berry)	1488, 2CH-60028 ◎ Wolf 2010CD
10080	**Bye Bye Johnny**	○ Chess 1754**a** ■ Chess LP-1448,
	(Chuck Berry)	Pye International NPL-28031, Chess
		LP(S)-1514D, CH2-8201,CH6-80001
		◎ Beat Goes On BGOCD-428
	Bye Bye Johnny *[stereo remix]*	■ Chess CH2-92521
	(Chuck Berry)	
10081	**Run Around** -1	■ Chess LP-1456, Pye International
	(Chuck Berry)	NPL-28039, Marble Arch MAL-702
		◎ Ace CDCH-397, Beat Goes On
		BGOCD-428
	Run Around *[stereo version]* -1	■ Marble Arch (UK) MALS-702
	(Chuck Berry)	
10082	**Jaguar And Thunderbird** -3	○ Chess 1767**a** ■ Chess LP-1480,
	(Chuck Berry)	Pye International NPL-28031, Chess
		2CH-60023, CH6-80001
		◎ Beat Goes On BGOCD-428

Note: LP-1480 was overdubbed with audience noise.

Towards the end of the 50s, Chuck had been expressing a desire to cut more blues and on this, his first session of the new decade, he got his wish. In addition to the usual crew of Johnson, Dixon and Hardy (or is it Jaspar Thomas again?), L.C. Davis makes another appearance and, to enhance the blues feel, the highly-regarded Matt 'Guitar' Murphy.

Murphy, or 'M.T.' as Sonny Boy Williamson II affectionately called him, had a considerable blues pedigree, having started out in Tuff Green's Memphis-based band, progressing to playing lead guitar for Bobby Bland and Junior Parker on formative records by these artists in the early 1950s. He relocated to Chicago in 1952 and became Memphis Slim's guitarist, playing on some of Slim's best sessions. He went on to team up with Sonny Boy Williamson II in 1963, and later that year also played Europe with Sonny Boy and Memphis Slim as part of the *American Folk Blues Festival* package. He eventually found real fame in 1980 when he played Aretha Franklin's hen-pecked husband in *The Blues Brothers*.

Murphy's rhythm guitar on this Berry session meant that the practice of overdubbing Chuck's lead guitar on the rhythm track could be dispensed with, as a result of which the tracks have a more cohesive feel.

Where better for Chuck to start his blues session than with **Drifting Blues**, a song by a major influence of his, Charles Brown? The number was first recorded in 1945 on the Los Angeles-based Philo label by Johnny Moore's Three Blazers with Brown on vocal and piano. When it started to catch on, it was remastered and released on Imperial under Brown's own name and became his first big seller, winning the *Cash Box* 'Best R&B Record of 1946' award. The song has since become a blues standard, cut by Bobby Bland and Lowell Fulson amongst many others. Indeed, Brown himself has re-recorded it on numerous occasions.

Berry's version cannot match the delicate simplicity of Brown's original. The unknown vocal group (which might be the Ecuadors again) chant "I ain't got nobody" incessantly behind Chuck's plaintive, heavily-echoed vocal which gives the track an over-produced feel. Strangely enough, he makes no attempt to replicate Johnny Moore's guitar solo and the melody is carried by L.C.'s sax instead. The last two verses of Brown's original song are substituted by one alternative verse from Berry's pen and, on the whole, it is not fully realised. Chuck's version is okay, I suppose, if you are unfamiliar with the original, but somehow it leaves one wanting... drifting almost.

Although he is frequently listed as the composer of **I Got To Find My Baby**, Chuck did not write the song, which was actually first recorded six years earlier at Chess by Little Walter Jacobs. Walter, too, is often credited with its authorship, as is Willie Dixon (who, incidentally, played on both cuts). My money is on Walter because Dixon wrote a completely different *I Got To Find My Baby*, recorded in 1955 by Muddy Waters, and what we have here is yet another case of the old '*Mixed-Up Copyright Blues*'!

Here's a strange thing though: the original version by Little Walter and Berry's version have two common verses, but an alternative version of the song by Walter also has a third common verse: "I've got to search this town from door to door/ The love I crave I can't find no more" — the same couplet that opens Berry's 1960 cut. This alternative take was, however, only released in 1992! Was Chuck psychic, did he hear the unissued track at Chess, or did Willie Dixon contribute to the lyrics?

Chuck also adds a verse of his own ("Ever since she said we were through/ I've been nervous and shook up too"), which achieves little apart from pulling the narrative together. He chose, however, to leave out Walter's most colourful couplets: "If I was the good Lord, pretty wimmens would never die/ You may be good-looking, baby, but you'd hang your head and cry" and "I'm gonna walk the floor till my moustache drags the ground/ I'm gonna find my baby and see what she's puttin' down". Walter is searching for his "big-legged brownskin", while all Chuck is looking for is his "little girl" — an altogether more suitable subject for his perceived audience.

Musically, Berry's song is taken at a faster lick than Walter's blues, but has no guitar solo. The harmonica is replaced by some pretty heavy saxophone from L.C. Davis and A.N. Other (or is it just L.C. double-tracking?). There is also some pretty neat drumming and a guitar figure played on the bass strings by Matt Murphy which really makes the cut something else. Chuck's instrumental contribution is confined to a very typical boogie rhythm played during the sax break.

The stereo alternative is the one of several new mixes of previously released songs which were issued in 1986 on the *Rock'n'Roll Rarities* and *More Rock'n'Roll Rarities* albums, and in this case it makes a great track super-great! Chuck's vocal is raised out of the musical maelstrom and the instruments are more clearly defined. As they say in the business, the stereo really does lift and separate — honest, cross my heart.

Despite the dubious authorship, it was the Berry cut, issued as it was on a single and on the influential *Rockin' At The Hops* album, which subsequently inspired the likes of the Animals to cut the song.

Chuck Berry is also sometimes credited as the composer of **Don't You Lie To Me**, as is Fats Domino, but in truth the song was written and first recorded in 1940 by the prolific blues singer, famous slide 'Guitar Wizard' and infamous kazoo-player, Tampa Red (known to his mother as Hudson Woodbridge and to his song publisher as Hudson Whittaker). Interestingly, at the same session that he cut this song, Red also recorded another of his most famous compositions, *It Hurts Me Too*, which Chuck would later record.

However, it was probably Domino's 1951 recording of *Don't You Lie To Me* that Chuck picked up on, as he follows the latter's version fairly closely, substituting just one verse with his own. More convincing is the strong New Orleanian second-line backbeat which underscores the whole record from the very wonderful sax-and-drums intro to the faded ending with the same repetitive sax and drums. Here's a proposition though: a non-Chuck Berry guitar solo on a Chuck Berry record! A rarity indeed, with the honour in this instance going to Matt 'Guitar' Murphy.

For the next number, Chuck reached deep into his blues bag for Big Maceo Merriweather's **Worried Life Blues**. Maceo himself must have found the song in his own bag, for it is based on Sleepy John Estes's *Someday Baby Blues*, first cut in 1935 and recut three years later as *New Someday Baby*. Estes doubtless based his song on some earlier composition, too — such is the blues continuum.

Big Maceo's *Worried Life Blues*, cut in 1941, was his very first record. It was a major R&B hit and has subsequently become a blues standard. Merriweather was a powerful blues pianist who went on to cut some tremendous blues in his own right as well as playing on several Tampa Red sessions. On this record, Red returned the favour by providing some seamless guitar accompaniment.

Chuck follows Merriweather's opus closely, with only minor lyrical variations. The tempo is speeded up and, much as I like Chuck's vocal, it is no match for the smokey tones of Big Maceo, who seems to really mean what he sings and is truly saddened by his old lady's mean mistreatment. Listen to the venom in his spoken aside: "No boy, I ain't gonna worry *my* life no more," just before the piano solo.

Nevertheless, Berry's *Worried Life Blues* is a pretty smooth outing with an instinctive interplay between the two guitars, Chuck taking the rhythm part and Matt Murphy the lead. An altogether thoroughly satisfying Berry blues which, when released on the back of *Bye Bye Johnny*, must have struck a chord with a fair few budding blues boys in the early sixties.

Take the tune of Sonny Boy Williamson's *Good Morning Little*

Schoolgirl, mix in the guitar lick from Memphis Minnie's *Me And My Chauffeur Blues*, add some topical lyrics about orbiting the earth (the USSR had launched the first Sputnik satellite in 1957) and you have **Our Little Rendezvous** — a trite little ditty that somehow found its way onto the 'B' side of *Jaguar And Thunderbird*.

A true romantic at heart, Berry extols the twin virtues of love and marriage time and again in his songs (*Vacation Time, Almost Grown, Diploma For Two*, etc) and here they are again in *Our Little Rendezvous* — even including the promise of grandkids for grandma and grandpa. Once again, he concentrates on the racing rhythm (complete with a strummed intro this time), while Matt Murphy contributes guitar fills over a tinkling piano.

On his sequel to *Johnny B. Goode*, **Bye Bye Johnny**, Chuck makes a power-play to top the original and damn near makes it. The by-now-familiar guitar intro (played on the bass strings this time) leads us into the powerful

chugging rhythms constructed from Murphy's chunky chords, supported by some pretty off-centre drumming. There's no solo, but, because of the sheer locomotive power of the track it's not missed.

Chuck fills us in on Johnny's biography since Episode One and we learn of his mother's sacrifice, first to get him his guitar from money made by gathering crops, and then to send him off to "make some motion pictures out in Hollywood". Johnny's mom is ambivalent about the trip but all ends well because her beloved son writes of his success in both love and commerce and announces that he will soon be home with his new bride (note that 'love and marriage' thing again) to build a mansion for them by the railroad track. There is probably more than a hint of wish-fulfilment in the desire to make it in Hollywood and, if things hadn't turned sour for Chuck, with three feature films under his belt he may well have followed Elvis to the Promised Land. As they say, every cloud has a silver lining!

The stereophonic version of *Bye Bye Johnny* separates the two guitars and reveals that the powerful rhythm which makes this track so wonderful emanates from the fingers of Matt 'Guitar' Murphy with Berry adding the fills and frills. Of the two, the mono version is my favourite, but this might just be old-fashioned nostalgia. I do love the distorted feedback on the last chord, and it sounds so much better in mono.

Bye Bye Johnny was issued as the 'A' side of Chess 1754 on 9th May

1960. It reached a No. 64 in the *Cash Box* 'Top 100' in June but inexplicably never featured in any *Billboard* chart. However, this relative lack of success should not cloud the influence of the song on others, which has enjoyed reasonable popularity in the cover stakes. The Rattles, Germany's answer to the Beatles, cut it twice; Eddy Mitchell, France's answer to Cliff Richard (there is no answer to *that*!) also attempted a version; and the Rolling Stones yet again displayed their immaculate musical taste by cutting the song and using it as a rabble-rousing finale at their gigs in the early days.

On **Run Around**, Chuck sets aside his Gibson for his pedal steel guitar and kicks off with that well-worn Elmore James riff again, playing some fairly predictable slide figures before Johnnie Johnson takes over with a dominant piano pattern.

The song is thematically and melodically a kissing cousin of Guitar Slim's *The Things That I Used To Do*, a highly-influential blues recorded by a myriad of bluesmen and later by Berry himself. Over the loping beat, he sings his sad blues in a weary, lovelorn tone. Having tried his best, he becomes resigned to his fate: "So long, so long baby, there's no future for me and you/ I love you too much to let you run around the way you do."

The cut was tacked onto the tail-end of the *New Juke Box Hits* album, which had a great cover but little else going for it. Its more recent inclusion on Ace's 1993 *On The Blues Side* CD collection has elevated it to a more respectable position in the Berry songbook. The stereo version appears on the stereo pressing of the UK *You Never Can Tell* album on Marble Arch. The steel guitar is on the right track with the piano, while the rhythm guitar appears far more prominently on the left.

Jaguar And Thunderbird is a case of 'here we go again', with the singer heading at "99" for the county line, though this time it's in Indiana not Pennsylvania where the action takes place. The Jag is still sky blue and, although we aren't informed, my guess is that the 'bird is probably a cherry red '53. In this reworking of 1959's *County Line*, Chuck virtually talks his way through the song except when, accompanied by the unknown male vocal group, he interjects the chorus: "Slow down little Jaguar/ Keep cool little Thunderbird Ford." Meanwhile, Johnnie tinkles away on the piano keys in a manner reminiscent of Lafayette Leake's playing on many of Bo Diddley's outings.

Like Diddley's *Road Runner*, Chuck's fast-driving song was released in 1960 at the height of the early sixties' dragging/hot-rodding craze — a pastime popular amongst budding rebels without causes — but inexplicably missed the mark with the record buying public, struggling to No. 93 in the *Cash Box* 'Top 100' and only managing to scrape 109th position in *Billboard*'s 'Bubbling Under The Hot 100' chart. In recent years, the integrity of the process by which *Billboard* charts were compiled has been called into question. Could it be that the negative publicity surrounding Chuck's personal problems at this time had an effect on the record missing the lists? Or was it just that the temperature was already cooling for hot rock as those 'damn Bobbys' were pushed centre stage by the corporate record moguls.

SESSION 24
CHUCK BERRY

Chuck Berry, vocal/guitar, steel guitar-1; Leroy C. Davis, tenor saxophone -2; unknown tenor saxophone -2; Johnnie Johnson, piano; Matt Murphy, guitar -4; Willie Dixon, double bass; Ebby Hardy *or* Jaspar Thomas, drums; unknown vocal group -3; unknown female vocal -5

Chess Records studio
2120 South Michigan Avenue   **15 February 1960**
Chicago, Illinois   **(12 April 1960)**

10092	**Diploma For Two** -2-3 *(Chuck Berry)*	○ Chess 1853**b** ■ Chess LP-1456, Pye Int'l. NPL-28039, Marble Arch MAL-702 ◎ Beat Goes On BGOCD-428
	Diploma For Two *[stereo version]* -2-3 *(Chuck Berry)*	■ Marble Arch MALS-702
10093	**Little Star** -2-3 *(Chuck Berry)*	○ Chess 1779**b** ■ Chess LP-1456
10094	**The Way It Was Before** -2-3 *(Chuck Berry)*	■ Chess LP-1456, Pye International NPL-28039, Marble Arch MAL(S)-702 ◎ Beat Goes On BGOCD-428
10095	**Away From You** -2-3 *(Chuck Berry)*	■ Chess LP-1456
10096	**Down The Road Apiece** -4 *(Don Raye)*	■ Chess LP-1448, 2CH-60023, CH6-80001 ◎ Ace CDCH-397
	Down the Road Apiece *[stereo remix]* -4 *(Don Raye)*	■ Chess CH-9190
10097	**Confessin' The Blues** -4 *(Jay McShann, Walter Brown)*	■ Chess LP-1448, 2CH-60028, CH6-80001 ◎ Ace CDCH-397
10098	**Sweet Sixteen** -4 *(A. Nugetre)*	■ Chess LP-1456 ◎ Ace CDCH-397
10099R	**Thirteen Question Method** -4 *(Chuck Berry)*	■ Chess LP-1456, CH6-80001
10100	**Stop And Listen** -4-5 *(Chuck Berry)*	■ Chess LP-1456 ◎ Ace CDCH-397
10101	**I Still Got The Blues** -4 *(Chuck Berry)*	■ Chess LP-1480 ◎ Ace CDCH-397
10102	**I'm Just A Lucky So And So** -4 *(Duke Ellington, Mack David)*	■ Chess CH6-80001
	I'm Just A Lucky So And So *[alt. take]* -4 *(Duke Ellington, Mack David)*	unissued
10103	**Mad Lad** *[instrumental]* -1-3 *(Billy Davis)*	○ Chess 1763**b** ■ Chess LP-1448, 2CH-60023
10104	**Surfin' Steel** [Crying Steel*] *[instrumental]* -1-3 *(Chuck Berry)*	■ Chess LP-1480, CH6-80001*

Note: LP-1480 was overdubbed with audience noise.

1960, and Chuck Berry is under the hammer. In March, a series of trials and court hearings commenced, concerning allegations involving two young ladies, Janice Escalante, a Native American and Joan Mathis, a French girl. The incident with Mathis had happened in 1958, and Berry's crime appears to have been that he was a black man driving a white girl in an expensive car through a Southern state. In this case, Chuck was acquitted — mainly thanks to the testimony of Mademoiselle Mathis — but not so in the Indian girl indictment. This began in December 1959 and ran through until October 1961, when Chuck was found guilty of offences under the *Mann Act* (namely transporting a minor across state lines for immoral purposes) and given a five year sentence and a $5,000 fine. This was subsequently commuted to three years and $5,000 upon appeal because the original judge was found to be racially biased.

I mention all this not to dwell on Chuck's misfortunes, but because of its undoubted effect on his music. As he put it: "With the condition my head was in regarding the trials, it shows I was less concerned in the results of what was going down then, than in what was coming up."

Chess, fearing the worst, wanted to get some new cuts in the can and this session and the previous one, recorded three days earlier, were rush-recorded. The non-original songs which were familiar to the band fare reasonably well, but the original Berry compositions are way below par, particularly the first four cuts of this session.

Diploma For Two (*ie* a wedding licence) is an archetypal Chuck Berry 'moon in June' tune expressing the sentiments previously heard in *Vacation Time, 21, 21 Blues*, etc. about the 'love and marriage' ethic of middle class America. The stereo version of *Diploma For Two* on the UK-released Marble Arch album adds little to the cut. The saxes appear on the right track with the guitar solo, but unfortunately fail to drown out the dreadful female chorus.

In **Little Star** and **The Way It Was Before**, the unknown girl group come to the fore sounding like rejects from the *Perry Como Show* (is it only me who is haunted by "Dear Perry, would you be so kind to fill a request and sing the song I love best?"). This group does for Chuck what the Jordanaires did for Elvis... absolutely nothing! One can only assume that he was trying to emulate his idol Nat 'King' Cole who did this kind of middle-of-the-road schlock weekly on his television shows.

Away From You is slightly better than the three previous songs. For this, Chuck adopts his 'plaintive' voice and, no doubt contemplating his imminent incarceration, sings the lyrics with a degree of feeling.

If, as Berry says, this session was recorded over two days, my guess is that these first four tracks with sax and female backing, and without Matt Murphy's guitar, were cut on the first day. All four were included on the *New Juke Box Hits* album and contributed to it being the weakest Berry LP Chess ever produced.

Fortunately, for his next cut, Chuck travels **Down The Road Apiece** back to his musical roots: 1940's boogie woogie (it was Tommy Dorsey's stomping *Boogie Woogie* that started Berry on his musical adventures in the first place). The number is a classic of its genre, and influential too: *House Of Blue Lights*, for instance, followed its lead in both mood and melody even down to the jive talk introduction. This isn't surprising, as both songs were penned by

Chuck poses on the set of 'Go, Johnny, Go!'

Don Raye, who also wrote the masochistic-sounding *Beat Me Daddy, Eight To The Bar*.

The song first appeared in 1940, recorded by the Will Bradley Trio with vocal by Ray McKinley, supported on piano and jive by Mr. Freddie Slack. Bradley (born Wilbur Schwichtenburg) formed his band in 1939, which he co-led with McKinley. As a result of this joint leadership, *Down The Road Apiece* was released separately under both Bradley's and McKinley's names. Interestingly, Bradley was a trombonist and didn't actually feature on the disc.

Quite rightly, *Down The Road Apiece* immediately became a standard with the boogie woogie fraternity. Before Chuck got his chops around it, it had already been covered by Ella Mae Morse (as *A Little Further Down The Road Apiece*), Merrill E. Moore and the great Amos Milburn who produced a frenetic version on which he talks to himself!

Berry's version cuts the 'Slack' and gets straight to the boogie bone. Johnnie Johnson works hard on the eighty-eights, but is forced into the back seat by the powerhouse twin guitars of Chuck and Matt, who mesh perfectly together. Following a typical intro set-up, Berry starts up his patented romping boogie, allowing Murphy the freedom to pick over the mess. Three brief verses introduce us to the wonderful roadhouse juke joint which features, amongst other delights, "Kicking McCoy, that rubber-legged boy", "home-cooked chicken fried in bacon grease" and "an eight-beat like an old steam drill". The verses are interspersed first by a Murphy solo, then a Berry solo, until the whole gang truck on down that road which can only be Route 66.

If you think the mono version is good, wait till you hear the stereo version: un-bloody-believable! If you ever plan to take a trip to boogie heaven, Jack, take my tip, slip the stereo cut into the old CD player, set the dial on repeat, don a decent pair of headphones and, boy, you're there! Don't you just love that stomping boogie fade — is it *perfect* or what?

The Rolling Stones must have thought so because, when they recorded at 2120 South Michigan Avenue in 1964, they included a version of *Down The Road Apiece* that is clearly based on Chuck Berry's. Drummer-man Kicking McCoy becomes 'Charlie McCoy' (*ie* Mr. Watts) and Keith Richards throws all his best Berry licks into the pot. When visiting during the sessions, Berry is reported to have said: "Swing on, gentlemen. You are sounding most well, if I may say so." About *Down The Road Apiece* he commented: "Wow, you guys are really getting it on!" Rare praise indeed from the usually reticent St. Louis legend.

Next up come covers of two blues hits. The first, **Confessin' The Blues**, was the song Chuck sang in his first public performance at the Sumner High School '*All Men's Review*'. The tune was a big seller in 1941 for its originators, pianist/bandleader Jay McShann and his vocalist, Walter Brown. It quickly became a blues standard, covered within weeks by Doctor Clayton and later on by B.B. King, Little Walter, Esther Philips and many others. Brown's relaxed, mellow tones and McShann's delicate piano make the original a difficult act to follow, and Berry's pepped-up version is simply not in the same class. It's still pretty good though, particularly the great single-string guitar runs from Murphy while Chuck confesses. The lead briefly reverts to our man for a fairly typical instrumental break. All in all, *Confessin'* is one of Berry's better blues cuts.

The aforementioned B.B. King was riding high in the R&B charts with his tremendous two-part *tour de force* **Sweet Sixteen** when Chuck decided to cover it in 1960. His version is, however, based on Big Joe Turner's original reading of the song penned by Atlantic boss Ahmet Ertegun under the pseudonym 'A. Nugetre' (Ertegun spelt backwards). It could well have been retitled *'Sickly Sweet Sixteen'* because in his hands it becomes a slow lament in which the plaintive vocals are pushed to the 'pathetic' side of pathos. The power of Big Joe's recording and B.B.'s stunning stop-time climax at the end of his epic are completely overlooked by Berry, who is content to settle for a low-key reading and an even lower-key ending. Not one of his best, I'm afraid. The sweetest thing on the cut is the busy filigree guitar from Matt Murphy.

Chuck's musical creativity must have been stretched at the time he cut this session, because he resorted to re-recording **Thirteen Question Method**, a minor composition from three years before. Or maybe he was dissatisfied with the original, because this version is given a completely different treatment. Out come the wood blocks and we are off down South America way to samba the night away in true *Come Dancing* fashion (if you'll pardon the expression). The questions change from the earlier version but we still don't learn exactly what the thirteenth question is — however, I'm sure you can all guess!

Judging from the questions he asks, Ryland P. Cooder's 1987 cover — one of only three so far — is based on this version. But what happened to Question Number 4, Ry?

Stop And Listen has got to be one of Chuck Berry's worst recordings ever, and certainly one of the worst from his tenure at Chess. The lyrics of this slow blues — which Chuck half-speaks — make no sense at all, and, to top it all there is an unknown female a-moanin' and a-wailin' in the background. The song has been described as 'haunting'... 'haunted' is probably nearer the mark.

"How many times have you heard this song/ If I had what he has, my blues would be gone." This profoundly philosophical line starts **I Still Got The Blues**, a jaunty little original number from the mind and pen of Mr. Berry which features Johnnie Johnson's tinkling piano as much as Chuck's guitar. The composition is lightweight by Berry's standards, but didn't deserve to be buried beneath the fake audience that overlaid the track on the *Chuck Berry On Stage* album. Strangely though, I still anticipate the surge from the audience at the start of the guitar solo when listening to the clean version on the 1993 Ace CD.

Considering his personal predicament, one might have expected a tinge of irony to creep into Chuck's recording of **I'm Just A Lucky So And So**. If it's there, I can't detect it. This is the type of song he would play for his own pleasure, and this recording probably started as just that: a studio warm-up perhaps never intended for release. It was finally issued on the 1988 *Chess Box* set, and boy I'm so glad it was! I just love its relaxed 'amicable' feel, the lovely fat guitar chords, the neat brushwork from Ebby Hardy and the precisely-pronounced vocals. Three chords and a clearing of the throat bring this cut to an artistic conclusion.

The tune was written by Duke Ellington and Mack David and recorded in 1945 by the Duke with Al Hibbler, his band vocalist at this time. Hibbler's wonderfully mellow tones are evocative of a relaxed bygone era before the rats left the starting blocks. Ellington's version also features two beautiful solos from Johnny Hodges on alto sax and Lawrence Brown on trombone. Berry had toured with the blind Hibbler in 1956 and no doubt heard him sing the song at first-hand. It is little wonder then, that Chuck — together with quite a few others along the way — chose to record this great composition.

The unreleased alternative take is taken at a slower pace but otherwise follows the arrangement and lyrics exactly, even down to the mistake(?) where Berry sings: "The birds in every tree seem all so near to me", whereas the correct line is: "The birds in every tree [are] all so neighbourly" — which makes better sense.

For the last two tunes of the session, Chuck returns to his Gibson Electraharp to produce two distinctive instrumentals, *Mad Lad* and *Surfing Steel*.

Mad Lad is unusual because it is a Berry slide piece that *isn't* based on *Deep Feeling*. Instead, we get a strolling beat workout with neat interplay between slide and lead guitars. It also contains the deepest recorded bass since the Deep River Boys recorded *Deep In The Heart Of Texas* at the bottom of a Texas oil well!

The song is credited to one 'B. Davis' (presumably the prolific Billy Davis, who also penned *Too Pooped To Pop*) and, as far as can be determined, Berry's recording is the original. Sir Charles Thompson's All Stars cut an instrumental by the same title in 1947 — named after the band's tenor player, Leo 'Mad Lad' Parker — but this is a completely different tune.

The title of Berry's cut probably alludes to E. Rodney Jones, a Chicago disk jockey whose nickname was 'The Mad Lad'. Jones was closely associated with the Chess organisation — he was the fake MC on the *Chuck Berry On Stage* album — and later became programme director and top jock at their radio station, WVON (the 'VON' incidentally, stood for 'Voice of the Negro').

Surfing Steel is yet another version of *Deep Feeling* but, with the benefit of the second guitar from Matt Murphy and some steady rollin' piano from Johnnie Johnson, it is, in my view, the best variation on the theme.

It was first issued as *Surfing Steel* beneath waves of adulating adolescents on the infamous *Chuck Berry On Stage* LP (the 'surfing' tag was appended to cash in on the latest teenage craze) and we had to wait until the release of *The Chess Box* in 1988 to hear it minus the flotsam and jetsam. Here, it was finally issued under its proper title, *Crying Steel* — altogether more befitting than that "surfing shit" (to quote Jerry Lee Lewis).

SESSION 25
CHUCK BERRY

Chuck Berry, vocal/guitar; Johnnie Johnson, piano; poss. Reggie Boyd electric bass, Ebby Hardy or Jaspar Thomas, drums

Ter-Mar Recording Studio
2120 South Michigan Avenue
Chicago, Illinois

10 January 1961
(19 January 1961)

10636	**Route 66** -1 *(Bobby Troup)*	■ Chess LP-1456
	Route 66 *[stereo alt. take]* -1 *(Bobby Troup)*	■ Chess CH-9190
10637	**I'm Talking About You** *(Chuck Berry)*	○ Chess 1779**a**, 1853**a** ■ Chess LP-1456, 2CH-60023, CH2-8201, CH6-80001
	I'm Talking About You *[stereo remix]* *(Chuck Berry)*	■ Chess CH-9190
10638	**Rip It Up** *(Robert 'Bumps' Blackwell, John Marascalco)*	■ Chess LP-1456

After two prolific sessions, this three-song gig must have been quite relaxed. The backing vocals which contaminated the previous sessions are dropped, and even guitar overdubs are eschewed to provide a back-to-basics rhythm and rock session. It is also the first Berry session to have an electric bass guitar (possibly played by Reggie Boyd) instead of the ubiquitous string bass of Willie Dixon. Boyd seems to have been a protégé of Dixon, who used him on a number of sessions he produced or was involved with, including Otis Rush's *Three Times A Fool* and *She's A Good 'Un*, Jimmy Rogers's *Rock This House* and *My Last Meal*, and Billy 'The Kid' Emerson's *The Whip (Parts 1 & 2)*. Boyd also played bass on Etta James's 1962 smash, *Something's Got A Hold On Me*. On Berry's sessions he plays with distinction and makes his presence felt.

There have been countless songs about roads — *Route 90*, *Highways 49, 51* and *61* all readily spring to mind — but none can be as famous as **Route 66**. The legendary thoroughfare had a TV series named after it, which in turn spawned a hit theme tune by Nelson Riddle — though the latter has nothing to do with the song in question. Sweden's 'Mr. R&B', Jonas Bernholm, named his most popular imprint 'Route 66' and on each record we were urged to get our 'kixs' from the music therein. BBC-TV broadcast a documentary about the legendary highway, but as it didn't mention Chuck Berry we won't talk about it either, except to note that the composer of *Route 66*, Bobby Troup, was interviewed and shown playing the piece on piano. Troup's other main claim to fame is as composer of Little Richard's *The Girl Can't Help It*. Richard's wild version came as quite a shock to the old jazzer (whose wife, Julie London, coincidentally played the dreamy chanteuse in the film).

The tune was, of course, first waxed by Berry's idol, Nat 'King' Cole in 1946, and is very much in his cool 'supper club' style. Cole's version begins with a lengthy introduction followed by a log of the towns to be seen on the two thousand mile plus journey from Chicago to L.A. and closes with a smooth guitar/piano passage.

Berry spurns the long intro and cuts straight to the travelogue. He spices up the beat, adds a tinge of tango and finds time to repeat the advice on the best way to traverse the States within the two minutes thirty-eight seconds duration of the cut. The alternative take is very similar to the track issued on *New Juke Box Hits* except for the odd additional "Jack" and the fact that it is in sterling stereo. It ends with Chuck advising: "Get your kicks on Route 66 and I'll meet you on Route 62"... wherever that might be.

Just as Berry upped the tempo of his idol's version, the Stones, for the first track of their first album, upped the tempo of *their* idol's version. If Nat and Chuck chose to cruise the highway, the Britishers decided to burn up the blacktop in a car "that would eat up the road".

Sadly, Route 66 is now a shadow of its former self, usurped by US Highway 40, but its memory lives on in Bobby Troup's wonderful song.

I'm Talking About You is the best cut of the session — the meat in the burger, as it were. A powerful electrical force pervades the song, starting with a distorted chord and continued throughout by Boyd's heavy pumping bass which powers its way across the pauses as though they don't exist.

"Let me tell you about a girl I know/ I met her walkin' down an uptown street." Nadine maybe? Whoever it is, Chuck has the hots for her in a big way: "Lovely indeed, that's why I ask her if she/ Will promise me someday she will be my bride?" (The 'love and marriage' ethic again.)

This song, the only original of the session, owes more than a little to Memphis Minnie's *I'm Talkin' 'Bout You*, particularly the thrice-repeated "I'm talking about you" refrain. Minnie first recorded the number in February 1930 and it proved so popular that she cut a remake entitled *I'm Talking 'Bout You No. 2* in July of the same year. These songs were firm favourites with the blues and hillbilly fraternity and were recorded on several occasions throughout the years. The great blueslady was also one of Berry's old-time favourites and it's not surprising that he used one of her most popular songs as a basis for his composition. It's rumoured that when Chuck first started to record for Chess he met Minnie (who had cut a session herself at Chess back in 1952) and recorded some duets with her. These tapes are supposedly stashed away in his possession. Of course, rock and roll is littered with such tales, and who knows whether or not this one is true?

The stereo remix does little more than place the vocal and bass in your left ear and piano and drums in your right. The vocals are clearer, however, and don't you just love the slur on the end of Hollywood?

I'm Talking About You was issued in February 1961 as Chess 1779 with the appalling *Little Star* on the flip, and again in May 1963 coupled with the little-better *Diploma For Two*. Neither release made the charts. Despite this, the song — which shouldn't be confused with Ray Charles's call-and-response workout, *Talkin' About You* — was a firm sixties group fave. The heavyweights, Beatles and Rolling Stones (of course) cut versions; middleweights Hollies and Yardbirds did it; as did featherweights Wayne Fontana & The Mindbenders and Bern Elliott & The Fenmen. In the 1970's and 1980's, the British covers continued with rockabilly revivalists the Milkshakes and blues-rockers Dr. Feelgood.

Chuck's recording of **Rip It Up** was a mistake, pure and simple. His previous covers had been of swing and R&B favourites from the forties. Here he tackles a contemporary rock and roll song from the Georgia Peach's tree and Little Richard's raucous, rebellious rant is toned down to a point were it could have been retitled '*Fold It Up And Put It Safely Away In A Box*'! The fire and fury, the essence of rock and roll that made *Let It Rock* and *Roll Over Beethoven* so great is completely lacking here. I was always contemptuous of Bill Haley's version because he changed "shag on down by the Union Hall" to "*rock* on down..." (but then, I didn't know at the time that "shag" was a dance). In Berry's version this line becomes "*cruise* on down..." Need I say more?

SESSION 26
CHUCK BERRY

Chuck Berry, vocal/guitar, overdubbed guitar -1; Leroy C. Davis, tenor saxophone -2; Johnnie Johnson piano; *possibly* Reggie Boyd, electric bass; Phil Thomas, drums; Martha Berry, second vocal -3

Ter-Mar Recording Studio
2120 South Michigan Avenue
Chicago, Illinois   **29 July and 3 August 1961**

11072	**Come On** -1-2-5 *(Chuck Berry)*	○ Chess 1799**b** ■ Chess LP-1465, Pye International NPL-28039, Chess 2CH-60023, CH2-8201, CH6-80001 ◎ Beat Goes On BGOCD-428
	Come On *[alt. take] [stereo]* -1-2-3 *(Chuck Berry)*	■ Marble Arch MALS-702, Chess CH2-92521
11073	**Adulteen** -2-3 *(Chuck Berry)*	unissued
11074	**The Man And The Donkey** -1-2-3 *(Chuck Berry)*	■ Chess LP-1480, 2CH-60028
	The Man And The Donkey *[takes 2,3 and 4]* -2-3 *(Chuck Berry)*	unissued
12593	**The Man And The Donkey** -1-2 -3 [Nashville] *(Chuck Berry)*	■ Chess CH-9318 ◎ Chess CHD-9318
11075	**Go Go Go** -2-3 *(Chuck Berry)*	○ Chess 1799**a** ■ Chess LP-1480, 2CH-60023
	Go Go Go Johnny B. Goode *[stereo remix]* -2-3 *(Chuck Berry)*	■ Chess CH-9190
	Go Go Go *[alt. take]* -2-3 *(Chuck Berry)*	unissued
11076	**Trick Or Treat** -2-3 *(Chuck Berry)*	■ Chess LP-1480

11077R	**Brown Eyed Handsome Man** -2 (Chuck Berry)	■ Chess LP-1480
12594	**Brown Eyed Handsome Man** -2 (Chuck Berry) [stereo remix]	■ Reelin' 001, Chess CXMP-2011, Checkmate LP-1955, Chess CH-9190
11078	**All Aboard** -1-2 (Chuck Berry)	■ Chess LP-1480

Note: 12593/4 remastered 1 August 1963. LP-1480 was overdubbed with audience noise.

One might expect that the last session before Chuck's second internment would have been a downbeat affair. Not so, as it produced the first class *Come On*, the almost-first class *Go Go Go*, as well as some 'not so bads' and 'also rans'. The session was enhanced by L.C. Davis on sax and, for her one and only outing on wax, Chuck's baby sister, Martha Luvenia Berry on vocals. More's the pity, because Martha adds a new dimension to Berry's music and is far more complementary than the previous female vocalists he had used. The session also features drummer man Phil Thomas who hung around the Chess studios and recorded with Buddy Guy. He later moved into jazz, cutting with Sonny Stitt and Zoot Sims.

Come On, the first cut of the session, is the best: a real-life, streetwise story in the "Why do everything happen to me?" vein. With lyrics such as: "Laid up from my job and can't afford to check it *[his car, that is]* / I wish someone would come along and run into it and wreck it" and "Every time the phone rings, sounds like thunder/ Some stupid jerk tryin' to reach another number", *Come On* is thematically similar to, and just as lyrical as the classic *Too Much Monkey Business*.

Martha sings in unison with her brother on the verses (except when he slips in the odd additional word) and sounds rather tentative and inexperienced in parts. This, however, adds to the charm of her contribution. In the fade-out she sings: "Tell me something baby" which sounds like an ad lib but, as it occurs in both versions, it can't be.

The alternative version is a different take with very minor variations in the lyrics. The biggest difference is that it is in stereo — which enhances the high-pitched, overdubbed guitar and subdues the piano, and to these ears does not sound as good as the mono cut. The speeded-up overdubbed guitar sounds like a bit of Chess audio trickery, similar to that used on John Lee Hooker's *Walkin' The Boogie*. A Gibson on speed! Fortunately the short but gritty guitar break is undubbed and therefore untainted. It sounds better, however, on the stereo cut.

The alternative take first appeared on the mega-rare twelve-track stereo version of the UK Marble Arch *You Never Can Tell* LP, which doesn't actually mention the track on the sleeve or on the label. However, it is now more readily available on the Chess *Rock'n'Roll Rarities* album. (Incidentally, on the Marble Arch issue, the stereo tracks are reversed.)

Come On was released as a single in September 1961 and, considering its quality, hasn't been covered by that many people (there are several recordings with the same title which shouldn't be confused with Chuck's song — Bo Diddley, Smiley Lewis and Earl King readily spring to mind). Probably the best known cover is that by the Rolling Stones, which was their very first single release. However, unlike many of their early recordings, the Stones' *Come On* has not survived the test of time, as the original has, and Jagger's singing and Jones's tinny harmonica are embarrassingly bad. The Blues Band version is much better, but then they have had forty years to practise.

Adulteen remains unissued and probably just as well. The song is one in which Mr. Berry advises teenagers to get it while they can for tomorrow may be too late. "Once you're grown, you can't repeat the scene," he advises, "So love and live your life as an adulteen."

"Adulteen" is Berryspeak such as "motorvatin' " or "botheration", but, whereas the latter two fit naturally into their respective compositions, this expression seems altogether too contrived. The title is sometimes prefixed with '*(Everything I Do Is Wrong)*', but as this doesn't appear in the song and doesn't reflect the song's message either, it appears to be a perpetuated error. Musically, the irritatingly familiar melody line is carried by L.C. Davis's sax and there is no guitar break.

"Down the road came the junco partner" sang James Wayne in his classic 1951 recording, *Junco Partner;* "Down the road came a tired little donkey" sings Chuck Berry in his 1961 adaptation of the tune, **The Man And The Donkey**. It's not, however, in the same class as the original which has long been a standard, especially in New Orleans, cut by the likes of James Booker and Dr. John amongst others. However, knowing Berry's penchant for all things Jordan, it could be that it was the latter's version of the *Junco* theme that led him to develop his interpretation of the tune.

Chuck's simple tale of a weary burro, rejuvenated by the demon drink from the man with no name (Lazy Pedro maybe?) is sung in unison with his little sister and is spiked with a killer — albeit somewhat incongruous — guitar solo. The high-pitched overdubbed guitar is present again, pestering the track like a fly on the donkey's behind. The tune was first featured on the *Chuck Berry On Stage* LP, buried under a welter of false audience noise.

The alternative take, *sans* audience, is mucho better. This take is subtitled '*Nashville*', added when the track was remastered along with *Brown Eyed Handsome Man* (matrix 12594) on 1st August 1963. The reason for this subtitle is obscure, unless, of course, matrix 12593 was incorrectly attributed to *The Man And The Donkey* and there is an entirely different song by Berry about Music City, USA still lurking in the vaults. The early takes are no more than false starts, counted in by Berry himself and fouled up when he mashes the words.

Go Go Go is the last in the trilogy of songs mapping the career of the celebrated Mr. Goode. Previously we heard that Johnny was off west to make some motion pictures... seems now he's back home playing guitar at the weekly record hop. Any lingering doubts that Johnny B. Goode wasn't Chuck Berry's alter ego are dispelled in this song as Johnny turns it up and turns it on: "Duck walking on his knees, peckin' like a hen/ Lookin' like a locomotive, here he comes again." Who else could this possibly be?

Johnny has finally made it. His parents give him tentative approval ("Used to sound goofy, but I guess it's alright") and someone's told him — somewhat unbelievably — that "Stan Kenton's cutting *Maybellene*". However, it is Berry's rather than Goode's aspirations which surface when he sneaks Erroll

Garner into his *Sweet Sixteen* and mixes Ahmad Jamal into *Johnny Be Goode.*

Each verse, sung in unison by Chuck and Martha, is punctuated by alternate guitar and sax solos leading to a long run-out beneath which mutterings and laughter can be heard. The sax breaks from L.C. are some of his best and Johnnie Johnson's piano sparkles as ever.

The stereo version bereft of overdubbed crowd noise is a big, big improvement, but better yet is the unissued version. Here, the band pick up the tempo by about 100% and blast out the song until it comes out like a different tune. This is a tremendous performance, full of the raw energy and spunk that's needed to make rock and roll great — and this is *great* rock and roll. Chuck's celebratory: "Yes, yeah, yeah" as the track ends says it all. Rough and ready as it is, this cut should be issued immediately!

Go Go Go became the 'A' side of Chess 1799, released in September 1961. It failed to register on any charts Stateside, but two years later in the good old UK, as Pye International 7N.25209 (backed with *Come On*) it entered the charts on 13th July and reached No. 38 in the Top 40 by 25th July 1963. One week later, the Rolling Stones made their first-ever appearance in the same chart with their version of *Come On*. Things were finally beginning to stir for Chuck Berry across the Pond.

In stark contrast, **Trick or Treat** is a marketing ploy gone bad. Okay, so we've done Christmas with *Run Rudolph Run*, what else is there? I know: Hallowe'en!" Come back Freddy Krueger, all is forgiven!

Berry's re-recording of **Brown Eyed Handsome Man** was an ominous precedent of things to come when he later moved to Mercury, though this remake — unlike the Mercurys — is in a very different mould from the original. Slowed down and given a conga beat with the sax taking a prominent part, a song with such great lyrics deserved another outing. Only one minute forty-eight seconds long (the final 'baseball' verse doesn't make it to last base this time) but Chuck's vocals are a treat: dig the way he rolls those R's at the start, and the way he pronounces "wrastling". The stereo mix, remastered on 1st August 1963, and devoid of intrusive crowd noise, gets the full five-star rating.

And finally, it's **All Aboard** as the Chuck Berry travelogue show hits the road — or to be precise, the *rails*. The much-beloved automotive mode is replaced by locomotive power as we travel from Newburgh, fifty or so miles north of New York, to Oklahoma City in the Midwest. The journey takes us via Chicago, St. Louis and Kansas City, but we also hear mention of little bitty towns such as Kingston, Lorain and Sanddusky *en route*. After switching locos in St. Louis to the M–K–T *[Missouri–Kansas–Texas]* lines, we pass through Chuck's adopted hometown, Wentzville, and then on down into Oklahoma.

All Aboard is a two-verse song that is literally a list of stops on the line. I bet Chuck wrote it with a railroad timetable on his lap! The Iron Horse has, of course, figured large in black music — often as a symbol of escape — from *Shorty George* to *Smokestack Lightnin'*, and from *Choo Choo Ch' Boogie* to *Take The 'A' Train*.

In 1956, Muddy Waters cut a song called *All Aboard*, from which Chuck filched the porter's call and steam hiss for his tune. The arrangement and phrasing of Berry's song and *Good News* by Eugene Church, cut the previous year, cannot be coincidental either; hell, even the buzzing sax is the same.

There are also notable similarities with the lyrics to *Night Train*, written for the Swans back in '54 by Oscar Washington.

Trick Or Treat and All Aboard are the only remaining songs that have not been released clear of the fake audience which pervades the *Chuck Berry On Stage* LP. This is no great loss in the case of *Trick Or Treat*, but it's a pity about *All Aboard*. I'm convinced that there must be a clean version in the vaults that continues the journey to the West Coast (or maybe even Mexico) instead of running out of steam in Oklahoma City.

Billboard, February 1964

SESSION 27
CHUCK BERRY

Chuck Berry, vocal/guitar, overdubbed guitar -1, double-tracked vocal -2; James Robinson, tenor saxophone -3; Leroy C. Davis, tenor saxophone -3; Johnnie Johnson, piano; unknown bass; Odie Payne, drums

Ter-Mar Recording Studio
2120 South Michigan Avenue
Chicago, Illinois

15 and 16 November 1963
(14 January 1964)

12907	**Nadine (Is It You?)** -3 *(Chuck Berry)*	○ Chess 1883**a** ■ Chess LP-1485, Pye International NPL-28031, Chess LP(S)-1514D, CH2-8201, CH6-80001 ◎ Beat Goes On BGOCD-428

	Nadine (Is It You?) *[stereo remix]* -3 *(Chuck Berry)*	■ Chess CH2-92521
12908	You Never Can Tell -2-3 *(Chuck Berry)*	○ Chess 1906**a** ■ Chess LP(S)-1488, Pye Int'l. NPL-28039, Marble Arch MAL-702, Chess 2CH-60023, CH6-80001 ◎ Beat Goes On BGOCD-428
	You Never Can Tell *[stereo remix]* -2-3 *(Chuck Berry)*	■ Marble Arch MALS-702, Chess CH2-92521
12909	The Little Girl From Central [The Girl From Central High] *(Chuck Berry)*	■ Pye International NPL-28039, Marble Arch MAL-702, Checkmate LP-1955
	The Little Girl From Central *[stereo]* *(Chuck Berry)*	■ Marble Arch MALS-702, Chess CH-9318 ◎ Chess CHD-9318, Beat Goes On BGOCD-428
	The Little Girl From Central *[alt. take]* *(Chuck Berry)*	unissued
12910	(The) Things I Used To Do -1 *(Eddie Jones)*	○ Chess 1916**b**, Pye International NEP-44033 ■ Pye Int'l NPL-28031, Chess LP(S)-1488, CH6-80001 ◎ Ace CDCH-397, Beat Goes On BGOCD-428
12911	I'm In The Danger Zone -3 *(Chuck Berry)*	unissued
	I'm In The Twilight Zone -3 *(Chuck Berry)*	unissued
12912	Fraulein -1-3 *(Lawton Williams)*	○ Pye International NEP-44033 ■ Pye International NPL-28031 ◎ Beat Goes On BGOCD-428
12913	Lonely All The Time [Crazy Arms] -2-3 *(Chuck Seals, Ralph Mooney)*	○ Pye Int'l NEP-44033 ■ Pye Int'l NPL-28031, Chess CH6-80001 ◎ Beat Goes On BGOCD-428
12914	Dust My Broom *(Elmore James)*	unissued
	Mean Old World *(Aaron 'T-Bone' Walker)*	unissued
12924	O Rangutang *[instrumental, faded]* -3 *(Chuck Berry)*	○ Chess 1883**b** ■ Pye International NPL-28031, Checkmate LP-1955 ◎ Wolf 2010CD
	O Rangutang *[instrumental, unfaded]* -3 *(Chuck Berry)*	◎ Beat Goes On BGOCD-428

From 19th February 1962 until 18th October 1963 (his 37th birthday), Chuck Berry was in imposed exile from his public at the pleasure of Uncle Sam. Whilst serving his time, he didn't waste it, reading up on accountancy and business studies. A practical result of this endeavour was the

The 'Nadine' session, 15-16 November 1963.
Left to right: Johnnie Johnson, Chuck Berry
and (obscured by mike) Odie Payne.

establishment of his publishing company, Isalee Music, registered at Berry Park, which carried all his songs from 1965 onwards. As well as taking care of business, the physical restrictions did not in any way limit his musical juices, and in the short stay at the Springfield Medical Center he wrote five songs which are the equal of some of his best fifties' compositions.

On his release, Chuck was keen to regain his musical chops. One of his first public appearances was sitting in with Little Walter at a West Side Chicago club called 'Pride & Joy', playing his own songs and supporting Walter on *Blues With A Feeling* and *Mean Old World*.

Chess were also keen to cut some new Berry product, and Marshall Chess recalls that, within three weeks of his release, their star was recorded playing a gig in Flint, Michigan with a pick-up band that just happened to be the Motown rhythm section. The idea was to produce a *bona fide* live album in an attempt to emulate the success of *Chuck Berry On Stage*.

"I never got the tapes from Berry Gordy because, at that time, he thought the Motown rhythm section was worth a royalty on the record," is how he recalled it in a 1980 interview. Is it too much to hope that this session may currently reside 'somewhere in Hollywood' with the other dusty Detroit Hit Factory tapes and could one day be issued?

Notwithstanding this dream, within one month of hitting the streets Chuck Berry was back in the studio cutting two of the five great songs he had composed in Springfield: *Nadine* and *You Never Can Tell*.

Nadine is an urban — and urbane — update of *Maybellene*. Instead of chasing his girl along country blacktops, the scenario switches to the bright lights, big city. The cinematic equivalent would be the *Bonnie and Clyde* chases as compared with the race beneath the el line in *The French Connection*. The urbanisation is reflected musically as well, with two saxes providing a solid R&B base in contrast to *Maybellene*'s country leanings. The main feature, however, is the insistent, mesmeric bass figure played in unison by bass and guitar over rock-solid drumming.

Johnnie Johnson is adamant that Jaspar Thomas plays on this session. However, photographic evidence points to Odie Payne, who has always been listed and was a blues drummer *par excellence*. A veritable permanent fixture in the Chicago studios, he cut sides with Sonny Boy Williamson, Jimmy Rogers, Otis Rush and, most famously, Elmore James, on whose sides he featured for years.

The urgency of the beat is perfect for Berry's story of 'desperately seeking Nadine'. Like a nightmare in which you never quite achieve your goal, Chuck pursues his "future bride" on foot, by bus, by taxi, always somehow remaining one step behind the elusive lady.

The imagery is so sharp that, if ever a promo video were required, there'd be no need for a storyboard. Bruce Springsteen's comment that he'd never seen a "coffee-colored Cadillac" but knew exactly what one looked like when he heard the song, encapsulates the feel of this Cinemascope, all-action, Technicolor tale. Lines such as: "I caught a loaded taxi, paid up everybody's tab/ Flipped a twenty dollar bill and told him: Catch that yellow cab!" and "I's pushing through the crowd, tryin' to get to where she's at/ I was campaign-shouting like a Southern diplomat" demonstrate Berry's complete mastery of the idiom. Springsteen hasn't covered *Nadine* (yet) but a couple of dozen others have, including Waylon Jennings, John Hammond, George Thorogood and... the Great Dames of Rock & Roll.

The so-called 'stereo remix' ought to be reported to the Trading Standards Office. As the original is in stereo, the 'remix' is really just a retread — virtually indistinguishable except for the longer fade-out which is, admittedly,

very pleasant.

Nadine was issued as a single in the middle of February 1964 and by March it was a hit on both sides of the Atlantic, peaking at No. 23 and No. 32 in the *Billboard* and *Cash Box* pop charts, No. 7 in the Cash Box R&B chart and No. 27 in the British 'Top 50'.

"Such is life say the old folks/ It goes to show *You Never Can Tell*"... and such is Chuck's story of Pierre and the beautiful mademoiselle (unnamed, but my guess is 'Cherie'). This tale of teenage lovers and the angst they cause their parents is a truly tremendously optimistic fable from Mr. Berry's poetical pen. The old folks really don't think Pierre and his young bride are going to make it, but they don't reckon with the couple's mutual vibes: a "coolerator" crammed with TV dinners and ginger ale, a hi-fi phono with 700 little records "all rock, rhythm and jazz", and a "souped up jitney, a cherry red '53" in which they drive to New Orleans (a jitney incidentally, was a type of taxi cab that could be hired for a nickel or 'jitney').

'New Orleans by way of Nashville' is the musical style of the song, with its robust rolling piano and saxes and nary a spark of guitar except for the obligatory opening. The rhythm is so infectious that it made Vincent Vega twist like John Travolta at Jackrabbit Slim's! The country influence comes in the double-tracked "C'est la vie" vocal part, and it isn't surprising that amongst the forty-odd covers are some by country artists including Waylon Jennings & Jessi Colter, Billie Jo Spears, the New Riders Of The Purple Sage, Kenny Loggins and — the best of the bunch — Emmylou Harris.

Released in July 1964, *You Never Can Tell* was another Transatlantic hit for Chuck, reaching No. 14 and No. 15 respectively on the *Billboard* and *Cash Box* pop listings and No. 23 in the UK 'Top 50'.

As regards the 'stereo remix', there isn't a gnat's knob of difference between the two versions. "C'est la vie," say the old record collectors, "it goes

to show you never can believe the record sleeve!"

Listening to *Nadine* and *You Never Can Tell*, one might think that Chuck had left his guitar back at Springfield, but not so, as **The Little Girl From Central** proves. Quite appropriately, the tune commences with the *Little Schoolgirl* riff, then quickly drops into the *Sweet Little Sixteen* rhythm.

The song is about a gym-slipped temptress, the archetypal jail bait, who knows she's got it, flaunts it, but no way is she going to give it away! She's got her heart set on fame and is moving on to higher things.

The cut trucks along until it reaches the guitar break, then catches fire as the volume of the guitar increases. The guitar sound has a harder, metallic ring to it, and it's been suggested that this came about when Berry switched to the thinner-bodied ES-335 TDC Gibson. Chuck, however, claims the guitar makes no difference and it's all in the mixing board.

The Little Girl From Central was only available for many years on the UK long-players NPL-28039 and MAL-702 (both titled *You Never Can Tell*), finally appearing in the USA on the 1990 LP, *Missing Berries: Rarities (Volume 3)*. The song is sometimes subtitled *'The Girl From Central High'*, which appears to have been the title used in the Chess files. However, this title has never been used on record releases and isn't quoted in the lyrics. Maybe it was felt there was a need to explain that 'Central' was a high school and not a bus station!

The stereo version of the song can only be found on the ultra-rare stereophonic version of the UK Marble Arch LP (look for the 'S' on the end of 'MAL', record hunters!).

The unissued cut is very similar to the released version except that it is twice as long, clocking in at five minutes twelve seconds. This extension consists of a repeat of the first three verses plus a prolonged closing guitar passage which ends abruptly. The tape I've listened to is decidedly lo-fi and I would dearly love to hear it in its full glory.

The 'B' sides of many of Chuck Berry's singles, starting with his very first release, have been blues. It was perfectly natural then, for Chess to choose **The Things I Used To Do** as the 'B' side of Chess 1916.

The song is Eddie 'Guitar Slim' Jones's masterpiece that has became a solid blues standard covered almost as frequently as Berry's own *Johnny B. Goode* or *Memphis*. I've yet to hear a cover, however, that comes close to Slim's *Things* — and that includes Berry's. Slim's original contains an extraordinary time-warp space guitar and impassioned vocals laid over a plodding band riff (with vamping piano from none other than Brother Ray Charles, who can be heard exclaiming a satisfactory "Yeah" as the song ends).

Slim, by all accounts, was as flamboyant as Berry himself, if not more so. Decked out in brightly-coloured suits with hair dyed to match, he played a solid-bodied guitar and used feedback a decade before Hendrix, and, with an extended guitar lead would walk the floor in a fashion that Albert Collins made his own twenty years later. He was the same age as Chuck, but he didn't last. Burned out by booze and fast living, Slim was dead before he reached the age of thirty-three.

Berry's version of *The Things I Used To Do* is decent enough, but frankly doesn't hold a candle to Slim's. In place of Slim's declamatory vocals, Chuck adopts a resigned tone, and instead of the flowing guitar of the original, he turns in some rather routine picking spiked with occasional high-register overdubs.

The unissued **I'm In The Danger Zone** is a slow dirge of a blues with little to offer lyrically built as it is around the repeated line: "Alone, I'm in the danger zone." **I'm In The Twilight Zone** is the same song with just the one word substituted, possibly to tie in with the *Twilight Zone* TV show. The tune is reminiscent of Leroy Carr's *Midnight Hour Blues* with piano and droning saxes featuring heavily. These songs have nothing in common with the Ray Charles's/Percy Mayfield's *The Danger Zone*, a far superior composition.

Fraulein and **Crazy Arms** expose Chuck's country roots to the daylight. Both were originally Number One C&W hits: *Crazy Arms* for Ray Price in 1956 and *Fraulein* for Bobby Helms in 1957. Berry's arch-rival Jerry Lee Lewis also cut a sterling version of *Crazy Arms* which was released as his debut Sun single the same year as the original, 1956.

The original *Crazy Arms* by Ray Price is pure Hank Williams country: fiddle, steel guitar and a straight-eight country beat. Berry injects an additional beat into his reading which corrupts the country feel, turning it into 'rhythm and country' or 'country and blues'. The twin-tracked vocal from Price's version is, however, retained by Chuck in the chorus. In 1960, Bob Beckham enjoyed a sizeable hit with an upbeat country version of the song and it's possible that this may have influenced Chuck to cut his own interpretation.

Similarly, the country fiddle of Bobby Helms's *Fraulein* is replaced by soothing saxes and a choppy rhythm guitar in Berry's version. Helms's high tenor is replaced by Chuck's lowest-register tenor, trying for all his worth to achieve the husky tones of Nat Cole. Berry refers to *Fraulein* in his autobiography as a First World War song he heard as a child, so Helms's hit version possibly wasn't the one that influenced him to cut it.

Both cuts initially appeared in the UK on the Pye International LP, *The Latest And The Greatest*, on which *Crazy Arms* was erroneously titled '*Lonely*

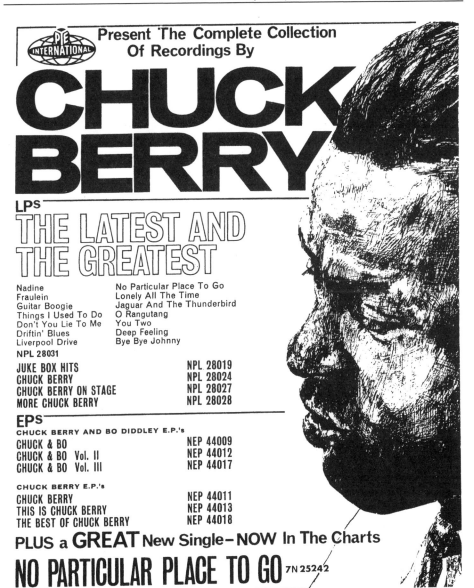

All The Time'. They also formed half of the Chuck Berry UK EP, *Blue Mood*. *Crazy Arms* was eventually released in the USA on the 1988 *Chess Box* set, but the elusive *Fraulein* remains unissued to this day. Europeans have fared better, however, with Chuck's fair maiden being readily available on Charly reissues for most of the '80s and early '90s.

After the country comes the blues, but these covers of Elmore James's **Dust My Broom** and Little Walter's **Mean Old World** remain unissued and unheard to this day. I have it on good authority, however, that Chuck's interpretation of the Elmore epic isn't worth releasing — though this, of course, is purely subjective. Not to worry. Both songs were subsequently re-recorded by Chuck and released, and Elmore's famous '*Broom*' lick graced many a Berry tune over the years — not least **O Rangutang**.

This spirited and intriguingly-titled instrumental, which is to be found on the flipside of *Nadine*, demonstrates Chuck's new found tintinnabulatory guitar sound. He really *does* play that guitar like ringing a bell! It's a great workout by the entire band and not just some tired instrumental to end the session. Virtually all the releases of this cut are faded out at about two-and-a-quarter minutes, however, the British Beat Goes On release from 1998 is unfaded and the band boogie on for a further forty-five seconds before bringing matters to an artistic conclusion.

SESSION 28
CHUCK BERRY

Chuck Berry, vocal/guitar; Ellis 'Lafayette' Leake *and/or* unknown, piano; unknown guitar; Willie Dixon, double bass; Odie Payne drums.

Ter-Mar Recording Studio
2120 South Michigan Avenue
Chicago, Illinois   **20 February 1964**

13048	**Big Ben** (Blues) *(Chuck Berry)*	■ Pye Int'l. NPL-28039, Marble Arch MAL-702, Checkmate LP-1955 ◎ Beat Goes On BGOCD-428, Official 4012-FS
	Big Ben (Blues) *[stereo version]* *(Chuck Berry)*	■ Marble Arch MALS-702, Chess CH-9318 ◎ Chess CHD-9318
13049	(The) **Promised Land** *(Chuck Berry)*	O Chess 1916**a** ■ Chess LP(S)-1488, Pye Int'l. NPL-28039, Marble Arch MAL-702, Chess 2CH-60023, CH6-80001 ◎ Beat Goes On BGOCD-428
	(The) **Promised Land** *[stereo remix]* *(Chuck Berry)*	■ Marble Arch MALS-702, Chess CH2-92521
13050	**Brenda Lee** *(Chuck Berry)*	O Chess 1906**b** ■ Chess LP(S)-1488, Pye Int'l. NPL-28039, Marble Arch MAL(S)-702 ◎ Beat Goes On BGOCD-428

For this session, the band is stripped to the bare essentials: guitars, piano, bass and drums. Out go the saxophones and the overdubs, and in comes Lafayette Leake (well, maybe — see later) on his first Berry session since *Johnny B. Goode*.

Big Ben sees our hero revisiting *School Day*. The number uses the same distinctive stop-time tune, and the storyline is an update of the school day traumas which have now become workaday hassles. Twenty years of schooling and they put you on the day shift! Instead of trouble from the guy behind him and mean-looking teachers, the singer now has to contend with "Work, work the same routine/ Either the boss or the old machine". Unlike the school day freedom at three o'clock, there seems to be no respite from the tedium of "another dollar, another day". Three verses, three ringing guitar solos, two minutes twenty seconds and it's over, the tale told.

Big Ben (often referred to as *'Big Ben Blues'*, no doubt because of the sentiments expressed rather than its musical structure) was first issued in the UK on the 1964 Pye International LP, *You Never Can Tell*, then three years later on the budget Marble Arch LP of the same name. It would be twenty-six years before it saw the light of day Stateside on the 1990 *Missing Berries: Rarities (Volume 3)* album with the *'Blues'* addendum to the title. Strangely enough, *Big Ben* isn't mentioned in the song at all, and I can only surmise that anything remotely British was considered saleable in 1964. However, this album contains the relatively rare stereo version previously only available on stereo pressings of the Marble Arch LP. The cut separates Chuck's guitar, so that on headphones you get the full force in your right lughole. The mono cut is also readily available on UK Charly's 1992 *Chess Years* box set and other reissues.

And so, to another Berry classic. *Route 66* and *All Aboard* were mere day trips when compared to **Promised Land**, a Trans-American journey of epic dimensions written — ironically — while Berry was banged up in Springfield. He reportedly had problems obtaining a map of the USA to assist him with composing his tale of great escape to California, the land of dreams, the Promised Land.

The story begins in a cool Norfolk, Virginia and ends in the diametrically-located hot L.A. In-between, the "poor boy" travels by Greyhound bus, smoking steam train and jet-propelled plane to reach his goal, encountering all kinds of trouble "that turned into a struggle halfway 'cross Alabam". However, people who care about him set him up when he finally hits New Orleans. Before you can say "Johnnie Johnson", he finds himself in a silk suit tucking into an *à la carte* steak at 30,000 feet over Albuquerque on a jet to his desired destination!

Based on the rhythm and drive of Roy Acuff's 1938 country hit, *The Wabash Cannonball*, the number is a rip-snorter from start to finish. A ringing Berry introduction sets the band off at a tearaway pace and they cut through the song like a Kansas tornado. It all sounds spontaneous but, according to an eyewitness report in *Jazz Beat*, it took one-and-a-half hours and twenty takes to get it in the can. The article also reports the recording date as Thursday, 20th February, not the previously-listed 25th (which may have been the mastering date).

The session started at 6 pm, and the report notes the presence of Willie Dixon on bass and a session rhythm guitarist. It also adds that Leake left half-way through the session and was replaced by a young studio pianist. Could this it be Paul Williams who turns up on a couple of subsequent Berry sessions? It's not clear, however, who plays piano on which cuts.

Promised Land b/w *Things I Used To Do* was released as a single in December 1964 and made its mark Stateside, reaching No. 41 and No. 35 on the *Billboard* and *Cash Box* pop charts and No. 16 on the *Cash Box* R&B listing. Issued on Pye International in the UK, the same coupling peaked at No. 26 towards the end of January 1965. Given its success, there are surprisingly few covers of this Chuck Berry classic and I've only heard one that comes close to the original: Johnnie Allan's stunning Cajun garage band outing, with Belton Richard's wonderful accordion emulating Berry's guitar licks is the one that almost cuts Berry at his own game. In reality, the record is a bit of a shambles: Allan misses out one verse, which blows the story line, and then buggers up the zone/telephone rhyme in the last verse. Not to worry, for the exciting spontaneity carries it through and the rough edges only add to its charm. Unfortunately — in the UK at least — Allan's record was swamped by King Elvis's staid version, released at the same time, which wound up at No. 9 on the UK charts in January 1975.

The stereo remix of Chuck's *Promised Land* is an improvement on the originally-released cut. Although the latter is also in stereo, the remix provides a heavier bass and drums and more prominent piano — both of which serve to emphasise the urgency of the song. It also runs on for five seconds longer in the fade out.

One time when I saw a Chuck Berry concert, at the point where he asks: "You say 'em, we play 'em," someone yelled out "*Brenda Lee*!" "*Brenda Lee*?" came the surprised response from Chuck. He didn't play it, and probably hadn't done so since the day he recorded it. In fact, according to the eyewitness report of the session, Chuck expressed his dissatisfaction with the song at the time.

The number has nothing to do with Little Miss Dynamite, but it does have a lot to do with *Little Joe From Chicago* from which it takes its melody. The original *Little Joe* was recorded in 1938 by Andy Kirk & His Twelve Clouds of Joy. The song was written by Kirk's pianist, Mary Lou Williams and trombonist Henry Wells, about the band's agent, Joe Glaser, who came from Chicago.

Chuck's favourite ballad singer, Nat 'King' Cole, also featured the song in his repertoire and his version seems to take its lead from Cole's faster reworking. However, Cole's only known recording of the number appears on a 1944 radio transcription disc. Maybe Chuck heard the show and remembered the arrangement?

Brenda Lee, we learn, is the little girl from Central High. Unlike the other *femmes fatales* in Chuck's songbook — Nadine, Betty Jean and the very beautiful Delilah — Brenda studies hard, hoping to pass and rejects the flirty guys all through her schooldays. She only emerges in her full glory at the senior prom where she sings, she entertains and waves her alma mater goodbye. The tale is related to the accompaniment of a bouncy beat and some cool jazzy chords *à la* Johnny Moore.

Brenda Lee was chosen as the 'B' side of *You Never Can Tell* and was also included on Berry's *St. Louis To Liverpool* album (released when all things Liverpudlian were fab gear), on the cover of which Chuck, in a raw silk suit, holding a blond Gibson, takes a giant leap for rock and roll.

It has been stated (by Krista Reese, in the first-ever book about Berry), that *Brenda Lee* was replaced on some copies of *St. Louis To Liverpool* by the old gospel song *How Great Thou Art*. I've yet to find anyone who has a copy of this version of the album and look forward to being enlightened.

SESSION 29
CHUCK BERRY
Chuck Berry, vocal/guitar; Paul Williams, piano; unknown bass; Odie Payne, drums.

Ter-Mar Recording Studio
2120 South Michigan Avenue
Chicago, Illinois   **26 March 1964**

13126	**No Particular Place To Go** *(Chuck Berry)*	◉ Chess 1898**a** ■ Chess LP(S)-1488, Pye Int'l. NPL-28031, Chess LP(S)-1514D, CH2-8201, CH6-80001 ◎ Beat Goes On BGOCD-428
	No Particular Place To Go *[stereo remix]* *(Chuck Berry)*	■ Chess CH2-92521
13129	**You Two** *(Chuck Berry)*	◉ Chess 1898**b** ■ Chess LP(S)-1488, Pye Int'l. NPL-28031, CH6-80001 ◎ Beat Goes On BGOCD-428
13130	**Liverpool Drive** *[instrumental]* *(Chuck Berry)*	■ Checker LP(S)-2991, Chess LP(S)-1488, Pye Int'l. NPL-28031, Chess CH6-80001 ◎ Chess CHD-9170, Beat Goes On BGOCD-428, Official 4012-FS

Chuck Berry, poet laureate of rock, Shakespeare of roll, and... king of rock and roll conservation! Well, he certainly knows a thing or two about recycling his old tunes. **No Particular Place To Go** is a prime example, being *School Day* with new lyrics.

The new song, if anything, is better than the old, its storyline alternately overflowing with anticipation ("I stole a kiss at the turn of a mile/ My curiosity running wild") and frustration ("Can you imagine the way I felt/ I couldn't unfasten her safety belt"). For 'safety belt' read 'chastity belt', and you really *can* imagine the way he felt!

Chuck's guitar sound on the cut is wonderful, it really does sound like he's ringing a bell (one wonders if he got this expression from the bell emblem on the head of his Gibson?). What is more, he gets to stretch out at the close of the track in a way he had only previously hinted at before the inevitable fade that occurs on many of his cuts. This is matched by the sweeping piano fills from newcomer Paul Williams, whose fingers must have been red hot by the end of the session.

Williams is a complete mystery. He isn't Paul Williams, the forties band leader of *Hucklebuck* fame, nor is he the Paul Williams who sang with Motown's Temptations, nor the bassist who appeared on Tommy Tucker's tracks. He pops up on two, maybe three, Berry sessions, then disappears.

Whoever he was, he certainly makes his presence felt here.

The original version of *No Particular Place To Go* is in stereo, so the 'stereo remix' adds little to the cut. Chuck's vocals are enhanced, but at the expense of a slight loss in guitar volume.

No Particular Place To Go holds a special place in my psyche as it was the song that locked me into the Berry groove — a time warp I've yet to escape. The nostalgia quotient was reinforced when Shell UK featured the song in a TV commercial together with an image of a rotating Pye International red-and-yellow 45 just like the one I used to have, but don't have no more.

This was another great song written by Berry whilst he was in Springfield "riding the rap" (as Elmore Leonard put it). The simple things in life, "riding along in my automobile... cruising and playing the radio... with no particular place to go" must have been particularly poignant to his free-travelling spirit.

For such a good song, *No Particular Place To Go* has received surprisingly little patronage from other artists, although it apparently holds a special appeal for Scandinavian and northern European groups, who have accounted for well over half the total cover versions. The best of these has got to be the hilarious version cut by the Swedish group Byfånarna... hearing is believing! UK psychobilly group, the Guana Batz also excreted a version, but this is — yep, you guessed right — a right load of old mammal droppings.

Like its predecessor, *Nadine*, *No Particular Place To Go* hit the charts on both sides of the Pond, making No. 10 and No. 9 in the *Billboard* and *Cash Box* pop listings as well as No. 2 in the *Cash Box* R&B chart, and a very respectable No. 3 in the UK 'Top Twenty' — the highest spot yet attained in Britain by a doubtless positively merry Mr. Berry.

Chuck's renaissance was on the rise, helped by covers of his songs by the Beatles and the Rolling Stones. Indeed, his first-ever UK tour was just weeks away. This, together with the fact that at the time all things related to Merseyside were eminently bankable, must have suggested **Liverpool Drive** as a perfect title for the powerful instrumental that sat on the 'B' side of *No Particular Place To Go* on the aforementioned UK Pye 45. An alternative title — *Liverpool Beat* — is quoted in some discographies, but I've yet to find a release which used this name.

Liverpool Drive is a Berry instrumental of the first order, essentially an extended workout on the *Rock At The Philharmonic* theme but with a harder-edged guitar sound, sparkling piano and a pounding bass. The track rolls along with Chuck playing some of the most intimate jazzy licks that he has ever laid down. Suddenly, about three-quarters of the way through, he lets rip with a series of double-stop notes that seem to ricochet around the studio. Oldsters amongst us may recall that deejay Mike Raven featured the track as the theme tune for his influential Radio London *Mike Raven Blues Show* in the sixties.

In **You Two**, we discover that Chuck has progressed from the juvenile twosomes of songs like *Vacation Time* and *Diploma For Two* to a more sophisticated lifestyle of twilight cookouts, jazzy sounds and cosy clans of four ("You two, we two, no more"). As he encourages his friends to "roast the wieners" and "chow 'til the night grows nigher", the jazzy sounds are laid down by the cosy clan of guitar, piano, bass and drums. Previous discographies list a second unknown guitar on this session, but, try as I might, I cannot detect it.

SESSION 30
CHUCK BERRY & BO DIDDLEY
Chuck Berry, guitar; Bo Diddley, guitar; Ellis 'Lafayette' Leake, piano; Jesse James Johnson *or* Chester Lindsey, bass; Billy 'Dino' Downing *or* Edell 'Red' Robertson, drums; Jerome Green, maracas

Ter-Mar Recording Studio
2120 South Michigan Avenue
Chicago, Illinois   **April 1964**

| 13369 | **Chuck's Beat** *[instrumental]*
(Chuck Berry) | ○ Checker 1089*a ■ Checker
LP(S)-2991, Chess CH6-80001
◎ Chess CHD-9170 |
| 13370 | **Bo's Beat** *[instrumental]*
(Ellas McDaniel) | ○ Checker 1089*b ■ Checker
LP(S)-2991 ◎ Chess CHD-9170 |

* Edited.

Chuck Berry and Bo Diddley, Chuck'n'Bo, *Chuck & Bo* — for anyone who bought those three UK Pye EP's in 1963, the names are as synonymous as ham and eggs or pork'n'beans.

Bo Diddley's recording career started slightly ahead of Chuck's in 1955 with his classic *Bo Diddley* b/w *I'm A Man* single. Together with Berry, he spearheaded the Chess assault on the rock and roll era. The Chess brothers probably couldn't believe their luck. Just as their blues giants began to wane, they had two young rock and roll Turks to wax. Bo's music is blacker and bluesier than Chuck's and, in consequence, he never achieved the mainstream crossover status that his labelmate enjoyed. During the sixties, his jungle rhythms were grabbed, rattled and hummed by as many white R&B groups as were grappling with *Johnny B. Goode*. *Mona* by the Rolling Stones, *Before You Accuse Me* by the Creedence Clearwater Revival and *Pretty Thing* by the Pretty Things spring to mind as notable examples of his wide-ranging influence.

The two 'big daddies' have played together on occasion throughout their careers and these Titan clashes have been filmed on at least a couple of occasions. There appears to be a genuine affinity and affection between the two men which transcends the usual showbiz bullshit that often passes for friendship. It's not surprising then, that Chess should get them together in the studio.

This was, in fact, the first Chess 'super session', cut three years before those more famous (some would say infamous) *Super Blues* and *The Super Super Blues Band* get-togethers which featured Diddley playing with Chess's other heavyweights: Little Walter, Howlin' Wolf and the mighty Muddy Waters. However, if Dick LaPalm's sleevenotes are to be believed, the session was as spontaneous as a Californian earthquake: *'Chuck was in Chicago for a meeting with officers of Chess Records, while Bo was in the Chess studio, one floor above, actually doing one of his own recording sessions. Chuck simply happened to wander into the recording studio, picked up a guitar that a musician left lying around and started to play, then Bo, then together, etc. Someone yelled "Take One" and all of a sudden it was a Bo Diddley–Chuck Berry session.'* From such are myths born.

Actually, there is a deal of credence to this story, as the band was Bo's current group and each of the two tracks cut that day is a long, loose, unstructured Bo–Berry jam. The album, *Two Great Guitars*, on which **Chuck's Beat** and **Bo's Beat** appeared also seems a little unplanned and opportunistic — a classic Chess rush job, slinging together these cuts with a couple of other recently-recorded instrumentals by the two guitarslingers. *Chuck's Beat* (10:40) and *Bo's Beat* (a mighty 14:08) represent a goodly proportion of the total playing time of the album (30:37), which was so measly that it had to be beefed up with four additional tracks for reissue on CD.

The cover sleeve doesn't even depict the two main protagonists but instead features a shot of their guitars — Bo's mis-shapen Gretsch and Chuck's blond Gibson — draped over not a Caddie or T-Bird but a cherry red Porsche!

Around the time of these recordings, Berry and Diddley seemed to be closely musically linked. Bo cut a song called *Hey Good Lookin'* which was credited to 'Chuck Berry Music Inc.' (although I'm not at all convinced it was penned by Chuck) and had also recently cut his one and only Berry cover ever, *Memphis*, in instrumental form on the live *Bo Diddley's Beach Party* LP.

Chuck's Beat itself is loosely based on *Memphis*. Chuck chugs and clucks along while Bo plays his shimmering figures above the polyrhythm. Both throw snippets from their hits into the pot and pass the greasy spoon to stir their licks. First Chuck, then Bo, then Leake gets a turn, then Bo brings it back to Jerome to shake his thing. At one point, about four-and-a-half minutes into the opus, Bo takes off into the stratosphere with a wonderfully distorted run. Despite the title, this is primarily a Diddley track with Berry in secondary mode: Chuck fiddles while Bo burns.

Bo's Beat is more of the same, but this time set to that timeless 'shave and a haircut, two bits' *Bo Diddley* monkey beat. Maracas and drums to the fore — the drummer man even takes a semi-solo towards the close — the two great guitars at times parry and thrust, and at others gel and meld into a metamorphic musical mass. Nine minutes into the cut, Chuck seems to want out — you can almost picture him backing out the studio door, guitar held in out-stretched arm, strap hanging loose — only to be enticed back by Diddley's infectious beat.

Big Bad Bo.

These tracks are considered by some to be overlong, and I guess it's how the mood grabs you. Play them in the car on the open road, or through headphones whilst reclining on a velvet chaise longue with a glass of claret, and it sometimes cannot get any better.

As well as forming the bulk of Checker LP(S)-2991, Chuck's and Bo's respective *Beats* were issued in truncated form as a Checker single, at just under three minutes each side (it was Chuck's only Checker label release in his long and chequered career). The tracks were also shortened when reissued on the 1988 Charly *Chess Years* box set (to 6:27 and 3:15 respectively).

SESSION 31
CHUCK BERRY WITH KINGSIZE TAYLOR & THE DOMINOES
Chuck Berry, vocal/guitar; Ted 'Kingsize' Taylor, guitar; Sam Hardie, piano; John Frankland, guitar; Howie Casey, tenor saxophone -1; Dave Wood, tenor saxophone -1; Bobby Thompson, bass; Gibson Kemp, drums; Brian Matthew, interviewer

Saturday Club (BBC Light Programme)
BBC Playhouse Theatre
Northumberland Avenue
London, England   **11 May 1964**

School Day -1   ◎ Official 4012-FS
(Chuck Berry)

Memphis Tennessee   ■ Merseyside's Greatest
(Chuck Berry)   MG BOX 801005-8*
                                    ◎ Official 4012-FS

*Chuck rocks out with Kingsize and the lads.
Sheffield, 14 May 1964.*

Sweet Little Sixteen *(Chuck Berry)*	■ Merseyside's Greatest MG BOX 801005-8* ◉ Official 4012-FS
Interview	■ Merseyside's Greatest MG BOX 801005-8
Nadine -1 *(Chuck Berry)*	■ Merseyside's Greatest MG BOX 801005-8*
Johnny B. Goode -1 *(Chuck Berry)*	■ Merseyside's Greatest MG BOX 801005-8

* Incomplete

"Now R&B fans, here's the moment lots of you have been waiting for, because here — for the first time in person on British radio — is the great Chuck Berry!" This is how British R&B fans (note, not rock and roll fans) were introduced to Chuck Berry by Brian Matthew on the BBC Light Programme's premier pop show, *Saturday Club*, broadcast 10 till 12 each Saturday morning.

The session was recorded on the Monday prior to its broadcast the following Saturday, 16th May. Chuck also made a brief appearance on another BBC radio show called *Pop Inn* which was broadcast on the 12th. Here he was interviewed by Keith Fordyce, who also spun his latest release, *No Particular Place To Go*.

Chuck was four shows (two days) into his first UK tour when he cut this set. He had previously toured Australia in '58 and '59, and then Jamaica in '60, but this was his first trip across the Big Pond. At this time he was hot news in Britain. His songs were probably better known by their beat boom cover versions, but things were changing as Chuck Berry singles released by Pye began charting and his LPs started being snapped up by the growing R&B movement. The tour lasted twenty-two days, the first twenty-one scheduled dates taking him on a round trip of all the major cities of England plus an excursion to Glasgow, and finished with a return date to London's Hammersmith Odeon (or 'Heymaarsmith' as Chuck pronounced it one time) by public demand.

Supporting him on the tour were the Swinging Blue Jeans (who had covered *Around And Around* and *Johnny B. Goode*), the Animals (who also cut *Around And Around* as well as *Almost Grown*, *How You've Changed*, *Let It Rock*, *Memphis Tennessee*, *Sweet Little Sixteen* and *Too Much Monkey Business*), Kingsize Taylor & The Dominoes (who recorded *Broken Arrow*, *Memphis Tennessee*, *Roll Over Beethoven* and *Sweet Little Sixteen*), the Other Two (who?) and Carl Perkins, also on his first British tour. Perkins himself cut Berry's *Brown Eyed Handsome Man*, *Roll Over Beethoven* and later on *Maybellene*, so all in all Chuck's influence on the tour entourage was significant. The final concert featured special guest Gene Vincent, who had likewise cut a couple of Berry tunes in his time (*Maybellene* and *Roll Over Beethoven*).

As well as playing their own spot on the tour, Kingsize Taylor & The Dominoes provided backing for Berry and Perkins. They were a second-league Merseybeat group who had cut their musical chops in the wake of the Beatles at the Star-Club in Hamburg. By 1964, however, they had turned into a

pretty tight unit and on these BBC cuts they provide very credible support for Chuck (he has had a lot worse since!).

In the interview with Brian Matthew, Chuck comes across as very enthusiastic, with little of the cynical attitude that would later taint his reputation. "These four shows," he enthuses, "have been superb, believe me. I started to do a no-hand flip. I know I can't but I was inspired to."

Asked about the backing group, he said: "They're great! I really was surprised at the unity that we compiled at our first rehearsal *(rehearsal!!!)* and we're really tight, so we'll be ready for the road."

The five tracks here are proof of this, in particular those featuring saxes which build up a strong head of steam, stomping all down the line. Chuck plays well and is in good voice even though the endings are a little raggedy.

In deference to the location and his new found 'R&B' status, Chuck cannot resist working some appropriate references into his compositions. In **School Day** he interjects "Long live rhythm and blues... ahhhh, it'll never lose", and in **Nadine** when he stops the yellow cab he flips a five pound note instead of his customary twenty dollar bill.

Over the very familiar boogie beat Brian Matthew introduces **Memphis** thus: "And here's the one that really started it all happening for fans here in Britain after we played on *Saturday Club* the disc of *Memphis Tennessee*." It is a great version up until the abrupt and discordant ending. **Sweet Little Sixteen** and **Johnny B. Goode** both come across as though Chuck really means it, good powerful singing and strong decisive guitar.

In an interview years later, Ted 'Kingsize' Taylor said that there had been no rehearsals and that Berry had tried to catch out the drummer on the changes. He also claimed that Chuck had forgotten his own guitar licks! Can ducks forget how to duckwalk? His memory is clearly failing him, as is evidenced by these tracks.

It's a great pity then, that this session hasn't been issued in a better fashion. The tracks were for a long time only available on a 4-LP box set of Taylor's early recordings. They are the best tracks on the set and, frustratingly, three of them are faded out after the first verse. However, with the recently-released Official CD, *Chuck Berry In London*, *Memphis* and *Sweet Little Sixteen* are now available in a complete form, albeit the hi-fi is much lower than the LP versions. In addition, *School Day* has finally been issued on the same CD, twenty-six years after it was recorded.

That same year, Kingsize & Co. recorded the only known cover version of *Broken Arrow*. They struggled on for a couple of years, made a couple of blues singles with Alex Harvey, then called it a day. Instead of cutting records, Taylor returned to cutting meat in the family butcher business in Southport.

SESSION 32
CHUCK BERRY

Chuck Berry, vocal/guitar, overdubbed guitar -1, double-tracked vocal -1; Ellis 'Lafayette' Leake *or* Paul Williams, piano; unknown bass; Odie Payne, drums

Ter-Mar Recording Studio
2120 South Michigan Avenue
Chicago, Illinois   **16 August 1964**

13451	**Little Marie** -1	◉ Chess 1912**a** ■ Chess
	(Chuck Berry)	LP(S)-1488, 2CH-60028, CH6-80001
	Little Marie *[stereo remix]* -1	■ Chess CH2-92521
	(Chuck Berry)	
13452	**Go, Bobby Soxer**	◉ Chess 1912**b** ■ Chess
	(Chuck Berry)	LP(S)-1488, 2CH-60028

Six years after placing a call via Long Distance Information, Chuck's alter character receives a return phone call from his estranged partner, the mother of **Little Marie**. Inevitable, but perhaps a little late, this is the sequel to Chuck's own personal soap opera, *Memphis Tennessee*, and, like most sequels, it doesn't quite measure up to its predecessor. *Little Marie* isn't particularly bad, it just lacks originality and hasn't got sufficient strength in itself to override this deficiency.

Here, Berry chooses to overdub a second vocal over the base track rather than simply twin-track one vocal. The slight variation in the two voices adds a certain charm to the proceedings, as does the naïve happy ending to the saga in which Marie's mother invites her dad to "come back and see Marie and live together in our home in Memphis, Tennessee."

The stereo version adds very little to the mono original. Chuck counts in the song and his two vocals and guitar overdubs are distinctly separated into the left and right stereo channels.

Little Marie became the 'A' side of Chuck Berry's thirty-first Chess single and became a modest US hit, reaching No. 54 and No. 51 in the *Billboard* and *Cash Box* pop charts and No. 30 on the latter's R&B survey. Ironically, *Memphis* itself, languishing on the 'B' side of *Back In The USA*, never charted in its own right although it has since become a world-famous composition, spawning in excess of 260 covers to *Little Marie*'s one and only revival by George Thorogood — and then only in a medley with *Memphis*!

The other song cut at this brief session, **Go, Bobby Soxer**, became the 'B' side of *Little Marie*. It is a typical Berry rocker, totally derivative, the type of song Chuck could turn out at the drop of a plectrum.

Bobby sox were short white ankle socks worn by teenage girls in the late forties and into the fifties. The girls, known as 'bobby soxers', became synonymous with the first wave of hysterical fans of the first true teenage idols such as Frank Sinatra and a little later, Johnnie Ray. By 1964, however, the term was surely *passé* — a throwback to Berry's youth?

The reference to this particular attire may actually have stemmed from Chuck's own idol, T-Bone Walker, who in 1949 cut *Bobby Sox Baby* — a song about a young girl who chases famed autographs for her scrapbook. Now, does that ring any bells?

Swamp bluesman Slim Harpo cut another *Bobby Sox Baby* in 1961, though this one had no connection with the T-Bone song other than the title and no discernible influence on Berry's tune.

Back in 1964, the USA was in the grip of Beatlemania with the faberoonies holding the No. 1 spot for three solid months, February thru April. Quite naturally, in his role of rock and roll chronicler, Chuck makes reference to the phenomenon in his song. The teenage attention has shifted from the ageing Johnny B. Goode to "the Beatles in the bobby band" for whom the bobby soxer "wiggles like a whimsical fish"!

SESSION 33
CHUCK BERRY

Chuck Berry, vocal/guitar, overdubbed guitar -1; Bobby Caldwell, guitar; Harry Simon, tenor saxophone -2; Jules Blattner, bass; Johnny Catallano, drums

Ter-Mar Recording Studio
2120 South Michigan Avenue
Chicago, Illinois   **15 December 1964**

13625	**Lonely School Days** -2 *(Chuck Berry)*	◉ Chess 1926**b** ■ Checkmate LP-1955
13626	**His Daughter Caroline** *(Chuck Berry)*	■ Chess LP(S)-1495 ◎ Official 4012-FS
13627	**Dear Dad** -1 *(Chuck Berry)*	◉ Chess 1926**a** ■ Chess LP(S)-1495, CH6-80001 ◎ Official 4012-FS
13628	**I Want To Be Your Driver** -1 *(Chuck Berry)*	■ Chess LP(S)-1495, CH2-8201
	I Want To Be Your Driver *[stereo remix]* -1 *(Chuck Berry)*	■ Chess CH2-92521
13629	**Spending Christmas** -2 [My Blue Christmas] *(Chuck Berry)*	unissued
13630	**The Song of My Love** -2 *(Chuck Berry)*	■ Chess LP(S)-1495 ◎ Official 4012-FS
13631	**Butterscotch** *[instrumental]* -1-2 *(Chuck Berry)*	■ Chess LP(S)-1495 ◎ Official 4012-FS

In 1964, anything English was selling product, so it isn't that surprising that these tracks (excepting 13625) cut at 2120 South Michigan Avenue in the heart of South Side Chicago ended up on the album *Chuck Berry In London,* its front cover sporting the declaration *'Recorded in England'.* (Coincidentally, Louisiana swamp-rocker Rod Bernard cut a great Berry soundalike in 1966 called *Recorded In England.*) The session is unusual in that it does not include a piano — one of only a handful of Berry outings that lacks this instrument.

The backing band on this occasion was led by Jules Blattner, whom

Chuck had met at the Butterscotch Lounge, a club in St. Louis. Blattner was something of a teenage boy-wonder, having scored a regional rockabilly hit, *Rock And Roll Blues* [Bobbin 105] with his band, the Teen Tones, in 1959. By the time of this recording, the Teen Tones (after a brief period as the Twist Tones) had become the Jules Blattner Group, and Blattner himself had switched to electric bass. An avowed Chuck Berry fan (he cut *No Money Down* shortly before this session, and later on, in 1971, recorded *School Day* and *Downbound Train*), he unfortunately remembers the gig with some displeasure: apparently Berry was really uncooperative and the guys only made $122 apiece for their contribution. To cap it all, they didn't even receive a credit on the album.

For the first number, **Lonely School Days**, Chuck adopts his teenage/schooldaze persona and a plaintive vocal to sing his sad song of juvenile rejection: "I saw you eating in the lunchroom," he whines, "right where we used to dine/ With someone sitting close beside you, enjoying pleasures that were mine." His heartbroken tale is sung to the accompaniment of a flayed guitar vibrato which intensifies the blue mood. The guitar concentrates on the chords while a lonesome sax injects the melody which lingers long after the last sad chord has decayed.

Lonely School Days became the flipside of Chess single 1926, but has to date never had a legitimate release on a Stateside album, although it was made available on several UK CDs by Charly.

From teenage tears to paternal pain in the course of one song is a big jump, but with **His Daughter Caroline** Chuck leaps the chasm with one mighty bound. To a measured beat, he imparts the ambiguous feelings of a father giving away his dear daughter to some predatory male: "Cheer was sparkling from his eyes, but tears were in behind/ When he gave his heart away, his daughter Caroline." He would later revisit both *Lonely School Days* and *His Daughter Caroline* and re-record them at a faster tempo.

The next time someone says rock and roll died when Beechcraft Bonanza N3794N crashed in an Ohioan field, or when a black man of diminutive stature threw his rings into Sydney Harbour, or when a young Memphian became private 53 310 761 in Uncle Sam's army, just place the 'A' side of Chess 1926 on your Dansette and ask them to reconsider.

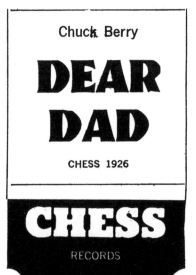

Dear Dad is a rush of pure, unadulterated rock and roll energy, a *tour de force* that forces all other tours off the road. It is the hottest thing Berry cut this side of the fifties. Not a single note is wasted, nor a second's pause permitted throughout the proceedings as, within the space of 110 seconds, Chuck belts out six verses and hits two storming guitar solos.

Singing about his favourite subject — automobiles — he imparts some of the wittiest lines of his career. In the form of a letter to his old man, he describes the shortcomings of his raggedy old Ford in the hope of getting a replacement, a "Cadillac '62 or '3" maybe: "Dad I'm in grave danger out here tryin' to drive/ The way this old Ford wiggles when I'm approaching forty-five/ I have to nurse it along like a little stubborn pup/ Cars whizzing by me Dad, look like I'm backing up!" He just can't get any power out of his old jalopy and almost gets a violation for driving too slowly on the freeway despite having made some modifications: "Dad, I've got four carburettors hooked up on it now/ I tried to hook another [to] see if it'd do a little good/ But ain't no place to put it 'less I perforate the hood". The sting in the tale comes when he signs the letter "Sincerely, your beloved son, Henry Jr. Ford"! Underpinning these great lyrics, the band is as tight as O.J.'s glove, pounding power-drumming from Catallano and rumbling bass from Blattner accentuating Berry's rolling rhythm and pecking lead guitar. Minimalist rock and roll of the first order.

Strangely, *Dear Dad* has never featured highly in Chuck's repertoire (perhaps because it wasn't a big hit — it only reached No. 95 in the *Billboard* 'Hot 100', though it did make No. 29 on the *Cash Box* R&B chart), nor has it been overly covered. Dave Edmunds, who knows a good groove when he hears one, cut a version of it, as did pub-rockers the Count Bishops and bar-rockers Mudboy & The Neutrons.

It has been speculated that **I Want To Be Your Driver** was Chuck Berry's response to the phenomenal success of the Beatles and was influenced by the Fab Four's *I Want To Hold Your Hand*. This just isn't so. Berry's tune is clearly based on Memphis Minnie's 1941 hit, *Me And My Chauffeur Blues*, both lyrically and in its *Good Morning Little Schoolgirl* melody which Minnie also borrowed. Of course, Chuck's intentions are far more carnal than holding hands. When he sings of mountains and valleys, his mind isn't on geographical topography — as he makes clear with: "I will ride you home with ease/ You will enjoy every journey, it will be my aim to please." A motorvatin' and copulatin' sort-of busman's holiday mixing pleasure with, well, pleasure!

The 'stereo remix' emphasises the guitar and vocal, which in my book cannot be a bad thing.

To date there have been a mere four cover versions of this song, including one by blues-rocker Bobby Mack & Night Train.

It appears that Chuck did learn something from his encounter with Janice Escalante other than not to mess with spring chicken, because the first five verses of **The Song Of My Love** are in the Spanish tongue, and only the last is in English. My friendly neighbourhood translator describes it as "sounding like it was sung by a South American peasant in very poor Spanish"... but don't worry — he's from Barcelona!

The song is a languid lament with a vibrato guitar and sax lead melody sounding so typically Mexican that it might actually be based on a traditional theme. It is a rambling account of mountain travels in search of Mexicali roses: "If anybody wants to cut it — I saw it first — I want to steal it — even if I haven't got a garden" seems to be the gist. Later on, Chuck sings: "Aqui vine porque vine *[I came here because I came]* / A la feria de las flores *[To the flower festival]* / Y canto con mis amigos *[And I sing with my friends]* / El cantar de mis amores *[The song of my love]*." Certainly, Berry himself was sufficiently 'amored' with the song to return to it later in his career.

Remember those sixties' sub-Bond caper movies such as *Our Man Flint* or *Matt Helm*? Remember the scene where James Coburn or Dean Martin attend some party full of girls, old before their age, dancing in boots and crocheted mini-dresses with guys old enough to be their fathers? Remember the music? **Butterscotch** sounds just like the music they would be boogalooing to. Despite this, it develops into a half-decent groove with that rare phenomenon for a Chuck Berry tune, an extended saxophone solo. The song's title stems from the Butterscotch Lounge, where Chuck and the band may have worked out the number.

Matrix 13629, **Spending Christmas**, alternatively called *My Blue Christmas* and apparently featuring saxophone, remains unissued and unheard. From the title, it sounds like it could be sort-of a festive *Lonely School Days*.

SESSION 34
CHUCK BERRY

Chuck Berry, vocal/guitar, overdubbed guitar -1; Peter John Hogman, harmonica -2, backing vocals -3; Bob Scrivens, piano; Jeff Krivet, guitar; Louis Cennamo, bass; Brian David 'Chick' Kattenhorn, drums; Bill Armstrong, Mike Boocock, Neil Carter, Roger Eagle, Roger Fairhurst, Rick Green and Brian Smith, backing vocals -3

Pye Studio
Cumberland Place
London, England   **9 January 1965**

13677	**After It's Over** *[instrumental]* -2 (Chuck Berry)	■ Chess LP(S)-1495 ◎ Official 4012-FS
13678	**Why Should We End This Way** -2 (Chuck Berry)	■ Chess LP(S)-1495
13679	**You Came A Long Way From St. Louis** -3 (Bob Russell, John Benson)	■ Chess LP(S)-1495 ◎ Official 4012-FS
13680	**She Once Was Mine** (Chuck Berry)	■ Chess LP(S)-1495 ◎ Official 4012-FS
13681	**Jamaica Farewell** -1 (Lord Burgess)	■ Chess LP-1495 ◎ Official 4012-FS
	Jamaica Farewell *[stereo]* -1 (Lord Burgess)	■ Chess LPS-1495

Following on from the success of his first UK tour, Chuck was back in January 1965 to tour again, this time taking time to cut tracks for his up-coming LP, *Chuck Berry In London*, and, no doubt, hoping to grab some of the Anglophilic fervour sweeping the United States at this time.

He had, in fact, been due to tour in November 1964 as a replacement for the infamous trouser-splitting Texan, P.J. Proby, who had been thrown off the show by promoter Robert Stigwood because of his antics. Although Berry turned up in London on time to start the tour, his famous brinkmanship for once got the better of him when Stigwood cancelled it because he hadn't signed the contract by the due date. It seems, however, that the pair parted amicably with Chuck clutching a contract to return in the New Year for a 24-day jaunt starting 8th January 1965 at the Lewisham Odeon in London.

'*Chuck Berry — The King of Rhythm And Blues*' proclaimed the posters, reflecting the popularity of R&B over the then-perceived as jaded 'rock and roll' tag. The tour line-up also reflects this: the Graham Bond Organization, Long John Baldry (who didn't actually perform), the Moody Blues (in their R&B pre-pretentious/mystical mode), together with one Winston G. who had the gorilla balls to include *Little Queenie* in his set.

Also on the tour were the Five Dimensions, who opened the show with their own spot and also backed Chuck on stage and in the studio for this and the following recording session. When they were backing Berry in concert, the Dimensions' harmonica-player, Peter Hogman, didn't play the whole set.

Chuck would, however, invite him on stage to blow during slow blues such as *Wee Wee Hours* or *Mean Old World* that he would invariably include in his act.

The Five Dimensions had previously backed Jimmy Powell and cut a raucous number with him called *That's Alright*. Included in the line-up for a short period was Rod Stewart, which contributed to 'Rod the mod' being erroneously credited with the harp-playing on Millie Small's 1964 ska smash, *My Boy Lollipop*. It was, in fact, Hogman. The group had also backed Sister Rosetta Tharpe and that old goat Sonny Boy Williamson II on UK tour dates, so they had a reasonable blues pedigree and this bias pervades both of their sessions with Chuck.

The first two numbers of this session are both slow blues. **After It's Over** is a melancholy instrumental based on *Deep Feeling* with prominent harmonica substituted for Chuck's steel guitar. Berry certainly appears to have taken a shine to Hogman because his harp is featured more than his own guitar.

Why Should We End This Way is a heartfelt song of a broken relationship in which Chuck sings: "I could scream, I want you to know/ It hurts me so bad that you should go," with a sincerity bordering on biography. The tune is based on Elmore James's memorable *It Hurts Me Too*, a song that has featured in Berry's repertoire for many years. The harmonica is again prominent, as is the tasteful piano tinkling of Bob Scrivens.

I suppose it was inevitable that Chuck would cut **You Came A Long Way From St. Louis** while he was six thousand or so miles away from his hometown. The gang listed on backing vocals — the "Olé's" that punctuate the song — were the nucleus of the British Berry appreciation society (officially called the 'Chuck Berry Information Centre') and the editors of *R'n'B Scene* magazine. Chuck was in full control of the session, nipping back and forth between studio floor and the control room. He conducted the backing vocalists by pointing at them when he wanted an "Olé!" to be inserted in much a similar manner as he controls backing bands at his gigs with his left leg to conclude a song. Included in the group was that intrepid flasher Brian Smith, whose photographs adorn many blues and rock and roll publications including this one.

Composed by Bob Russell *(words),* who also supplied the lyrics to *Time Was*, recorded earlier by Chuck, and John Benson *(music)*, the number was first introduced by Ray McKinley & His Orchestra in 1948 and subsequently covered by Harry James and Bing Crosby — thereby providing another link with the music of Berry's formative years: big band swing. Bill Jennings — Louis Jordan's one time guitarist and a major Berry influence — also cut a version in '55, so even the connections have connections.

It is a wonderfully witty ditty about a *femme fatale* sung by Chuck with panache and more than a hint of a fleshy muscular organ stuck in the side wall of the mouth: "I've seen a lot of crazy cars that were parked outside of your fancy address." Olé! — and say no more!

Another taste of the Caribbean is served up with Berry's brief version of **Jamaica Farewell**, whose theme about leaving loved ones behind echoes that of his own *Havana Moon*. The song was adapted from an old West Indian folk-song by calypso man Lord Burgess in 1955, but Chuck picked up on it from the 1956 Harry Belafonte hit and cites him as the source in a contemporary

Pye publicity.

interview.

Whilst Berry's version has a certain charm of its own and he tries hard to get the West Indian vocal intonations right, it doesn't match the folky *naïveté* and delicate enunciation of Belafonte's version.   He also misses out the colourful verse which describes a country market where ladies cry out while on their heads they bear ackee, rice and salt fish.

Chuck Berry In London was issued in both mono and stereo in the USA. On the mono version, *Jamaica Farewell* is faded prematurely, whilst the stereo version is permitted to run its full course and reaches an artistic conclusion with a crash of cymbals. The mono track checks in at a mere one minute forty-four seconds; the stereo version lasts just over two minutes. Both American versions are also blessed with an additional overdubbed guitar part by Berry which is more audible on the stereo release. Needless to say, the UK pressing of the album [Chess CRL-4005] appeared in mono only, faded and without the overdub.

SESSION 35
CHUCK BERRY

Chuck Berry, vocal/guitar; Peter John Hogman, harmonica -1; Bob Scrivens, piano; Jeff Krivet, guitar; Louis Cennamo, bass; Brian David 'Chick' Kattenhorn, drums

Pye Studio
Cumberland Place
London, England   **31 January 1965**

My Little Love Light *(Chuck Berry)*	■ Chess LP(S)-1495, 2CH-60028 ◎ Official 4012-FS
I Got A Booking -1 *(Chuck Berry)*	■ Chess LP(S)-1495 ◎ Official 4012-FS
St. Louis Blues *(William Christopher Handy)*	■ Chess LP(S)-1495, 2CH-60028 ◎ Official 4012-FS

Minus the Berry fan club, the band returned to the studio towards the end of the tour to cut three further tracks for what was to become the *Chuck Berry In London* album. Sadly, by this time things had turned sour: Chuck had started to work to rule, there was a riot at the Cardiff gig, and when asked about his backing group he reportedly answered: "Forgive them, for they know not what they do!" I suspect most of this was media hype, because if it *was* true it certainly doesn't show in these recordings.

The session starts with *My Little Love Light*, a secular version of the gospel song, *This Little Light Of Mine*, which probably harks back to Chuck's youth when he sang with his parents and sisters in the Antioch Baptist Church Choir. In the black gospel world, the song was a massive hit in 1952 for Clara Ward & Her Famous Ward Singers and was later lifted lock, stock and cassock by Ray Charles for his 1955 recording, *This Little Girl Of Mine*. The main riff of Berry's song is based on Brother Ray's *What'd I Say*, which no doubt was itself lifted from some sacred song, although blues pianist Champion Jack Dupree always claimed it as his own.

Chuck must have been looking forward to getting back in the USA when he cut *I Got A Booking* — which turns out not to be a contract to play a gig, but an airline ticket reservation: "I got a booking with the airlines, packed up and prone to go/ I'm gonna leave here by plane, darling, because railway is much too slow." Sound familiar? It will to blues fans who will immediately recognise it as the blues standard, *Key To The Highway*, which articulates the desires of the black man to move on to find better things down that big road. His key was his own two feet; Berry upgrades to jet plane.

Key To The Highway was first recorded by Charlie Segar in February 1940, followed in quick succession by Jazz Gillum in May 1940 and Big Bill

Broonzy in May the following year. Its authorship is commonly attributed to Broonzy, but in truth the song is probably as old as the highway itself. Chuck has cited Big Bill as an influence, but it is more likely Little Walter's 1958 R&B hit with Muddy Waters and Otis Spann in the band that was the precursor of *I Got A Booking*: both songs are set to a plodding beat, unlike the earlier recordings. However, Hogman's thin, reedy harp cannot compare to the plump tones achieved by Walter, even though he was already past his 'use by' date at the time he cut his version.

There have been two covers of *I Got A Booking*, one of which deserves mention not so much for the featured artist, Tim Williams, as for his guitarist, Pee Wee Crayton, who with his T-Bone-influenced style may well have influenced Chuck in his formative years.

From one song that may be as old as the hills to another that definitely is. *St. Louis Blues* was published in 1914 by the self-styled 'Father of the Blues', W.C. Handy. However, it wasn't until Bessie Smith, 'the Empress of the Blues', recorded her ethereal 1925 version — with piercing cornet from Louis Armstrong and churchy reed organ by Fred Longshaw — that the song became established. Since then, of course, it has become a blues standard recorded by dozens of artists as diverse as Jimmy Smith and Billy 'Wakey Wakey' Cotton. Many of Chuck's influences and idols cut it too, including Basie, Goodman, Nat Cole, Joe Turner and Les Paul. So, it was perfectly natural for Berry to tackle the tune — doubly so in that the city mentioned in the title is also his birthplace.

Chuck's cut of *St. Louis Blues* is a belter: if you didn't know, you'd swear it came out of South Michigan Avenue and not Cumberland Place. Following a stuttering guitar intro, the band hit a *Down The Road Apiece* boogie groove propelled by some hard-driven drumming and rolling piano of which Spann, Johnson or Leake would have been proud. Chuck sings it with considerable commitment and takes a lengthy imaginative solo. He must have been pretty pleased to be heading back home with this one tucked underneath his arm.

SESSION 36
CHUCK BERRY
Chuck Berry, vocal/guitar; Bob Scrivens, piano; Jeff Krivet, guitar; Louis Cennamo, bass; Brian David 'Chick' Kattenhorn, drums

Top Gear (BBC Light Programme)
Aolean Hall Studio
Bond Street   *Recorded:* **1 February 1965**
London, England   *Broadcast:* **6 February 1965**

Nadine	◎ Official 4012-FS
(Chuck Berry)	
Promised Land	◎ Official 4012-FS
(Chuck Berry)	
No Particular Place To Go	◎ Official 4012-FS
(Chuck Berry)	

The tracks listed above have recently surfaced on an Official CD — which seems to be anything but — called *Chuck Berry In London*. It is a mixed bag of tracks from the sixties (plus *London Berry Blues* from 1972) emanating from two 1965 UK sessions with the Five Dimensions, the Kingsize Taylor & The Dominoes 1964 *Saturday Club* session, some sides cut in Chicago, and songs that have an English title such as *Liverpool Drive* and *Big Ben Blues*.

These three tracks in fact appear *twice* on the CD, erroneously listed as *'recorded in 1964'* and again as *'Saturday Club 1964'*. Despite these claims,

they almost certainly emanate from a BBC radio recording for the Saturday afternoon *Top Gear* programme which was broadcast at 4 pm on 6th February 1965. The likely recording date is the previous Monday, just before Chuck flew home (the last show of the tour was at the Edmonton Regal on Sunday). Berry's backing band on the tour were the Five Dimensions, so it is safe to assume that they appear here too. Also on the hour-long programme (which, like *Saturday Club*, was introduced by Brian Matthew and produced by Bernie Andrews) were the Rockin' Berries, who were anything but rockin', but who had nevertheless chosen their name in deference to you-know-who.

The artwork for the CD uses the cover of the mid-Sixties Dutch release of *Chuck Berry In London* — a great photograph of Berry reading his fan mail. As befits most bootlegs, the tracks come complete with poorly-recorded, muffled sound, probably taped on a reel-to-reel straight from the wireless on a cold and wintry Saturday afternoon by some avid Chuck Berry fan. Who is that man? Stand up and be counted! Whoever it was should be thanked because, despite the iffy sound quality and a very tinny-sounding piano, the songs drive along with Chuck in good voice and playing strong guitar.

Nadine is sung with great expression. It follows the single version closely in its structure and lyrics but is, of course, minus the sax of the Chess release. As with the previous British live version, Chuck is still paying for the "loaded taxi" in Sterling.

"Olé! I was the poor boy. I'd like to do our latest recording, **Promised Land**," is how Chuck introduces his famous paean to travel. This too follows the well-travelled route of the original with the only concession to his location being the substitution of "coach" for the 'hound that breaks down in Alabam.

No Particular Place To Go is also pretty decent, except instead of the glorious stretched-out instrumental exit of the original, this version is brought to a juddering halt. Despite the poor hi-fi and the dubious provenance, it is good to have these sides available.

SESSION 37
CHUCK BERRY
Chuck Berry, vocal/guitar, overdubbed guitar -1; Johnnie Johnson, piano; Chuck Bernard, bass; Jaspar Thomas, drums

Ter-Mar Recording Studio
2120 South Michigan Avenue
Chicago, Illinois   1 September 1965

14152	**Run Joe** *(Joe Willoughby, Walter Merrick,* *Louis Jordan)*	■ Chess LP(S)-1498, CRL-4506
14153	**It's My Own Business** *(Chuck Berry)*	■ Chess LP(S)-1498, CRL-4506, CH6-80001
14154	**One For My Baby** **(And One More For The Road)** *(Harold Arlen, Johnny Mercer)*	■ Chess LP(S)-1498, CRL-4506
14155	**Every Day We Rock And Roll** *(Chuck Berry)*	■ Chess LP(S)-1498, CRL-4506
14156	**My Mustang Ford** -1 *(Chuck Berry)*	■ Chess LP(S)-1498, CRL-4506
	My Mustang Ford *[stereo remix]* -1 *(Chuck Berry)*	■ Chess CH-9190

Over three consecutive days in September 1965, Chuck was back in the studio at 2120 South Michigan Avenue cutting tracks that were to sit in the can for eight months before finally appearing on his next album, *Fresh Berry's.* Old faithful Johnnie Johnson was back on the eighty-eights with a brand new rhythm section consisting of Chuck Bernard on bass and Jaspar Thomas on drums. Thomas, of course, was not new to Chuck Berry's music, having played off and on in his road band since 1956 after Ebby Hardy quit, and possibly having played on several earlier Berry sessions. He had previously been a jazz drummer with the Eddie Johnson big band, so was well suited to Berry's swinging, boogie approach to rock and roll.

Bernard may be the vocalist who cut a single with Ike Turner's band in St. Louis in 1958 as Chuck Bernard & His Blue Notes (*Calling Your Name* b/w *Everytime I Think Of You* on Joyce 305 — the latter song was recut by him later on the Bobbin label). Although he was not known to play bass during his time in St. Louis, he relocated to Chicago in the mid-sixties and may have subsequently taken up the instrument. Alternatively, it could be that Chuck asked Johnnie to bring his current band with him up to Chicago, and that this is a completely different Chuck Bernard.

No matter, for after this trio of dates they disappear from Chuck's discography — which is a pity because the unit turned out to be pretty tight, with some inventive electric bass and effective drums being provided by the newcomers.

With his recording of **Run Joe**, Berry nails his colours to the mast. After years of dipping into Louis Jordan's bag of tricks for his own compositions, he finally comes clean and cuts a Jordan original. It cannot be emphasised too much how Jordan influenced Berry. His music, his wit, his stage presence, his guitar style, all owe a debt to Jordan and his band, and if you had to pick just one tune as an example, the Caribbean-tinged *Run Joe* isn't a bad one to start with.

The song was a No. 1 Juke Box R&B hit for Jordan in June 1948. He recorded it at the same April 1947 session that also produced the enduring *Early In The Morning*. For both songs, his band was augmented by the 'Calypso Boys' on maracas and claves. *Run Joe* was written by two West Indians, Joe Willoughby *(words)* and Dr. Walter Merrick *(music)* — who also happened to be Jordan's personal physician.

In his version, Chuck cuts out the jive talk prologue of the original and gets straight into the narrative of the song which is about illicit fortune telling "behind the door" and the subsequent bust by the 'man', or as Chuck puts it, "the fuzz". Compared to Jordan, he rushes through the story, sticking closely to the original lyrics, but cutting down on the choruses. After all, who in their right mind would want to mess with lines such as: "When the judge ask how I plea/ Not guilty sir, most decidedly/ You can see, judge, at a glance/ I'm a victim of circumstance"? The words must have struck a strong personal chord with Berry, as he later reworked the theme for 1970's *Tulane*.

Set in a framework of throbbing electric bass, tinkling piano and steady, rimshot drumming, Chuck exposes his 'live and let live' philosophy in **It's My Own Business**, a sort-of 'adult' update of *Almost Grown* with an echo of the sentiments expressed by Hank Williams in his *Mind Your Own Business*. In just over two minutes, by using some choice analogies, Mr. B lays it on the line:

"If I go buy a convertible Cadillac coupe and all I've got at home to eat is just onion soup — it's my own business!"

"If I's a dignitary on Capital Hill and up and married a waitress in a hot dog grill — it's my own business!"

Two or three more verses of this calibre and the song would have been a classic. As it stands, it emerges as a rather undeveloped composition: Nutrasweet rather than sugar-sweet.

A phased guitar and drums introduce the Harold Arlen–Johnny Mercer standard, **One For My Baby (And One More For The Road)**. The song was first featured by Fred Astaire in the 1943 movie, *The Sky's The Limit*, but is indelibly linked with Francis Albert Sinatra, a singer whose phrasing could not fail to influence someone of Chuck's musical disposition, particularly as its theme is one of drinking in the wee wee hours (or, as Frank the Voice put it in 1955, *In The Wee Small Hours Of The Morning* — another song with echoes of Berry's own *Wee Wee Hours*).

Chuck's version is okay, but try as he might, his crooning cannot compete with the Sinatras, Coles and Crosbys who inhabit this sophisticated twilight world. On the plus side is the trilling piano from Johnnie Johnson which, together with the bass, features heavily on the track.

Back on familiar ground, **Every Day We Rock And Roll** is just an excuse for a rock and roll blowout. The number consists of a string of banal lyrics sung in short sequence between guitar phrases lifted from Berry's past catalogue — most noticeably the introduction from *Around And Around*. A nothing LP filler track played with consummate skill that might have been better developed as an instrumental.

In 1964, the President of the Ford Motor Company, Lee Iacocca, as part of Ford's commitment to 'total performance', introduced the Mustang to replace their Thunderbird, by then an ageing ten year old model. Not to be left trailing in the exhaust fumes, in **My Mustang Ford** Chuck duly upgrades his wheels to a "1966 cherry red Mustang Ford". His model is, of course, customised with a "three hundred eighty-five horsepower overload" — 10 hp more than the most powerful V8 7030 cc production model. This, however, proves to be too powerful even for Chuck who relates in the song an incident at J.F.K. Airport where he hits the gas and almost drives into Jamaica Bay (possibly an allusion to a recent incident at San Francisco Airport where Berry, with Marshall Chess at the wheel, was involved in a car wreck). Fear not though, our man has the answer: a windbreaker parachute! Not your usual optional extra.

This flight of fancy is sung to a typical Berry musical backdrop. My only regret is that a compressed guitar sound was used in place of the bell-ringing tones of earlier cuts. The stereo version differs from the mono original by separating and emphasising the overdubbed lead guitar from the rhythm guitar part. At the end of this track, Chuck adds: "I can't get it all in one [breath], let's call it a day," and thus endeth the thirty-seventh session.

SESSION 38
CHUCK BERRY
Chuck Berry, vocal/guitar; Johnnie Johnson, piano; Chuck Bernard, bass; Jaspar Thomas, drums

Ter-Mar Recording Studio
2120 South Michigan Avenue
Chicago, Illinois   **2 September 1965**

14157	**Merrily We Rock And Roll** (Chuck Berry)	■ Chess LP(S)-1498, CRL-4506
14158	**Vaya Con Dios** (Larry Russell, Inez James, Buddy Pepper)	■ Chess LP(S)-1498, CRL-4506
14159	**Wee Hour Blues** (Chuck Berry)	■ Chess LP(S)-1498, CRL-4506 ◎ Ace CDCH-397
	Loving You In Vain (Robert Johnson/ Sonny Boy Williamson?)	unissued

After a good night's sleep, the band reassemble in the studio and the first song up, **Merrily We Rock And Roll**, is basically *Every Day We Rock And Roll* with different — but equally banal — lyrics: "Mary had a wee little lamb/ He had music in his soul/ And every record that Mary played/ That lamb would ..." (you fill in the blank). The guys chip in with off-mike 'ughs' at appropriate points and Chuck exhorts "Sing, children!" as though the song might be a rabble-rouser tryout for his concert set.

The Mexican-styled love song **Vaya Con Dios** *[Go With God]* was

Backstage at the Birmingham Hippodrome, 17 January 1965.

written in 1953 by Larry Russell, Inez James and Buddy Pepper, but I suspect that the melody may be of a much older folk-song vintage. Jazz singer Anita O'Day first introduced it to the listening public and Chuck may have heard her sing it at the 1958 *Newport Jazz Festival* when they appeared on the same bill (if you've seen the film, she's the one with the hat). It's more likely, however, that he heard Les Paul & Mary Ford's 1953 waxing and picked it up from this source.

Berry's version is a nice lilting rendition in which he concentrates on the singing and leaves Johnnie Johnson to tinkle the piano keys to his heart's content.

Johnson also plays a major part in the last issued song of the day, **Wee Hour Blues**, and even gets to take a solo — a pretty rare event on a Chuck Berry recording. A minor key 'long-lost-lover' blues, the song is a close relation of *Wee Wee Hours* with similar lines and musical composition. This is the type of slow blues that Chuck and Johnnie could churn out *ad infinitum* — that is, in their sleep without disturbing the bed-springs. I'll bet this was played in the early hours in the early days at the Cosmo Club in St. Louis. Nice, but not exactly taxing.

The unissued title, **Loving You In Vain**, is intriguing — one wonders if it is related to the famous Robert Johnson/Sonny Boy Williamson II song of similar name.

SESSION 39
CHUCK BERRY

Chuck Berry, vocal/guitar, overdubbed guitar -1; Johnnie Johnson, piano; Chuck Bernard, bass; Jaspar Thomas, drums; Mike Bloomfield, overdubbed guitar -2; Paul Butterfield, overdubbed harmonica -3

Ter-Mar Recording Studio
2120 South Michigan Avenue
Chicago, Illinois   **3 September 1965**

14160	**It Wasn't Me** -2-3 *(Chuck Berry)*	⦿ Chess 1943**a** ■ Chess LP(S)-1498, CRL-4506, CH6-80001
	It Wasn't Me *[stereo remix]* *(Chuck Berry)*	■ Chess CH2-92521
14161	**Ain't That Just Like A Woman** -1 *(Fleecie Moore)*	■ Chess LP(S)-1498, CRL-4506
	Ain't That Just Like A Woman -1 *(Fleecie Moore) [stereo remix]*	■ Chess CH-9190 ◎ Ace CDCH-397
14162	**Right Off Rampart Street** *(Chuck Berry)*	■ Chess LP(S)-1498, CRL-4506
14163	**Welcome Back Pretty Baby** *(Chuck Berry)*	⦿ Chess 1943**b** ■ Chess LP(S)-1498
14225	**Sad Day, Long Night** *[instrumental]* -3 *(Chuck Berry)*	■ Chess CRL-4506, CH6-80001
	Forgive Me *(Chuck Berry?)*	unissued

Back on the third and final day of recording, the creative juices really started to flow. The best song of the whole three days was *It Wasn't Me*, in which Chuck innocently denies involvement in all manner of situations to authority figures: bosses, women, sergeants, police officers, state troopers and army captains all get a palms-up "It wasn't me" shrug. As well as these well-versed hassles, there is an oblique reference to the inter-racial tensions in the South: "I met a German girl in England who was goin' to school in France/ Say we danced in Mississippi at an Alpha-Kappa dance ... Wasn't me, officer!"

It Wasn't Me comes in two flavours, 'original' and 'new and improved'. The original version, issued in October 1965 as the 'A' side of Chess 1943, has Mike Bloomfield's guitar and Paul Butterfield's harp overdubbed. These two guys were hot stuff in '65, doyens of the white blues movement in the States. In 1965, together with Elvin Bishop, Jerome Arnold and Sam Lay (the last two late of Howlin' Wolf's band), they became the Paul Butterfield Blues Band. Here, they provide an exciting overlay to Berry's strong rhythm base, Bloomfield taking the lead guitar part throughout while Butterfield's harp wails atop of the mess. The question remains: was it always the intention to overdub their contributions, or had Chuck originally planned to overdub his own lead guitar as he had done on previous occasions?

The two Fields went on to back Bob Dylan when he converted to electricity, and later also played on Muddy Waters's *Fathers And Sons* album

— probably the best collaboration ever of older bluesmen with their younger, paler counterparts.

The 'stereo mix', which only surfaced in 1986, comes minus the overdubs and in consequence the vocal is louder and clearer, but the track lacks the drive of the original cut.

For such a good song, it is a little strange that only three other artists have recorded it. Of these, George Thorogood liked it sufficiently to cut it twice!

Next, Berry tackles one of his old maestro's best songs, **Ain't That Just Like A Woman**. This classic was a big hit for Louis Jordan in 1946 and contains some wonderfully witty lyrics all about Biblical frails (Lot's wife gets salty and Samson gets clipped by beautiful Delilah). Ironically, although Jordan wrote the song in collaboration with Claude Demetrius, he published it under the maiden name of his third wife, Fleecie Moore. In return, Fleecie not only fleeced him of the royalties for this song and the even more lucrative *Caldonia*, but also cut him every which way but loose.

Ain't That Just Like A Woman also contains a guitar introduction from Carl Hogan that will be instantly recognisable to Berry fans: Chuck borrowed it note-for-note to introduce an unsuspecting public to *Johnny B. Goode*.

Surprisingly, he doesn't use this intro in his version of the Jordan song, but starts with one similar to *Roll Over Beethoven*. Indeed, his interpretation turns out to be only a vague approximation of the original, with only the first verse containing anything resembling Jordan's lines. (The best cover of this classic has got to be B.B. King's storming, near-instrumental arrangement with its powerful guitar and the band's robust chant of: "Ain't that just like a woman!")

The stereo version adds very little: it separates the piano and guitar tracks, and the boogie at the end of the track continues for a few extra bars rather than being faded.

Down in Louisiana, way behind the sun, in the city of New Orleans, Rampart Street forms the east boundary of the Vieux Carre, the old French quarter. Just off this thoroughfare (Congo Square maybe), there's an old boy playing a funky electric guitar while a go-go dancer shakes to a mojo beat. This is the scene set in **Right Off Rampart Street**, a moody, funky blues with plenty of steamy guitar and rock-steady drumming to evoke the humid atmosphere of southern Louisiana. It was probably no accident that Berry chose the location of Cosimo Matassa's legendary J&S Studio — the home of New Orleans funk — as the setting for this atmospheric song.

After this brief excursion south, for his next cut Chuck heads out west. **Welcome Back Pretty Baby** is a mid-tempo blues very reminiscent of those cut a decade earlier by T-Bone Walker, a major influence on a whole legion of blues guitarists mainly based in Texas and out on the West Coast and, of course, a long-time influence on Chuck Berry. Compare Walker's *Bobby Sox Baby* with Berry's *Sweet Little Sixteen*; note the similarity between 'Bone's big blond Gibson electric guitar and his flamboyant stage style and Berry's; contrast the single-string runs of the two guitarists.

In this song, Chuck welcomes his baby back from her vacation: "It's really boss to hold your hand, to talk and dance with you again," he explains between some very sharp extended T-Bone-type runs, supported by metronomic hi-hat tapping and tinkling piano.

Sad Day, Long Night is an alternative version of *Welcome Back Pretty Baby* with the vocal track replaced by some very muscular Little Walterish harp, courtesy of Paul Butterfield. For many years this cut was only available as a substitute for *Welcome Back Pretty Baby* on the British pressing of the *Fresh Berry's* album.

Forgive Me is an unheard track, presumably a Berry composition.

SESSION 40

CHUCK BERRY

Chuck Berry, vocal/guitar, overdubbed guitar; Johnnie Johnson, piano/organ -1; Chuck Bernard, bass; Jaspar Thomas, drums; unknown overdubbed saxes -2

Ter-Mar Recording Studio
2120 South Michigan Avenue
Chicago, Illinois   **13 April 1966**

14667	**Ramona, Say Yes** -1-2 *(Chuck Berry)*	○ Chess 1963**b** ■ Checkmate LP-1955
	Ramona, Say Yes *[alt. mix]* -1 *(Chuck Berry)*	■ Chess CH6-80001
14668	**Viva** (Viva) **Rock & Roll** *(Chuck Berry)*	■ Chess CH-50008, 2CH-60028, CH6-80001
14669	**His Daughter Caroline** *[fast version]* *(Chuck Berry)*	unissued
14670	**Lonely School Days** *[fast version]* -1 *(Chuck Berry)*	○ Chess 1963**a** ■ Chess CH-50008

This session was to be Chuck Berry's last at Chess for some three-and-a-half years and provides an indication of things to come, with a subtle change in production values and Johnnie Johnson featured for the first time on organ. Chuck's overdubbed guitar has more echo than usual (which separates it more distinctly from the base track) and the single issue of 14667 features overdubbed saxes.

Two of the four songs recorded were revised uptempo versions of earlier Berry songs (both cut, incidentally, at the same session in 1964). Whether this indicates a lack of new material or a desire to improve on the earlier recordings is a matter for conjecture. This session, at least, produced some pretty reasonable tracks with Chuck in good vocal form throughout.

Ramona, Say Yes isn't a plea for some nefarious pleasure, but an exhortation for us all to say "yes" to Ramona, her dress and her monkey (sung without the slightest innuendo). Ramona's dress is something else, on a par with Sugar Pie's soulful *haute couture* and the garment that made Big Joe shake, rattle and roll: "Ramona, Ramona, where you get that dress?/ The neckline's down South and the hemline's way out West!"

Throughout the number, the organ pipes along in the background while Berry's echo-laden guitar punctuates each line of the song. The alternative mix is exactly the same take except that the overdubbed saxophones riffing quietly

141

in the mix of the single are omitted. The original cut with the saxes has only ever been issued as a single and on the Checkmate bootleg LP. All the Charly releases and others use the 'alternative' version, which first appeared on the 1988 *Chess Box* set.

Viva Rock & Roll (this is the correct title as written on the original LP, not *Viva, Viva Rock & Roll* which is what Chuck sings and therefore theoretically more correct — but what's a 'Viva' between friends anyway?) has a more traditional Berry sound due to Johnnie Johnson switching back to piano. The song sounds like a rabble-rousing yell that might have virtually written itself — another *Every Day / Merrily We Rock And Roll*, albeit with rather more substance. In fact, it's a tough little rocker with Berry in good voice singing the praises of 'that teenage music of the fifties' ("Go on and shake it — I can take it!") and hitting some unusual guitar licks in the process. He even refers to a childhood memory reflecting on a time when he would compete with his sister Lucy to play the family piano: "My Mother had my sister learning Bach and Strauss/ For years it was the only music in our house/ But I got my guitar and I rearranged Bach/ And came up with some good old folk and country rock."

RAMONA, SAY YES
(Chuck Berry Music, Inc.)

Isalee Music
Publishing
BMI (14667)
Time 2:40

CHESS

CHUCK BERRY
1963

MANUFACTURED BY CHESS PRODUCING CORP., CHICAGO, ILLINOIS, U.S.A.

The faster revised version of **Lonely School Days** drops the plaintive feel of the earlier attempt and adopts an infectious Jimmy Reed *Big Boss Man*-type beat. Lyrically, it is similar to the former, except for an amended first verse and a repeat of the chorus at the end of the song.

This cut appeared as the 'A' side of Chess single 1963 with *Ramona, Say Yes* on the flip. The record was subsequently reissued later that year with *Ramona* promoted to the 'A' side and *Havana Moon* replacing *Lonely School Days* on the dark side of the disc. The remade *Lonely School Days* then disappeared for four years to rise again as a filler track along with *Viva Rock & Roll* on the 1971 *San Francisco Dues* album.

The sad aura that surrounds the issued version of **His Daughter Caroline** is absent from the unissued remake here, which is underpinned by a bouncy, mid-paced beat and whining guitar. The lyrics are virtually identical, except at the very end we discover that Chuck himself is the suitor of the bride as he sings: "Oh Caroline, now she's mine." This is a pretty good version of the song and would certainly merit release.

THE PYRITES PERIOD (1966-69)

*Chuck Berry's three-year tenure at Mercury Records
saw him cutting 'fool's gold' covers of his Chess classics
alongside new material in a funky modern style.*

SESSION 41
CHUCK BERRY

Chuck Berry, vocal/guitar; Johnnie Johnson, piano/organ -1; Carey Enlow, tenor sax -2; Quincy Macon, guitar; Forrest Frierson, bass; Ebby Hardy, drums; unknown tambourine -3

Technisonic Studio
1201 South Brentwood Avenue
Clayton, Missouri   **20 September 1966**

YWI-39066	**Campus Cookie** *[instrumental]* -1-2 *(Chuck Berry)*	◎ Mercury 836 073-2
YWI-39067	**Mum's The Word** -2 *(Chuck Berry)*	■ Mercury SR-61176 ◎ Mercury 836 073-2
YWI-39068	**My Tambourine** -2 -3 *(Chuck Berry)*	■ Mercury SR-61176, SRM2-6501 ◎ Mercury 836 073-2
YWI-39069	**Laugh And Cry** *(Chuck Berry)*	● Mercury 72643**b** ◎ Mercury 836 073-2

Eleven years and one month after he first recorded for Chess, Chuck Berry's so-called 'golden decade' came to a close. On 17th June 1966, he signed a three year contract with the Chicago-based Mercury Records for a sum reported to be as high as $150,000, but by Chuck's accounting was actually nearer $60,000. Whatever the figure, it seems that Mercury wanted Berry badly because they fielded their vice-president, Quincy Jones, to conduct the negotiations. For Chuck's part, he must have been pretty comfortable with the move to the label, whose roster since their inception in 1945 had included many of the artists he admired so much: Louis Jordan, Buddy and Ella Johnson, Illinois Jacquet and Jay McShann all cut for this 'minor major' company (which, incidentally, was founded by Louis Jordan's long-time manager, Berle Adams).

In many ways, Berry's stint at Mercury mirrors that of his hero. Jordan's first task was to recut his Decca hits in an upbeat rock and roll style. Chuck was required to do the very same thing, and it has to be said that neither artist improved on the originals. It was obviously part of the deal that Berry recut his hits for Mercury so that they could trade on his past glories. They have certainly recycled them *ad infinitum* to a sometimes unsuspecting public who must wonder what the fuss is about if they haven't heard the Chess cuts. Phil Chess was philosophical about the move: "He'll be back in three years" was his only comment — and he was.

A pair of two-day studio dates during September and October 1966 inaugurated Chuck's tenure at Mercury. The sessions took place at the conveniently-located Technisonic Studio in Clayton, a suburb to the west of St. Louis, about twenty-five miles from Wentzville. Johnnie Johnson and Ebby Hardy from the old days were joined by newcomers Quincy Macon, Forrest Frierson and Carey Enlow, who may have been regulars in Johnnie's St. Louis band at the time or possibly house musicians connected to the studio, because after these sessions at Clayton they disappear from Berry's discography.

Of Chuck's Mercury recordings, Johnson said in his biography: "I've never heard what Chuck did at Mercury, but from what I've been told, they ain't too good". This is a strange statement to make, as he is known to have played on several Mercury sessions. Maybe he didn't know they were Mercury sessions or maybe the drink made him forget. Or perhaps he simply didn't want to be associated with the cuts.

Campus Cookie, possibly inspired by one of the young ladies from the nearby university, starts the session off and sounds like the usual warm-up common to Berry's method of working. It's a jaunty instrumental with pumping saxophone and what sounds like a rattling tambourine placed on the drum kit prominent in the mix. Chuck's echo-laden guitar sounds as if he's playing it from the bottom of a well and Johnnie contents himself by fingering his organ. *Campus Cookie* remained unissued until its appearance in 1989 on the expanded CD release of *From St. Louie To Frisco*. This was one of five CDs which came out at this time in the USA, Germany and France containing previously unissued tracks which were not even identified as such on the discs.

Mum's The Word finds Chuck at the epicentre of a potential family ruckus if Aunt Sue finds out what Uncle Joe has been up to and, conversely, if Uncle Joe finds out what Aunt Sue's been up to while he was "doin' what he shouldn't have been doin'." This dilemma, played out to a stuttering stop-start bass line in ninety-two seconds, isn't satisfactorily resolved but ends surreally with the line: "He said: 'I heard some talk/ You ain't got no squawk/ I've been checking stone for stone!"

My Tambourine is far more interesting historically than musically because it is the first recorded version of the song that would develop into *My Ding-A-Ling*, Chuck Berry's biggest-ever international hit, six years later. It was originally recorded by Dave Bartholomew, the New Orleanian bandleader, ace trumpeter and musical maestro to Fats Domino. Bartholemew apparently picked up the song for a song from a guy by the name of Hayes, cleaned up the words somewhat and recorded it in January 1952 as *My Ding-A-Ling* — complete with blue lyrics, a blue beat (before the term was invented) and a corny '*Pop Goes The Weasel*' lick.

Released on the King label, the record did zilch, but Bartholemew had faith in the dirty ditty and returned to the studio in November of the same year to recut it for Imperial as *Little Girl Sing Ding-A-Ling*. (Incidentally, the other side of the platter, *Who Drank My Beer While I Was In The Rear*, is far wittier and much more fun.) Two years later his 'ding' popped up for a third time, this time in a faster version called *Toy Bell* by the Bees, a vocal group which included Billy Bland, later of *Let The Little Girl Dance* fame.

In Chuck's first stab at the number, he redrafts the lyrics and cleans them up a little: his 'ding-a-ling' becomes his 'tambourine'. The best — and most risqué — verse goes: "Once I remember in grammar school/ I was talking to a girl in the vestibule/ She dug my music and my routine/ I showed her how to shake my tambourine."

The verses are punctuated by fruity saxophone and an insistent tambourine probably jangled by Johnnie Johnson, whose piano is noticeably absent from the cut.

Laugh And Cry, which was released as the 'B' side of Chuck's first Mercury single, is by far the best song to emanate from the session. It is a slow blues cast from the same mould as *Wee Wee Hours*, starting with a traditional 'floating' lyric most likely picked up from Big Joe Turner's *Wee Baby*

Blues. "It was early one morning and I was on my way to school" in Chuck's version becomes "It was late one Friday evening and I was on my way from school". And, instead of breaking the teacher's rule, it's his mother's rule that gets broken. The highlight of the track is Johnnie Johnson's atmospheric piano playing to which Berry's guitar takes a subservient role.

SESSION 42
CHUCK BERRY

Chuck Berry, vocal/guitar; Johnnie Johnson electric piano/organ -1; Carey Enlow, tenor saxophone -2; Quincy Macon, guitar; Forrest Frierson, bass; Ebby Hardy, drums; unknown tambourine

Technisonic Studio
1201 South Brentwood Avenue
Clayton, Missouri   **21 September 1966**

YWI-38879	**Maybelline** -1 *(Chuck Berry)*	■ Mercury MG-21103/SR-61103, Pickwick SPC-3327, Mercury 6463 044 ◎ Mercury 826 256-2
YWI-38880	**unknown title**	unissued
YWI-38881	**School Days** *(Chuck Berry)*	■ Mercury MG-21103/SR-61103, Pickwick SPC-3327 ◎ Mercury 826 256-2
YWI-38882	**Sweet Little Sixteen** *(Chuck Berry)*	■ Mercury MG-21103/SR-61103, Pickwick SPC-3327, Mercury 6463 044 ◎ Mercury 826 256-2
YWI-38883	**Johnny B. Goode** -2 *(Chuck Berry)*	■ Mercury MG-21103/SR-61103, Pickwick SPC-3327, Mercury 6463 044 ◎ Mercury 826 256-2
YWI-38884	**Memphis** *(Chuck Berry)*	■ Mercury MG-21103/SR-61103, Pickwick SPC-3327 ◎ Mercury 826 256-2
YWI-38885	**Roll Over Beethoven** *(Chuck Berry)*	■ Mercury MG-21103/SR-61103, Pickwick SPC-3327, Mercury 6463 044 ◎ Mercury 826 256-2
YWI-38886	**Rock'n'Roll Music** -2 *(Chuck Berry)*	■ Mercury MG-21103/SR-61103, Pickwick SPC-3327, Mercury 6463 044 ◎ Mercury 826 256-2

Note: The matrix numbers of these recordings are lower than those of the previous session but are placed here on the basis of information gleaned from Chuck Berry's autobiography.

Second day in the studio and the band get to the main purpose of the gathering: to cut Mercury masters of Berry's back catalogue. However, the meat of the meet turns out to be Spam!

It's hard to place what goes wrong. Chuck is in good voice and guitar, but somehow the Chess sparkle is missing. It's as if the economic necessity of the session subverts the artistic endeavours. The production is undoubtedly part of the problem and, as Chuck was the producer, we know who to blame. The bass is too prominent, the piano too far back, and the persistent tambourine-banger should have been locked in the broom cupboard.

Maybelline (note the change in spelling) has Johnson on organ, which again is a complete miscalculation. *Memphis* is taken far too fast and lacks all the intimate charm of the Chess version. The best cut is *Roll Over Beethoven*, with Chuck sounding like he means it, but even this has an inappropriate choppy rhythm guitar.

I feel sorry for the casual record buyer who, maybe wanting one representative Berry album in their collection, purchased *Chuck Berry's Golden Hits* on Mercury which contains this session. But then again, what would you think of these 'music by numbers' versions if you had never heard the Chess masters?

SESSION 43
CHUCK BERRY

Chuck Berry, vocal/guitar; Johnnie Johnson, electric piano; Forrest Frierson, bass; Eugene Washington, drums

Technisonic Studio
1201 South Brentwood Avenue
Clayton, Missouri   **26 October 1966**

YWI-39169	**Oh Captain** *(Chuck Berry)*	■ Mercury SR-61176 ◎ Mercury 836 073-2
YWI-39167	**Around And Around** *(Chuck Berry)*	◎ Mercury 826 256-2
YWI-39174	**Back In The USA** *(Chuck Berry)*	■ Mercury MG-21103/SR-61103, Pickwick SPC-3327, Mercury 6463 044 ◎ Mercury 826 256-2
YWI-39173	**Thirty Days** *(Chuck Berry)*	■ Mercury MG-21103/SR-61103 ◎ Mercury 826 256-2
YWI-38900	**Club Nitty Gritty** *(Chuck Berry)*	● Mercury 72643**a** ■ Mercury MG-21103/SR-61103 ◎ Mercury 826 256-2
YWI-39176	**Misery** *(Chuck Berry)*	■ Mercury SR-61176, SRM2-6501 ◎ Mercury 836 073-2

The three retreads on this session are marginally better than the product of the previous one. This is because the band has been stripped to the bone and we have lost the rhythm guitar and the dreaded tambourine. New drummer Eugene Washington drives the band on, particularly on *Back In The USA*, which is the best of the recuts, with the band whoop-whooping in the background as Chuck scats along, clearly enjoying himself. The big mistake is placing Johnnie at the electric piano rather than the real thing: instead of rattling the ivories, he merely patters the plastic. Moreover, the scrappy endings of *Thirty Days* and *Back In The USA* smack of low or no rehearsal.

Club Nitty Gritty is the best of the three new songs cut at the session, and with proper piano it could have equalled many of those gracing the Chess label. This tale of a funky backwoods juke joint "way down in Tennessee close to Mississippi" has a heavy shuffle beat that is reminiscent of Berry's later Chess sides. What makes it stand out is his vocal delivery. Soul songster Dan Penn said Chuck Berry "never went to church", meaning that he didn't have soul in his voice. Generally I'd agree, but this is the exception that proves the rule. Here, Chuck lets out a choked scream that Brother Ray would surely recognise.

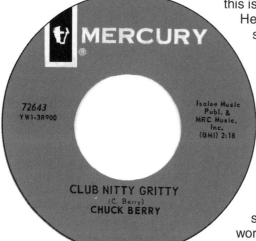

Mercury's files state that Club Nitty Gritty was recorded at Wentzville on 4th November, while the liner notes to the Mercury *Golden Hits* album say that he developed the song at Berry Park but recorded the final version in one take at Technisonic. The dates here are from Berry's own files, as stated in his autobiography. The worthwhile *Club Nitty Gritty* was released as a single in January 1967 but saw no chart action.

Misery is a hot little rocker which hits off with the *Roll Over Beethoven* opening but doesn't really go anywhere. It is based loosely on *Don't You Lie To Me* and is totally derivative of past glories. The song is not fully realized and suffers from lack of rehearsal: Johnnie appears to miss his cue for the piano break.

Oh Captain has got to be in the running for Chuck Berry's worst-ever record. It's an interesting song about a football quarterback giving advice to his team captain, set to a stumbling beat, which is completely blown by the production. It begins reasonably enough, from the left speaker, but is then inexplicably repeated in the right speaker after a six second delay, making the lyrics virtually unintelligible. It's like listening to a very badly tuned radio. One for schizoid sports fans only.

Chuck himself was none too pleased with the track. In an interview with Charlie Gillett in 1974 he said: "I did a song about football called *Hey Captain [sic]*, which was about three plays. When Mercury got the tape, they took the first verse out and overlapped it with the third one. So, when the song came out, it started with the second play and then moved on to one that was a mixture of the third and the first. My friends heard it, they said: 'Hey, Chuck?'."

This version of **Around And Around** is one of the eleven previously unreleased tracks which surfaced when Mercury reissued Berry's catalogue on CD. Was it worth the wait? Well, hardly, but as the Chess cut of this song was an unpolished home recording, I guess this version doesn't sound *too* bad in comparison, with some spirited piano and an unusual rhythm guitar riff.

SESSION 44
CHUCK BERRY

Chuck Berry, vocal/guitar; Johnnie Johnson, electric piano; Forrest Frierson, bass; Eugene Washington, drums

Technisonic Studio
1201 South Brentwood Avenue
Clayton, Missouri   **27 October 1966**

YWI-39168	**Carol** *(Chuck Berry)*	■ Mercury MG-21103/SR-61103, 6463 044 ◎ Mercury 826 256-2
YWI-39170	**Brown Eyed Handsome Man** *(Chuck Berry)*	◎ Mercury 826 256-2
YWI-39171	**Let It Rock** *(E. Anderson)*	■ Mercury 6463 044 ◎ Mercury 826 256-2
YWI-39172	**Reelin' And Rockin'** *(Chuck Berry)*	■ Pickwick SPC-3327, Mercury 6463 044 ◎ Mercury 826 256-2
YWI-39175	**Almost Grown** *(Chuck Berry)*	◎ Mercury 836 073-2

The fourth session at Clayton consists entirely of re-recordings of earlier Berry hits and is probably the most consistent of the four.

Mercury's *Carol* is no match for Chess's. However, the song hits off at a terrible pace with bags of energy. Chuck entices the lady of his dreams with a bucket-seated cruiser to a joint where "Everybody's shaking up and feeling gay/ And every time you check it out, you find them rocking away". As he rolls out the lyrics, Johnnie's electric piano takes the lead over his guitar.

Brown Eyed Handsome Man is taken at a more relaxed pace — rollin' rather than rockin'. Musically, it's closer to Berry's 1961 Chess version, but the words are identical to his original 1956 cut.

Let It Rock and *Reelin' And Rockin'* are also word-perfect to the originals without a hint of the risqué lyrics that Chuck was by now employing for live performances of the latter (contrast this with the Fillmore version recorded twelve months after this session). Despite some powerful drumming and rolling piano, both cuts lack the sharp-edged Berry guitar of old.

Almost Grown hasn't matured from the Chess days either, although some of the words have changed: "I'm cruising right along in class/ [The] way I'm rolling, I'm bound to pass" and "Gonna buy myself a little car/ Steady work on my guitar." The dodgy start and the 'leg out' stop gives the cut the feel of a run-through rather than a finished product. Perhaps that's why it stayed in the can until it was digitised in 1989.

In fact, the only track from this session that was originally released in the USA was *Carol*. *Brown Eyed Handsome Man* finally crept out on the *Golden Hits* CD in 1989. *Let It Rock* and *Reelin' And Rockin'* — also on this CD — had been previously issued, but only on a 1972 US Pickwick budget album and an obscure 1980 West German LP titled *Rock! Rock! Rock'n'Roll* [Mercury 6463 044].

SESSION 45

CHUCK BERRY

Chuck Berry, vocal/guitar; Reggie Young, guitar; Bobby Emmons, piano (omit piano -1), Gene 'Bowlegs' Miller, trumpet; James Mitchell, baritone saxophone; Andrew Love, tenor saxophone; Tommy Cogbill, bass; Jerry 'Satch' Arnold, drums

Royal Recording Studios
1320 South Lauderdale Avenue
Memphis, Tennessee   **21 March 1967**

YWI-39489	**Ramblin' Rose** *(Noel & Joe Sherman)*	■ Mercury MG-21123/SR-61123 ◉ Mercury 836 071-2
YWI-39490	**Check Me Out** *(Chuck Berry)*	■ Mercury MG-21123/SR-61123, SRM2-6501 ◉ Mercury 836 071-2
YWI-39491	**I Do Really Love You** -1 *(Chuck Berry)*	❍ Mercury 72680**b** ■ Mercury MG-21123/SR-61123, SRM2-6501 ◉ Mercury 836 071-2
YWI-39492	**Back To Memphis** *(Chuck Berry)*	❍ Mercury 72680**a** ■ Mercury MG-21123/SR-61123, SRM2-6501 ◉ Mercury 836 071-2

Having completed his obligations to re-cut his back catalogue, Chuck was free to experiment a little and, five months after his Clayton sessions, he turned up in Memphis, Tennessee for three sessions held over three consecutive days. These yielded four tracks per day, eleven of which were subsequently released on the *Chuck Berry In Memphis* album and his second Mercury single.

In 1966, Mercury Records took Jerry Lee Lewis back to Memphis in order to recapture some of his former glories, and it seems altogether logical for them to have given Chuck Berry the same treatment.

Although Mercury files list Sam Phillips's Sun Studios as the recording

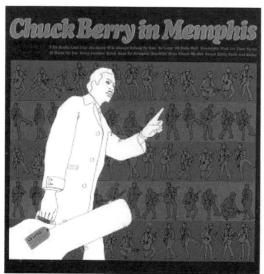

venue, Ray Harris, co-owner of Hi Records and the Royal Recording Studios, has confirmed that the recordings were made at his studios. Indeed, Harris also engineered and mixed the sessions. (This location has also been confirmed by country-rock singer Narvel Felts, who recalls seeing Chuck recording at Royal.)

The band is one hell of a cutting crew — the cream of Memphis sessionmen: Reggie Young, Bobby Emmons and Tommy Cogbill were the backbone of the house band at the famous American Studio.

They had started out as rock and rollers (Young was in Bill Black's Combo and also backed Eddie Bond on his *Rockin' Daddy*), but as the sixties progressed they developed into a crack team of rhythm-and-bluesers, laying down many classic cuts for the Goldwax label (including James Carr's seminal *The Dark End Of The Street*). Cogbill also recorded at Stax behind Wilson Pickett (*Mustang Sally*) and at Fame behind Aretha Franklin (*I Never Loved A Man (The Way I Love You)*). Later still, they accompanied Elvis Presley on two of his best late sixties sides, *Suspicious Minds* and *In The Ghetto*.

Gene 'Bowlegs' Miller had a long pedigree as a Memphis R&B bandleader, employing — amongst many others — a young Andrew Love in the band. He later moved to Hi when Willie Mitchell took over the business from Ray Harris and was instrumental in introducing the great Ann Peebles to the label.

Love, together with his partner Wayne Jackson, started out as the Mar-Keys and later became the Memphis Horns. They virtually wrote the script for the Southern horn sound during their tenure at Stax, playing for the likes of Otis Redding (including his masterwork *Otis Blue* album), Sam & Dave and Booker T. & The MGs, as well as gracing Albert King's best-ever sides. Baritone saxophonist James Mitchell also occasionally featured in the Memphis Horns line-up and went on to work with Ann Peebles and Al Green at Hi on their fabulous early seventies recordings (don't let anyone tell you soul died in the sixties with Otis!). The Memphis Horns of course are still at it today, sub-contracting their soul to the likes of U2, Keith Richards and Robert Cray.

Engineer Ray Harris also had a long history in Memphis music, recording two classic rockabilly singles at Sun before launching the Hi label in 1957 with Joe Cuoghi, Bill Cantrell and Quinton Claunch.

So, all in all, not a bad backing band for Chuck to record with. But even so, after the relative failure of the previous sessions, Mercury felt the need to bring in producers Boo Frazier and Roy Dea to oversee things. One wonders how they coped with the taciturn control freak, Mr. Berry. Nonetheless, these cuts are a marked improvement on what had gone before.

A baritone saxophone sounding like a Mississippi riverboat foghorn introduces **Ramblin' Rose** and sets the tone for these horn-rich sessions. The tune had been a huge hit for Nat 'King' Cole in 1962, reaching No. 2 in the *Billboard* 'Hot 100'. This was some time after Cole had left his jazz roots behind and sang every song with a permanent smile on his face to an accompaniment of lush strings and heavenly backing vocals. Fortunately, Chuck eschews the schmaltz and turns in a pretty loose version. It's clear that Berry was a Cole fan from his early 'King Cole Trio' days (as demonstrated by the recording of *Bring Another Drink* at the following session) and often featured this song at his shows in the early '70s, to the surprise of many fans.

Check Me Out is a tight little rocker with the characteristic Berry guitar to the fore, underscored by staccato horns. The guitar break is shared 50/50 between Chuck and Reggie Young, Chuck's half being his usual run-through, Reggie's being more typical of the funky Memphis soul style. Lyrically, the song has little new to offer, just a flash from the master in the shape of: "I can't dance by Tchaikovsky/ Nay and Johann Se-Bach/ No compree Franz Schubert/ I'm goin' stick to my style/ Come on up to me baby/ 'Cause I wanna rock"

The opening lines of *I Do Really Love You* ("It's you I'm in love with/ It's not what you are/ It's not how you treat me or your fancy car") set out the stall for this slowish bluesy number, reminiscent of Jimmy Reed's *Honest I Do*. There is no instrumental break and the guitar content is minimal, with the horn section stepping up to the mike to vamp throughout. Chuck proves the claim that he is no soul singer by singing the song particularly clearly and straight with no attempt at all to 'worry' the words, though it is remarkable to hear such a renowned wordsmith mis-pronounce ecstasy "ectasy". The cut is relatively short and, just as one is anticipating another verse, Berry draws it to a close — you can almost see his leg shoot out — with a perfectly-balanced minor chord.

I Do Really Love You was selected as the 'B' side of Chuck's second Mercury single, the top deck being **Back To Memphis**. With the horns vamping and the rhythm section hitting a sub-*Land Of 1,000 Dances* groove, Chuck extols the virtues of Memphis compared to the cold hard metropoli of New York and Chicago. He seems to have a fixation with night attire, riding "barefooted" and walking down Beale Street in his pyjamas. The instrumental break is a particularly well-structured exchange of licks between the two guitarists.

The sheer quality of *Back To Memphis* made it the natural selection for the single. It is a decent release, but out of time for the mid-sixties high on a diet of Motown and *Sgt. Pepper*. Had Chuck taken up the offer to play the *Monterey Pop Festival*, things might have taken a different turn. The composition wasn't overlooked, however, by George Thorogood and the Band who are among the handful of the faithful who subsequently recorded it.

SESSION 46
CHUCK BERRY
Chuck Berry, vocal/guitar; Reggie Young, guitar; Bobby Emmons, piano; Gene 'Bowlegs' Miller, trumpet; James Mitchell, baritone saxophone; Andrew Love, tenor saxophone; Tommy Cogbill, bass; Jerry 'Satch' Arnold, drums

Royal Recording Studios
1320 South Lauderdale Avenue
Memphis, Tennessee   **22 March 1967**

YWI-39493	**Bring Another Drink** (Roy Branker, Robert Bell)	■ Mercury MG-21123/SR-61123 ◉ Mercury 836 071-2
YWI-39494	**It Hurts Me Too** (Hudson Whittaker)	■ Mercury MG-21123/SR-61123 ◉ Mercury 836 071-2
YWI-39495	**Goodnight, Well It's Time To Go** (James Hudson, Calvin Carter)	■ Mercury MG-21123/SR-61123, 6463 044 ◉ Mercury 836 071-2
YWI-39496	**So Long** (Russ Morgan, Remus Harris, Irving Melsher)	■ Mercury MG-21123/SR-61123, SRM2-6501 ◉ Mercury 836 071-2

The second day of recording produced four cover versions... or at least a close approximation in the case of the third number. The first cut of the day, however, faithfully follows its progenitor, a 1944 waxing by the King Cole Trio. Berry's **Bring Another Drink** doesn't swing as smoothly as Cole's original, with

Chuck drops a tanner.
Manchester, 17 February 1967.

its *Route 66*-style opening and fluid guitar break from Oscar Moore followed by Nat's equally-fluid piano, but it is nevertheless a smooth meld of guitar and horns. Chuck's desire for crystal-clear diction leads him to adopt a very English accent, which he loses with his pronunciation of the pure-American "deuce". The subject-matter — a Berry favourite — addresses the dangers of "lushing" and getting some "mellow chicks" high on mother's ruin.

As previously noted, Elmore James was another artist who had a significant influence on Chuck Berry's music. His 1952 recording, *Baby What's Wrong*, was the source of one of Chuck's most familiar guitar licks; his *Dust My Broom* provided the basis for *Childhood Sweetheart*, *Run Around*, *O Rangutang* and later on, *Bio*; and the melody and sentiment of his **It Hurts Me Too** was utilised by Berry for his 1965 waxing, *Why Should We End This Way*. Here, Chuck has a crack at covering the prototype.

Although it was the prolific bluesman Tampa Red who wrote and recorded the original in 1940 for Bluebird, it is almost certainly Elmore's posthumous 1965 smash (No. 9 and No. 25 on the *Cash Box* and *Billboard* R&B charts respectively) that Berry wired into. James had originally cut the tune in 1957 for the Chief label, but the Enjoy remake, with its rolling rhythm and atmospheric guitar and vocals, has the edge. Chuck's version isn't bad in a low-key sort of way, but it isn't a patch on either of Elmore's waxings, being delivered in a resigned tone without a hint of passion.

Goodnight, Well It's Time To Go is a loose approximation of the 1954 hit by the Spaniels. The song, originally titled *Goodnite, Sweetheart, Goodnite*, was written by lead singer James 'Pookie' Hudson and Calvin Carter, co-founder of the Vee–Jay label, for whom it was the very first hit. A private tape of Chuck playing some of his favourite tunes exists in which *Goodnite, Sweetheart, Goodnite* is linked in medley with the standards *These Foolish*

Things and *Blue Moon* — again underscoring his penchant for the mellow sounds of the forties.

In the Spaniels' hands, it is a languid, intimate love song, with Hudson intoning: "Goodnight sweetheart, well it's time to go/ I hate to leave you, I really must say/ Goodnight, sweetheart, goodnight," as the group bill and coo in the background. Berry's recording uses the song as a vehicle to close his stage show: "Goodnight, sweethearts *[note the plural]* it's time to go now/ Arrivederci, tally-ho, au revoir, adios, you've been wonderful/ I don't want to go, but this completes my show." Transmuted into *Bonsoir Cherie*, the song was used in medley with *Johnny B. Goode* as a closing number for his shows. Having grown accustomed to these, one waits in anticipation for the power surge of *Johnny B. Goode* to cut in. That doesn't happen here, but what we do get is Gallic lyrics sung in the worst French accent this side of the Channel Tunnel.

The last cut of this session is also the best: a moody, low-key reading of **So Long** with truly superb integration of guitar, piano and horns. The tune was twenty-one year old Ruth Brown's first recording and first R&B hit on Atlantic Records in 1949. Brown, sounding very young, already had that characteristic catch in her voice which became her trademark, but the backing by Eddie Condon's band sounds rather old fashioned, like a thirties' throwback danceband. She apparently learned the song from an eccentric blues singer, Little Miss Cornshucks (real name: Mildred Cummings) who had cut it back in 1947, but it was actually first recorded back in 1940 by Russ Morgan & His Orchestra (Morgan co-wrote it with Remus Harris and Irving Melsher, and subsequently used it as his theme song). Given his love of forties' swing band music, Chuck may well have had this version in the back of his mind when he decided to cut it.

SESSION 47
CHUCK BERRY

Chuck Berry, vocal/guitar; Reggie Young, guitar; Bobby Emmons, piano; Gene 'Bowlegs' Miller, trumpet; James Mitchell, baritone saxophone; Andrew Love, tenor saxophone; Tommy Cogbill, bass; Jerry 'Satch' Arnold, drums

1320 South Lauderdale Avenue
Royal Recording Studios
Memphis, Tennessee   **23 March 1967**

YWI-39497	**My Heart Will Always Belong To You** *(Arbee Stidham)*	■ Mercury MG-21123/SR-61123, SRM2-6501 ◎ Mercury 836 071-2
YWI-39498	**Flying Home** *[instrumental]* *(Benny Goodman, Lionel Hampton)*	◎ Mercury 836 071-2
YWI-39499	**Sweet Little Rock'n'Roller** *(Chuck Berry)*	■ Mercury MG-21123/SR-61123, 6463 044 ◎ Mercury 836 071-2
YWI-39500	**Oh Baby Doll** *(Chuck Berry)*	■ Mercury MG-21123/SR-61123 ◎ Mercury 836 071-2

The final day's play commences with **My Heart Will Always Belong To You**, a song consistently credited to 'C. Berry' and registered with his Isalee

Music publishing company registered at the Berry Park premises in Wentzville. However, the original version was actually written and recorded by Chicago bluesman Arbee Stidham in 1947, becoming successful enough for him to cut a sequel, *Your Heart Belongs To Me*, the following year. Stidham, a vocalist who fronted blues 'orchestras' was more sophisticated than most Chicago bluesmen and possessed a wonderfully grainy voice which he used to good effect on this sad story of lost love.

Chuck also renders the song well, with a convincing catch in the throat towards the end. The tempo is slower than Stidham's version and, as is usual when he records non-original material, he modifies the lyrics considerably whilst retaining the feeling and sense of the song. The famous Berry guitar is to the fore and he takes a fully-rounded single-string solo in the break. The rest of the band vamp along behind the vocal, each line being punctuated by a muted trumpet. All in all a very good cut, one of his best for Mercury.

Chuck's love of big band swing and his desire to play guitar in such a band surfaces once again with his recording of **Flying Home** — a tune he was to cut again three months later. This version, full as it is of enthusiasm and vigour and yells of enjoyment, unfortunately lacks co-ordination between the guitar and horns. Though this improves as the track progresses, it is probably the reason why it didn't get released until the expanded CD edition of *Chuck Berry In Memphis* hit the racks in 1989.

Flyin' Home is, of course, the swing standard cut by almost everyone who is anyone in jazz from Charlie Barnett to Charlie Watts, its classic tearaway riff anticipating rhythm and blues by about fifteen years. The number was written by Benny Goodman and Lionel Hampton and first recorded by the Benny Goodman Sextet in 1939. As well as Goodman and Hampton, this ensemble also included one of Berry's all-time guitar heroes, Charlie Christian, who makes his presence felt with a fine guitar solo. However, compared to what was to come in the next decade, Goodman's version was pretty restrained.

One suspects that the tune was more of a Hampton creation than Goodman's because, on forming his own outfit in 1940, it became Hamp's theme tune which he recut in quick succession, first with sax-man Illinois Jacquet in '42, then with Arnett Cobb in '44. With each attempt, the treatment became more raucous, increasingly emphasising the basic riff and the pounding beat. I suspect, however, that it was the 1945 version of *Flyin' Home* by Illinois Jacquet & His All Stars — the inaugural recording for the Mesner brothers on their Philo label (later to become Aladdin) — that blew Berry away.

The final two cuts of the Memphis sessions are remakes of Chuck's own **Sweet Little Rock And Roller** (or as Mercury would have it, *'Rock'n'Roller'*) and **Oh Baby Doll** which, because of the horns and excellent piano, are by far the best two revivals of Chess material he cut for Mercury — even if the songs themselves are not *Premier League* Berry.

SESSION 48

CHUCK BERRY (CHUCK BERRY–THE MILLER BAND on Mercury 72748)
Chuck Berry, vocal/guitar; Steve Miller, harmonica, guitar -1; Jim Peterman, keyboards; James 'Curley' Cooke, guitar; Lonnie Turner, bass; Tim Davis, drums; Bill Graham, introduction

LIVE RECORDINGS
Fillmore Auditorium
1805 Fillmore Boulevard
San Francisco, California   **27 June 1967**

YWI-35677	**Rockin' At The Fillmore** *[instrumental]* *(Chuck Berry)*	■ Mercury MG-21138/SR-61138, SRM2-6501 ◎ Mercury 836 072-2
YWI-35678	**Everyday I Have The Blues** *(Aaron Sparks)*	■ Mercury MG-21138/SR-61138, SRM2-6501 ◎ Mercury 836 072-2
YWI-35679	**C.C. Rider** -1 *(Gertrude 'Ma' Rainey)*	■ Mercury MG-21138/SR-61138, SRM2-6501 ◎ Mercury 836 072-2

YWI-35680	**Driftin' Blues** *(Charles Brown, Johnny Moore,* *Eddie Williams)*	■ Mercury MG-21138/SR-61138, SRM2-6501 ◎ Mercury 836 072-2
YWI-35681	**Feelin' It** *[instrumental]* -1 *(Chuck Berry)*	○ Mercury 72748**b** ■ Mercury MG-21138/SR-61138, SRM2-6501 ◎ Mercury 836 072-2
YWI-35682	**Flying Home** *[instrumental]* -1 *(Benny Goodman, Lionel Hampton)*	■ Mercury MG-21138/SR-61138, SRM2-6501 ◎ Mercury 836 072-2

Note: YWI 35677 and YWI 35678 are played in medley.

June 1967: the Summer of Love. The *Monterey Pop Festival* from the 16th to the 18th of the month had made stars of Jimi Hendrix and Otis Redding with the white audience and the hippies concentrated in the Haight–Ashbury district of San Francisco. A few blocks north-east at the junction of Geary Boulevard and Fillmore Street, Chuck Berry had a week's gig at the Fillmore Auditorium backed by the up-and-coming Steve Miller's Blues Band and supported by Eric Burdon & The New Animals. It was actually his second appearance at the Fill that year — a celebratory return after successful gigs on the 17th, 18th and 19th of February with the Grateful Dead and Johnny Talbot & De Thangs.

Widely touted as the next big thing, the Miller band had a strong local following in the Bay Area and this recording with Chuck was their very first outing on vinyl. They had played the Monterey festival to much acclaim and were being courted by the big record companies, eventually being bagged by Capitol. Miller soon dropped the 'Blues' tag and went on to cut a dozen or so albums and a couple of No. 1 hit singles, *The Joker* and *Abracadabra*.

These sets backing Berry were, however, most decidedly in a blues bag — a step Mercury may have insisted on because rock and roll was not selling at the time. Of the eleven cuts on the original album, *Live At Fillmore Auditorium*, eight were blues standards and only *Johnny B. Goode* an out-and-out rocker. When the album was re-issued on CD in 1989, a further five tracks were added, only one of which was a Berry rock and roll original.

The Fillmore Auditorium itself opened on 10th December 1965, although it didn't really come into its own as the leading hippie venue until March 1966 when Frisco impresario Bill Graham acquired the lease and began promoting psychedelic rock bands such as the Jefferson Airplane and Quicksilver Messenger Service, using psychedelic *art nouveau* posters designed by Wes Wilson to publicise the gigs. This idiosyncratic style is mimicked on the cover of *Live At Fillmore*, albeit with Mr. Berry looking very un-hippie in a brown suit, shirt and tie.

Bill Graham gets the proceedings started thus: "You meet him as a person and you don't forget him. As a performer he's the big, big daddy of them all, Mr. Chuck Berry!" — to which Chuck responds: "We gonna see if we can get in tune here a little with **Rockin' At The Fillmore**. See how you like it."

This is, of course, an update of *Rock At The Philharmonic* which, after a tentative few bars, slowly builds to a crescendo with Berry's guitar battling against Miller's harp and Peterman's electric keyboard for top billing. Four-and-a-half minutes or so into the tune the band segues into a romping, stomping version of **Everyday I Have The Blues**, a song written and first recorded by Aaron 'Pinetop' Sparks in 1935. In 1948, Peter Chatman (alias Memphis Slim) adapted it as *Nobody Loves Me* and later copyrighted it in his own name under its original title. It was subsequently picked up by West Coast bluesman Lowell Fulson who scored a hit with it in 1949, and enjoyed further chart success in the fifties in the hands of B.B. King and Joe Williams, whose 1952 version with the King Kolax Band and 1955 remake with the Count Basie Band both made the R&B charts. Since then, of course, it has gone on to become a blues standard of gigantic proportions. Berry's hoarse vocalisation of this old blues warhorse comes across well and the band boogie along nicely, preferring to roll with it rather than go for the dynamic dramatics of, say, the B.B. King version.

After the storming start, the tempo drops to a stuttering pace as Chuck tackles the ancient blues, **C.C. Rider**. This song stems back to the beginnings of recorded blues with Gertrude 'Ma' Rainey who, with Louis Armstrong in support on cornet, cut it in 1924 as *See See Rider*. In his autobiography Chuck recalls that, in his formative years, he would dig the blues and boogie woogie sounds of Tampa Red, Lonnie Johnson, Lil Green, Sister Rosetta Tharpe, Big Maceo, and Buddy and Ella Johnson. In this formidable list of blues greats he also includes Bea Booze, who had a No. 1 R&B hit with her version of the song, *See See Rider Blues*, in 1942. Muriel Nicholls, billed as '*Wee Bea Booze, The Famous See See Rider Girl*', was one of a small band of female guitar-playing singers around in the forties, but her languid version harks back to Rainey's style rather than the burgeoning rhythm and blues ahead.

Likewise, Berry's slow, lurching treatment has far more in common with Booze's recording than the better-known 1957 Atlantic hit by Chuck Willis, whose melodic rendition featuring a wonderful sax part by Sam 'The Man' Taylor earned him the title '*King of the Stroll*'. Atlantic tried again in 1962, cutting an upbeat version with LaVern Baker that presented her with a No. 9 R&B hit in the twilight of her career as a chart artist.

From one slow blues to another — this time Chuck's second attempt at Charles Brown's **Drifting Blues**, which is pretty run-of-the-mill stuff, with some good guitar but marred by dodgy vocals. There must surely have been some uptempo numbers separating these two songs on the night .

A couple of instrumentals finish off the first Fillmore set. Chuck counts in **Feelin' It**, a funky original with much interplay between guitar and piping organ which he obviously enjoys immensely, judging by the vocal interjections he makes. This theme is one he would develop in later songs such as *It's Too Dark In There* and *Your Lick*. The tune was issued as the 'B' side of *It Hurts Me Too*.

His second go at Hamp's theme, **Flyin' Home**, is a *tour de force* guitar workout from start to finish, with Berry playing the shit out of Jacquet's lick. Listen to the joy as he hits the 'rapapapapapop-pow' bit. Two minutes forty-four seconds that pass in a flash.

SESSION 49
CHUCK BERRY (CHUCK BERRY–THE MILLER BAND on Mercury 72748)
Chuck Berry, vocal/guitar; Steve Miller, harmonica, second vocal -1, guitar -2; Jim Peterman, keyboards; James 'Curley' Cooke, guitar; Lonnie Turner, bass; Tim Davis, drums; Bill Graham, closing remarks

LIVE RECORDINGS
Fillmore Auditorium
1805 Fillmore Boulevard
San Francisco, California   **29 June 1967**

YWI-35683	**I'm Your Hoochie Coochie Man** *(Willie Dixon)*	■ Mercury MG-21138/SR-61138, SRM2-6501 ◎ Mercury 836 072-2
YWI-35684	**It Hurts Me Too** -1 *(Hudson Whittaker)*	● Mercury 72748**a** ■ Mercury MG-21138/SR-61138, SRM2-6501 ◎ Mercury 836 072-2
	Good Morning Little Schoolgirl *(John Lee Williamson)*	◎ Mercury 836 072-2
YWI-35685	**Fillmore Blues** *[instrumental]* -2 *(Chuck Berry)*	■ Mercury MG-21138/SR-61138, SRM2-6501 ◎ Mercury 836 072-2
YWI-35686	**Wee Baby Blues** *(Joe Turner, Art Tatum)*	■ Mercury MG-21138/SR-61138, SRM2-6501 ◎ Mercury 836 072-2
	Bring Another Drink *(Roy Branker, Robert Bell)*	◎ Mercury 836 072-2
	Worried Life Blues *(Maceo Merriweather)*	◎ Mercury 836 072-2
	Reelin' And Rockin' *(Chuck Berry)*	◎ Mercury 836 072-2
	My Ding-A-Ling -2 *(Dave Bartholomew, Chuck Berry)*	◎ Mercury 836 072-2
YWI-35687	**Johnny B. Goode** *(Chuck Berry)*	■ Mercury MG-21138/SR-61138, SRM2-6501 ◎ Mercury 836 072-2

Chuck had already cut Muddy's *I Just Want To Make Love To You* back in 1959, but with **I'm Your Hoochie Coochie Man** he really was 'messing with the man'. Whilst it is unfair to make comparisons with one of Muddy's most famous and toughest blues, Chuck's version is pretty tough itself with mighty heavy guitar and hoarse vocals which by no means disgrace the song. As with many Berry covers, his version is merely a close approximation of the original, although he does leave two of the three verses and the "Black cat/ John the Conqueror root" couplet untouched. In place of the third verse, however, he inserts a topical reference to marijuana smoking, undoubtedly for the benefit of his audience. The last verse of this version is lifted from another Waters classic, *I'm Ready* (also written by Willie Dixon) but, whereas Mud's weapon is "a ax-handle pistol on a graveyard frame, shooting tombstone bullets wearing a ball and chain", Chuck's gun is "a Fresno pistol on a Frisco frame, shooting Monterey bullets, wearing Diego chains".

After freely using the lick from **Good Morning Little Schoolgirl** on several of his earlier compositions (*Our Little Rendezvous, Little Girl From Central, I Want To Be Your Driver*, etc), Chuck finally gets around to cutting a version of the influential John Lee 'Sonny Boy' Williamson' composition, originally titled *Good Morning, Schoolgirl*. Surprisingly, on the LP this is credited to Don Level and Bob Love, alias the 'Don & Bob' who cut a hyped-up cover in 1961 for the Chess subsidiary Argo, the arrangement of which was subsequently copied by the Yardbirds and a plethora of US punk bands in the sixties.

Berry's blues is clearly based on the Sonny Boy recording rather than Don & Bob's, using the same verse structure and identical lyrics in two of the three verses. The cut is taken at a fair lick compared with Williamson's and includes two extended instrumental passages in which the guitar and harp battle for supremacy. Miller's harmonica-playing doesn't hold a candle to Williamson's flowing, fluttering flourishes, nor can it compete with Berry's axe, which carries the distinctive '*Schoolgirl*' riff instead of the harp.

Chuck's second attempt at Elmore James's **It Hurts Me Too** became his third Mercury single, and it's easy to see why it was chosen: the waxing, with Miller providing a loose second vocal and laid-back harmonica, quite simply has immense charm. Berry's plaintive rendition — his best ever — is far closer to Elmore James's broken-hearted readings both lyrically and musically than to Tampa Red's 1940 original, which by comparison is a jolly romp, replete with Red's kazoo and swinging piano from Blind John Davis.

There is a telling comment at the close of the song when Chuck remarks apologetically: "Oh you sweet people, suffer with us a wee bit longer," as though blues-playing is not what they want to hear and he would soon get back to rock and roll. There *must* have been more rockers recorded at these dates which remain unissued.

Fillmore Blues is a slow, moody instrumental improvised around a funky stop-time theme on which Steve Miller gets to play some distorted fuzztone guitar as a foil to Berry's clear picking. The band seem to enjoy the workout, and this impression is confirmed at the close with Chuck's exclamation: "We shall call that one '*Fillmore*'!"

Wee Baby Blues is a dirge-like reworking of the Big Joe Turner classic. Joe re-recorded the song at intervals throughout his long career and Berry's cover is almost word-perfect to the superlative 1941 original which he made as featured vocalist with the Art Tatum Band: he sticks with the three basic verses and doesn't include lyrics from the later versions. (Had he heard

Tiny Bradshaw's 1945 reworking of the song, *School Day Blues*, Chuck would surely have connected with the amusing berry-picking verse.) No matter, it's still good with a great single-string guitar break and Miller blowing his best harmonica of the whole gig; despite this, however, it's no match for the combined talents of Tatum and Turner.

Bring Another Drink was obviously still fresh in Chuck's mind from the recording he made in Memphis. Pity it wasn't in the minds of the rest of the band! The cut is a shambles, with the band clearly unfamiliar with the song. To his credit, Chuck quickly seems to realise this and mercifully brings the proceedings to a swift conclusion. No wonder it didn't make the original LP release!

The blues standard, **Worried Life Blues** finds Berry and the boys back on safer ground. Chuck had previously recorded the song in his Chess days and Miller's band would have been familiar with this version at least, if not the earlier incarnations by Sleepy John Estes or Big Maceo. However, the performance here adds nothing to the Chess cut and it is again understandable why it was not included on the LP.

Reelin' And Rockin' is the first recorded example of Chuck's bawdy development of his 1957 hit and includes the immortal lines: "Looked at my watch and it was quarter to two/ She said she didn't but I know she do!" and "Looked at my watch and it was quarter to six/ Man, I was standing there firm like a cement mix!" Maybe it was too close to the bone for the time, or perhaps it just didn't fit in with the album concept, but the cut didn't make the original LP and only saw light of day twenty-one years later in digital form. It does, however, have a bluesy feel about it, being slower in tempo than the Chess original and featuring a rolling boogie backdrop, piping organ and thin, reedy, yet quite effective harmonica.

Chuck would take the raunchiness a step closer to 'disgusting' five years later in Coventry, the audience participation on that occasion making this version sound flat and tame. Whether this is the fault of producer Abe Kesh in not miking the auditorium properly, or whether the Fillmore crowd was just too spaced out to care, we'll never know.

My Ding-A-Ling also makes its debut on the CD release and is likewise an update of an earlier song — in this instance *My Tambourine*, here reverting to its original Dave Bartholomew title. Like *Reelin' And Rockin'*, this number is also at an interim stage in its development, again to reach its zenith (or nadir, depending on your view) at Coventry in 1972. And, like *Reelin' And Rockin'*, it sounds positively tame compared to the latter — primarily because Berry doesn't work the crowd sufficiently. Less Moroccan Brown and more brown ale might have made all the difference. As he sings his little ditty, Chuck advises that there is a little jerk in it (I don't *think* he was referring to Harvey Kornspan, 'business associate' of the Miller band, who somehow wangled a credit on the album!).

The last song of the set is, inevitably, **Johnny B. Goode** prefaced with a brief snatch of what later came to be titled *Bonsoir Cherie* — the song Berry had recorded in Memphis as *Goodnight, Well It's Time To Go*. If the lyrics are accurate, this was cut at the first show of the day. After a couple of lines of lethargy, Chuck bursts into *Johnny B. Goode* at breakneck speed, losing all the subtlety and feeling of the Chess classic — a rather inauspicious ending to a generally good concert and album. He apparently got paid, too, as his closing remarks ("I'd like to say this is the most wonderful promoter I have ever worked for. Let's give Graham a big hand.") are probably unique, given his well-publicised aversion to promoters. If you've seen the BBC1 *Omnibus* documentary *Johnny Be Good* from 1979, you will have seen his public humiliation of some poor sap who didn't get the stage set-up right.

SESSION 50
CHUCK BERRY
Chuck Berry, speech

Unknown location   1967

YMCA commercial   ○ Y.M.C.A. DJS-1/2**b**

Years before the Village People praised the facilities of the Young Men's Christian Association, Chuck Berry was giving the organisation his hard-sell patter on this little platter. His plug for the 'Y' appears on this 33⅓ rpm microgroove single titled *YMCA DJ Special*. Seventeen diverse acts are featured on the disc: Aretha Franklin, the Royal Guardsmen, Brenton Wood, Lou Rawls and Sonny & Cher get sixty seconds each; the Association, the Easybeats, the Four Tops, the Young Rascals, the Grass Roots and Dionne Warwick get thirty seconds apiece; tucked away on the 'B' side, Chuck gets a twenty-second spot alongside John Lee Hooker(!), Janis Ian, Tommy James, the Nitty Gritty Dirt Band and the Seeds. His contribution is spoken in a matter-of-fact sort of way in the hip argot of the time over the guitar break from *No Particular Place To Go*: "This is Chuck Berry. Where's the 'in' crowd' in these days? Why it's the 'in' place of course, the YMCA. That's where the whole gang goes for fun, sports and all sorts of great activities. Do you like to swim? The 'Y' pool's just right for keeping in shape. Join the fun, join the YMCA." The record sports a yellow label with a crudely drawn guitar above the title and states '*All music cleared. Produced by the National Council YMCA's*', and was presumably designed to permit radio jocks to insert portions between discs.

SESSION 51
CHUCK BERRY

Chuck Berry, vocal/guitar *possibly with* Augie Meyer, organ; Doug Sahm, guitar; Martin Fierro, trumpet, Francisco 'Frank' Morin, saxophone, Harvey Kagan, bass, George Rains, drums

916 Kearny Steet?
San Francisco, California   21 December 1967

YWI-41633	**I Can't Believe** *(Chuck Berry)*	■ Mercury SR-61176, SRM2-6501 ◎ Mercury 836 073-2
YWI-41634	**Soul Rockin'** *(Chuck Berry)*	■ Mercury SR-61176, SRM2-6501 ◎ Mercury 836 073-2

At the close of the year, Chuck Berry returned to California for this brief recording date. In his autobiography, he describes an aborted session in San Francisco with the Sir Douglas Quintet — cut short because the band paid more attention to illegal substances than to the job in hand. I think that these two tracks are the meagre product of that session. The instrumentation, with its prominent organ, matches the group's profile and the reverse of the *From St. Louie To Frisco* album on which the tracks appear sports a photo montage of Chuck and the boys, the unmistakable figure of the stetson-hatted Augie Meyer looming over the slight Doug Sahm, leader of the quintet.

The Sir Douglas Quintet started out in the Lone Star State, recorded by the Crazy Cajun, Huey P. Meaux in San Antone as an answer to the Beatles. They cut the wonderfully cheesy classic, *She's About A Mover* in 1965, but absconded to San Francisco a year later following a drugs bust. Signed to Mercury (hence the tie-up with Berry), the band went on to record their other classic, *Mendocino*, in 1969, which in turn was to inspire one of Berry's later recordings, *California*.

At the time, most of the recording in San Francisco took place in various studios located at 916 Kearny Street in the Fisherman's Wharf district of the city, and this is the probable location for these two numbers and the following session. The cuts themselves show little evidence of the frustrations Berry describes in his book and come across as spontaneous, straight-from-the-studio-floor cuts with no indication of overdubs or other tinkering. In fact, the songs, **Soul Rockin'** (a rocker) and **I Can't Believe** (a blues) feature some excellent Berry guitar and extra-fine bass and drum work. The only drawback is that both are totally derivative: *Soul Rockin'* starts as a carbon copy of *Back In The USA* and *I Can't Believe* is similar to a number of typical plaintive love ballads. Nevertheless, these two tracks, had they been lifted from the album for 45 release, would have made an honest little single that may have garnered more sales for the long-player.

SESSION 52
CHUCK BERRY

Chuck Berry, vocal/guitar, overdubbed guitar -1; Ingrid Berry, second vocal -2; *possibly* Johnnie Johnson, piano (omit -3); unknown trumpet -4; unknown trombone -4; unknown saxophone -4; unknown bass; unknown drums (omit -5)

916 Kearny Street?
San Francisco, California   **1 July 1968**

YWI-42554	**Ma Dear** -2-4 *(Chuck Berry)*	◉ Mercury 72840**b** ■ Mercury SR-61176, SRM2-6501 ◎ Mercury 836 073-2
YWI-42555	**Rock Cradle Rock** -1-3-4 *(Chuck Berry)*	■ Mercury SR-61176 ◎ Mercury 836 073-2
YWI-42556	**The Love I Lost** *(Chuck Berry)*	■ Mercury SR-61176 ◎ Mercury 836 073-2
YWI-42557	**Louie To Frisco** *(Chuck Berry)*	◉ Mercury 72840**a** ■ Mercury SR-61176, SRM2-6501 ◎ Mercury 836 073-2
YWI-42558	**I Love Her, I Love Her** -1-4 *(Chuck Berry)*	■ Mercury SR-61176 ◎ Mercury 836 073-2
YWI-42559	**Little Fox** -1-2 *(Chuck Berry)*	■ Mercury SR-61176, SRM2-6501 ◎ Mercury 836 073-2
YWI-42560	**Rock Cradle Rock** *(Chuck Berry)*	unissued
YWI-42561	**Song Of My Love** -1-2-3-5 *(Chuck Berry)*	◎ Mercury 836 073-2

Back again in San Francisco to finalise tracks for his new album, Chuck embarks on an extensive session of original songs. To cut seven songs in one day seems excessive and my guess is that it probably took two days. These are the first recordings to feature Chuck's seventeen year old eldest daughter, Darlin Ingrid, and her presence adds a new dimension to the tracks. Apart from Chuck and Ingrid, the band is anonymous — though the piano player sounds suspiciously like old 'blue hand' Johnnie, especially on the slower numbers.

If the matrix numbers are to be believed, the session started in a decidedly New Orleanian vein with **Ma Dear**, which is based on the tune and changes from Chris Kenner's 1961 waxing, *Something You Got* (a national hit in 1964 for Alvin 'Shine' Robinson). The song is sung in unison by the Berrys over a plodding beat and prominent horns. In the course of three short verses, Chuck's 'ma' advises him that he will find true love, and by the second verse he does. By the third, however, his love is gone and he's asking *Ma Dear* what he should do. *Ma Dear* was picked as the 'B' side for the album's 45 taster.

"I was born under the sign of Libra, October 18th, seven o'clock," is the line (biographically correct, give or take a minute) which starts Chuck's shortest-ever song, **Rock Cradle Rock**. Yet another paean in praise of rock and roll, this song had the potential of a great track had it been developed. One wonders what the unissued take (matrix YWI-42560) is like, and how the number might have come across had it been cut at Chess?

The Love I Lost treads some *very* familiar ground as a lovelorn blues ballad loosely based on *Wee Wee Hours* with prominent rippling piano from a pianist who, if not named Johnson, is a Johnson clone. Chuck plays some neat T-Bone chords as he sings of the pain he feels in his heart: "After the sun goes down in the evening, that's when your leaving hurts me most/ The times when you would nestle to me and dwell within my heart so close/ And although

FROM ST. LOUIE TO FRISCO   CHUCK BERRY

you stand just two steps away now, the distance seems from coast to coast." One is almost persuaded until he interjects a guitar quip from *Jingle Bells* as the song fades.

Louie To Frisco (subsequently retitled *St. Louie To Frisco* on some reissues) makes reference to Berry's absolutely independent lifestyle ("footloose and fancy-free" is how he puts it), unencumbered by manager, band or entourage: "I only have one cradle to rock now and I'm gonna rock it everywhere I go/ From St. Louis to San Francisco, ah from Canada to Mexico."

This declaration is made over a Jimmy Reed *Big Boss Man*-type beat, again with some very Johnsonian piano in the background. Whilst it is a workmanlike track, it lacks the spark of originality that makes a good song great. No way should it have been chosen for release as the 'A' side of the album's single. Nevertheless, George Thorogood liked it enough to record the one and only cover version so far.

With the exception of the 1964 instrumentals with Bo Diddley, ***I Love Her, I Love Her***, at nearly six minutes, is the longest track Chuck had cut to date. Clocking in at two minutes fourteen seconds, the intro is almost a Berry record in itself, the short, sharp guitar figure of old replaced with a funky insistent beat, rolling piano and punchy horns. The number comes across as a sub-*Papa Was A Rollin' Stone* without the tensions and dynamics of that great Temptations track. An 'against all odds' love story, with the older generation warning against getting spliced while the youngster declares "I love her, I love her/ Ain't no problem as big as the one living without her", this is a good laid-back track with fine instrumentation and a well-delivered lyric which deserves to be more widely known.

The subject of ***Little Fox*** is none other than Darlin Ingrid, who coyly responds to Chuck's invitation to "boogaloo" with soft, sexy "Alrights" and "Well, okays" and "If you say so's". There is something incongruous about daddy Chuck inviting his daughter to boogaloo, but if you can repress this

Chuck walks that walk.

uneasy feeling in the belief that it's only dancing, then I suppose it's "alright". Musically, the song has little new to say, opening with the *Back In The USA* lick and boogieing on through.

The real gem of the session is the remake of **Song Of My Love**, which ironically never got a contemporary release. This is a rare instance where the Mercury recut is actually superior to the Chess recording. Father and daughter harmonise perfectly and bring a charm and passion to the song not heard in the original. The backing is restrained and tasteful, with the beat patted out on the open strings of the guitar supported by subdued bass and an overdubbed Tex-Mex-flavoured guitar break. A wonderful cut which, with the current interest in world music, could strike a chord with many people.

SESSION 53
CHUCK BERRY

Chuck Berry, vocal/guitar, overdubbed guitar; Billy Peek, guitar, harmonica-1, organ -2, piano -3, tambourine -4; Halveen 'Kermit' Cooley, bass; Dale Gisher, drums

Berry Park studio,
691 Buckner Road
Wentzville, Missouri   **pre-May 1969**

YWI-44678	**Good Lookin' Woman** -1-4 *(Chuck Berry)*	○ Mercury 72963**b** ■ Mercury SR-61223 ◎ Mercury 836 074-2
YWI-44679	**My Woman** -1-3 *(Chuck Berry)*	■ Mercury SR-61223 ◎ Mercury 836 074-2
YWI-44680	**It's Too Dark In There** -1-2-4 *(Chuck Berry)*	○ Mercury 72963**a** ■ Mercury SR-61223, SRM2-6501 ◎ Mercury 836 074-2
YWI-44681	**Put Her Down** -2 *(Chuck Berry)*	■ Mercury SR-61223 ◎ Mercury 836 074-2
	Put Her Down *[instrumental version]* *(Chuck Berry)*	unissued
YWI-44682	**Concerto In B Goode** *[instrumental]* -2 *(Chuck Berry)*	■ Mercury SR-61223 ◎ Mercury 836 074-2
	Concerto In B Goode *[instrumental — slow version]* *(Chuck Berry)*	unissued
	Untitled Instrumental *(Chuck Berry)*	unissued
	Funny That Way *(Chuck Berry?)*	unissued
	If I Was *(Chuck Berry?)*	unissued
	Get A Little *(Chuck Berry?)*	unissued

Note: YWI-44680 also mastered as YWI-44373.

These recordings, which were to become the *Concerto In B Goode* album, were to be the last that Chuck cut for Mercury and it sounds like he was just going through the motions to fulfil his contract before re-signing with Chess. The exact date is unknown but must have been prior to May 1969 because at a question-and-answer session with Berkeley University students on 9th May he made reference to his "new single, *It's Too Dark In Here*" [sic]. This interview was published in the 14th June edition of *Rolling Stone* magazine, with Berry receiving the ultimate accolade of having his picture on the cover of the *Rolling Stone*.

For this session, Chuck assembled a new band which included the young multi-instrumentalist Billy Peek, who was to continue to play with him on and off for nigh-on six years until he hit the big time with Rod Stewart. (Stewart

spotted him backing Chuck on a late-night TV show and poached him to help create the Berry boogie beat on his own records.) Back in 1961, Peek had had his own fifteen minutes of fame when he scored a local hit in St. Louis with *Can A White Boy Sing The Blues* on the Marlo label.

As well as the new band, these were also the first recordings from Chuck's own Berry Park studio to be released. Herein, perhaps, lies the problem: with no restraint on time, the session is full of over-produced over-indulgences.

Like a child with a new toy, Berry twiddles with the volume controls, trips between stereo channels at random and distorts the guitars to sound like anything from a duck on speed to Sparky's magic piano to a hump-backed whale with stomach-ache. The songs themselves have very little to add and the whole album is really rather dull, lacking the fire and spontaneity of his classic work.

The shadow of the great Elmore James makes its presence felt again as **Good Looking Woman** revisits the *Dust My Broom* theme (it must be a close-run thing who used this lick the most, Chuck or Elmore), but the harmonica-playing is pretty inept and the lyrics banal in the extreme with Berry resorting to farmyard animal impressions to make the lines scan. This abomination is topped by an irritating tambourine bashed in true Salvation Army fashion.

My Woman fares a tad better due to Peek's fine piano-playing and better if not exactly original lyrics. The song is loosely based on Little Walter's *Last Night*, but the rudimentary harp-blowing bears no resemblance whatsoever to the maestro.

It's Too Dark In There is the most original cut of the session and contains some of the old Berry wit in its tale of a lady who suffers from nyctophobia. There is just no way that Chuck is going to get his way as the scene switches from the front porch, to a night club, to the open countryside, to a scary movie show then, finally, back home where the light fuse has blown. Unfortunately, the cut is spoiled by unnecessary over-production, with the singer's voice jumping between stereo channels as he acts out the two characters in the song. The guitar is of the dreadful 'wah-wah' variety and the phantom tambourine-basher is back, floating between channels like a lost soul. At least the harmonica is reasonably palatable if you can cope with a sort-of swampy Bob Dylan sound.

It's Too Dark In There was remastered for single release as YWI-44373 minus the guitar solo and in mono, which improves the cut.

The final track on Side One of the LP is **Put Her Down**, and the ghost of Elmore rises again in the guise of *It Hurts Me Too*, which is used as the basis of the composition. To be fair, the instrumentation ain't half bad, with Peek taking the bluesy lead guitar up to the break, at which point Berry takes over. The melody is carried on a loping *Albatross*-type beat from Cooley and Gisher, whose performance is consistently steady throughout the session. This song may actually be a reworking of the unreleased 1965 Chess cut, *Loving You In Vain*, as this expression is contained in the lyrics.

The unissued instrumental version of *Put Her Down* is a slow dirge of a blues in the *It Hurts Me Too/Deep Feeling* mode with plenty of echoey guitar, fading out at just over the two minute mark.

The final released number of the session — and also of Chuck Berry's tenure at Mercury — is the longest studio cut he has ever made and one which covered an entire side of the original LP. To be brutally frank, the best thing about it is its title: **Concerto In B Goode**. It bears no resemblance to its namesake and has none of the excitement or immediacy of Berry's masterpiece. It's just an eighteen forty-four bore: a meandering melisma of musical mush, gloated on gimmicky guitar and full of fanciful fluctuations of the control-board knobs. In other words: great concept, shame about the actuality.

If you think the issued *Concerto In B Goode* is bad, then you really *don't* want to hear the unissued slow version. The good thing is, it only (only?) runs for half the duration of the issued cut... it just seems a hell of a lot longer. Sadly, it is more of the indulgent same: a lumbering slow-to-medium tempo jam with the drums and bass setting a heavy pattern to which the organ pipes a response overlaid Chuck's freaky-deaky psychedelic guitar.

The **Untitled Instrumental** is another cut that deserves its anonymity. It's yet more of the '*Concerto*' crap with a jerky, staggering beat that falls in the musical gutter after about four-and-a-half minutes of aimless lurching around the studio.

The remaining unissued tracks are unheard and may well have been lost because none appeared when Mercury reissued Berry's catalogue on CD in 1989. Maybe they perished in the fire that later consumed the Berry Park studio, or it could be they are so bad that even Mercury couldn't bring themselves to let them escape? If they are/were anything like the unissued instrumental cuts, then their fate is sealed. **If I Was** looks as though it may have been the same song that Chuck later cut for Chess and Atco (the latter titled *If I Were*).

SESSION 54
CHUCK BERRY

Chuck Berry, vocal/guitar; *probably* John Richardson, guitar; Hughie Leggatt, bass; Danny Taylor, drums

LIVE RECORDINGS
Toronto Rock'n'Roll Revival
Varsity Stadium
University of Toronto
Toronto, Canada   **13 September 1969**

Rock And Roll Music *(Chuck Berry)*	■ Magnum MR-703 ◎ Mandarim MR-03978, Newsound/Penny PYCD-260, MasterTone 0301
Nadine *(Chuck Berry)*	■ Magnum MR-703
School Day (Long Live Rock And Roll) *(Chuck Berry)*	■ Magnum MR-703 ◎ Mandarim MR-03978, Newsound/Penny PYCD-260, MasterTone 0301
(In The) **Wee Wee Hours** *(Chuck Berry)*	■ Magnum MR-703 ◎ Mandarim MR-03978, Newsound/Penny PYCD-260, MasterTone 0301
Johnny B. Goode/ Carol/ Promised Land *(Chuck Berry)*	■ Magnum MR-703 ◎ Newsound/ Penny PYCD-260
Hoochie Coochie Man *(Willie Dixon)*	■ Magnum MR-703 ◎ Newsound/ Penny PYCD-260, MasterTone 0301
Memphis Tennessee *(Chuck Berry)*	■ Magnum MR-703
Too Much Monkey Business *(Chuck Berry)*	■ Magnum MR-703 ◎ Mandarim MR-03978, Newsound/Penny PYCD-260, MasterTone 0301
Reelin' And Rockin' *(Chuck Berry)*	■ Magnum MR-703 ◎ Mandarim MR-03978, Newsound/Penny PYCD-260, MasterTone 0301
Sweet Little Sixteen *(Chuck Berry)*	■ Magnum MR-703 ◎ Newsound/ Penny PYCD 260
My Ding-A-Ling *(Dave Bartholomew, Chuck Berry)*	■ Magnum MR-703
Bonsoir Cherie *(Chuck Berry)*	unissued
Johnny B. Goode *(Chuck Berry)*	■ Magnum MR-703
Maybellene *(Chuck Berry)*	■ Magnum MR-703 ◎ Newsound/ Penny PYCD-260, Mandarim MR-03978, MasterTone 0301

By the end of the sixties, Chuck had reached a turning point in his career and found himself 'standing at the crossroads'. He could have developed his blues tendencies (which he did to some extent with his studio recordings) but as far as live performances went, he opted to go down the far more lucrative rock and roll oldies route. The *Toronto Rock'n'Roll Revival* concert, staged in the Varsity outdoor sports stadium of the University of Toronto on 13th September 1969 was one of the first gigs he played in his new role as a rock and roll 'legend', and certainly one of the most memorable.

With temperatures soaring into in the eighties, the stadium rocked all day to the sounds of some of its finest exponents — Berry, Bo Diddley, Gene Vincent, Jerry Lee Lewis and Little Richard — as well as lesser lights Tony Joe White, Doug Kershaw, the Chicago Transit Authority, Cat Mother & The All Night Newsboys, Alice Cooper and England's very own Screaming Lord Sutch, fitting in the gig between elections. (As it happened, what had started out purely as a rock and roll spectacular was quickly renamed the '*Toronto Pop Festival*' or alternatively '*Toronto Peace Festival*', when it was announced that John Lennon was to be the surprise headliner. Lennon, one of the great rock icons and the most vocal pop peacenik, had last appeared on stage with the Beatles at Candlestick Park, San Francisco in 1966, so his evening performance with the Plastic Ono Band — which included Eric Clapton specially for the occasion — was a pretty momentous event.)

The whole festival was filmed by D.A. Pennebaker, who had made his name in the world of rock *ciné verité* with a documentary of Bob Dylan's 1965 tour of Britain, released in 1967 as *Don't Look Back*. The film of the Toronto gig was initially released in 1970 as *Sweet Toronto*, then re-edited to include only Diddley's, Lewis's, Richard's and Berry's performances and re-released in 1972 as *Keep On Rockin''*. The most accessible way to view this performance is on the 1991 videotape, *Rock & Roll Music*, which contains nine of the fourteen songs listed above *(Nadine, Memphis Tennessee, My Ding-A-Ling, Reelin' And Rockin'* and the closing *Bonsoir Cherie/Johnny B. Goode* are missing). However, two songs on the video are mysteriously mistitled and, even more mysteriously, the composer credits are changed! *School Day* becomes *Long Live Rock & Roll* written by one Tony Bryce (who he?) and *Wee Wee Hours* becomes *In The Wee Wee Hours (I Think Of You)* written by none other than Soul Brother No. 1, James Brown, who recorded a song of this title in 1964. Hail, hail, rock and rip-off!

For completists only, **Memphis Tennessee** can be seen in *Alice In Den Städten (Alice In The Cities)*, a 1974 arty-farty film by German director Wim Wenders, famed for his other art house smash, *The Goalie's Anxiety At The Penalty Kick*. In this black-and-white film the Berry footage is doctored — none too convincingly — to give the impression that it is a gig in an Amsterdam club on a cold winter's evening. The main character, played by Rüdiger Vogler, sort-of stumbles on the gig *en route* from America to Germany. Strange but true. Maybe Wenders was a friend of Pennebaker, who allowed him access to his cutting room floor?

A contemporary report of the festival states that Chuck sang *Roll Over Beethoven*, but this doesn't feature either in the film or the numerous audio releases, so maybe this was a slip of the pen.

Berry's performance is excellent, about the best commercially-released concert footage available. Introduced as "the Guitar King of Rock and Roll" by MC Kim Fowley, he strides on stage looking lean, mean and magnificent, hair slicked back gypsy fashion, sporting a neat triangular moustache, bedecked in a waistcoat and trousers which look like they are made from tapestry upholstery material. The look is completed with a white blouse finished off with a 'Ban the Bomb' medallion and a cherry red Gibson strung round his neck.

He greets the throng with his customary "Olé! Olé!" before crashing into **Rock And Roll Music**. This turns out to be a bit of a shambles and he quickly closes it down before too much pain is caused with a quip about now being tuned up and not knowing which key he is playing in until he starts. Many a true word...

The three young white backing musicians were members of a local Toronto band called Nucleus. They quickly hit the groove on the next song and generally perform pretty well for a pick-up band — albeit better on the fast numbers than on the blues songs. More importantly, Chuck is in good voice and plays some excellent fiery guitar, particularly during the **Johnny B. Goode/ Promised Land/Carol** medley and on Muddy's **Hoochie Coochie Man**. He's in good spirits, laughing and joking with the band and the audience, which rubs off on them. A good time is had by all.

During **Reelin' And Rockin'** — which by this point in his career had become pretty raunchy — a sign is held up in the crowd reading '*Recommended as Adult Entertainment*', which elicits a wry smile from Mr. Berry.

Like *Reelin' And Rockin'*, **My Ding-A-Ling** had by now been developed by Chuck into a *double entendre* song with very little *double* about it. In fact, the narrative of *My Ding-A-Ling* borders on the crude. At one point he jokes: "You know I don't do any dirty songs. No, no, not Chuck Berry. Every song I start playing is clean [but] it may get a little dusty in the middle."

Chuck obviously recognised the event as a 'peace and love' gathering, shouting "Peace! Peace!" when he first hit the stage. As well as his nod to the movement by sporting a 'Ban the Bomb' medallion, he makes reference to Vietnam in **Too Much Monkey Business** and proffers support for marijuana use in several songs. A strange contradiction for a confirmed teatotaller who says he doesn't drink and can't stand drunks because he (and they) need to be in full control of their faculties at all times. This clearly doesn't apply to the mellow mood marijuana induces.

Despite the shortcomings of the backing band (they struggle with **Wee Wee Hours** and need instruction from Berry, who conducts them with his guitar and leg gestures), they pull the gig off. Chuck is on top form, duckwalking, scooting and performing splits.

Not surprisingly, this atmospheric set has been reissued very frequently, mainly on cheapo releases, cut and shuffled, some with Berry's comments interspersed, others with shortened versions of the songs. Strangely, **Bonsoir Cherie**, (the song developed from the Spaniels' *Goodnite, Sweetheart, Goodnite*) which precedes *Johnny B. Goode* has never been issued on record or CD and can only be accessed on the film soundtrack itself.

The Toronto audience, as well as being treated to the full Berry works, were also witness to that exceedingly rare phenomenon: a Chuck Berry *encore*! After a blistering GBH of JBG, St. Louis's most famous son actually returned to the stage to sing his personal alma mater, **Maybellene** — an occurrence as rare as the proverbial hen's dentures.

SECOND COMING
(1969-76)

1969 saw Chuck Berry return to Chess with a mellower,
countrified studio sound that gained him
both critical acclaim and a measure of success.
His artistic achievements, however, were overshadowed by the
unprecedented 'My Ding-A-Ling' phenomenon.

SESSION 55
CHUCK BERRY

Chuck Berry, vocal/guitar, overdubbed vocal -1; Ellis 'Lafayette' Leake, piano; Robert Baldori, harmonica; Phil Upchurch, bass; unknown drums; band, backing vocals -2

Ter-Mar Recording Studios
320 East 21st Street   **21 November 1969**
Chicago, Illinois   **(22 December 1969)**

18420	**Tulane** -1 *(Chuck Berry)*	○ Chess CH-2090**a** ■ Chess LPS-1550, CH6-80001
18421	**Have Mercy Judge** *(Chuck Berry)*	○ Chess CH-2090**b** ■ Chess LPS-1550, CH6-80001
18556	**My Ding-A-Ling** -2 *(Dave Bartholomew, Chuck Berry)*	unissued
18557	**That's None Of Your Business** *(Chuck Berry)*	unissued
	Untitled Instrumental *(Chuck Berry)*	unissued

Brian Shephard, a producer at Mercury/Philips Records in London who was trying to develop a British blues roster, had the idea of recording a Chuck Berry blues album. The idea received approval from Berry and studio time was booked to coincide with his next visit to the UK. A number of well-known British blues musicians were lined up for the recording session, including Keith Tillman on bass, Dick Heckstall-Smith on sax, Victor Brox on keyboards, Mick Taylor on guitar and Aynsley Dunbar on drums. John O'Leary was to play harmonica and John Mayall was also pencilled in for a guest appearance. This might have been a musical watershed for Chuck had it proceeded. However, it was not to be: the proposed tour did not materialise and the project was aborted when his Mercury contract expired.

On 9th May 1970, he re-signed with Chess Records almost four years after leaving the label. Intriguingly, it would appear that he actually cut this session several months before his official return to the Chess fold. Maybe he was just sitting out his Mercury deal and did a little moonlighting with a track that just wouldn't wait?

The song in question was **Tulane**, a cracker of a composition as good as any stuff recorded during his first tenure at the label. Berry says he wrote the number during his 1962-63 sojourn at the Springfield Medical Center along with *Nadine, No Particular Place To Go, You Never Can Tell*, and *Promised Land*. If so, why did he keep it under wraps for seven years, particularly during his creatively lean years at Mercury? Be that as it may, this first session back at Chess's Chicago studio produced the wonderful Chess CH-2090 single.

Bob Baldori, who later helped Chuck cut his *San Francisco Dues* album, has confirmed that it is he and not the Five Dimensions' Peter Hogman who plays harmonica on this session. (For some reason, discographers frequently list Hogman, but why would an English musician who played on a

Berry UK tour four years earlier suddenly pop up in Chicago to play on a solitary session?) He also confirmed the presence of Lafayette Leake on piano and a second (unknown) guitarist at the session. Baldori himself was invited along by Chuck following a successful Detroit gig the previous evening. They flew together from Detroit to Chicago with the intention that Baldori would play piano, but, with the prodigious piano prowess of Lafayette Leake available on site, young Bob was relegated to mouth harp.

After Chuck, the most famous musician present at the session was Phil Upchurch on bass. A recording artist in his own right, usually on guitar rather than bass, Upchurch had started out cutting uptown Chicago soul with Jerry Butler and in 1961 hit the big time with the million-selling instrumental, *You Can't Sit Down* (later something of a UK mod anthem in the hands of Georgie Fame and his ilk). He subsequently became a Chess house guitarist and played mainly on soul-blues sides such as those by Little Milton and the infamous 'psychedelic' albums by Muddy Waters (*Electric Mud*) and Howlin' Wolf (*This is Howlin' Wolf's new album. He doesn't like it. He didn't like his electric guitar at first either.* — quite a mouthful, which was more succinctly retitled by Wolf as 'Dogshit'). Latterly Upchurch has recorded albums in a jazz vein and also with the Crusaders and Michael Jackson.

According to the sleevenote of the *Back Home* album [Chess LPS-1550], Chess engineer Roy Black was in the studio twiddling the knobs, and veteran record producer Ralph Bass supervised the session with Esmond Edwards in executive control. However, there can be little doubt as to who was really running the show.

Upchurch's bass certainly helps to power-drive *Tulane* on, with the harp carrying the tune rather than Berry's guitar. However, it's the story of Tulane and Johnny and the wonderfully intricate lyrics that make it so memorable. The song is, in fact, an update of Louis Jordan's 1947 hit, *Run Joe* (covered by Chuck in 1965). Instead of Moe and Joe selling fortunes behind the door of a candy store, we now have Tulane and Johnny running a "novelty shop" and selling illegal substances ("the cream of the crop") from under the counter. The cops raid the joint and, as Johnny is apprehended, he shouts all manner of advice and very specific instructions to Tulane as he urges her to "go 'head on". The advice given hasn't changed much since Jordan's day: feign sickness ("swallow some perfume") and get the good Dr. Keller to endorse your alibi; get rid of the evidence by hiding it in the van and get a lawyer "in the clique with politics" who can pull the right strings and get him out of that "rotten funky jail." A terrific song, sung by Chuck with perfect diction in near-perfect unison with himself via the medium of overdubbing.

Strangely for such a good composition, it has only been covered a handful of times — most famously by the committed Berryite Steve Gibbons, who scored a UK 'Top Twenty' hit with it in 1977. (Gibbons also recorded an excellent Berry tribute, *Chuck In My Car*, about cruising and playing the radio with you-know-who blasting out over the airwaves.)

The saga of Johnny and Tulane continued on the other side of Berry's platter. In **Have Mercy Judge**, Johnny has to face the consequences of his nefarious "trafficking of the forbidden". Chuck sings this song with the conviction of the unjustly convicted, perhaps thinking of Judge George E. Moore when he hits the lines "Have mercy, I'm in a world of trouble", "I go to court tomorrow morning and I got the same judge I had before" and "He'll send me away to some stoney mansion in a lonely room and lock the door". By the end, Johnny is resigned to serving his time, and his thoughts inevitably turn to Tulane and her "needs" while he is away: "She's too alive to be left alone," he bemoans.

Have Mercy Judge is a straight-ahead blues supported by expressive wailing harmonica and one of Berry's best. The only known cover comes from onetime Animal Eric Burdon.

Next, Chuck's **Ding-A-Ling** pops up yet again — he just wouldn't let it lie, would he? The number was by now a staple of his live show and (excluding the Mercury *My Tambourine* cut) this is his only known studio recording of it. This unissued version was most likely recorded at the *Tulane* session as it has the same instrumentation. All the lines of the song are in place, but with no audience participation it comes across as what it essentially is: a silly little ditty. This particular reading is, however, interesting because it is very much in a country vein, played in waltz time with the band singing harmony on the chorus and the harp sounding at times like a mountain fiddle. Berry's guitar licks are also as country as hay seeds.

The unissued **That's None Of Your Business** turns out to be a variation of *It's My Own Business* which Chuck first recorded back in 1965. Unfortunately, it is inferior compared to the earlier cut, adding nothing musically or lyrically to the composition. Whereas the earlier song ran through a series of scenarios ending with Berry declaring "It's my own business", the sentiment is now more forceful and in effect tells 'them' to stay out of his face: "You ought to practise what you preach and leave other folks alone." However, it still remains his own business if he buys a Lincoln Continental Coupe or slurps his mashed potato soup. This hardening of attitude comes across particularly strongly in the vocal delivery, in which, if one didn't know better, the nasal nuances of Bob Dylan might be detected.

The **Unissued Instrumental** remains just that, unheard by these ears.

SESSION 56
CHUCK BERRY

Chuck Berry, vocal/guitar, unknown guitar -1; Robert Baldori, harmonica, overdubbed piano -2, unknown bass, unknown drums

Ter-Mar Recording Studios
320 East 21st Street
Chicago, Illinois   **27 April 1970**

18595	**Instrumental** -2 *(Chuck Berry)*	■ Chess LPS-1550
18596	**Christmas** -1 *(Chuck Berry)*	■ Chess LPS-1550
18597	**Gun** *[instrumental]* *(Chuck Berry)*	■ Chess LPS-1550
18598	**I'm A Rocker** -1 *(Chuck Berry)*	■ Chess LPS-1550
18599	**Flyin' Home** *[instrumental]* -2 *(Chuck Berry)*	■ Chess LPS-1550
18600	**Fish & Chips** -1 *(Chuck Berry)*	■ Chess LPS-1550
18601	**Some People** -1-2 *(Chuck Berry)*	■ Chess LPS-1550

This session, together with *Tulane* and *Have Mercy Judge*, formed the aptly-named Chess LP, *Back Home*. Unfortunately none of the seven cuts here approach the quality of the two tracks cut five months earlier. Despite the consecutive matrix numbers, the songs seem to divide themselves into two camps — those with piano and those without — and may well have been recorded over two sessions divided along these lines. The musicians sound very similar to those used on the *Tulane* date and all the cuts have the same thin harmonica sound. Narratively and musically very little new emerges from the session, just a rehash of Berry's patented licks and lyrics.

Three of the cuts are instrumentals. ***Instrumental*** (could this be the same track as listed in the previous session?) is a typical fast-rocking Berry boogie — virtually a backing track for *Tulane* — in which the archetypal Berry guitar, pounding piano and wailing harp all hit the breaks at the right time. Competent and totally acceptable but nothing new. The harmonica takes the lion's share of the lead, as it does on ***Gun***, a more measured composition, with the harp and guitar intertwining to produce a pleasant if hardly earth-shattering blues. Baldori's harp carries the melody as Chuck boogies along on the bass strings. The third instrumental, ***Flyin' Home***, turns out not to be the Goodman–Hampton standard, but a Berry original. The tune has the celebratory feel of Hamp's famous theme, but the strong melody — carried by the harmonica rather than guitar — is clearly Berry's own. Playing at a fast tempo, the guitar, harp and piano all gel together to create an exhilarating instrumental with a very distinctive melodic riff.

Christmas comes but once a year (what a shame for Santa!) and

This striking portrait of Chuck was used on the front cover of the 'Back Home' album and also for the rear of the follow-up, 'San Francisco Dues'.

that's also about the frequency with which you'd want to listen to this track.

There is precious little seasonal feel to the song which is a loping bluesy number featuring Berry's plaintive vocals and Little Junior Parker-style harmonica. Chuck spells out the pleasures to be had if his woman will spend the Yuletide with him, but it's all been done before and with more panache. One wonders if this is the same composition as the unissued *Spending Christmas* (a.k.a. *My Blue Christmas*) from 1964.

I'm A Rocker is another totally competent but again totally derivative Berry rock and roll composition. The mother of this progeny is *Reelin' And Rockin'*, as is indicated by the numerical sequence for each verse and the inclusion of several choice lines from this classic. Musically the band click, working up a good head of steam — but, as they say: 'Been there, heard it, done it all before'. Still, I love the sharp-edged 'clucking' guitar played by Berry over the boogie base. *I'm A Rocker* spawned a handful of covers, mainly of European origin. In the USA, George Thorogood's is probably the best-known cover, but in Europe it will be Slade's 1980 hit in the Benelux countries that will be remembered.

It's hard to decide if the lyrics of **Fish & Chips** are intentionally crass or just plain stupid. Perhaps the "little Coke" complementing the great British dish is not of the cola variety? More likely they are just stupid. This is a shame, because the instrumentation itself is rather interesting. The two guitars intertwine, creating a distinctly oriental flavour (*Prawn Balls & Chips?*) reminiscent of Robert Ward's Magnatone sound on early 60's cuts by the Ohio Untouchables like *I'm Tired* and *Forgive Me Darling*.

In **Some People**, Chuck chronicles the disparity between the rich and the poor, and places himself — without a hint of irony — in the 'have not' camp. The 'free love' hippie ethic is espoused as the better of the two conditions, a view so far from Mr. Berry's true philosophy as to be completely out of sight. The song is sung in short three- or four-word bursts punctuated by a harmonica squall at each pause, and closes with a layered instrumental passage of piano, harp, and guitars — probably the best thing about this uninspired cut.

SESSION 57
CHUCK BERRY
Chuck Berry, vocal/guitar; unknown accompaniment

Ter-Mar Recording Studios
320 East 21st Street
Chicago, Illinois   **circa July 1970**

18735	**My Pad**	unissued
	(Chuck Berry)	

My Pad hasn't been heard, so it is pure speculation that Chuck plays an instrument on the track (on the other hand, it could just as easily be an instrumental). One wonders if it could possibly be an early version of *My Dream*, recorded at the following session, which is about Chuck's dream abode?

SESSION 58
CHUCK BERRY
Chuck Berry, vocal/guitar, speech -1, piano -1; Robert Baldori, electric piano, harmonica -2; Jeffrey Baldori, guitar; Jack 'Zocko' Groendal, bass; Bill 'Bee' Metros, drums; Johnnie Johnson, overdubbed piano at a later date -3

Lansing Sound Studio
2719 Mt. Hope Road
Okemos, Michigan   **8-12 January 1971**

19112	**Oh Louisiana**	■ Chess CH-50008
	(Chuck Berry)	
19113	**Festival** -3	■ Chess CH-50008
	(Chuck Berry)	
19126	**Let's Do Our Thing Together**	■ Chess CH-50008
	(Chuck Berry)	
19127	**Your Lick** -2-3	■ Chess CH-50008
	(Chuck Berry)	
19128	**Bound To Lose**	■ Chess CH-50008
	(Chuck Berry)	
19129	**Bordeaux In My Pirough**	■ Chess CH-50008
	(Chuck Berry)	
19130	**San Francisco Dues**	■ Chess CH-50008
	(Chuck Berry)	
19131	**My Dream** *[poem]* -1	■ Chess CH-50008, CH6-80001
	(Chuck Berry)	

Chuck was no doubt pleased to be back in the bosom of Chess, but soon started to get disillusioned. The record company he returned to was not the one he had left. No longer was it a patriarchal dynasty run by the brothers

Chess, but a corporate business sold in January 1969 to GRT *[General Recorded Tape]* Corporation in return for a $6.5 million plus GRT company stock. Phil and Marshall Chess were initially retained in executive roles but Leonard's interest in the label was never to be the same and he died of a heart attack on 16th October 1969. The task of updating their ageing stars was given to Marshall Chess, who had been responsible for Muddy Waters's *Electric Mud* and Howlin' Wolf's *Electric Dogshit*.

Chuck recalls that the new owners would ship him about to various recording locations as it suited the executives' business. The man in charge of this particular recording session was Esmond Edwards, who mainly handled Chess's jazz product, but it is doubtful that he chose Lansing Sound. During the recording of *Back Home*, Chuck had struck a chord with Bob Baldori and had threatened to turn up one day to cut a session at his studio — which is likely how he came to spend five days in January 1971 cutting material with Baldori's group, the Woolies.

Berry had previously gigged around with the Woolies, who had scored a hit record in 1967 with a cover of Bo Diddley's surreal *Who Do You Love* and went on to record an extended two-sided 45 version of *Reelin' And Rockin'*. With Baldori and his partner Dean Breadwell handling the engineering, the scene was set for something special, and that is exactly what we get.

Chuck spent five days at the studio writing lyrics and recording with the band, and in this relaxed setting produced some of his best post-Mercury recordings to date. The masters he left Lansing with at the end of the week were later overdubbed with Johnnie Johnson's piano and possibly additional Berry guitar on some of the sides. His 'sound' was updated by sophisticated production techniques providing stereo separation, channel crossover, reverb and echo. The wah-wah guitar is played by Baldori's brother, Jeff alongside the more familiar-sounding Berry lead, while Bob Baldori himself contributes electric keyboards.

The tracks cut at this session became the *San Francisco Dues* LP — Berry's most cohesive album ever, despite the inclusion of *Viva Rock & Roll* and *Lonely School Days* from his last pre-Mercury Chess session in 1966 and the use of cover photographs left over from the previous year's *Back Home* album. The cover credits the 'Baldor' brothers rather than 'Baldori', but the latter is the correct spelling.

The first cut, **Oh Louisiana**, is a beaut: a deep, moody chant with intertwined guitar figures, supported by intricate bass lines and rippling keyboards. You can just *feel* the Spanish moss dripping from every note. Chuck sings the praises of Louisiana as though it were a beautiful woman, not simply a tract of land: "Your beautiful delta and valleys in green... oh Louisiana." The recurring travel theme occurs again, this time to escape a shattered relationship from the cold Yankee North to the bosom of the South, Louisiana. An excellent opening track making full use of the Lansing recording facilities.

In the late '60s and early '70s Chuck had developed his home base, Berry Park, into a country club resort and during this period he staged several rock festivals on the site. None, however, could come close to that conjured up for the song **Festival**.

The first verse sets the scene: duration, fourteen days; location, Paducah to Cairo along the banks of the Ohio; size, 54 bands playing to a million punters! The imaginary line-up of performers is formidable with "some of the greatest guitar-players in the Western Hemisphere". The rock roll-call is a veritable who's who including the Who, the Band, Canned Heat, the Grateful Dead, the Rolling Stones, Led Zeppelin and Vanilla Fudge. Berry's contemporaries are also included: Ike Turner, Ray Charles, the Drifters, the Coasters, Bo Diddley, Little Richard, Elvis Presley and his favourite duo, the Everly Brothers... but no Jerry Lee. "Old Brother Hendrix, Sister Joplin, we wish you were here," Chuck declares. "All night Howlin' Wolf and Muddy Waters in a battle of blues" (dream on brother, dream on!). In amongst the

great and the good, he finds space to mention his backing group, the Woolies.

Chuck's wish list is sung to a tight rocking track with plenty of typical Berry guitar and Johnnie Johnson's sparkling piano trips cutting through the wah-wah and electric keyboards.

Festival was featured in *National Lampoon's Class Reunion*, a chronic so-called comedy movie about a high school reunion with a mad killer on the prowl (Chuck sings *It Wasn't Me*, *My Ding-A-Ling* and *Festival* at the fraternity dance).

Next up is **Let's Do Our Thing Together**, a rocking little number with a throbbing guitar and piping electric piano undercurrent over which Chuck cuts a sharp, precise solo. The song is an invitation to his lady to get it on with him. "I'm not a blueblood or a scholar, just a hard-working boy," he explains, "and after five long days a body needs a little joy." Olé! Olé!

The puritanical bent regarding drink crops up again too, with: "I don't need no pills and whisky, don't indulge in beer or wine" and "I am solid, sane and sober, and I'm over twenty-one." In fact, all he needs is to "dig you doing your thing" and he'll "turn you on when I do mine!"

In three short verses Chuck gets his message across and promptly closes the thing down. No point in wasting energy needed for other activities!

Your Lick is a near-instrumental based on a sexy harmonica riff played over a moody groove. The tune is a development of the *Feelin' It* theme from the '67 Fillmore gig. The wah-wah guitar is rested and perhaps it is Jeff Baldori who plays the minimal but effective harp in its place. It is possible that the eccentric guitar lick was an echo of that played by Hubert Sumlin, Howlin' Wolf's long-suffering guitarist on Wolf's 1964 killer cut, *Killing Floor*. To heighten the intimacy, Chuck interjects "What are you doing?", "Oh wow!", "Yeah!" and other vocal utterances that make one wonder whether "your lick" is purely a musical term.

The weakest cut of the session is **Bound To Lose** a meandering country type of song with hardly any discernible melody and little in the way of memorable lyrical content or vocal delivery. A loser.

Bordeaux In My Pirough once again illustrates Chuck's penchant for country tunes. This Berry 'original' is essentially Hank Williams's *Jambalaya (On The Bayou)* with new lyrics, and not even these are totally original.

Hank sings: "Goodbye Joe, me got to go, me-oh my-oh/ Me got to go pull the pirough down the bayou"; Chuck sings: "So long Jean, me got to go, me-oh my-oh/ Me got to go push my pirough down the bayou." Hank Williams was to country music songwriting what Chuck Berry was to rock and roll, but both masters of metre struggled to extend the bayou–pirough–Bordeaux rhyme: where Hank resorted to "gay-o", Chuck contents himself with "guitar-o"!

The story in *Bordeaux In My Pirough* is also a secondhand theme, being a tale of drinking and missing the boat as happened back in Havana many moons ago. The wah-wah guitar on this cut is really over the top, sounding like 'Sparky's magic piano plays the *Grand Ole Opry*'. (Incidentally, the 'Jean' to whom Chuck bids farewell is thought to be Jean-Pierre Ravelli, a fan Chuck first met in Paris in 1964. Ravelli showed him some Parisian nightlife and from then on their friendship grew into a lifelong relationship — a rare occurrence considering Berry's well-known reclusiveness.)

San Francisco Dues is another very effective number, immaculately executed by Chuck and the Woolies. The tune is a timeless blues reminiscent of numerous Berry blues, but the vocal phrasing is particularly redolent of *Have Mercy Judge*. Chuck, it must be said, had something of a fixation with the Golden Gate City, referring to it in several songs, and in this number he sings of the relaxed atmosphere in this most European of American cities. A great number and a worthy title song for the album, it is also notable as one of the few occasions where Berry does not take the lead opening guitar figure.

My Dream is a six-minute tone poem recited over a background of bass, guitar and drums well down in the mix, overlaid with Chuck's own free-form piano playing which, whilst not played on an "upright piano with pure ivory keys" is "surely improvised".

This is a rare instance of Berry at the piano. He can be seen at the keyboard rattling out a boogie in the 1959 movie *Go, Johnny, Go!* and in the late seventies was heard playing piano versions of *Johnny B. Goode*, *Worried Life Blues* and *Wee Baby Blues* on German radio, providing a fascinating insight into his musicality. Of course, his skills in this area are limited, and at one point he hits a wrong key but manages to retrieve the situation with some jazzy, free-form sleight of hand.

Berry's ability as a poet is to the fore here, and he also draws upon his carpentry experience with his father to describe his dream home with a roof "with peak lines and contours that dip to form shadowy eaves". His descriptions of "raindrops at play", "storm gods racing across the sky" and "roses heavy with dew" conjure up images of those wonderful forties' Disney cartoons. The poem is imbued with a sad melancholy which is explained towards the end when Chuck reveals that all these material dreams are meaningless without his "angel" to share them with. Sheer brilliance.

SESSION 59
CHUCK BERRY

Chuck Berry, vocal/guitar; Owen McIntyre, guitar; Dave Kaffinetti, piano; Nic Potter, bass; Robbie McIntosh, drums; piano/bass/drums (omitted -1); original piano/bass/drums probably omitted and replaced with unknown piano/bass/drums in New York City -2

LIVE RECORDINGS
Lanchester Arts Festival
Locarno Ballroom
Smithford Way
Coventry, England   **3 February 1972**

	Roll Over Beethoven *(Chuck Berry)*	unissued
	School Day *(Chuck Berry)*	unissued
	Back In The USA *(Chuck Berry)*	unissued
	Maybellene *(Chuck Berry)*	unissued
	Around And Around *(Chuck Berry)*	unissued
CH2223	**Roll 'Em Pete** -2 *(Joe Turner, Pete Johnson)*	⊙ Chess CH-2140**b**, Bellaphon BF-18214**b**
	It Hurts Me Too *(Hudson Whittaker)*	unissued
	Sweet Little Sixteen *(Chuck Berry)*	unissued
	Nadine *(Chuck Berry)*	unissued
CH2227	**Reelin' And Rockin'** *(Chuck Berry)*	⊙ Chess CH-2136†**a** ■ Chess CH-60020, CH6-80001
CH2228 (2028E*)	**My Ding-A-Ling** -1 *(Dave Bartholomew, Chuck Berry)*	⊙ Chess CH-2131*†**a**, 6145 019**a** ■ Chess CH-60020, CH6-80001†
E2229 (2029E*)	**Johnny B. Goode** *(Chuck Berry)*	⊙ Chess CH-2131*†**b** ■ Chess CH-60020, CH6-80001

† Edited version

1972, and in England there is an undercurrent resurgence in real rock and roll: the music hadn't died, it had only been resting between gigs. The organisers of the Coventry University *Lanchester Arts Festival* were hip to the trick and as part of the fest they booked the most dynamic of the original rockers, the merry Mr. Berry, for an exclusive one-off date. His last visit to the UK had been in 1967, when he played Brian Epstein's Saville Theatre in London. The concert had ended in a fracas when some jobsworth prematurely dropped the safety curtain, so there was quite an anticipatory buzz about.

The location was the Locarno Ballroom in the centre of Coventry (now the public library), where two concerts were scheduled for that Thursday evening — the first headlined by Chuck, the second by the Pink Floyd. The line-up for the former included Uncle Dirty, a middle-aged comedian of dubious character, Billy Preston (of *Get Back* fame), Slade (latterly of Cupa-Soup fame) and the Roy Young Band (a Scottish group of no fame whatsoever). The rhythm section of Young's band plus former Rare Bird pianist Dave Kaffinetti provided the backing for Chuck. Owen 'Onnie' McIntyre and Robbie McIntosh later found international success as members of the blue-eyed soul outfit, the Average White Band (short-lived success in the case of McIntosh, who died from a heroin overdose in 1974).

Like all good concerts, the show was not running to time and Young's ego was such that he over-ran his allotted slot, which meant that by the time Chuck hit the stage he was a good hour-and-a-half late. However, on this night the band was hot, Chuck was hotter and the crowd were steaming, waiting to hear the message from their rock and roll guru — and there can be no doubt whatsoever that they got what they desired.

Berry hit the boards with *Roll Over Beethoven* and immediately realised something special was going down — the audience knew his songs backwards and forwards, and were singing them to *him*! He played, they sang, unholy boogie communion was consummated.

Fortunately for posterity — and Chuck's career — Chess executive producer Esmond Edwards had arranged for the Pye mobile recording unit to be on hand and capture the entire event on tape. Apparently it recorded poorly (maybe the crowd sang too loudly?) and at one point the microphone blew causing Chuck to play a blues instrumental while it was being fixed. However, on the evidence of the three cuts that formed the second side of *The London Chuck Berry Sessions* LP, the audio quality is perfectly acceptable and perhaps one day, when MCA/Universal tire of reissuing Chuck Berry's greatest hits for the umpteenth time, they will do the decent thing.

Of course, it is the infamous **My Ding-A-Ling** that is remembered from the gig. Released as a single, it sold a couple of million, gave Berry an international chart-topper on both sides of the Atlantic and revitalised his career for at least another ten years. Much scorn has been dumped from a great height on this recording by music pundits (one prominent female blues reviewer referred to it as Chuck's 'limp ding' — ouch, they sure know how to hit a guy where it hurts!) and fans, as well as by self-appointed upholders of public morals led by the righteous Mrs. Mary Whitehouse.

Would this have happened had it not been such a huge hit? I think not, because where were the condemnations of the earlier versions? What makes *My Ding-A-Ling* so memorable isn't so much Chuck's performance — good as it is, honed to perfection after years of practice — but the reaction of the audience, who were really up for it, which makes the recording a truly remarkable artefact of the common man. This cannot be denied no matter whatever your musical or moral stance.

Throughout the near-twelve minutes Berry instructs, taunts and cajoles his congregation to sing (not that they need much persuasion) and eventually has them eating out of his hand, so that by the end not a single one of them is "playing with their own ding-a-ling."

For the single, Chuck's long 'Ding' was pared down to a more user-friendly four minutes sixteen seconds of salaciousness by removing the "there's nothing wrong with sex, it's just the way you handle it" preamble and some of the lewder passages (did Mrs. Whitehouse ever hear *these*, one wonders?).

Upon its release in the USA, the single shot to the top of the *Billboard*

and *Cash Box* pop charts in August 1972 with none of the moral backlash experienced in the UK, and even inspired an 'answer' record by a certain Miss Chuckle Cherry called *My Pussycat*. Say no more!

By November 1972, it was also No. 1 in the UK, doubtless helped by somehow avoiding a BBC airplay ban. As the top-selling single in the country, *My Ding-A-Ling* was featured several times on the Beeb's prime time TV show, *Top Of The Pops*, while a still photograph of Chuck was displayed on screen (it would have been impossible for him either to mime to the recording or re-create it live in the studio, as was customary at the time).

It has been postulated that the guitar, drums and bass on *My Ding-A-Ling* were over-dubbed later. This is clearly not the case, because the song is sung by Chuck to his own guitar accompaniment and a chorus of two thousand like-minded raunchy souls. A contemporary report of the concert states that Chuck sang the song *a cappella*, but I also doubt that his guitar was overdubbed because the recording contains feedback and Berry himself refers to having his hands full holding his plectrum.

This "fourth grade ditty", as Chuck describes it, had been in his repertoire for at least five years. With this recording it finally came together and paid dividends beyond his highest expectations. Musically it is nothing, but as a record of a spontaneous happening it is priceless. Admittedly, it sits rather uneasily alongside his classic songs on the numerous 'Greatest Hits' packages, but in its own right it is a classic of the dirty ditty genre.

Speaking of dirty ditties, *My Ding-A-Ling* was preceded on this occasion by the raunchiest version of **Reelin' and Rockin'** yet heard — not just the ripest, but also the hardest-rocking treatment of the number to date (Chuck has referred to this version as "*Rockin' and Reelin'*", but it has never been titled in this way to my knowledge). With such class lines as: "Looked at my watch and it was a little past six/ Man, I jumped back firm like a ce-ment mix" and "Looked at my watch and it was quarter to eight/ She made a little move which made me stretch out straight" it's no wonder the prudes were baying for blood!

Reelin' And Rockin' was released as a follow-up to *My Ding-A-Ling* and likewise made the best seller lists on both sides of the Atlantic: No. 27 in the *Billboard* 'Hot 100', No. 30 in the *Cash Box* 'Top 100' and No. 18 in the UK 'Top Fifty'. For the 45, three minutes were chopped out of the album cut by omitting the two guitar solos and two stanzas where Chuck duplicates the same time frame (including the ce-ment line) and the rather distasteful "We boogied in the kitchen, we boogied in the hall/ I got some on my finger so I wiped it on the wall" couplet. This editing tightens up the performance and improves the recording, even though it does lose the ce-ment from the mix.

Having fired the crowd up to fever pitch, Chuck applies the *coup de grace* when he hits *that* intro. He hardly needs to sing the words of **Johnny B. Goode** — two thousand people in the audience do it for him! In fact, it is *Johnny B. Goode's* sequel, *Bye Bye Johnny*, that Berry kicks off with, but when his followers cut in with the "Go Johnny go" refrain he reverts to the original. No-one notices and no-one cares, all they want is more of that famous boogie beat. Just listen to the roar during the guitar break as he duckwalks and ambulates across the stage. They want more and, of course, he leaves them wanting — in the arms of the management if some reports are to be believed, virtually strong-armed off the stage, having over-run his allocated time with another concert waiting in the wings.

The throng go frantic, chanting: "We want Chuck! We want Chuck!"

Ted Little, the MC, tries to cool things down, advising that there are two thousand people waiting outside the door.

"We want Chuck! We want Chuck!"

"If you want to see the Pink Floyd..."

Fuck the Floyd: "We want Chuck!"

Enter the patronising management: "Hold it kids — thirty seconds, that's all I ask..."

"We want Chuck! We want Chuck..."

But, of course, Chuck was gone like a shadow in the night, and was probably already "down the road apiece" even before the chant had died down.

With the exception of **Roll 'Em Pete**, the remaining titles from this extraordinary concert remain in the can, which is more than a pity: it's a crying shame, no matter what the quality of the recording. *Roll 'Em Pete* itself didn't make the *London Sessions* album but slipped out quietly in 1973 as the 'B' side of the US *Bio* single [Chess CH-2140] and its West German equivalent [Bellaphon BF-18214]. It has yet to appear on CD: Charly missed it off their 1992 (almost) comprehensive *Chess Years* 9-CD box set.

Berry's *Roll 'Em Pete* is an approximation of Big Joe Turner's 1938 waxing, with Chuck singing half-remembered lyrics to a *Reelin' And Rockin'*-type melody rather than the original tune. It is perhaps unfair to compare this scratch rendition with Turner's *tour de force*, as the latter became something of a theme song that Big Joe recorded at least eight times during his long and illustrious career. The 'Pete' in *Roll 'Em Pete* is Joe's piano-pounding pardner Pete Johnson, who constituted one third of the Boogie Woogie Trio with Meade Lux Lewis and Albert Ammons. In the late thirties and early forties this corpulent threesome virtually defined the boogie woogie piano style, but Johnson's playing on the '38 version of *Roll 'Em Pete* has never been bettered. Much of the exuberance and excitement of these early boogie masters was transformed via forties' R&B combos led by the likes of Amos Milburn and

Floyd Dixon into rock and roll. Chuck was, of course, more than a little influenced by these piano boogie rhythms and successfully transferred them to his red-hot Gibson.

It has been stated that the contributions of the musicians on *Roll 'Em Pete* were wiped and overdubbed by studio musicians in New York City. Comparing the ambience of this cut with the other released songs from the Coventry gig, this assertion is probably correct.

The remaining titles were mentioned in contemporary reports of this memorable concert (don't you wish you'd been there?) and, sadly, all remain unissued.

SESSION 60
CHUCK BERRY
Chuck Berry, vocal/guitar; Derek Griffiths, guitar; Rick Grech, bass; Ian McLagan, piano; Kenny Jones, drums

Pye Studio No. 2
Cumberland Place
London, England   5 February 1972

CH2230	**Let's Boogie** *(Chuck Berry)*	⊙ Chess CH-2136**b**, 6145 019**b** ■ Chess CH-60020
CH2231	**Mean Old World** *(Aaron 'T-Bone' Walker)*	■ Chess CH-60020
CH2232	**I Love You** *(Chuck Berry)*	■ Chess CH-60020
CH2233	**I Will Not Let You Go** *(Chuck Berry)*	■ Chess CH-60020
CH2234	**London Berry Blues** *[instrumental]* *(Chuck Berry)*	■ Chess CH-60020 ◎ Official 4012-FS

The plan had been to record a whole album's-worth of songs at the *Lanchester Arts Festival* for release as *Chuck Berry Live At Coventry* but circumstance, in the form of poor recording quality, did not permit this. However, contingency plans had also been made and, two days after the Coventry happening, Chuck was in the Pye Studio in London cutting the five tracks that would go to make up Side One of what was to become his most commercially successful album ever (forty-seven weeks on *Billboard's* 'Top LPs' chart make it so by far).

To put the decoration on the cake, the backing musicians chosen were, if not the icing, at least the marzipan of British rock. Producer Bob Scerbo gathered together Ian McLagan and Kenny Jones who had played their way through the Small Faces and then the Faces, Rick Grech, a survivor of the 'supergroups' Blind Faith and Traffic who had also played with Muddy Waters on his *London Sessions* the previous December, and Derek Griffiths, who began his career in the 1960s with the commercially unsuccessful Artwoods but later achieved success in the '70s with Argent.

The gig was a back-to-basics, no overdubs, no wah-wah guitar, no fancy electronics, live-in-the-studio session. Straight-ahead rock'n'roll, with the stress on the 'rock', plus a big slice of blues. Five tracks — one side of an album and two 'B' sides (*I Will Not Let You Go* ended up as the flip of the *Reelin' And Rockin'* single in the UK) — all laid to rest in five hours on a wet February afternoon. The sound places an emphasis on heavy bass and drums with Berry's guitar and vocals sounding good. The piano is tasteful but subdued, while Griffiths's guitar is barely audible on some tracks.

Of the five tracks, **Lets Boogie** is the least cohesive and perhaps it took this cut to get it together. It does sound suspiciously like a sequel to *Lets Do Our Thing Together* as, to that old *Memphis* beat, Chuck entices his partner to "boogie woogie".

Still from 'Let The Good Times Roll'.

As ever, Mr. B is up for it: "I wouldn't walk a block, but I'd dance a mile," he sings. Of course, it is not entirely clear if he wants to dance or "ball awhile": "You gonna feel my hands all around you, not a finger will you miss." Take it as it suits you.

Chuck Berry is a closet bluesman who loved to sing 'em the way he felt 'em — particularly standards such as *Worried Life Blues*, *It Hurts Me Too*, *Everyday I Have The Blues* and **Mean Old World**, which he had previously recorded at Chess in 1963 (but which to this day remains unissued).

The song originated with his guitar idol, T-Bone Walker, who cut it in 1942, 1945 and again in 1956, but it is surely Little Walter's version that is the closest to Chuck's heart. The wayward Chicago harmonica ace was also something of an influence on Berry, who cut several of his songs including *I Got To Find My Baby*, *My Babe* and *Key To The Highway*. Here, Chuck chooses Walter's grittier line, "Can't get the one you loving, have to use somebody else" in preference to 'Bone's "When you can't get the woman you love, then you know she's loving someone else." In actual fact, he sings three verses, two of which are from Walter's rendition of *Mean Old World* and the third from his introspective *Last Night*. At almost six minutes with only three verses, the band has the chance to stretch out — and stretch they do with

Berry playing an expressive break, combining well with piano and drums.

The best cut of the date is *I Love You*, a superb hard-rocking number with a churning beat, great drumming and fine guitar, economical and sharp. The song has echoes of the earlier *I Love Her, I Love Her*, but is far more earthy. The lyrics may not say much beyond "I love you", but they are sung with real commitment and expression. An altogether compelling track that deserves to be recognised as such.

I Will Not Let You Go starts off with the tune of the old spiritual/protest song, *We Shall Not Be Moved*, set to a heavy rocking beat but quickly metamorphoses into a secular plea of — and demand for — fidelity. Berry sings his heart out: "I'm tied to you with chains of love and I can't let you go," and burns up the strings of his Gibson with the determination of a desperate man. It's the shortest song of the session: no time is wasted getting the message across, and not a single note is wasted getting it there.

London Berry Blues is an almost-six-minute rocking blues instrumental workout in which Chuck employs his entire trick bag of licks. The rock-hard drum and bass pattern is almost heavy metal in places but, unlike most songs of this genre, the cut retains subtlety and dynamics and is not restricted in a full metal jacket. The backing musicians allow Chuck free flow to lead them where he may and he takes full advantage of the opportunity, dropping the tempo and volume at one point to a whisper before resurrecting it for a final fling in the dying moments of the track. It sounds like the whole band were thoroughly enjoying this end-of-session romp, and I'll bet there were wide grins all round as the closing notes faded.

SESSION 61
JOHN LENNON
John Lennon, vocal/guitar; Chuck Berry, vocal/guitar; Yoko Ono vocal/bongos; Wayne 'Tex' Gabriel, guitar; Gary Van Scyoc, bass; Adam Ippolito, piano; Stan Bronstein, tenor saxophone/tambourine -1; Jerry Rubin, bongos; Richard Frank Jr, drums; John Lennon and Mike Douglas, introductions

LIVE RECORDINGS
The Mike Douglas Show (WBC-TV/CBS)
Westinghouse TV Studio
Philadelphia, Pennsylvania   **3 February 1972**

Memphis Tennessee -1 (Chuck Berry)	■ Trade Mark of Quality TMQ-71046
Johnny B. Goode (Chuck Berry)	■ Trade Mark of Quality TMQ-71046

Note: TMQ-71046 is a bootleg record. These tracks are also included on bootleg LPs *Telecasts* [Trade Mark of Quality TMOQJL-517], *Telecasts* [Contraband Music CBM-3711], *Lennon with Berry and Hendrix* [Gun 062-11506] and *Working Class Hero* [Chet Mar Records CMR-75].

"If you ever tried to try and give rock and roll another name you might call it 'Chuck Berry'. Right! In the 1950s a whole generation worshipped his music and when you see him perform today, past and present all come together and the message is 'Hail, hail rock and roll' — right on!"

This is how John Lennon, nervously reading from an autocue, introduced Chuck Berry on Mike Douglas's afternoon chat show. Lennon, even more so than the other three Beatles, was a stone Berry fan (it was nearly always he who sang the Berry covers with the group) and to have his hero on a TV show that he was co-hosting was one big thing.

Having confessed his admiration for Chuck earlier on in the show ("I think he's the greatest. I really love him. It's an honour to be here today backing him."), Lennon went on to enthuse: "He's the greatest rock'n'roll poet. When I hear rock — good rock of the calibre of Chuck Berry — I just fall apart and have no other interest in life. The world could be ending if rock'n'roll's playing. It's a disease of mine." Praise indeed from one of the world's most renowned songwriters. Even when speaking to reporters after the show he could still barely contain his excitement: "It was worth it just to be with Chuck Berry. Man, it was just *worth* it!"

Lennon and his permanent partner Yoko Ono were at this time fighting hard to obtain his US citizenship, whilst simultaneously lobbying hard for most things from world peace to vegetable rights. They were temporarily resident in New York City and from 31st January to 4th February 1972, pre-recorded five shows as co-hosts of the *Mike Douglas Show* in nearby Philadelphia. The shows were aired a fortnight later between 4:30 and 6:30 pm (Douglas's usual slot) on the Westinghouse Broadcasting Corporation's network — a week that Douglas later confessed was one of the most difficult for him to deal with on account of the strange set of militants and misfits the couple chose as guests: Jerry Rubin, anti-Vietnam activist; Bobby Seale, co-founder with Huey Newton of the Black Panthers, George Carlin, counter-culture comedian; Ralph Nader, consumer protection thorn-in-the-side of corporate business, and the Chambers Brothers, West Coast blues brothers. On the strength of the interview with Chuck, it seems that Douglas was ill prepared, asking stupid questions mainly about a concert he had attended that meant little to the others.

Day three, Wednesday 16th February, was reserved for Chuck Berry. Both Lennon and Berry had played the *Toronto Peace Festival* gig in 1969, but apparently Chuck had split before the Plastic Ono Band arrived, so this was actually the first time the two giants of popular music had met.

After an effusive introduction from John, Chuck strides up to the mike and immediately hits the boogie chords of **Memphis Tennessee**. Toe-to-toe and nose-to-nose, the pair belt out the song, and it immediately becomes clear that the number is completely unrehearsed (perhaps it was considered unnecessary). John fluffs the lines and is thrown off-balance when Chuck exclaims: "Hello John!" midway through the song. The ending is a bit raggedy too, but otherwise Elephant's Memory, Lennon's backing group at the time, cope well under the circumstances. (Between 1969 and 1974 these guys recorded five albums under their own name, played on the Lennon albums *Somewhere In New York City* and *Approximately Infinite Universe,* and later backed Chuck on his *Bio* LP.)

However, also in the line-up was John's better half, Yoko Ono (or should that be Yoko Oh-no?), who, together with Jerry Rubin potters about on bongos. This would be innocuous enough, but things take a turn for the worse when she bends to the mike and commences to caterwaul in the worst possible taste. As the noise cuts in, is that a roll of Berry's eyes I detect? He's kicked better men (Richards and Rebennack for starters) off the stage for less. John really should have told her that the avant-garde and rock and roll just do not mix. Baggism should have been the order of the day for Yoko when John and Chuck played.

After *Memphis*, Chuck, John and Yoko join Mike Douglas for a short interview in which much backslapping occurs, John clearly wanting the world to know of his admiration and love for Berry's music. Unfortunately, he lets himself down by forgetting the title of *I Got To Find My Baby*, which he claims is a big band number. Two saxophones and an additional guitar do not constitute a 'big band'. Too much *'Lucy In The Sky With Diamonds'* seems to have taken its effect! Just as John cites Chuck as a great influence, Chuck, in response to the inane statement that he invented rock and roll, cites Louis Jordan, T-Bone Walker, Freddie Slack, Glenn Miller and the big bands as those who 'intrigued' him.

Following this rather vacuous interlude the trio return to the bandstand: John first, eager to strike another chord with his idol; Chuck, ever the ladies' man, escorting Yoko back.

"Johnny," poses Chuck.

"Yeah?" John replies.

"Let's be good."

Good? Well, maybe, but not *that* good. On *Memphis*, they sang in duet, with John's flat vowels making Chuck's sound round and fruity. Here on **Johnny B. Goode**, Chuck sings the verses with the Ono-Lennons joining in on the "Go, Johnny, go's" Thankfully Yoko is inaudible (maybe after her performance on the first song the producer switched off her microphone?) Chuck cuts a rug, duckwalking and body-popping as far as the short guitar lead will allow, but when he offers John the guitar break, he proves why he played rhythm for the Beatles. For such an historic meeting, it is sad that the music doesn't live up to the occasion.

Chuck later joins John and Yoko in a macrobiotic cookery demonstration given by another cooky guest, Hilary Redleaf.

The two songs and the now-famous Lennon introductory quote (a snatch of which appears at the start of the film, *Hail! Hail! Rock'n'Roll*) have been issued on at least four bootleg LPs catering for Beatles collectors. The first was the Trade Mark Of Quality album (a misnomer if ever there was one!) titled *Telecasts*. In the USA, a videotape of the show was issued by Rhino in 1998 as part of a five-tape box set of all the Lennon Mike Douglas shows, and more recently as a single tape of Day Three.

The meeting with Chuck must have still been fresh in the ex-Beatle's mind a month later when he cut an impromptu version of *Roll Over Beethoven* at one of his recording sessions. In the event, this was never released. However, his version of *Brown Eyed Handsome Man,* which was recorded around the same time, later appeared on *The Lost Lennon Tapes.*

SESSION 62
CHUCK BERRY
Chuck Berry, vocal/guitar; Mick Snow, piano; Jimmy Campbell, guitar; Billy Kinsley, bass; Dave Harrison, drums

LIVE RECORDINGS
Sounds For Saturday (BBC2)
BBC Television Theatre
Shepherds Bush Green
Shepherds Bush
London, England 29 March 1972

Roll Over Beethoven
(Chuck Berry)
■ Driving Wheel LP-1001 ◎ Archivio ARC CD-001, Newsound/Penny PYCD-260, Wolf 2010CD

Sweet Little Sixteen
(Chuck Berry)
■ Driving Wheel LP-1001 ◎ Archivio ARC CD-001, Newsound/Penny PYCD-260, Wolf 2010CD

Memphis (Tennessee)
(Chuck Berry)
■ Driving Wheel LP-1001 ◎ Archivio ARC CD-001, Newsound/Penny PYCD-260, Wolf 2010CD

South Of The Border
(Jimmy Kennedy, Michael Carr, Chuck Berry)
● Chess 6145 027**a** ■ Driving Wheel LP-1001, Checkmate LP-1955 ◎ Archivio ARC CD-001, Newsound/ Penny PYCD-260, Wolf 2010CD

Beer Drinking Woman
(Peter Chatman)
■ Driving Wheel LP-1001 ◎ Archivio ARC CD-001, Newsound/Penny PYCD-260, Wolf 2010CD

Let It Rock
(E. Anderson)
■ Driving Wheel LP-1001 ◎ Archivio ARC CD-001, Newsound/Penny PYCD-260, Wolf 2010CD

Mean Old World
(Aaron 'T-Bone' Walker)
■ Driving Wheel LP-1001 ◎ Archivio ARC CD-001, Newsound/Penny PYCD-260, Wolf 2010CD, MasterTone 0301

Carol
(Chuck Berry)
■ Driving Wheel LP-1001 ◎ Archivio ARC CD-001, Newsound/Penny PYCD-260, Wolf 2010CD

Liverpool Drive *[instrumental]*
(Chuck Berry)
■ Driving Wheel LP-1001 ◎ Archivio ARC CD-001, Newsound/Penny PYCD-260, Wolf 2010CD

My Ding-A-Ling *(Dave Bartholomew, Chuck Berry)*	unissued
Nadine *(Chuck Berry)*	■ Driving Wheel LP-1001 ◉ Archivio ARC CD-001, Newsound/Penny PYCD-260, Wolf 2010CD
School Day *(Chuck Berry)*	unissued
Too Much Monkey Business *(Chuck Berry)*	unissued
Rock And Roll Music *(Chuck Berry)*	unissued
Promised Land *(Chuck Berry)*	unissued
Reelin' And Rockin' *(Chuck Berry)*	unissued
Bye Bye Johnny *(Chuck Berry)*	■ Driving Wheel LP-1001 ◉ Archivio ARC CD-001, Newsound/Penny PYCD-260, Wolf 2010CD
Bonsoir Cherie / Johnny B. Goode *(Chuck Berry)*	■ Driving Wheel LP-1001 ◉ Archivio ARC CD-001, Newsound/Penny PYCD-260

In the early 1970s, the BBC were starting to develop colour TV and broadcast programmes in colour on their 'minority' channel, BBC2. To receive these colour transmissions, viewers needed the new generation of television sets with 625 lines instead of the old monochrome 405 line boxes.

Returning to the UK just one month after his landmark Coventry gig, Chuck was filmed in glorious colour for an episode of the BBC2 *Sounds For Saturday*, the soundtrack of which was quickly bootlegged on an album appropriately called *Six Two Five*. Cut from the BBC tape, it was issued in coloured vinyl on Driving Wheel 1001 and subsequently on Mabellene *[sic]* MBL-676. Much later, in 1991, it surfaced again on the Italian Archivio CD complete with pops and crackles from the vinyl, and later still on Newsound/Penny and Wolf. So, you see, little fleas have littler fleas!

The recording was made at the BBC Television Theatre in Shepherds Bush, London, and was first broadcast on 22nd July 1972, then again in a shortened form on 4th January 1973 — just as Chuck's engorged *Ding-A-Ling* was ousted from the No. 1 spot by Little Jimmy Osmond, the long-haired lover from Salt Lake City. The footage still exists because a snippet was recently shown on BBC2's *Top Of The Pops 2* when acknowledging Berry's 70th birthday.

Taking full advantage of the colour recording, Chuck, sporting long slicked back hair, mutton-chop sideburns, pencil-thin moustache with a hipster semi-goatee lower lip growth, is decked out in his '70s trademark multi-coloured, crazy paisley psychedelic shirt, royal blue velvet strides, white belt and stars-and-stripes red and white shoes which he cannot resist mentioning in **Roll Over Beethoven**. While his sartorial style may occasionally leave something to be desired, his taste in guitars cannot be faulted: the axe he wields with unfettered abandon is a top-of-the-range, semi-solid, deluxe Gibson ES-355TD in cherry wood, its twin 'f' holes and body edges picked out with cream inlay.

The recently-shown clip is an edit of **Bye Bye Johnny** and **Johnny B. Goode** spliced together. Now, wouldn't it be nice if someone at BBC Enterprises had showed a little and resurrected this gem from the vaults in its entirety?

The unissued tracks are listed in the same order as they appear in the sleevenote of the Driving Wheel album, except where the dialogue on the released tracks indicates a different running order. For instance, at the end of **Liverpool Drive**, Chuck leads into "We must do our alma mater" indicating that his 'greatest hit' was next.

Berry's backing group, Rockin' Horse, included the original bassist and vocalist of the Merseybeats, Billy Kinsley, who told me that the band accompanied Chuck on a European tour at the time this recording was made. As well as the BBC show, Chuck also appeared on German TV and, when he found out that Billy could sing, he would get him to vocalise with him on stage on songs like *Back In The USA*.

The setting for the show was a small stage with a politely subdued audience 'in the round', creating an intimate, comfortable ambience. The group lays down a solid backing on which Chuck can cruise with confidence. Perhaps the drummer drags a little rather than propelling the beat, but piano-

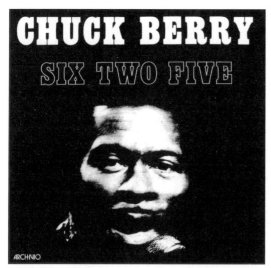

man Mick Snow makes up for any deficit with a fine rolling performance. Chuck is relaxed and at ease, joking with the audience ("We thought we'd open with one of the Beatles' numbers," he quips at the close of *Roll Over Beethoven*), explaining the origins of **Sweet Little Sixteen**, and thanking them for their response ("Sounds like one of those groovy festivals").

All the hits are present, including notable extended workouts of **Memphis** and **Let It Rock**, but as usual it is the unusual songs which catch the attention. The Archivio CD nonchalantly proclaims *'All songs by Chuck Berry'* but three of them in fact have a different provenance.

South Of The Border has the distinction of being the only cut from this session to receive a legitimate release — as the 'A' side of UK Chess single 6145 027. This was a 1973 follow-up (missed off the Charly 'complete' *Chess Years* box) to Chuck's two chart successes, *My Ding-A-Ling* and *Reelin' And Rockin'*, and the company presumably hoped for a repeat success with this risqué little number. On the 45, the song is credited to *'J. Kennedy/M. Carr.*

Additional lyrics by Chuck Berry'.

South Of The Border (Down Mexico Way), to give it its full title, was written by Jimmy Kennedy and Michael Carr in 1939, when it was a best-seller for Shep Fields & His Rippling Rhythm. More significantly, however, it was Gene Autry, the singing cowpoke, who brought it to true prominence a year later. The song quickly became a standard, straddling both the popular and country catalogues with covers by Bob Wills, Patsy Cline, Carl Mann, Frank Sinatra, Al Bowlly and not forgetting Blackpool's finest, Reginald Dixon, at the mighty Tower Ballroom organ.

Chuck's version turns a lament for a dusky señorita down Mexico way into an amusing tale of deceit and retribution where a travelling salesman, cuckolded by some "jerk from Albuquerq" who plays with his wife south of *her* border, gets his come-uppance: "I shot him right between his Rio Grande and his Santa Fe!" This two-minute ditty contains more wit and wisdom than a dozen extended *My Ding-A-Lings* ever would. It is clearly a song Chuck nurtured, because he was to return to it in a later studio recording.

Beer Drinking Woman, a blues composed and recorded in 1940 by Peter Chatman — alias pianist Memphis Slim — is not without wit itself, being about a lady with an enormous capacity for quaffing the 'amber nectar'. In a typical Berryism, Chuck sings "She was the beer drinkinest woman, don't you know." In fact, true to form, he Berryfies the song to suit his nature, using only the opening verse from Slim's song *in toto*. In recognition of the London location, Slim's beer tavern becomes an English 'beer pub'. He adapts a verse of Slim's to produce: "She said: Daddy won't you excuse me, I want to go back there/ When I come back to the table, I'll have more room for another beer" — a familiar scenario from the 1972 version of *Reelin' And Rockin'*. In the end, he advises the beer-drinking woman "to go way back up in the country, way beyond Leeds" because he's tired of her criticising London. Who knows, maybe she prefers Tetley's to Fuller's? Amidst all this froth we are treated to an extended piano solo as smooth and full of body as a pint of Boddington's.

Prefacing the seven-minute thirty-seven second version of **Mean Old World** are instructions on how to pronounce blues ("not blews, but blooooze") followed by a rambling monologue: "Into each life a little rain must fall. Quite a bit *[a veritable downpour]* has fallen into mine... makes one's heart melancholy... turns their attention to the blues, way over across the railroad track. Some of you have never been. Did I say 'been'? *[instead of 'bin']* It's catching, isn't it?"

The first verses follow Berry's previous rendition, after which he dips into Jimmy Reed's songbook for some well-worn floating blues lines from *You Don't Have To Go* and *Baby What You Want Me To Do*. The song closes with the admonition: "Thank you very kindly. You can't play too many of those blues because they get to you and make you think of those olden days in south America."

Let It Rock and **Carol** benefit from lengthy workouts and — unusually — the latter is performed in its entirety without the now-familiar segue into *Little Queenie*. Only **Nadine**, played at the request from the audience, is perfunctory. Interestingly, "Southern diplomat" here becomes a "Georgia democrat" — a clear reference to the world's most famous peanut farmer, Jimmy Carter, for whom Chuck was to play on 6th July 1979 on the South Lawn of the White House.

Liverpool Drive is, as Chuck puts it, "an instrumental challenge" to take the band "round the Horn". Erroneously, he hits the *Johnny B. Goode* intro button and pulls up short to ask: "Boy, if that isn't Chuck Berry, what is? Now, I'll do the number for you," and proceeds to burn up the strings on his Gibson, seeking approbation at its end with: "Did we strike a groove? Shall we maintain this groove?" Yes, you surely did and you surely must, is the answer of any sane man.

A short rocking version of **Bye Bye Johnny** is followed by the **Bonsoir Cherie** passage — now a common feature before the climactic **Johnny B. Goode**.

This a tremendously strong and varied concert, one of best Berry gigs ever committed to any recording medium. It is therefore all the more frustrating that half the sound recording and almost all the video footage still lies hidden deep in the BBC's vaults, for the librarians' eyes and ears only.

SESSION 63
CHUCK BERRY
Chuck Berry, vocal/guitar; Aaron 'T-Bone' Walker, vocal/guitar -1; Willie Dixon, double bass -3; Ellis 'Lafayette' Leake, piano; Louis Myers, guitar (except -4); Dave Myers, bass -2; Fred Below, drums

LIVE RECORDINGS
Montreux Jazz Festival
Montreux Pavilion
Montreux, Switzerland   **16 June 1972**

CH2440	**Guitar Boogie** *[instrumental]* -2 *(Chuck Berry)*	unissued
CH2441	**Roll Over Beethoven** -2 *(Chuck Berry)*	unissued
CH2442	**Sweet Little Sixteen** -2 *(Chuck Berry)*	unissued
CH2443	**Memphis Tennessee** -2 *(Chuck Berry)*	unissued
CH2444	**Nadine** -2-4 *(Chuck Berry)*	unissued

CH2445	**Everyday I Have The Blues** -1-2 *(Aaron Sparks)*	unissued
CH2446	**Maybellene** -3 *(Chuck Berry)*	unissued
CH2447	**Wee Wee Hours** -3 *(Chuck Berry)*	unissued
CH2448	**Let It Rock** -3 *(E. Anderson)*	unissued
CH2449	**Rock And Roll Music** -3 *(Chuck Berry)*	unissued
CH2450	**Little Queenie / Carol** -3 *(Chuck Berry)*	unissued
CH2451	**You Never Can Tell** -3 *(Chuck Berry)*	unissued
CH2452	**Johnny B. Goode** -3 *(Chuck Berry)*	unissued
CH2453	**School Day** -3 *(Chuck Berry)*	unissued

In 1967, Claude Nobs, jazz fan and entrepreneur extraordinaire, organised the first *Montreux Jazz Festival*, which over the next thirty years would develop into the leading European jazz festival. By 1972, the Montreux fest had expanded and the blues hit big town in the form of Chess artists Muddy Waters, Bo Diddley, Koko Taylor, Willie Dixon and Chuck Berry. The backing on this occasion was provided by the Aces (brothers Louis and Dave Myers, and Fred Below) augmented by 'ace' piano-man Lafayette Leake. T-Bone Walker and his own rather avant-garde group were there also. Saturday night was blues time, but the previous evening, the first day of the festival, the joint rocked to the sounds of Chuck and Bo.

The 'joint' in question was the Montreux Pavilion, because the usual venue, the Casino de Montreux, had burned down the previous December during a Frank Zappa concert. The whole Chess shebang was recorded and some titles were subsequently issued on the various artists 2-LP, *Blues/Rock Avalanche*. Two of Chuck's songs, **Let It Rock** and **School Day**, were earmarked for release but never made the final selection.

The Berry concert was matrixed by Chess — hence the inclusion here of a totally unissued session. It's not certain why the planned cuts were excluded. It has been suggested that Chuck possibly pulled the plug because of his dislike of compilation LPs. (Another example of this was the veto of his performance appearing on the *Let The Good Times Roll* soundtrack album.)

It is equally possible, however, that the quality just wasn't up to scratch, as the whole set is musically poor and beset by microphone problems. Certainly, *Let It Rock* is about the best of the numbers I've heard, being a near-instrumental rock'n'roll flight of fancy with a furious string-bass solo by Willie Dixon. This view is based on a seriously dodgy video recording with poor sound which runs out at *Rock And Roll Music*. Maybe things did finally improve beyond this point and by the time *School Day,* the second song selected for the album, was reached (strange that this song should close the show), the standard was acceptable. The Chess tapes will undoubtedly be better than the video, but presumably not good enough.

The Aces, of course, had been around on the Chicago blues scene since the early fifties, first backing Junior Wells, then Little Walter when he hit with *Juke*. Joining them on piano was Lafayette Leake, Willie Dixon's cohort and the guy who gets overlooked in favour of Johnnie Johnson when people speak of the guitar/piano magic of Berry's early hits. Remember (discounting Johnson's recent claims) that it was Leake radiating those eighty-eights on *Rock And Roll Music, Sweet Little Sixteen, Reelin' And Rockin'* and *Johnny B. Goode*.

The video shows the Pavilion packed to the gills as Chuck eases into things with **Guitar Boogie** (which has nothing to do with the *Guitar Boogie*, but is merely a guitar workout to exercise his fingers). Although it was allocated a separate matrix number, it is in effect just an extended introduction leading straight into **Roll Over Beethoven**. He doesn't seem too committed to the song and quickly but graciously gives Louis Myers leave to solo before passing the baton over to Leake.

Sweet Little Sixteen follows, and the cameraman's eye is caught by a loony in powder blue, you know the type — there's one at every gig, gyrating and getting on down in his own private world to the irritation of most of the audience, here to see the stage-show not the floor-show. "Is that alright? Is that alright?" Chuck asks Dave Myers at the close. Ever the gentleman, Myers answers in the affirmative, but one wonders what he really thought of the lacklustre performance.

Up to this point, Berry has been relatively static, but during **Memphis** he takes a tentative scoot across the stage. Absence of rehearsal is sadly evident in the botched cacophony masquerading as an ending. During this number, he apparently breaks a string, so for the next one he borrows Louis Myers's guitar while Myers exits to repair the damage to his beautiful Gibson (the same instrument he used on the 1972 BBC-TV *Sounds For Saturday* show).

Maybe it's the strange guitar, or maybe the lack of rhythm support, but **Nadine** is just plain awful. The whole band seem out of sync with each other and Chuck retreats into an extended instrumental passage with no light at the end of it. When he finally returns to the microphone, he asks: "What song was I singing?" — which really says it all.

The best part of the show is when a dapper T-Bone Walker saunters up to the microphone, G&T in hand, to sing **Everyday I Have The Blues** with consummate ease. In the presence of his hero, Chuck immediately adopts a subservient role of backing musician and what proceeds is the best guitar of the whole concert, with cool chords and jazzy runs aplenty. Standing a good six inches taller than 'Bone, he reaches over his idol's head and places his guitar in the hands of the master. An act of complete homage and a rare occurrence indeed from a man with such a enormous ego, but when it comes down to the music Chuck really loves, he has never had a problem in praising and crediting his musical forebears.

In fact, of all the guitarists who have had a major influence on Berry (a list which includes Muddy Waters, Elmore James, Carl Hogan and Les Paul),

T-Bone Walker must be ranked at the top. The essence of his style literally drips from Berry's guitar, be it in the fast rockers or the smooth blues. Any doubters need only listen to a small selection of Walker's work: take, for instance, the uptempo jumpin' jive of *Strollin' With Bones*, *T-Bone Jumps Again* or *Riffette* with Freddie Slack's band; or contrast Berry's guitar style with the flowing, extravagant introductions on tunes such as Walker's *Too Much Trouble Blues*, *I'm Gonna Find My Baby* or *That's Better For Me*; or bend an ear to the single-string runs on *The Hustle Is On*, or the riffing chords of *T-Bone Shuffle*, or the piano/guitar interplay of Walker's most famous song, *Call It Stormy Monday*, if further convincing is necessary. What *is* strange is that Chuck never cut this masterwork!

So, while T-Bone plays some tasty sounds, Chuck gets down and boogaloos so deep in the groove that he misses the signals when 'Bone wants to pass back the guitar. A touching and historical moment that must have been worth the cost of admission alone.

For **Maybellene**, Dave Myers exits stage left and the formidable figure of Willie Dixon appears, handling his double bass as if it were a mere cello. Unfortunately, all the skill and blues knowledge contained in Dixon's fingers can't seem to rescue the musical day, and things are not helped by microphone "trouble that turns into a struggle" for two roadies and a mess of electrical insulation tape. Berry deigns to tune up for **Wee Wee Hours** and his performance is better for this, with both Dixon and Louis Myers taking turns to solo. In Dixon's presence, Leake also seems to liven up.

More brewer's droop microphone problems beset **Rock And Roll Music**, but Chuck provides a nice touch by acknowledging his piano player by crouching at his side — maybe recalling the original recording of the song sixteen years before?

The remainder of the concert remains unseen and unheard, but ain't it a pity and ain't it a shame that what looks on paper like a dream team in actuality turned out to be a bit of a nightmare. Lack of rehearsal and imagination in the song selection — had he seized the initiative, this could have been Berry's blues renaissance — has, quite rightly, consigned this set to *'Room 101'* of the Chess vaults.

SESSION 64
CHUCK BERRY
Chuck Berry, speech; Pim Oets, interviewer

The Hilton Hotel
Apollolaan 138-140
Amsterdam, Netherlands   **20 January 1973**

Introduktie (Introduction)	■ Sun/Chess NQCS-1, Bellaphon
[Interview*]	BI-15119*, Checkmate LP-1955*
	◎ Wolf 2010CD*

At the start of 1973, Chuck was on a grand tour of Europe, playing dates in England, France (Paris and Strasbourg), Belgium, Denmark, Switzerland, Sweden, Germany and — on 20th January — Amsterdam in the

Netherlands. There, he paused to grant a press conference in the same hotel that John and Yoko had bedded down for peace. It is from this interview that this one-minute thirty-six second soundbite is taken: "My name is Carlos Berrino," he quips, then proceeds to answer several rather asinine questions with appropriately obtuse answers.

If you wish to hear this verbiage, the best place is on the 1997 Wolf CD, *Our Little Rendez-vous*. Failing this, try the 1986 Dutch bootleg LP, *Let It Rock* [Checkmate LP-1955], which also includes a selection of previously-issued Chess tracks that at the time of its release were hard to come by. The Sun/Chess and Bellaphon releases are Dutch and German compilations of interviews with Chuck, Bo Diddley, Carl Perkins and Jerry Lee Lewis interspersed with their Sun and Chess hits.

SESSION 65
CHUCK BERRY
Chuck Berry, vocal, overdubbed vocal -1, piano, overdubbed guitar -2; Billy Peek, guitar; Greg Edick, bass; Ron Reed, drums

Technisonic Studio
1201 South Brentwood Avenue
Clayton, Missouri   1 March 1973

CH2918	**Rain Eyes** -1 *(Chuck Berry)*	■ Chess CH-50043
CH2919	**You And My Country** *(Chuck Berry?)*	unissued
CH2920	**Sue Answer** -1 *(Chuck Berry)*	■ Chess CH-60032
CH2921	**Got It And Gone** -1-2 *(Chuck Berry)*	■ Chess CH-50043
CH2922	**A Deuce** -2 *(Chuck Berry)*	■ Chess CH-60032, CH6-80001

Back in the USA after his extensive travels in Europe, Chuck returned to familiar ground at the Technisonic Studios in Clayton, west of St. Louis. This session is unusual because his chosen instrument on this occasion was piano, not guitar, which is handled here like a true master's apprentice by Billy Peek.

The band also included bassist Greg Edick, son of George Edick, impresario of the Club Imperial, the famous St. Louis night-spot of the fifties and sixties. Chuck occasionally played the club, but it was more Ike Turner territory. However, the venue was racially integrated from the early days and he loved to walk in the front door of the ritzy place as a paying guest. Edick the Younger was a big Berry fan and claims to have played on two Berry albums — the second of which remains unidentified — and also toured Europe with Chuck. In the mid-nineties, Edick's band, the Joint Jumpers, played gigs in St. Louis and have on occasion been joined on stage by Chuck and daughter Ingrid.

The intriguingly-titled **You And My Country** remains unissued, but the other four titles have a distinct country trait to them, which comes from Chuck's overdubbed vocal duetting and the lightweight, springy drumming. His piano is in a meandering, jazzy mode that sits surprisingly comfortably within this musical setting.

Rain Eyes continues the theme of *Memphis Tennessee* in that it is a story of a broken family told from the child's perspective: through "rain eyes that blur the rays of sunshine". It's a sad tale of a mother's infidelity and the father's consequential departure even though he loves his son.   However, unlike *Memphis*, by the last verse all's well that ends well when daddy returns home and the trade winds part the clouds, allowing the sun to shine and dry the 'rain eyes'. Despite the sad subject-matter, the beat is jaunty with Chuck rolling the basses and singing in unison with himself.

Sue Answer (or *Sue Ann? Sir*, as it is called in the sloppy discography in Berry's autobiography) continues the African American musical tradition for stuttering song lyrics, practised amongst others by Willie Dixon, Champion Jack Dupree and John Lee Hooker (who really does stutter when he talks).

Billy Peek kicks off the song with a guitar lick from his master's songbook, but it is Berry's eccentric piano that dominates. Chuck doubles-up the vocal stutters in this story of an increasingly acrimonious exchange of letters in which the correspondents try to extract money from each other without success. The lyrics are 'writ' in a mock 'country hick' style with "be's" aplenty: "What be lookin' g-g-g-good to the goose, gotta be groovy to the g-g-g-gander," is a typical line.

Got It And Gone hits off with a variant of the *Bye Bye Johnny* opening lick and is the closest Chuck gets to rock and roll at this session. This is, however, *lightweight* country rock rather than the heavy blues-rock of Berry's finest hour.   This is down to the absence of any discernible backbeat, the drummer man being content to ride atop of a country hop beat. Chuck cuts in with a jabbing guitar figure, but the bulk of the soloing is by Billy Peek who plays in true Berry fashion.

The story is a familiar-sounding tale of a guitar-playing 'poor boy' who fumbles his way through life wanting only to play his good ol' rock music on his guitar as the sun goes down. On this occasion, he is hauled off to Vietnam, but even this experience doesn't dampen his spirit for his music.

A Deuce is the best cut of the session because it is in a jazz bag rather than a country sack. The overdubbed vocal is also dropped, which is a relief. The song is, in fact, a reworking of Nat Cole's *Bring Another Drink*, which Chuck had previously recorded in its original form. The update substitutes illegal substances for the original booze, a 'deuce' being an old-fashioned term for a pair of reefers or two people sharing a joint *à deux*.

Our man, however, is more interested in getting his end away ("honeycomb drips right at my fingertips") rather than getting high, and, after an abortive attempt to book a "no-tell motel" room, he has to content himself with a 'steamy windows' scenario in his Ford. Despite plying his date with best quality weed and good vibes from the FM waveband, it all ends in distress and he consoles himself with yet another 'deuce'. This is a great track full of Berry wit and wisdom.

Rain Eyes and *Get It And Gone* were issued on the *Bio* album in July 1973, while *Sue Answer* and *A Deuce* had to wait two years for issue on the 1975 *Chuck Berry* LP. The quality of *A Deuce* was, however, finally recognised in 1988 when MCA compiled the retrospective *Chess Box* set and it got the exposure it deserved.

SESSION 66

CHUCK BERRY

Chuck Berry, vocal/guitar; Wayne 'Tex' Gabriel, guitar; Gary Van Scyoc, bass; Adam Ippolito, piano; Stan Bronstein, tenor saxophone (omit saxophone -1); Richard Frank Jr, drums; Esmond Edwards, vocal comments, tambourine and handclaps -2; Linda Solomon, handclaps -2

Sound Exchange Studios
265 West 54th Street
New York City   **3 June 1973**

CH2958	**Talkin' About My Buddy** *(Chuck Berry)*	■ Chess CH-50043
	Tell You About My Buddy *[alternative short version]* *(Chuck Berry)*	unissued
CH2959	**Hello Little Girl, Goodbye** *(Chuck Berry)*	■ Chess CH-50043
CH2960	**One Sixty Nine AM** *(Chuck Berry?)*	unissued
CH2961	**Aimlessly Driftin'** *(Chuck Berry)*	■ Chess CH-50043
CH2962	**Tell Me About My Buddy** *(Chuck Berry)*	unissued
CH2963	**Woodpecker** *[instrumental]* -2 *(Chuck Berry)*	■ Chess CH-50043, CH6-80001
CH2964E	**Bio** -1 *(Chuck Berry)*	○ Chess CH-2140**a**, 6145 027**b,** Bellaphon BF-18214**b** ■ Chess CH-50043, CH6-80001
CH2965	**Roll Away** *(Chuck Berry?)*	unissued

Four years after they acquired the Chess empire, GRT closed down the Chess offices and studios in Chicago and moved all remaining operations to their home base in New York City. As a result, the Big Apple was to be the recording location for the remainder of Berry's Chess recording career.

Sixteen months previously, Chuck had played with John Lennon and his backing group, Elephant's Memory, and it was these guys who were drafted in to play on this session. They were a class act and assisted Berry in cutting his last great album and his last truly great song, both titled *Bio*.

The album cover itself is something else: a gatefold item sporting a photograph of a wean-year Berry on the front with an evocative photo collection inside including an intimate August 1937 snap of the eleven year old Chuck in his photographic darkroom in the basement of his family's home at 4319 Labadie Avenue (a hobby that would later be taken to dubious extremes), publicity shots, movie stills, Club Bandstand action shots, a reunion photo with Johnnie Johnson and Ebby Hardy, and — last but not least — a picture of our hero at the tenth *Rock & Roll Revival Show*, Madison Square Garden, New York on 13th October 1972 receiving a gold disc for the million-selling *My Ding-A-Ling* from the hands of Esmond Edwards with Richard Nader looking on.

Nader, the promoter of the first-ever *'Rock & Roll Revival'* shows, gave Chuck's career a much-needed boost when he booked him to headline his first spectacular on 18th October 1969 at New York's Felt Forum, but he later also proved to be his nemesis when he testified to making him undeclared 'under the table' cash payments for performances in the seventies.   This 'malparamanopo' (Chuck's own word for the crime), led in 1979 to another stay in that 'stoney mansion', this time in Lompoc, California.

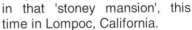

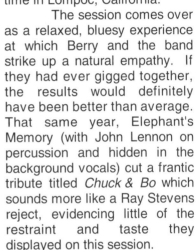

The session comes over as a relaxed, bluesy experience at which Berry and the band strike up a natural empathy. If they had ever gigged together, the results would definitely have been better than average. That same year, Elephant's Memory (with John Lennon on percussion and hidden in the background vocals) cut a frantic tribute titled *Chuck & Bo* which sounds more like a Ray Stevens reject, evidencing little of the restraint and taste they displayed on this session.

The first cut of the day was the easy-rollin' **Talkin' About My Buddy**, almost seven minutes of laid-back, loping blues based on the distinctive melody of Ray Charles's *Lonely Avenue*, itself a steal from the Pilgrim Travelers' *How Jesus Died*. The cut features great piano and sax from Ippolito and Bronstein respectively, while Mr. B gives out with some emotional vocalisation.

The song is the chat-up line of the century in which Chuck recounts various sexual encounters of his buddy in the hope of turning his own girl on. The 'buddy' is, of course, his own alter ego and the conquests he relates are his own.   His buddy, it seems, has had more hot dinners than Don Juan, starting with a faithful, devoted and true girl in Pennsylvania to a foxy German filly whom he takes between gigs in Toronto (a university student maybe?) and whose lustful whims become his fancy.   The scene then shifts to a swank suburb of Houston and a wealthy widow "in a mansion made of stone" (this has *got* to be Candace Mossler, who merits a whole chapter in his autobiography), then to a teacher in Miami Beach who taught him to "do it unto others as he used to just have them do." The ultimate challenge is a "virgin called to be a nun" who, I'm pleased to report, remains unsullied. It's not recounted if the thinly-disguised ruse succeeds and the seductive deal goes down, but what's sure is, it's not through want of trying!

Two further versions of the song remain in the can — both with a slightly amended title — and one wonders if these contain other adventures from the love conquistador.

After the lengthy narrative and slinky seduction of *Talkin' About My Buddy*, the lyrically-inconsequential **Hello Little Girl, Goodbye** comes as something of a relief. The song is little more than an excuse (if excuse be needed) for a rocking blow-through with some great driving drumming that powers the tune on like a juggernaut in the hands of a joy-rider. Piano from the Jerry Lee Lewis school of pyrotechnics and rooting sax *à la* King Curtis complete the picture. Clearly inspired, Chuck's guitar sounds like he really means it. Berry acolyte George Thorogood certainly thought enough of the song to cut a version himself — a relatively rare occurrence for a latter-day Berry composition.

A descending guitar phrase that must have graced a thousand blues introduces **Aimlessly Driftin'**, a slow number based on Charles Brown's timeless classic, *Drifting Blues*. Chuck had started out playing a "three change trick" which, with a little adjustment of tempo and rhythm, would accommodate dozens of blues. This is one of them — the type he could knock out in his sleep. It sounds reminiscent of the earlier unissued *I'm In The Twilight Zone*. Again the band back him ably, most of the blues licks coming from Tex Gabriel while Chuck concentrates on his vocals. Prominent piano and saxophone complete the mix. Just another 'think I'll go to California' saga, this song isn't one to email home about, though it is pleasant enough in its own way.

The instrumental **Woodpecker** is an amalgam of Charlie Christian's guitar figures on the Benny Goodman tunes *Air Mail Special* and *Seven Come Eleven* slowed down and given a measure of syncopation by way of tambourine and handclaps. While the influence of Christian is clear, the catchy little lick also sounds a little like Woody Woodpecker's manic call and might have suggested the title. But old Woody was never as funky as this and, in fact, this is about as funky as Chuck Berry gets, with some excellent interplay between the two guitars and a heavy sax break. He certainly sounds like he is enjoying himself, interjecting encouragements and comments to the band and exchanging banter with Esmond Edwards. (Linda Solomon, incidentally, was a journalist who attended the session and was privileged to be allowed to clap her hands for the great Chuck Berry.) MCA also seemed to like the track because it was deemed good enough for inclusion on the 1988 *Chess Box* set.

The last track of the session is **Bio**, a song which is almost as good as anything Berry cut in the fifties. Dusting off Elmore James's *Broom* lick yet again, in five verses and four minutes twenty-one seconds Chuck eloquently elucidates his biographical story. "Lord have mercy, gotta tell, tell it just like it is — every word" introduces a rather romanticised and expurgated version of his life. From humble beginnings in St. Louis, to his trip to Chicago and his meeting with the mighty Muddy Waters ("I asked him what I could do to make it, and it was he who showed me the way"), to the making of his first hit record, measured — typically — in monetary terms ("It netted over ten thousand dollars and added glory to my name"), to his trip to movieland (shades of *Bye Bye Johnny*), to his endless touring "doing the only thing I know", and finally — without a hint of irony — to his love of performing. It is a great song and a great performance and deserved better than the 'B' side billing it got in the UK.

Chuck certainly liked it sufficiently to sing it regularly at his gigs over the next ten years, albeit in a truncated form.

Roll Away, the oddly-titled **One Sixty Nine AM** (which should be 2:09 am by my watch!) and the similarly-named **Tell Me About My Buddy** and **Tell You About My Buddy** remain in the can. In view of the overall quality of the session, one hopes that when MCA get around to issuing the *Bio* album on CD, they will enhance it with these titles.

SESSION 67
CHUCK BERRY

Chuck Berry, vocal/guitar; Ingrid Gibson Berry, second vocal -1; Ernest W. Hayes, piano; Wilbur Bascomb Jr, bass; Earl C. Williams, drums; Elliott Randall, overdubbed steel guitar

Sound Exchange Studios,
265 West 54th Street
New York City   **26 August 1974**

CH3802	**I'm Just A Name** -1 *(Chuck Berry)*	■ Chess CH-60032
CH3803	**Too Late** -1 *(Chuck Berry)*	■ Chess CH-60032
CH3804	**Turn On The Houselights** *(Chuck Berry)*	unissued

This session and the next three, recorded over four consecutive days, produced twenty-two recorded tracks. Originally planned for release as a double album, only eleven out of the twenty-two cuts were actually issued — perhaps a reflection of their overall quality. These eleven, (together with two from an earlier session) became Chuck's last Chess album, titled *Chuck Berry* in the USA and *Chuck Berry '75* in Europe.

The recordings were again produced in New York City, but this time local session musicians were drafted in, including Wilbur Bascomb Jr. and Ernie Hayes who had played on some Bo Diddley Chess sessions in the previous year. Hayes was a well-established New York session pianist and a longtime associate of sax-man King Curtis. He had played on such great tracks as Mickey & Sylvia's *Love Is Strange* in 1956, LaVern Baker's *Voodoo, Voodoo* in 1958, and Joe Turner's *Chains Of Love* and *Honey Hush* in 1959, and was also an integral part of Curtis's Noble Knights during the sixties, playing on his big hit *Soul Twist* (and, incidentally, on Curtis's version of *Memphis*).

Also included was the overdubbed steel guitar of Elliott Randall, whose contributions were overdubbed some time after the sessions took place at the behest of producer Esmond Edwards. Randall was a prolific session guitarist who recorded three albums under his own name during the seventies and went on to play on dozens of other sessions including 1980's hit *Blues Brothers* film soundtrack album.

Also returning to the studio was Darlin Ingrid, appearing on her dad's recordings for the first time since his Mercury days. On **I'm Just A Name** and

Too Late, her contribution consists of singing in unison with Chuck, really just replacing the overdubbed second vocal that he used on many of his recordings. Randall's contribution is to add chickenshit country lap-steel licks above the bouncy boogie base. And it works too, lightening these country rockers considerably.

In England, the burgeoning pub rock movement and older Stiff rockers like Dave Edmunds and Nick Lowe must have been listening. Records such as Lowe's *I Knew The Bride*, Edmunds's *Crawling From The Wreckage* and Kirsty MacColl's *There's A Guy Works Down The Chipshop Swears He's Elvis* (written by Graham Parker) all owe more than a passing nod to Berry's country boogie concoctions.

I'm Just A Name recounts the feelings of a fan who knows she is only a name — one of many in the life of a rock star who loves 'em and leaves 'em. Couplets such as: "I'm just a name within your past you met while all alone/ Someone who shared a love with you and stayed behind unknown" and "It seems you're looking straight at me when I see you perform/ I often wonder if you know the power in your charms?" are no doubt directly inspired by personal experience.

Too Late, often credited to the pen of Chuck Berry was, in fact, written by Jimmy Wakely, an Okie who made it big over on the West Coast in the late '40s and early '50s. Always a fan of close harmony country music, Chuck probably picked up on the song from the 1957 recording by the Louvin Brothers who were a duo he is known to have admired. Berry's version follows Wakely's lyrics much more closely than he was inclined to do with other composers' material, but in speeding-up the tempo and turning it into a rocker, he loses the poignancy of this sad tale of a break-up of a long relationship related via a tearstained letter left on a pillow.

The unissued **Turn On The Houselights** is likely to be a variant of the tune that Berry featured regularly at the end of his concerts when he would ask the lighting man to turn up the auditorium lights so that he could see his 'children', and is probably an early version of the song that later appeared on his 1979 *Rockit* album.

SESSION 68
CHUCK BERRY

Chuck Berry, vocal/guitar, overdubbed guitar –1, overdubbed vocal -2; Ingrid Gibson Berry, second vocal -3; Ernest W. Hayes, piano; Wilbur Bascomb Jr, bass; Jimmy Johnson Jr., drums; Elliott Randall, overdubbed steel guitar -4

Sound Exchange Studios,
265 West 54th Street
New York City   **27 August 1974**

CH3796	**Hi-Heel Sneakers** -1 *(Robert Higginbotham)*	■ Chess CH-60032
CH3797	**Jambalaya** *(Hank Williams)*	unissued
CH3798	**The Song Of My Love** -3 *(Chuck Berry)*	unissued
CH3799	**If I Was** *(Chuck Berry)*	unissued
CH3800	**Vaya Con Dios** *(Larry Russell, Inez James,* *Buddy Pepper)*	unissued
CH3801	**South Of The Border** -2-4 *(Jimmy Kennedy, Michael Carr,* *Chuck Berry)*	■ Chess CH-60032

In November 1963, Tommy Tucker (real name Robert Higginbotham) entered a New York studio to cut the seminal ***Hi-Heel Sneakers***, destined to become a defining disc for the mod fraternity in the UK, appealing not only to their musical taste but also to their sartorial sensibilities. Tucker had taken Jimmy Reed's sparse boogie and funked it up with some hip guitar from Weldon Young and his own cheesy organ to create a classic that was covered by all and sundry but never bettered. Amongst the 'sundries' were Elvis Presley, Stevie Wonder, Jose Feliciano, Jerry Lee Lewis and... Chuck Berry.

Chuck's version increases the beat from the slinky relaxed throb of the original and, as with many Berry covers, it is only an approximation of the song as it was first conceived. After the first verse, he lapses into verses of his own making which add nothing to the story and long instrumental workouts from himself and Hayes, who, in response to his encouragement ("I'll make you a star" he declares at one point) plays some exceedingly jazzy runs. On this track, Randall is nowhere to be heard and Berry overdubs his own guitar .

The only other released cut from this session is Chuck's recasting of ***South Of The Border***, which he first committed to posterity at the BBC2 *Sounds For Saturday* concert in 1972. This version follows the earlier cut pretty closely, but without the audience reaction much of the humour falls flat. Chuck, however, works hard, overdubbing his vocals and adopting a brogue weirder than Loyd Grossman's and about as convincing as Dick Van Dyke's Cockney concoction in *Mary Poppins*.

The other four tracks are unissued. ***Jambalaya*** is the Hank Williams standard which Chuck had previously used as the basis for his *Bordeaux In My*

Pirough in 1971. ***The Song Of My Love*** was previously cut for Chess in 1964 and issued on the *Chuck Berry In London* album, then again for Mercury in 1968 (eventually released as an extra track on the 1989 CD reissue of *From St. Louie To Frisco*). This version remains in the can. ***Vaya Con Dios*** was previously issued in 1965 on the *Fresh Berry's* album and is likely to be another duet with Ingrid. ***If I Was*** is the second attempt at this composition — both of which remain unissued — and it is probably the same song as *If I Were* which appeared on the 1979 *Rockit* album.

SESSION 69
CHUCK BERRY
Chuck Berry, vocal/guitar, piano -1; Ernest W. Hayes, piano -2; Wilbur Bascomb Jr, bass; Jimmy Johnson Jr, drums; Elliott Randall, overdubbed guitar -3

Sound Exchange Studios
265 West 54th Street
New York City   **26 August 1974**

CH3805	**The Weight** -2 *(Robbie Robertson)*	unissued
CH3806	**Swanee River** -1 *(Stephen Collins Foster)*	■ Chess CH-60032
CH3807	**You Are My Sunshine** -1-3 *(Jimmie Davis, Charles Mitchell)*	■ Chess CH-60032
CH3808	**Johnny B. Blues** *[instrumental]* -2 *(Chuck Berry)*	unissued
CH3809	**Dust My Broom** -2 *(Elmore James)*	unissued
CH3810	**Don't You Lie To Me** -2-3 *(Hudson Whittaker)*	■ Chess CH-60032
CH3811	**Together Again** -2 *(Buck Owens?)*	unissued

One might well suspect that Chuck Berry had been listening to Brother Ray's records, judging by the song selection for this session. Charles's version of *Swanee River* (titled *Swanee River Rock*) came out in 1957 as a single on Atlantic; *You Are My Sunshine* was released as a single and as a track on his 1962 ABC–Paramount LP, *Modern Sounds In Country And Western Music (Volume 2)*; and, if the unissued *Together Again* is the Buck Owens composition, then Charles recorded this too, for his 1966 album, *Country & Western Meets Rhythm & Blues* (an equally apt description for probably 50% of Berry's output at this time).

Of course, Chuck's influences extend way back beyond the music of Ray Charles. Indeed, in many respects both artists drink from the same fountain, and Berry could just as easily have been reprising Albert Ammons's *Swanee River Boogie* here. Certainly, he was a sucker for that old refried boogie woogie that Meade Lux Lewis, Albert Ammons and Pete Johnson were

churning out in the thirties and forties. *Swanee River* flows back yet further —
to 1851 in fact, when it was written by Stephen Collins Foster as *The Old Folks
Back Home*. Often described as the 'Father of American Popular Music',
Foster wrote many classic 'darky' compositions including *Camptown Races* and
Oh Susannah, and one wonders what he would have made of Berry's rocked-
up version.

Chuck lays into the tune with abandon, taking it at one hell of a lick,
weaving in his own lyrics including a reference to *Johnny B. Goode* and a
commitment to "fix up his grandma's little shanty." The solid Berry guitar
boogie holds down the bottom while his more ephemeral piano floats above the
bassline rhythm. Elliott Randall's guitar isn't audible on this track.

You Are My Sunshine is another oldie-but-goodie dating back to
1940, when it was composed and recorded by country music star and future
Governor of Louisiana, Jimmie Davis, together with his steel-playing guitarist,
Charles Mitchell. It has since become a standard, covered by dozens of artists
including the likes of Gene Autry and Bing Crosby, and is reckoned to be the
most valuable copyright in country music.

The song had already been rocked-up by Jerry Lee Lewis and
Johnny & The Hurricanes amongst others before Chuck took his chances with
it. After singing the first verse straight, he lets rip with the most raucous vocal
delivery of his career, echoing Brother Ray. He may never have gone to
church, but here he certainly makes it to the vestibule. Again, he improvises
his own lyrics: "I woke up screaming, I had hallucinations, I had to hang my
head off the foot of the bed and cry," as he vamps on piano to the
accompaniment of his own muscular boogie guitar.

When Chuck first cut **Don't You Lie To Me** in 1960, it clocked in at
under two minutes. This second version is almost twice as long, turning a well-
paced classic into a less-successful epic. The tempo here is cooled from the
staggering, stuttering original beat to a slower, slinky, broody blues. Chuck
sticks strictly to the script except for a couple of excursions — one into
astrology ("I'm a Libra and I'm hip to you") and the other, a carnal proposition
delivered with a leer ("I'll give you mine, if you'll give me yours too").

Drummer Jimmy Johnson (who replaced Earl Williams after the first
day of this multi-day session) and bassist Wilbur Bascomb Jr. lay down a
moody foundation over which Ernie Hayes constructs some very tasty piano
chords and runs. Sadly, it all goes wrong with the inclusion of an irritating
overdubbed 'wah-wah' guitar that subverts Chuck's chops and cheapens the
rendition. It would have been oh-so-much better had Berry adopted his usual
technique of overdubbing his own second guitar pattern.

In the can from this session, but as yet unreleased, is another version
of Elmore's **Dust My Broom** (the first was recorded in 1963) and the
intriguingly-titled **Johnny B. Blues**, which is probably an instrumental based on
you-know-what.

Still more intriguing is **The Weight**, which with such an unusual title
can only be the Band's classic. The Band themselves had cut a version of
Promised Land for their 1973 chart album, *Moondog Matinee*, and as 'the
Hawks' had also backed Ronnie Hawkins on his 1959 hit, *40 Days*, so maybe
Chuck decided to repay the compliment.

Likewise, Buck Owens — the composer of **Together Again** — though a country artist, was not averse to the occasional rock and roll song and cut a No. 1 C&W hit version of *Johnny B. Goode* in 1969, accompanied by his very own Buckaroos.

SESSION 70
CHUCK BERRY

Chuck Berry, vocal/guitar, overdubbed guitar -1; Ingrid Gibson Berry, lead vocal -2; Ernest W. Hayes, piano; Wilbur Bascomb Jr, bass; Jimmy Johnson Jr, drums; Elliott Randall, overdubbed guitar -3; unknown percussion -4

Sound Exchange Studios
265 West 54th Street
New York City   **29 August 1974**

CH3812	**My Babe** -1 *(Willie Dixon)*	■ Chess CH-60032
CH3813	**Here Today** *(Chuck Berry?)*	unissued
CH3814	**I Just Want To Make Love To You** -3 *(Willie Dixon)*	■ Chess CH-60032
CH3815	**Rockin'** *[instrumental]* *(Chuck Berry)*	unissued
CH3816	**Shake, Rattle And Roll** -4 *(Charles E. Calhoun)*	○ Chess CH-2169**a** ■ Chess CH-60032
CH3817	**Baby What You Want Me To Do** -1-2 *(Jimmy Reed)*	○ Chess CH-2169**b** ■ Chess CH-60032

For his very last Chess recording session, Chuck ducks back into Blues Alley, cutting four stone R&B classics. As with all retreads of classic recordings, it is seldom that they meet or surpass the originals, and this is also the case here.

From the active mind and pen of the mighty Willie Dixon we get two of his best songs, **My Babe** and **I Just Want To Make Love To You** (titled *Just Make Love To Me* when originally recorded by Muddy Waters in 1954).

Though written by Dixon, *My Babe* is heavily based on the melody of *This Train*, a gospel number made popular in 1947 by Sister Rosetta Tharpe, but it is Little Walter's wonderful 1955 blues shuffle that Chuck attempts to emulate. Walter's recording is blessed with one of the most infectious walking guitar and bass figures, both played by Robert Jr. Lockwood, but, for reasons best known to himself, Berry chooses to ignore this and rocks it up instead, losing "the beauty of the melody" — as someone once so succinctly put it! As always, he injects his own lyrics to update the ditty: "My babe loves me steady/ My babe, she's always ready" and "My babe don't ever deny me/ Bend over backwards to satisfy me." Ooer, missis!

I Just Want To Make Love To You is the second time that Chuck cut the song (his first stab at it was 1959). This rendition would have been pretty good — there's a nice feel to the cut, with strong vocals and some neat lyrical additions ("I don't want you to be actin' tough/ I don't want you to be smokin' that stuff") — but unfortunately Chess chose to overlay it with a freaky guitar reminiscent of the excesses perpetrated on the '*Electric*' albums of Muddy and Wolf. Maybe one day they will issue it *sans* the shite?

   Shake, Rattle And Roll fares better and was considered good enough for the 'A' side of Chuck's final Chess single release (which, incidentally, inspired an exact copy from Swedish rocker Jerry Williams). The song was written by Jesse Stone under his pen name, Charles E. Calhoun, who also arranged and played the tremendous insistent rolling piano on Big Joe Turner's 1955 Atlantic original. Turner's is the definitive version of the song, which quickly acquired 'standard' status thanks to Bill Haley's anaemic hit. Even Presley's dynamic 1956 cover cannot compete, so what chance for a 1974 scratch cut from Berry? On this cut, as with many rock and roll versions, Turner's relaxed vocals loaded on a boogie frame are substituted with a frenetic tempo thereby gaining little but loosing a lot. Chuck inputs some suitably saucy lines in an effort to update the song, but nothing approaching the sheer poetry of: "The way you wear those dresses, the sun comes shining through/ I can't believe my eyes all that mess belongs to you" or "I'm like a one eyed cat peeping in a seafood store/ Well I can look at you, tell you ain't a child no more." Sometimes, even for the 'poet laureate of rock and roll', it is better to repeat than compete!

   Finally, Berry tackles the Jimmy Reed perennial, ***Baby What You Want Me To Do,*** first recorded in 1959 in Chicago for Chess's main rival in the city, Vee–Jay Records. The lazy, infectious beat and the insinuating vocals of the great Reed warbler are retained, but the innovation on Chuck's part is to let his daughter sing the lead vocal with dad taking the harmony part. Ingrid sings it well, but then, Reed's songs are not exactly arias, just plain old downhome blues.

   Here Today and the instrumental ***Rockin'*** remain unissued and unheard.

   With these final Chess cuts, another chapter in the recording history of Chuck Berry closes. His return to Chess after three fallow years at Mercury had started well but unfortunately failed to sustain the quality promised by *Tulane* — the beginning of an artistic downward spiral from which Chuck would only briefly emerge for the remainder of his career.

SESSION 71
CHUCK BERRY
Chuck Berry, vocal/guitar; Johnnie Johnson, piano; Billy Peek, guitar; Jim Marsala, bass; Terry Houser, drums

Berry Park studio
691 Buckner Road
Wentzville, Missouri
and
CBC *(Chuck Berry Communications)*
Market Street
St. Louis, Missouri   **before 29 March 1976**

   Floyd *[instrumental]*   unissued
      (Andy Kirk, Floyd Smith?)

Silver Threads   unissued
    (Dick Reynolds, Jack Rhodes?)

Vaya Con Dios   unissued
    (Larry Russell, Inez James,
       Buddy Pepper)

Jambalaya   unissued
    (Hank Williams)

      Throughout the whole of his recording career to date, Chuck Berry had only been signed to two record labels: Chess for sixteen years and Mercury for three. Now, with the once-great Chess label being sold and re-sold, Chuck chose to cut loose and freelance his wares. He had been developing his Berry Park studio since the late sixties, and during 1975 and 1976 he was hard at work there, recording tracks for a double-album project with the working title of *The Second Coming*, for which he hoped to negotiate a release with either Warner Brothers or ABC–Paramount. Some cuts may also have been laid down in St. Louis or at the All-Platinum Studios in New Jersey. Negotiations progressed to a point were he was informing friends that a Warner Bros. release was scheduled for 29th March 1976 (hence the recording date noted above before this date), but it was not to be. The tapes remained in the Berry Park studio and may well have perished in a fire there in March 1989.

      This unissued session is included as representative of the type of material he was cutting at the time. ***Floyd*** is rumoured to be a blues instrumental modelled on *Deep Feeling*. This is perfectly feasible, in that *Deep Feeling* was itself modelled on Andy Kirk's 1939 recording, *Floyd's Guitar Blues*. If this is the case, then Berry probably plays his steel guitar on the cut.

      Silver Threads is likely to be a version of the country classic, *Silver Threads And Golden Needles,* written in 1956 by Dick Reynolds and Jack Rhodes and recorded amongst many by Chuck's favourite harmony duo, the Everly Brothers, or possibly the traditional *Silver Threads (Among The Gold)*.

      This was the first time that bassist Jim Marsala cut with Chuck, and he remembers the band line-up as shown above. Marsala had started out playing in local bands around St. Louis, eventually hooking up with Billy Peek, whose outfit frequently backed Chuck on gigs. After Peek split to join Rod Stewart's band in 1976, Berry asked him to work with him — which he did, becoming his regular bassist and road companion on overseas trips until December 1998. By that time, his concert schedule had diminished to such an extent that Marsala went back to playing again with Billy Peek, albeit with the proviso that "Chuck's shows still and always will come first".

REELIN' AND REELIN' (1977-2000)

Almost a quarter of a century of recordings
— almost all of them live —
capturing Chuck Berry in action on the rock'n'roll oldie treadmill.
A classic demonstration of the law of diminishing returns.

SESSION 72
CHUCK BERRY AND MATCHBOX
Chuck Berry, vocal/guitar; Steve Bloomfield, guitar; Rusty Lupton, piano; Fred Poke, bass; Wild Bob Burgos, drums

LIVE RECORDINGS
De Zandkuil Open Air Theatre
Lochem, Netherlands   **19 May 1977**

Liverpool Drive *(Chuck Berry)*	◎ (white label) HRTCD-93003
Carol *(Chuck Berry)*	◎ (white label) HRTCD-93003
Little Queenie *(Chuck Berry)*	◎ (white label) HRTCD-93003
Hail, Hail, Rock'n'Roll [School Day] *(Chuck Berry)*	◎ (white label) HRTCD-93003
Sweet Little Sixteen *(Chuck Berry)*	◎ (white label) HRTCD-93003
Memphis Tennessee *(Chuck Berry)*	◎ (white label) HRTCD-93003
Let It Rock *(E. Anderson)*	◎ (white label) HRTCD-93003
Everyday I Have The Blues *(Aaron Sparks)*	◎ (white label) HRTCD-93003
Wee Wee Hours *(Chuck Berry)*	◎ (white label) HRTCD-93003
I Believe [Bio] *(Chuck Berry)*	◎ (white label) HRTCD-93003
Promised Land *(Chuck Berry)*	◎ (white label) HRTCD-93003
You Never Can Tell *(Chuck Berry)*	◎ (white label) HRTCD-93003
My Ding-A-Ling *(Dave Bartholomew, Chuck Berry)*	◎ (white label) HRTCD-93003
Johnny Be Goode *(Chuck Berry)*	◎ (white label) HRTCD-93003
Reelin' And Rockin' *(Chuck Berry)*	◎ (white label) HRTCD-93003

During May 1977, Chuck Berry was back out on the road again, touring extensively throughout Europe, taking in the UK, France, the Netherlands, Sweden, Norway (for the first time ever), Spain, Germany and Austria. Two of these dates were surreptitiously recorded and bootlegged. This session and the next are those recordings.

Chuck's backing band on the tour were rock and roll revival group the Flying Saucers, augmented by Jacko Buddin on piano. On 15th May they played together in Lille, France and on the 19th were due to play at an afternoon open air festival in Lochem, a small Dutch town to the east of Amsterdam. Chuck travelled by limo while the boys went by bus. The latter was involved in a crash *en route*, as a result of which the band didn't make the gig. Matchbox, who were also booked to play the festival, backed him instead and the event was recorded for posterity, eventually appearing on CD in 1994 as *Chuck Berry Meets Matchbox* [HRTCD-93003]. (The tray insert confusingly also bears the legend '*Promised Land Records PL72 1977*', although I know of no previous releases.)

It is not clear if this CD has any connection with the Driving Wheel bootleg described in the following session, but it does utilise the same contemporary photograph of Chuck, albeit reversed and reproduced in an ugly yellow monochrome tint.

Matchbox were a competent rock and roll/rockabilly fifties' throwback outfit (judging from the quiffs and drapes they sport in the photograph on the back of the CD) inclined to the country side of rock, who went on to ride the rockabilly wave in the late seventies/early eighties, chalking up eight UK hits between 1979 and '82, and recording a couple of Chuck Berry numbers along the way: *Carol* and the little-covered *It Don't Take But A Few Minutes*. They were also old hands at backing visiting US rock and roll stars and therefore had no trouble fitting in behind Berry. As far as Chuck was concerned, he probably didn't notice the difference. The group's lead vocalist, Graham Fenton, was surplus to requirements, but the rest of the band make a decent fist of it.

The main drawback is the very inadequate recording quality which sounds like the gig was taped from a microphone placed in front of the monitors with no balancing whatsoever. As a result, Berry's vocals are faint, the piano is practically inaudible, and the sound flits between the stereo channels like a bee in a bottle. The plus points are the driving beat set up by the bass and drums and Chuck's up-front guitar (if you can live with the odd bum note and off-centre chord).

A manic flying Dutchman makes the introductions, then Berry hits off with a very loose approximation of **Liverpool Drive** followed by the coupling of **Carol** and **Little Queenie**, which was to become the usual way he performed these two classics.

Hail, Hail Rock And Roll is, of course, *School Day* in which Chuck fluffs the lines he must have sung a thousand times and in which we are treated to the usual unmusical chant from the crowd seeking deliverance from the days of yore.

After a perfunctory *Sweet Little Sixteen*, he declares the show open. *Let It Rock* is set up with a tight rocking beat and develops into an extended workout with a bridge the length of the Golden Gate — so long, in fact, that he forgets what he is singing.

"Into each life a little blues must fall" goes the maxim, and it seems that this applies equally to Chuck Berry concerts. In this case, we are treated to Memphis Slim's *Everyday I Have The Blues* and his own *Wee Wee Hours*, from his first single. On these, the piano-man and the guitarist also get the opportunity to solo. The blues continue with *I Believe*, which turns out to be Berry's very own *Bio*, though he regrettably omits the verse in recognition of his mentor, Muddy Waters. The mis-titling comes from the very last couplet of the song, "I believe, I believe I'll go back home *x2* / Gonna leave my baby, gonna break up my happy home," which is derived from the Elmore James's *I Believe*. The mistaken attribution most likely stems from the compiler's ignorance of Chuck's later catalogue.

After a truncated *Promised Land,* Berry declares a need to speed up the proceedings because the show closes at 10:30 and explains that he will only do short renditions of his hits. He then promptly contradicts this by performing a full-length version of *You Never Can Tell*, in which he almost recites the lyrics.

"What do you want to hear? *My Ding-A-Ling*?!?!" He can't believe it himself, but obliges anyway with a very tired rendition which falls flat through lack of response to the now-hackneyed jokes. Even some new lines recently composed in Las Vegas fail to click.

The finale is reached with the almost-inevitable *Johnny B. Goode/ Reelin' And Rockin'* medley including a reprise of *Let It Rock* in the middle and the "we gotta go now; we got to close the show" interlude for good measure. The combined tracks rumble on for what seems much longer than their actual nineteen-and-a-half-minutes duration.

If you attended the gig, then you might want this release as a souvenir — otherwise it doesn't present much listening pleasure. But if you think this is bad, then wait, for worse is yet to come!

SESSION 73
CHUCK BERRY AND THE FLYING SAUCERS
Chuck Berry, vocal/guitar; Sandy Ford, guitar; Nigel 'Niggsy' Owen, guitar; Pete Pritchard, bass; Terry Earl, drums; Jacko Buddin, piano

LIVE RECORDINGS
Musikhalle
Karl-Muck-Platz
Hamburg, West Germany   **21 May 1977**

Roll Over Beethoven *(Chuck Berry)*	■ Driving Wheel C-7788
School Days *(Chuck Berry)*	■ Driving Wheel C-7788

Sweet Little Sixteen *(Chuck Berry)*	■ Driving Wheel C-7788
Let It Rock *(E. Anderson)*	■ Driving Wheel C-7788
Maybellene *(Chuck Berry)*	■ Driving Wheel C-7788
Memphis *(Chuck Berry)*	■ Driving Wheel C-7788
The Promised Land *(Chuck Berry)*	■ Driving Wheel C-7788
Nadine *(Chuck Berry)*	■ Driving Wheel C-7788
Too Much Monkey Business *(Chuck Berry)*	■ Driving Wheel C-7788
No Money Down *(Chuck Berry)*	■ Driving Wheel C-7788
Little Queenie *(Chuck Berry)*	■ Driving Wheel C-7788
Round And Round *(Chuck Berry)*	■ Driving Wheel C-7788
You Never Can Tell *(Chuck Berry)*	■ Driving Wheel C-7788
Hamburg Berry Blues [Dust My Broom] *(Chuck Berry)*	■ Driving Wheel C-7788
Reelin' And Rockin' *(Chuck Berry)*	■ Driving Wheel C-7788

Three days after the Lochem gig and three hundred kilometres to the north-east, the Flying Saucers caught up with Chuck for the Hamburg concert. This again was very poorly recorded, sounding like it emanates from a microphone in the fifth row stalls (at times the audience are almost as loud as the star of the show!). The whole production is a mess: poor audio quality, badly edited, mis-titling, one track not listed. About the only thing going for it is the full-colour sleeve with photos of the man front and rear (front and rear of the sleeve, not the man — that came later on!).

Unfortunately, the music matches the production: sloppy with little regard or respect for the classic songs by the man who wrote them. What can be heard of the backing group sounds okay, except the drumming seems a little heavy-handed. On the plus side, Chuck plays some great hard-driven guitar if one overlooks the occasional bum notes and fluctuations in tempo.

The Flying Saucers were another retro-Teddy boy outfit similar to Matchbox without the latter's success or stature. (One of their albums was called *Planet Of The Drapes*, which probably says it all! They did, however, have the good taste to record *Johnny B. Goode*.) Strangely enough, *Johnny* isn't featured here, so maybe everything that was played that evening didn't make it onto vinyl?

With no introduction at all, **Roll Over Beethoven** is faded in to start the album. This includes the unusual couplet: "Feel tomorrow, feel like I wanna cry *x2* / Gonna play my guitar until the day I die," but quickly segues into a loose-rocking instrumental that is a long-distance cousin of *Rock At The Philharmonic*. **School Days** becomes *'Singalongachuck'* and is mercifully short. **Sweet Little Sixteen** is poorly edited, and **Memphis** suffers from a bout of the old European 'clapping on the offbeat' malaise. **Nadine** isn't listed on the record label or sleeve, but is one of the better tracks — or at least would be if it could be heard properly over the audience's enthusiasm which rises in waves in response to Chuck's duck-walking antics.

At this point, he decides that he is in tune (and who would argue with him?) and with mock-deference 'requests' permission to open the show. He again proposes to do shortened versions of his classics — which is akin to Picasso painting by numbers or Michaelangelo artexing ceilings! **Too Much Monkey Business**, **Little Queenie** (which sounds like its usual companion, *Carol*, has been lopped off the front end) and **Round And Round** quickly flow like water off a Chuck's back.

In **No Money Down**, the salesman — appropriately for the location — offers the singer a Mercedes in exchange for his raggedy old Ford.

During **You Never Can Tell**, Chuck — ever the stickler for clear diction — requests a little more treble on the microphone so that his T's and P's can be heard.

Hamburg Berry Blues turns out to be *Dust My Broom* in which Berry declares that he "Don't want no woman, go with every Hamburg man she meet." This cut has more going for it than most of the others, with some distorted but fiery guitar and piano.

The final rabble-rousing number is, of course, **Reelin' And Rockin'**, which here never gets beyond quarter to three before it is faded out just as the piano-player takes hold.

This concert is a sad reflection of how far Berry had depreciated his wonderful catalogue of songs by this stage of his career, and the bootleg recording and production quality are frankly all his performance deserves.

SESSION 74
CHUCK BERRY
Chuck Berry, vocal/guitar; Wolfgang Melz, bass; Paul Griffin, piano; Don Poncher, drums; unknown, guitar; Al Aarons, trumpet; Gary Barone, trumpet; Jock Ellis, trombone; Anthony Brown, tenor saxophone; Buddy Collette, tenor saxophone; Steve Douglas, tenor saxophone; Don Menza, tenor saxophone; Tim McIntire, master of ceremonies

LIVE RECORDINGS
Wiltern Theatre
3790 Wilshire Boulevard
Los Angeles, California   **Late 1977**

Reelin' And Rockin' *(Chuck Berry)*	■ A&M SP-6500
Roll Over Beethoven *(Chuck Berry)*	■ A&M SP-6500

The two tracks here are from the movie soundtrack LP, *American Hot Wax*, a double album consisting of one disc of old recordings by the young stars of the fifties (including Chuck's *Sweet Little Sixteen*) and another of new recordings by old stars (Berry, Jerry Lee Lewis and Screamin' Jay Hawkins) and latter-day wannabes like the Chesterfields, Timmy & The Tulips and Professor LaPlano & The Planotones.

The film was released in February 1978, so it is likely that these performances were filmed in 1977. It chronicles a fictional week in the life of rock and roll deejay and entrepreneur, Alan Freed, and centres around his struggle with the authorities when promoting rock and roll to the masses. It culminates in his first anniversary rock and roll show at the fabled Brooklyn Paramount Theatre circa 1956.

The poster for the film states: *'New York City, 1959 — The Beginning Of An Era. You Shoulda Been There!'*. If you *had* been there, you would have been three years too late! This is, of course, mid-fifties New York viewed through the Hollywood gloss of a panoramic lens: the rock and roll era with late seventies sensibilities. For instance, if Chuck had sung the bawdy 1970s version of **Reelin' And Rockin'** to a predominantly white, teenaged audience in the fifties, as depicted here, he never would have made it to the sixties!

Berry, portraying himself twenty years younger, looks great, hardly aged from the fifties, all dressed up for the part in a spotted bow-tie and baggy cream tux. His performance is brief but spirited and we get the finest duckwalk, wheels and splits his crazy legs can muster during **Roll Over Beethoven**.

These two classic songs are sung in medley, but if Chuck thought he would achieve his ambition to front a large swing orchestra it was not to be. The band assembled is certainly big, but under the direction of baton-wielder Ira Newborn it was never going to swing. In fact, although the horns and reeds are there and appear to be playing, they can hardly be heard on the record. The audio recording is okay, but it is far better when seen in the film.

The best moment actually occurs *before* Berry hits the stage, when Alan Freed (played by Tim McIntire) is informed that the IRS have attached the house receipts and in consequence the two star performers aren't going on. The camera settles on Chuck's face as in the background the chant of "We want Chuck! We want Chuck!" is heard.

"A-ah, something else is going on," says Chuck as the implications dawn. "Mmmm," he mulls. Then without a trace of irony says: "You know, rock and roll's been pretty good to me. I think I'll do this one for rock and roll!"

This is priceless stuff from a man known to have held promoters to ransom in similar back-stage stand-offs and who, according to promoter Richard Nader, "raped rock and roll". Without doubt the best line of the film.

SESSION 75
CHUCK BERRY

Chuck Berry, double-tracked vocal/guitar, steel guitar -1, speech-1; Johnnie Johnson, piano; Jim Marsala *or* Bob Wray, bass; Kenny Buttrey, drums

Berry Park studio,
691 Buckner Road
Wentzville, Missouri   14 February 1979

Move It *(Chuck Berry)*	■ Atco SD38-118
Oh What A Thrill *(Chuck Berry)*	○ Atco 7203**a** ■ Atco SD38-118
California *(Chuck Berry)*	○ Atco 7203**b** ■ Atco SD38-118
Pass Away *[poem]* -1 *(Chuck Berry)*	■ Atco SD38-118
Boogie Tonight *(Chuck Berry)*	unissued

It had been four-and-a-half years since Chuck Berry's last issued studio recording when he laid down these tracks over a two-day period starting on St. Valentine's Day, 1979. He had been busy at Berry Park throughout this time cutting tracks for this and that project which never came to fruition. It is possible that these two sessions were for a release that he was trying to negotiate with Capitol, but this is only conjecture. It was also rumoured that Dave Edmunds was in the frame to produce the goods. In the event, the sessions, produced by Chuck at his home studio and engineered and mixed by him and Kyle Lehning in Wentzville and at Doc's Place in Hendersonville, Tennessee between February and May 1979, became his one and only Atlantic release on their Atco subsidiary.

The album, titled *Rockit*, featured on its cover a space-age Gibson guitar orbiting the world. It was released in the summer of 1979, by which time Chuck was yet again a reluctant guest of Uncle Sam, this time doing 120 days in Lompoc, California at the instruction of Judge Harry Pregerson. Perhaps it was because of this incarceration (or more likely the poor sales of the LP), but Atlantic didn't do any further business with him.

It's a pity that Dave Edmunds wasn't involved, because the production values of the album — which contains some interesting songs — let it down. Berry's inclination to double-track his vocals, for instance, is a mistake, dissipating whatever emotion they may have contained.

The band on this occasion included top Nashville sessionmen Bob Wray (now well-known for his bass-work with the likes of Ray Charles, Etta James and B.B. King) and drummer Kenny Buttrey who had previously backed Kris Kristofferson, Waylon Jennings, Linda Ronstadt and Elvis Presley, and had also played on Bob Dylan's landmark *Blonde On Blonde*, *John Wesley Harding* and *Nashville Skyline* albums.

London,
21 July 1979.

Jim Marsala was also there, sharing the bass duties with Wray (though it is not known who played on which tracks) and the ever-reliable Johnnie Johnson making a welcome return on piano. Although Marsala had previously cut an unissued album with Billy Peek in 1974 and had also played on Chuck's lost Berry Park sessions, this was his actual debut on vinyl.

Move It is a fine mid-tempo rocker with lashings of hot boogie guitar and a relentless beat. It is a relatively short song consisting of three unrelated verses of short staccato lines similar to those Berry used to tremendous effect in *Too Much Monkey Business*. The verses are all linked by the command to "Move it!" The first deals with a poor soul whose '55 Ford breaks down on the highway to be met by the "Move it!" instruction from the hard-nosed Officer Lamarr; the second has a "slugger at the plate" who hits a homer and urges his team-mates to "Move it!"; lastly, we are treated to a female who "dresses like a fish; makes you look and wish" and can most certainly "Move it". Above all, the song shows that Chuck Berry could still conjure up eloquent images of American life with just a few well crafted-lines.

The substantial shadow of Big Joe Turner is cast over ***Oh What A Thrill*** with its "Well oh well, I feel so good today"-derived lyrics and Pete Johnson-like triplet-rich piano boogie performed with great panache by his namesake. This cut made the 'A' side of the Atco single that was issued as a taster for the album, which wasn't a bad choice at all. It even attracted a trio of latter-day Berry cover versions including one from the Dave Edmunds

Rockpile.

Chuck evidently liked the song a lot, as can be seen in the BBC-TV *Omnibus* documentary profile, *Johnny Be Good*, filmed in the summer of 1979. Berry, Johnnie Johnson and Ebby Hardy are seen at the Club Bandstand. Flanked by his two old bandmates, Chuck reminisces and spins the LP disc for the crowd, singing along with this track and inviting them to dig the lyrics, particularly the bit that goes: "Squeezing and teasing and pleasing the evening away" and the "Yes, yes, oh what a thrill" chorus, which really gets them moving. The song also contains the enigmatic line: "While the clouds from the east go west to confess it is spring", which I particularly like.

During his Mercury tenure in the late sixties, Chuck cut a pretty unsuccessful session in San Francisco with the mighty high Sir Douglas Quintet. The connection continues here with **California**, which takes its melody from Sir Doug's 1969 hit *Mendocino*. In his song, Berry sings the praises of the Golden State — his 'promised land' from an earlier time — much as he did for the whole country in *Back In The USA*. He expresses his longing to visit its fabled sights: its "movies and showplaces, beaches and freeways", "mountains of snowtop, valleys of rich crops", "Hollywood, trolley cars, oranges and palm trees bending in the wind". ("Oh baby, don't you want to go?") A host of Californian locations are name-checked along the way — predominantly those ending in 'o' — San Francisco, Sacramento, San Diego, Fresno, Barstow... but strangely enough not Cape Mendocino. I wonder why?

As a child, Chuck's father would recite poetry to him, which instilled a love of words, rhyme and metre in the boy (he once confessed that poetry was his life-blood and in 1969, in an interview published in *Rolling Stone*, talked of a 45-minute poem he had composed called *Vagabond's Horse*). Later still, he observed that songs are only poems with music behind them, and even recorded a poem with musical backing titled *My Dream* on his *San Francisco Dues* album. With **Pass Away** he does it again.

This time, however, instead of tickling the ivories he chooses to stroke the strings of his pedal-steel guitar, adding a strange, exotic atmosphere to this *Arabian Nights*-style tale. Seems he only knows one tune on it though, as he again reprises a variation of the after-hours theme used on *Deep Feeling* and *Blues For Hawaiians*. *Pass Away* is also featured in the above-mentioned BBC *Omnibus* documentary, used as the background music to a sequence where Chuck cruises around Wentzville in his coffee-coloured Caddie, complete with air horns. The version used, however, is not the album cut but, as we see at the end of the sequence, a 'live' rendition with Berry reciting it in his studio over a tape of the music.

The narrative is a salutary story of a fabled King of Persia who knows that even his fabulous wealth, his unparalleled fame and his subjects' love will all eventually fade and pass away. There are, of course, parallels to be drawn here with Berry's own fame and fortune, not to mention his 'love' for his subjects, specifically the foxy fan element. Chuck employs his considerable skills of metre, rhyme and reason to spin his lengthy tale of the wise monarch: " 'What is wealth?' the King would say/ 'Even this shall pass away/ What is fame? Fame is but a slow decay/ Even this shall pass away/ Pleasures may come, but these cannot stay/ Even these shall pass away'."

Inevitably, sex rears its omnipresent head: "Most beautiful woman ever seen/ Was the bride he chose his queen/ Pillowed on their royal bed/ Whispering to her soul he said:/ 'Though a bridegroom never pressed/ A dearer bosom to his chest/ But mortal flesh must turn to clay/ Even this shall pass away'." The atmospheric music and indolent delivery of the words give the track a pleasant, dreamlike quality well befitting the subject-matter.

The last song of the session, **Boogie Tonight**, does not from its title sound like a lost *Roll Over Beethoven* or *Brown Eyed Handsome Man*, but as it remains unissued, who knows?

SESSION 76
CHUCK BERRY
Chuck Berry, vocal/guitar, double-tracked vocal -1; Johnnie Johnson, piano; Jim Marsala *or* Bob Wray, bass; Kenny Buttrey, drums

Berry Park studio
691 Buckner Road
Wentzville, Missouri   **15 February 1979**

I Need You Baby *(Chuck Berry)*	■ Atco SD38-118
If I Were -1 *(Chuck Berry)*	■ Atco SD38-118
House Lights -1 *(Chuck Berry)*	■ Atco SD38-118
I Never Thought -1 *(Chuck Berry)*	■ Atco SD38-118
Havana Moon -1 *(Chuck Berry)*	■ Atco SD38-118
Wuden't Me -1 *(Chuck Berry)*	■ Atco SD38-118

First to the crease for the second day's play is *I Need You Baby*, a blues from the *It Hurts Me Too* pavilion which benefits from a single vocal track that allows some feeling in the lyrics to seep out. There is some instinctively subtle interplay between guitar and piano proving that the Berry–Johnson partnership is still intact. The lyrics themselves go nowhere in particular and say little that Chuck hadn't expressed before, but it is a pleasant enough track nevertheless.

If I Were is a country-style rocker with a structure similar to Berry's early composition *It Don't Take But A Few Minutes*. The track contains some pretty neat guitar and piano, but the inane lyrics sung by the 'Berry twins' let it down. Chuck contemplates what it would be like if he and his girl were various animate and inanimate objects, culminating in a surreal scenario where he proposes that "If you were a Mercedes–Benz, I'd have to be a Fleetwood Rhone" and that they could "lodge in a double garage" and live happily ever after "bumper-to-bumper together"! *Weird* or what? The composition is probably the same as the two previously unissued, less grammatically correct, songs titled *If I Was*.

For many years, Chuck had closed his concerts by requesting that the auditorium lights be turned up to enable him to invite jivers and boppers to crowd the stage so that he could exit stage left after the requisite length of reelin' and rockin' had been done. Before anyone noticed and before the music had faded he would be gone ("Ladies and gentlemen, Chuck Berry has left the building!"), leaving everyone exhausted and begging for more — which, of course, they never got. 'Encore' is not a word in Berry's vocabulary. He would usually make his request with a little song titled **House Lights**. Here, it is finally transcribed onto shiny plastic (or vinyl if you prefer) for posterity. Hardly worth the effort really.

In *I Never Thought*, Chuck plays the naïve innocent, expressing his incredulity at incidents of racism from Southern rednecks ("I went down in Mississippi/ Asked Mr Charlie about my roots/ He said: 'Turn around, bend over boy/ They right here in my boots!"), violence from the police, revenge from a spurned lover ("My girlfriend's dating this here guy who's going out with some man's wife/ I lost my girl, the wife her husband/ The guy, he lost his life!"), what sounds like cigarette-lighter fetishism ("I used to have a gold Corina and at that time I had a chick/ She used to get her kicks just asking me to click my Bic") and surprise at the progress of his race ("My grandpa drove a horse and buggy, but my father used a train/ I worked and bought a Cadillac, but my son he flies a plane"). All this wrapped up in a Jimmy Reed beat punctuated by an excellent T-Bone-esque single-string guitar run solo with a snatch of *Jingle Bells* thrown in for good measure.

Berry has described this **Havana Moon** cut as a 'disco version' of his atmospheric 1956 composition. Need I say more? It is just plain awful — sacrilege of the worst order. Gone is the subtle intimacy of the original, substituted with thudding drums, a popping bass (could this be Bob Wray's contribution to the session?) and double-tracked cod-Caribbean vocals overlaid with a third Berry voice chanting "Wah-oh-wah" throughout. Chuck has made some duff recordings in his time and this is definitely one of them!

On the other hand, **Wuden't Me** is as glorious a tale of woe as Berry ever wrote. Never mind the mush-mouth spelling, this is a tale to match *Tulane*, almost a verbal version of Bruce Willis's *Pulp Fiction* mishaps without the gore. Some similarities can be drawn with *It Wasn't Me*, but whereas that song chronicled a series of unrelated incidents, *Wuden't Me* is a beautifully articulated continuous story of a young brother in trouble with the Mississippi law for a minor misdemeanour. Stuck in a Delta county jail without hope or help ("no phone, no plea, no bail"), he cuts loose and is hotly pursued by a posse of Alabama bloodhounds. Just seconds away from "canine jubilee", he seeks salvation with a passing trucker, only to discover that he's wearing a swastika KKK armband! A great song which, had it been cut in his halcyon days at Chess, would now be a classic featured on all the greatest hits compilations. It wasn't completely ignored, however. You'll be relieved to learn that it was covered in 1982 by the great Danes, Nalle, as *Ikke Mig*.

SESSION 77
CHUCK BERRY
Chuck Berry, speech

Unknown location   *Broadcast:* **18/19/20 January 1980**

        Interview   ■ *The Chuck Berry Special*
                          (NBC Radio Network - no number)

This interview was included in a Chuck Berry tribute programme that was issued on a double-LP for radio broadcast by NBC syndicated stations across the United States. It was obviously recorded some time before the broadcast dates, but it must have been after the release of *Rockit* because the album is referred to in the interview as his "latest" release. The narrative is chopped up and interspersed with twenty-one Chess cuts and — rather oddly — the Mercury cut of *Carol*. *Oh What A Thrill*, *Move It*, and *Havana Moon* are included from the *Rockit* LP, and Chuck probably consented to the interview to obtain publicity for the release.

The interview is not in a 'question and answer' format, just Berry's responses to unheard questions and prompts. He covers a wide range of subjects including his guitar influences, his start in music, his first meetings with Muddy Waters and Leonard Chess, the recording of *Maybellene* and the Freed/Fratto royalties fiasco, his popularity with both black and white audiences, drunks and his aversion to them, sex and his attraction to it, and his ambition to play in a big swing band.

The whole thing is pulled together by a narrative from Robert Christau, who has written perceptively about Berry and rock music in various publications including the *Village Voice* and *Rolling Stone*.

The LPs also include comments from Berry disciple George Thorogood, who doesn't stint in his praise of his hero's talents as a singer, guitarist, performer and songwriter, comparing him favourably to Dylan, the Beatles, the Stones and Elvis — none of whom possessed all four talents in abundance. Or, as Thorogood puts it: "Berry is the best all-round ball-player in the business." Perhaps to emphasise the point, his own raucous version of *It Wasn't Me* is also included.

Chuck's old sparring partner, Bo Diddley, also expresses his admiration for Chuck's musical ability and business acumen. He comments that Berry's beat is just an updated 'triplet' version of Jimmy Reed's boogie beat — not a half-bad analogy.

This extensive interview has been used time and again in later radio programme discs for the NBC network, but not in such a comprehensive form as on this *Chuck Berry Special*. However, one release (and there may also be others), *The Source – NBC Radio's Young Adult Network: The Fathers of Rock* from June 1984, contains a snippet of interview not included on the record listed above, which is clearly from the same occasion.

SESSION 78
CHUCK BERRY
Chuck Berry, vocal/guitar; Jim Marsala, bass; possibly Billy Ciofe's band: unknown guitar, piano and drums

LIVE RECORDINGS
Wolf & Rismiller's Country Club
18419 Sherman Way
Reseda, California   *Broadcast:* **19 April 1981?**

Maybellene *(Chuck Berry)*	■ Westwood One/ ABC Radio Network 81-1
Sweet Little Sixteen *(Chuck Berry)*	■ Westwood One/ ABC Radio Network 81-1
Carol / Little Queenie *(Chuck Berry)*	■ Westwood One/ ABC Radio Network 81-1

This LP is another of the 'recorded for syndicated radio broadcast only' variety, but, unlike others of its kind, it contains original live music rather than previously-issued records interspersed with interviews.

The set was recorded at Wolf & Rismiller's Country Club, a large dancehall/club located at Sherman and Canby in Reseda, California (a north-west suburb of Los Angeles) and sounds about as rural as a Tesco's car park. The date given above may be the radio broadcast date rather than the recording date. Chuck shares the album with one of his apprentices, George Thorogood, who gets the lion's share of the time with seven long tracks to Berry's three. Maybe this was because of Thorogood's relationship with the programme's sponsors, Anheuser–Busch, the Budweiser-brewing giant of St. Louis, for whom he recorded a very Berry-like *This Bud's For You* commercial around this time.

The album opens thus: "Welcome to *In Concert* brought to you by Budweiser. For all you do, this Bud's for you. Tonight's show features one of the hottest performing groups in the country, George Thorogood & The Destroyers. And now from Wolf & Rismiller's Country Club, the godfather of rock and roll: here's Chuck Berry!" This gives the impression that Chuck and George played the same night with George getting top billing but, listening to the album, this is doubtful. It is more likely that the two artists were recorded on separate dates.

Berry's three songs are clearly part of a longer set, and it's a pity the whole show wasn't issued because he really gets his rocks off, fronting a very competent band with fire in their belly and boogie in their soul. The excellent rhythm section power along like a Mustang on a four-day drive (to coin a phrase) allowing Chuck space to enjoy himself, singing well and almost melting the strings of his Gibson.

Maybellene is taken at one hell of a lick, with distinct country overtones courtesy of the rhythm guitarist and piano player. Chuck's guitar, however, is pure rock and roll. *Sweet Little Sixteen* is also taken at a breakneck pace, with the bass almost overpowering the vocal at times. Both of these are very short, but on *Carol/Little Queenie* the band really stretch out and blow. This has got to be one of the best live versions of this famous medley that Berry has ever cut: ultimate power and control with not a bum note in sight. Chuck incites the crowd to sing the "Go, go, go Little Queenie" refrain and — no doubt well-lubricated with Bud — they readily oblige.

George Thorogood's portion of the LP includes *House Of Blue Lights* (à la Berry) and *It Wasn't Me*. His two main men are undoubtedly Elmore James and Chuck Berry, and their influences are imbued into a great deal of his work. Indeed, Thorogood has recorded at least seventeen Berry compositions. As he once said: "Why should I write songs? Chuck Berry wrote them all!" Clearly, his heart is in the right place, and he is a storming guitarist, but his raucous vocals are an acquired taste.

SESSION 79
CHUCK BERRY
Chuck Berry, vocal/guitar; Jim Marsala, bass; Shigeru Narumo, piano; Tsutomu Maki, drums; Ingrid Berry, second vocal -1

LIVE RECORDINGS
Shinjuku Koseinenkin Hall
Tokyo, Japan   **27 April 1981**

School Day *(Chuck Berry)*	■ East World WTP-90072
Roll Over Beethoven *(Chuck Berry)*	■ East World WTP-90072
In The Wee Wee Hours [Wee Wee Hours] *(Chuck Berry)*	■ East World WTP-90072
Ding-A-Ling -1 *(Dave Bartholomew, Chuck Berry)*	■ East World WTP-90072
Memphis Tennessee -1 *(Chuck Berry)*	■ East World WTP-90072

In 1958 and 1959, Chuck toured Australia, in 1960 he hit Jamaica, and from 1964 onwards he toured Europe on a regular basis. However, it wasn't until 1981 that he made it to Japan, accompanied by daughter Ingrid and his faithful bassman and travelling companion, Jim Marsala. Two of his concerts were recorded a couple of days apart, and selections from these made up the East World *Tokyo Session* album. East World is part of EMI Japan and the LP is a top-quality product, released only in the Land of the Rising Sun with the excellent high-fidelity sound for which Japanese releases are renowned. The sleeve, which sports a contemporary full-colour guitar-slinging pose of Mr. Berry taken especially for the album, states that it is a *'live recording under licence from Chuck Berry Communications System Inc.'*, so it appears to have been released with his agreement. Surprisingly, however, Chuck seemed not to recognise the record when it was proffered for signature by a fan.

As is common with Japanese releases, the lyrics are printed on an enclosed flysheet from which we learn that Johnny carried his guitar in a 'granny' sack, lived way back in the woods amongst the 'verygreens' and, sitting in the shade could be heard 'stumping' to the rhythm that the driver made.

Together with the ever-reliable Jim Marsala on bass and Ingrid on second vocal ('side vocal' as the cover has it) are two Japanese musicians who are the weakest part of the assembly. The drummer comes across like a Tigo tub-thumper with a deaf wish, while the pianist is content to hammer the ivories in a staccato pastiche of Jerry Lee Lewis. Chuck, however, is on great form. Inspired by the location and occasion, and needing to work hard due to the lack of a rhythm guitar, he plays as though he is back in the fifties, hitting some of the hottest licks east of Java.

Clearly, more songs were recorded during the two concerts. In the absence of any other information, they are listed here as they appear on the album, not necessarily in the order they were performed. In fact, the division of the songs between the two sessions is arbitrary, based on Tommy Holmström's 1983 discography in *Jefferson* magazine.

Side One, Track One, **School Day** is not an inspired choice to open the album because the band hit a wrong groove which only gets sorted out after Chuck's solo. He also struggles to raise audience participation, even the failsafe "Hail, hail, rock and roll!" refrain failing to get a response from the reserved Japanese. However, by **Roll Over Beethoven** the Chuck Berry engine is firing on all pistons. This is a great cut — *the* cut of the album — with highly-charged guitar fills and a steaming solo.

"It's the blues, nothing but the blues," is Chuck's introduction to **Wee Wee Hours**, another excellent track full of dynamics, loping bass lines and improved piano work. He plays some beautifully-controlled blues chords and closes with a quote from *Jingle Bells*... nice.

By 1981, **My Ding-A-Ling** was well past its 'use by' date, but here Chuck unwisely chooses to inflict it upon the unsuspecting Japanese. The only reason it was such a hit in the first place was because of the audience reaction and participation. Here, his '*Ding*' flops yet again — this time because of the cultural and language barriers (if culture and *My Ding-A-Ling* can be mentioned in the same breath). Ingrid, who is brought on to sing the chorus, sounds decidedly uncomfortable and sings rather weakly. There is, however, something quite incongruously amusing about Chuck corrupting Japanese youth and insisting that they respond in Spanish ("Let me hear you say: Olé! "). He even adds to his Japanese vocabulary after asking how to pronounce 'sing' in the native tongue. Side One closes with an attractive version of **Memphis Tennessee** sung in unison by father and daughter.

SESSION 80
CHUCK BERRY
Chuck Berry, vocal/guitar; Jim Marsala, bass; Shigeru Narumo, piano; Tsutomu Maki, drums

LIVE RECORDINGS
Shibuya Kokaido
Tokyo, Japan   **29 April 1981**

Sweet Little Sixteen *(Chuck Berry)*	■ East World WTP-90072
Rock And Roll Music *(Chuck Berry)*	■ East World WTP-90072
Carol / Little Queenie *(Chuck Berry)*	■ East World WTP-90072
Bio *(Chuck Berry)*	■ East World WTP-90072
Johnny B. Goode *(Chuck Berry)*	■ East World WTP-90072

The second Tokyo concert was very much more of the same — in fact, very much like *any* contemporary Chuck Berry concert, which by this time had become not so much a musical performance as a ritual with the leader guiding the gathered multitude through a set formula of calls to "Go, go, go Little Queenie", "Go, Johnny go" and "Roll over Beethoven" in order to elicit the inevitable responses.

Sweet Little Sixteen and **Rock And Roll Music** are the usual fare, with the teenagers rocking "right here in Tokyo" as well as Philadelphia, Boston and all points east. **Carol/Little Queenie** gets a fiery reading propelled by Marsala's driving bass and incendiary guitar fills. After a few days' practice, Chuck was now addressing his audience in their native tongue: "Sukiyaki," he repeats. Not *quite* fluent, but come on, give the guy a break.

Bio — only the second live version of the song since its recording in 1973 — comes as a disappointment. The drive and power of the Elmore James-derived track is substituted with a gently-rocking beat and the verse about meeting Muddy Waters again gets lost in the shuffle. The Japanese musicians do not appear to be too familiar with the number.

The finale is... what else but **Johnny B. Goode**? This is a good, strong version with the crowd eating out of the palm of Berry's substantial hand. "Go, go Johnny go!" they chant, to which Berry responds: "I love you!" And, at that moment in time, preserved in vinyl, I do believe he does.

SESSION 81
CHUCK BERRY
Chuck Berry, speech

Unknown location   *Broadcast:* **week of 20 May 1982**

        Interview   ■ Weekly Music Magazine
                                      'Pop Pioneers'
                            (RKO Radio Networks – no number)

      The 'interview', this time for the RKO Radio Network stations' use, can hardly be described as such, as it merely consists of a brief telephone comment from Chuck sounding like a call from the Planet Wentzville: "I love words that rhyme like 'I' and 'my', 'be' and 'she', and so forth. Definitely rhyme. *[Is he pulling our ding-a-lings?]* Some of the lyrics in *Maybellene* are true. This *[Maybellene's success]* encouraged me to write about my experiences."
      These banalities appear on Side 1B of the disc about pop pioneers and are accompanied by his Chess cut, *Sweet Little Sixteen*, plus a snatch of *Johnny B. Goode* as well as cover versions of Berry songs by the Beach Boys (*Rock And Roll Music*), Linda Ronstadt (*Back In The USA*), ELO's (*Roll Over Beethoven*) and Rod Stewart's blinding *Sweet Little Rock And Roller* with Ron Wood on peak form.

SESSION 82
CHUCK BERRY
Chuck Berry, vocal/guitar; Rei Atsumi, keyboards; Ginji Shiokawa, bass; Tsutomu Maki drums

LIVE RECORDINGS
Yokohama Stadium
Yokohama City, Japan   **7 August 1982**

        Bio   ■ East World WTP-72403
          (Chuck Berry)

        Johnny B. Goode   ■ East World WTP-72403
          (Chuck Berry)

      Not much seems to have happened in Chuck Berry's recording career between his first visit to Japan and the second sixteen months later, though he did put in an appearance in the *National Lampoon's Class Reunion* film playing three songs (*Festival*, *It Wasn't Me* and *My Ding-A-Ling)* which have so far not been released on disc.
      On this return visit, he was backed an all-Japanese band including — unfortunately — the drummer from the previous tour. In 1956 Chuck sang: "Been to Yokohama, been fighting in the war" and now, twenty-six years later, he really did make it to the city, which lies just a few miles south of Tokyo.
      On 7th August he played the Yokohama Stadium together with Sam Moore and his Sam & Dave Revue and local band R.C. Succession. The concert was recorded by the Tamco Remote Recording System (the same people who recorded the *Tokyo Session* album), remixed at Onkyo Haus No. 3

Studio and released with a weird cartoon cover by East World as *The Day Of R&B*. Chuck's contribution was limited to just two tracks, the recording quality of which is sadly not up to the previous East World standard because the bass and drums are too prominent in the mix at the expense of the vocals.

Bio (seemingly a popular choice with the blues-loving Japanese) was

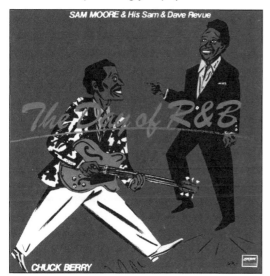

selected for release along with the immortal *Johnny B. Goode*. Berry's ringing guitar is pretty good but the leaden drumming tears the playhouse down. *Bio* is similar to the previous year's cut with the Muddy Waters verse missing, but the ten thousand yen Chuck netted for the little song he wrote is now worth ten thousand dollars — such is the situation in these inflationary times. Yokohama City also gets a name check in recognition of the location. **Johnny B. Goode** fares better, but the thudding of the drums is just 'too heavy, man'.

SESSION 83
CHUCK BERRY
Chuck Berry, vocal/guitar; William D. Smith, piano; Richie Zito, guitar; James R. Horn, saxophone; Jim Marsala, bass; Willie Orneals, drums; Tina Turner, vocal -1; Ingrid Berry, vocal -2

LIVE RECORDINGS
Roxy Theatre
9009 West Sunset Boulevard
Hollywood, California   **Summer 1982**

Roll Over Beethoven *(Chuck Berry)*	◎ Mandarim MR-03978, MasterTone 0301, Columbia River Entertainment Group VMK-1154
School Day *(Chuck Berry)*	◎ Newsound/Penny PYCD-260, Columbia River Entertainment Group VMK-1154
Sweet Little Sixteen *(Chuck Berry)*	◎ Mandarim MR-03978, MasterTone 0301, Columbia River Entertainment Group VMK-1154
Nadine (Is It You) *(Chuck Berry)*	◎ Mandarim MR-03978, MasterTone 0301, Columbia River Entertainment Group VMK-1154
Let It Rock *(E. Anderson)*	◎ Mandarim MR-03978, MasterTone 0301, Columbia River Entertainment Group VMK-1154

Promised Land *(Chuck Berry)*	◎ Newsound/Penny PYCD-260, Mandarim MR-03978, MasterTone 0301, Columbia River Entertainment Group VMK-1154
Memphis Tennessee *(Chuck Berry)*	◎ Mandarim MR-03978, MasterTone 0301, Columbia River Entertainment Group VMK-1154
Johnny B. Goode *(Chuck Berry)*	◎ MasterTone 0301, Columbia River Entertainment Group VMK-1154
Brown Eyed Handsome Man *(Chuck Berry)*	◎ Newsound/Penny PYCD-260, MasterTone 0301, Columbia River Entertainment Group VMK-1154
Too Much Monkey Business *(Chuck Berry)*	◎ Columbia River Entertainment Group VMK-1154
Carol / Little Queenie *(Chuck Berry)*	◎ MasterTone 0301, Columbia River Entertainment Group VMK-1154
Rock And Roll Music -1 *(Chuck Berry)*	◎ Columbia River Entertainment Group VMK-1154
Instrumental *(Chuck Berry)*	◎ Columbia River Entertainment Group VMK-1154
Reelin' And Rockin' -2 *(Chuck Berry)*	◎ Columbia River Entertainment Group VMK-1154

Originally made for television as *Chuck Berry Live At The Roxy*, this set has been available on video since 1990 but it took seven more years for the complete soundtrack to surface on CD, and even then the VMK-1154 release doesn't list four of the tracks on the packaging or on the disc itself.

Chuck has the assistance of a good band with competent musicians who appear to know and understand his work, yet the songs fail to catch fire — mainly due to the fact that he simply goes through the motions, hardly breaking into a sweat throughout the gig. It's not that it is *bad*, it's just sort of polite — and 'polite' is not rock and roll! The overall feeling is relaxed rather than raucous, with the emphasis squarely on the boogie rather than the rocking beat.

To his credit, he recognises the quality of the musicians and allows them opportunities to solo: the drummer is a pleasure to hear, providing a driving boogie beat without the thousand hammer blows that usually feature with Berry pick-up bands; Jim Marsala is a stoic figure at the back of the bandstand and steady as a rock; the piano-man knows his stuff too, and the saxophone brings a novel dimension to the proceedings. Chuck looks good in his dated white suit — like a five-year throwback to *Saturday Night Fever* — and, whilst exertion is definitely not on the menu, he does seem to enjoy himself.

All the oldies are wheeled out, as is only to be expected for the capacity crowd of enthusiastic Californians, but it's a pity that nothing unusual — like a good blues — was featured in the set.

Roll Over Beethoven starts the show and is one of the better cuts, with the pianist and second guitarist taking solos. On **School Day** and **Sweet Little Sixteen** the sax becomes more prominent and comes into its own quite naturally on **Nadine**.

The dash for freedom of the original **Promised Land** here becomes a leisurely Sunday afternoon drive for the residents of the Sunset Home for the Incontinent as Chuck literally walks the lyrics home.

Brown Eyed Handsome Man and **Too Much Monkey Business** are treated with even less dignity. Cut down to a shadow of their former magnificent selves, these compositions really deserve to be treated better by their creator. The **Carol/Little Queenie** hybrid does get a little more of an outing, but not much more and again far less than it deserves.

Let It Rock is one of the songs in Berry's repertoire that normally fares well at gigs, and that's the case here. With the emphasis on the boogie beat, Chuck stretches out on the guitar solo and injects a little of the old fire into the performance — only to blow it at the close by forgetting exactly what it is he is performing.

Memphis Tennessee is given the kid glove treatment with some delicate drumming, while **Johnny B. Goode** injects some much-needed heat into the proceedings with some neat interplay between piano and guitar.

Tina Turner, looking good like a *One Million Years BC* woman in a sparkling tigerskin mini-dress, high-heeled thigh boots and spiky wig-hat joins Chuck to duet on **Rock And Roll Music** — the precursor of his now far more famous duet with Etta James at his 60th birthday bash.

After a quick change of clothes, he returns to close the show and starts an instrumental that is a complete shambles, playing in a key seemingly unknown to the others on the stage. The only good thing about it is its duration, which is less than a minute.

The finale is — inevitably — a raunchy **Reelin' and Rockin'** on which he is joined, as he puts it, by his "wife's daughter", Ingrid. If Tina looked good, then Ingrid looks tremendous, upstaging her dad — in the cameramen's eyes at least. Her nerves and apprehension, all the more appealing at the start, soon dissipate when she gets into the song which, true to form, ends in a melée of gyrating bodies — including Tina's — on stage as Chuck exits, this time via the table tops.

SESSION 84
CHUCK BERRY AND KEITH RICHARDS
Chuck Berry, vocal/guitar; Keith Richards, guitar -1; unknown guitar, piano, saxophone, bass and drums.

LIVE RECORDINGS
Ritz Club
East 111th Street
New York City   **1982**

Roll Over Beethoven	■ *Let It Rock*
(Chuck Berry)	(Vinyl Gang Production - no number)
Sweet Little Sixteen	■ *Let It Rock*
(Chuck Berry)	(Vinyl Gang Production - no number)

Schoolday (Ring, Ring Goes The Bell) *(Chuck Berry)*	■ *Let It Rock* (Vinyl Gang Production - no number)
Instrumental *(Chuck Berry)*	■ *Let It Rock* (Vinyl Gang Production - no number)
Memphis Tennessee *(Chuck Berry)*	■ *Let It Rock* (Vinyl Gang Production - no number)
Let It Rock *(E. Anderson)*	■ *Let It Rock* (Vinyl Gang Production - no number)
Introduction	■ *Let It Rock* (Vinyl Gang Production - no number)
Mean Old World *(Aaron 'T-Bone' Walker)*	■ *Let It Rock* (Vinyl Gang Production - no number)
Carol *(Chuck Berry)*	■ *Let It Rock* (Vinyl Gang Production - no number)
Little Queenie *(Chuck Berry)*	■ *Let It Rock* (Vinyl Gang Production - no number)
Johnny B. Goode -1 *(Chuck Berry)*	■ *Let It Rock* (Vinyl Gang Production - no number)
Every Day I Have The Blues -1 *(Aaron Sparks)*	■ *Let It Rock* (Vinyl Gang Production - no number)
Reelin' And Rockin' -1 *(Chuck Berry)*	■ *Let It Rock* (Vinyl Gang Production - no number)

These recordings form three-quarters of a double album called *Let It Rock*. Three sides are devoted to Berry and the fourth to live versions of Berry's songs by the Rolling Stones spanning the period 1963–78 (the Stones, if nothing else, were consistent in their homage to Mr. B). One suspects, however, it is the presence of Keith Richard(s) on some of the Berry cuts that was the prime reason for this release, the group being eminently bootable in whatever guise.

The production on Berry's titles is decidedly bootleg quality, compiled by the 'Vinyl Rat' from amateur tapes recorded from amongst the audience, with no balancing and a great deal of extraneous noise. The venue was the Ritz Club (now Webster Hall) on East 111th Street, between 3rd and 4th Avenue in New York City, and, as might be expected from an American gig, the audience is very enthusiastic and need little encouragement to sing along with Chuck.

The backing group is larger than usual for a Berry gig, augmented by a tenor sax and, when Keef joins them, three guitars. The musicians are unknown but one wonders if they might be part of Richards's usual retinue. Maybe he needed some backup insurance playing with the unpredictable maestro? If this is the case, then it is likely to be Bobby Keys on sax, Chuck Leavell on piano and Steve Jordan on drums.

The show starts with a routine, nondescript run-through of a trio of classic Berry toons: **Roll Over Beethoven**, **Sweet Little Sixteen** and **School Day**. The sax man gets a chance to blow on *Beethoven* and the audience make their presence felt by singing the famous refrains, but that's about all there is to them — a pretty perfunctory performance.

For the fourth number, Chuck decides to tune up his guitar before hitting for the millionth time that immortal lick-to-end-all-licks which introduces the accurately, if somewhat unimaginatively-titled **Instrumental**. *'Rockin' At The Ritz'* would have been more appropriate, because it is in fact a short, distorted version of *Rock At The Philharmonic*.

Memphis Tennessee and **Let It Rock** quickly follow and again are of little consequence: just Chuck running through a mechanical, formulaic routine with little consideration for the end product. *Let It Rock* in particular, is peppered with off-schedule notes; only the pianist picks up the commitment factor when he solos. The drumming also starts to fall into that mechanical 'thud-thud-thud' mind-deadening tempo that is the curse of many live Berry recordings.

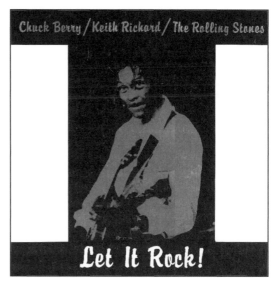

Side Two commences with a brief **Introduction** which hardly warrants a track listing, in which Chuck introduces the band (not by name of course, he wouldn't know them) but by way of "that's my piano-man over there, that's my sax-man over there", etc.

The track titled **Mean Old World** is prefaced with the comment: "Even in New York we have the blues," but it seems the Vinyl Rat isn't a blues fan because this track is, in fact, a medley of Jimmy Reed's perennial *Baby What You Want Me To Do* which morphs into T-Bone's/Little Walter's *Mean Old World* after the solo. The pace is that of a very slow snail, sounding for all the world like *Low Feeling*, the slowed-down version of *Blue Feeling*.

Eventually, Chuck tires of the tune and abruptly lets rip into that eternal crowd pleaser, **Carol/Little Queenie** which, although listed as separate tracks on the album, is sung in medley as usual. "You can't dance. I know the drummer can/ He beats his skin like a natural man," is the most memorable and — perhaps unintentionally — most amusing line. The crowd just lap it up and by the end are singing so loudly that they drown out the band.

By **Johnny B. Goode** time, the whole audience is singing. "Keith Richards of the Rolling Stones!" Chuck announces as the Stones' guitarist takes the stage in time to solo and jam with the piano and sax. By this time, the drummer is content to slam-dunk the kit as the Glimmer Twin lets rip with a steaming solo closer to rock than rock and roll.

Before starting into the next song, Chuck takes the opportunity to openly repent for punching Keith out in a dressing room of the Ritz the previous year: "For the bo-bo I did, I publicly apologise. This is my main man!"

Everyday I Have The Blues follows, expressed with some feeling when he sings the line: "Speaking of bad luck and taxes, you know I've had my share." With two other guitarists on stage, Berry has no need to exert himself and leaves the guitar chores to Keith and Co. "Play the blues, white boy," he exhorts, but the number appears to lose its momentum and peters out.

Side Three consists of one God-awful long version of ***Reelin' And Rockin'***, an excuse for some over-indulgent guitar pyrotechnics which bang on for an interminable time that seems a lot longer than its actual twenty-three minutes forty seconds duration. No doubt a great experience to have witnessed live, but as a listening experience, it is hard to endure. The drumming is by now reduced to nailing slats on a fence. Finally, with some relief, Chuck decides that "It's time to go now" and breaks into his 'house lights' routine: "Y'all want us to stay and boogie 'till the break of day"?

"Yeah!" the crowd yell, but both they and the band know there's not a cat in hell's chance of that really happening. The sands are running out, and sure as grits ain't groceries Chuck Berry will soon be gone.

I'd be a rich man if I had a dollar for every bum note Chuck had hit in his career and this session would substantially top up the coffers.

SESSION 85
CHUCK BERRY
Chuck Berry, vocal -1/guitar; Ingrid Berry, vocal -2; Billy Peek, guitar; Jim Marsala, bass; unknown drums

Rock'n'Roll Spectacular
Wirrina Sports Stadium
Bishops Road
Peterborough, England   3 September 1983

Schooldays -1 *(Chuck Berry)*	◎ Magnum Force CDMF-092
Sweet Little Sixteen -1 *(Chuck Berry)*	◎ Magnum Force CDMF-092
Roll Over Beethoven -1 *(Chuck Berry)*	◎ Magnum Force CDMF-092
Everyday I Have The Blues -1 *(Aaron Sparks)*	◎ Magnum Force CDMF-092
Bio -1 *(Chuck Berry)*	◎ Magnum Force CDMF-092
Maybelline / Mountain Dew -1 *(Chuck Berry) / (Traditional)*	◎ Magnum Force CDMF-092
Let It Rock -1 *(E. Anderson)*	◎ Magnum Force CDMF-092
Carol / Little Queenie -1 *(Chuck Berry)*	◎ Magnum Force CDMF-092

Keys To The Highway -2   ◉ Magnum Force CDMF-092
  (Big Bill Broonzy)

Got My Mojo Working -2   ◉ Magnum Force CDMF-092
  (Preston Foster / McKinley Morganfield)

Reelin' And Rockin' -1-2   ◉ Magnum Force CDMF-092
  (Chuck Berry)

Johnny B. Goode -1   ◉ Magnum Force CDMF-092
  (Chuck Berry)

Late summer 1983, and the merry Mr. Berry was back on the road again, touring the UK with the closest thing to a working band than he had used in years. He was supported on guitar by Billy Peek (appropriately attired at Peterborough in a French beret), his long-time associate from his Chess and Mercury days. On bass was the ever-present Jim Marsala and daughter Ingrid also came along to offer vocal support. The English drummer, Graham Hollingworth, acquits himself well — much better than the usual tub-thumpers Berry seems to attract.

The gig recorded here was promoted by Hereward Radio as a *'Rock'n'Roll Spectacular'* starring *'the one and only living legend of rhythm and blues, Chuck Berry'*. For a 'spectacular', the support was a little thin: Billy J. Kramer & The Dakotas, Screaming Lord Sutch, Tommy Bruce, the Glitter Band and Billie Davis... but then again, this was in East Anglia!

The bash was to be staged in a big top tent on the banks of the River Nene. However, due to strong gales, the location was switched at the eleventh hour to nearby Wirrina Sports Stadium — a smaller venue which left "two thousand waiting outside the door". The duration of the festival was shortened, but at 11 pm sharp, Chuck and Co. arrived on stage to play their contracted forty-five minutes.

Unlike the previous Ritz gig, this concert is reasonably well recorded, sounding like it was engineered straight through the mixing deck. However, the audience ought to have been higher in the mix to capture the excitement generated. The guys behind Chuck know just how to lay it down and provide a rock solid backing, permitting the man upfront to fly right and enjoy himself.

From kick-off with **School Day** and **Sweet Little Sixteen**, Berry gets the audience up for it. They sing the choruses with him and, in some parts, without him. "They singing my song!" he exclaims in mock surprise.

Things really hot up on **Roll Over Beethoven**, with Chuck hitting a stonking solo over a stomping, stormtrooper backing rhythm. Memphis Slim's **Everyday I Have The Blues** is wheeled out again with good vocals and guitar. Billy Peek trades licks with Chuck, sounding like Clapton in his Bluesbreakers years as Berry chomps down on those fat and juicy chords of his.

Despite the piercing Elmore James guitar, **Bio** is a disappointment. This fine biographical song is here cut down to three disjointed verses, rattled off with little thought for the narrative.

By song number six, however, Chuck is really enjoying it and it shows in this unusual coupling of **Maybellene/Mountain Dew**. *Maybellene* always was close to country, but here it really is down on the farm, perfectly combined with that good ol' *Mountain Dew*.

Although this is the first known Berry recording of the hillbilly standard, the song had been in his repertoire longer than even *Maybellene*: he had sung it as a member of Tommy Stevens's band in St Louis way back in '52 before his time in Johnnie Johnson's Sir John's Trio. As an avid listener to the *Grand Ole Opry*, Chuck probably picked up on the song from the show back in the forties. However, it was probably Willie Nelson's 1981 C&W hit that prompted him to resurrect it. He imbues the song — yet another about the demon brew — with an amusing 'country yokel' twang, and it stands out in the set from the tried and tested 'mouldy oldies'.

By the seventh number, Chuck decides to "open the show" (with the audience's permission of course) and rips into an excellent propulsive version of **Let It Rock**. Berry and the boys play as though they are back in the Chess studios in '59 and the famous off-schedule train never sounded as dangerous as it does here. Alas, like the original Chess cut, this version is also far too short.

To reproduce the locomotive's ringing bell, Berry has bent his guitar strings so much he needs to pause and re-tension them before he can continue the show and introduce us to the girl standing over by the record machine.

During the rendition of **Carol/Little Queenie**, guitarist Billy Peek plays a passage and receives the rare honour of being introduced by name. To the question: "Don't the music entreat you when we play so loud?" the crowd respond with a resounding affirmative: "Go, go, go!"

Having got his rock and roll vehicle into gear, Berry slams on the power-brakes as nepotism takes hold: "We'd like to bring Ingrid Berry to the stage to sing the blues. Come on baby, sing the blues," and Ingrid enters to the accompaniment of cheers and wolf whistles. If only she sang as good as she looks, things would be fine. Unfortunately, the Berry genes only extend as far as the fine brown frame, and her vocal prowess is not strong enough to carry a song solo. Her rendition of the Big Bill Broonzy/Little Walter standard, **Key To The Highway** is passable, but would never have been heard on stage or on disc had it not been for her famous daddy.

She fares better on the uptempo **Got My Mojo Working**, growling the lyrics in an approximation of Etta James, though frankly Etta has nothing to fear. This new addition to the Berry repertoire is, of course, taken from the Muddy Waters songbook.

Waters picked up the tune from New York songstress Ann Cole, with whom he toured the southern States in 1956. He cut the tune with revised lyrics in December of that year, several weeks before Cole herself got around to waxing it. (On this CD it is correctly credited to 'Foster' — that is, Preston Foster, who wrote the Cole original and who subsequently settled out of court with Chess over the authorship.) Both versions were released in March 1957 and Cole's platter actually beat Waters's up the R&B charts. However, these sides were eclipsed in importance when Muddy performed the song as the finale of his now-legendary 1960 live album, *At Newport*, which introduced him to the burgeoning white blues following almost a decade after his most famous fan of all, Chuck Berry, had crossed over.

After this pause for the family promotional cause, Chuck steps back to the microphone to render **Reelin' And Rockin'** in duet with his beautiful daughter and, while the music is better, there is something vaguely uncomfortable about father and daughter trading the lines of this lewd composition. It comes as a relief, therefore, when he cuts into *House Lights* half-way into this nine-minute track. He then continues to its conclusion with a high-powered guitar duel with Billy the Peek employing all his guitar clichés. Without a nanosecond's pause, they segue into **Johnny B. Goode** and, with his foot to the boards and the crowd crowing the famous refrain, Berry blows their musical sensibilities: "All my rockers, all my children, I love you!" he tells them in English, German, Italian, French and what sounds like Japanese. A fade-out ends the disc, winding up what must have been a great concert to have witnessed.

SESSION 86
CHUCK BERRY
Chuck Berry, vocal/guitar; Johnnie Johnson, piano; Keith Richards, guitar; Robert Cray, guitar; Steve Jordan, drums

Berry Park clubhouse
691 Buckner Road
Wentzville, Missouri   **10-14 October 1986**

I'm Thru' With Love *(Gus Kahn, Matt Malneck,* *Fud Livingston)*	■ M.C.A. MCA-6217
A Cottage For Sale *(Larry Conley, Willard Robison)*	unissued film version

The anatomy of a gig: 23rd January1986, and Chuck Berry is in New York waiting to be inducted into the newly-founded *Rock And Roll Hall Of Fame* as an inaugural member. Keith Richards is on hand to make the presentation and to perform with him. In the band is a young black drummer, Steve Jordan, who has been around, recording with John Mayall, George Benson, Cissy Houston, and the Rolling Stones on their *Dirty Work* album.

While in New York City, Chuck plays the Lone Star Cafe and during breaks he discusses the idea of a movie about his life and music with film producer Stephanie Bennett. Delilah Films is born, and the plot for what is to become *Hail! Hail! Rock'n'Roll* is hatched: a star-studded concert celebrating Berry's 60th birthday.

Robbie Robertson of the Band is offered the musical directorship on the strength of the good job he made in Scorsese's *The Last Waltz*. In the event, Robertson pulls out because he can't cope with Berry's ego (although he still gets a credit as 'Creative Consultant' at the end of the film) and Keith Richards, a lifelong Berryite, is proud to grasp the poisoned chalice.

For Richards, this is the gig of a lifetime. Imagine the challenge of directing and controlling a guy who has been nothing but trouble each time they've crossed guitar necks! Twenty years of handling Mick Jagger is but a rehearsal for the *big* one.

July 1986: Richards visits Berry Park for preliminary discussions about the band. Keith wants Johnnie Johnson: "Sure, he plays locally." Chuck remembers Steve Jordan from the January bash: "Sure, he's a phone call away and begging to be included." Jordan suggests Joey Spampinato, former bass player with NRBQ *[New Rhythm & Blues Quartet]* who can whack a Fender bass like an old bull-fiddle. Keith recruits Chuck Leavell on organ and Bobby Keys on tenor saxophone — both long-time members of the

Stones touring and recording entourage (Keys also having played on their exemplary version of *Let It Rock* in 1971). With this crack unit, the 'guest stars' are bound to come flocking.

August 1986: Chuck jets off to visit Keith and Steve Jordan in Jamaica to discuss the guests and the songs to be played in the set. There is an inkling of the trouble to follow as Richards and Berry clash over control of the gig. Away from his home turf, Chuck is very edgy — one minute warm and friendly, the next stone-cold. As he himself describes the condition: "At times I become very hot and cold, moody and schizophrenic — it's really controlled schizophrenia, and I'm controlling it."

September 1986: Chuck, Keith, Steve, Johnnie and Joey gather at Berry Park for preliminary rehearsals. These go pretty smoothly, with the band having fun jamming together on plenty of blues and country songs.

October 1986: More rehearsals at Berry Park, this time with the full assembly including guests Robert Cray, Etta James and Eric Clapton. Some of these are captured on celluloid by director Taylor Hackford for inclusion in the film. We glimpse Robert Cray and Ingrid Berry performing a delightful version of *Come On*, while the song's composer observes contentedly. Later, Eric and Chuck sing a very countrified version of *It Don't Take But A Few Minutes* *a capella* and Chuck doesn't seem to mind being the butt of the joke when he forgets the lines.

However, the mood quickly shifts, the temperature rises and the jukebox leaves the room! In one electrifying sequence during rehearsals of *Carol* — a song that didn't make the final concert song list — the shit *really* hits the fan. The problem seems to be the sound of Chuck's guitar that an off-screen soundman wants to change by adjusting his amplifier.

Chuck blows a valve: "That's my amp and I'm setting it the way I want it. It's to sound the way I want it to sound. Don't touch my amp!"

Richards interjects: "It's not recording well and that's the way it'll sound on the film."

"If it winds up on the film, that's the way Chuck Berry plays it. You understand?"

"I understand, but you've got to live with it afterwards."

"I've been living with it for sixty years."

"This is gonna be here after we're all dead and gone."

"Well, I ain't dyin'. Go ahead and sing your song!"

Later on, Keef has the temerity to suggest that Chuck should play the rhythm while he plays lead because it's too difficult to do both.

"Well, it wasn't!" is Chuck's terse reply, conveniently forgetting his liberal use of overdubs on his recordings.

He also instructs Richards on the finer points of his guitar technique: "If you wanna get it right, let's get it right," is his barbed comment. The 'lesson' continues in fits and frustration, and, if looks could kill, the world would now be less two great guitarists. It is to Richards's credit that he didn't succumb. He recognised that, to get the thing done, he had to eat this shit. Had he not, the whole thing could have folded: no show, no film, no recording, no nothing.

The vibes aren't always bad, however, and with tempers cooled, the two tracks listed here find the guys in a relaxed mood, cutting songs from the Nat 'King' Cole songbook and reflecting Berry's taste for sweet and mellow supper club blues.

Both originated in the early thirties: **A Cottage For Sale** was written in 1930 by Larry Conley and Willard Robison and premiered in the *Garrick Gaieties Of 1930* show (performed by the Lazy Levee Loungers). Cole recorded it, of course, as did other Berry favourite balladeers Billy Eckstine and Frank Sinatra.

I'm Thru' With Love is included on the soundtrack album as a peaceful antidote to the earlier frenetic sounds. This composition by Gus Kahn, Matt Malneck and Fud Livingston dates from 1931 and was introduced by Mildred Bailey, one of the first white female jazz singers. Chuck starts the number with a snatch of *The Frim Fram Sauce*, revealing that his interest in it stems from Cole's 1945 version. He may also have recalled it being sung by Marilyn Monroe in the classic 1959 comedy film, *Some Like It Hot*.

Whatever its provenance, Berry sings the lyrics — which are clearly very familiar to him — to the accompaniment of relaxed piano chording from Johnson and smooth, restrained guitar from Richards which elicits a rare complement from the master: "You sure play some purty, purty chords to be a rock and roller, Jack. Really, they're purty chords, you should have been a jazz artist." Keef's reply that there's no money in it cannot disguise his pleasure in receiving this uncommon praise from the guy from whom he once admitted to "lifting every lick he ever played".

Listening to the song's lyrics, it's clear where Chuck found some of his poetic inspiration: "I locked my heart, I'll keep my feelings there/ I've stocked my heart, like an icy frigidaire," are lines that Berry himself could have penned.

SESSION 87
CHUCK BERRY

Chuck Berry, vocal-1/guitar; Johnnie Johnson, piano; Keith Richards, guitar/backing vocals -2; Joey Spampinato, bass/backing vocals -2; Bobby Keys, tenor saxophone -3; Chuck Leavell, organ; Steve Jordan, drums/backing vocals -2; Robert Cray, vocal -4/guitar -5; Linda Ronstadt, vocal -6; Julian Lennon, vocal -7; Eric Clapton, vocal -8; guitar -9; Etta James, vocal -10; Ingrid Berry, vocals -11

LIVE RECORDINGS
Fox Theatre (first show)
527 North Grand Boulevard
St. Louis, Missouri   **16 October 1986**

Maybellene -1 (Chuck Berry)	unissued
Around And Around -1 (Chuck Berry)	■ M.C.A. MCA-6217
No Money Down -1 (Chuck Berry)	unissued film version
Sweet Little Sixteen -1 (Chuck Berry)	■ M.C.A. MCA-6217
Memphis Tennessee -1 (Chuck Berry)	■ M.C.A. MCA-6217
Brown Eyed Handsome Man -1-4-5 (Chuck Berry)	■ M.C.A. MCA-6217
Roll Over Beethoven -1-5 (Chuck Berry)	unissued
Nadine -1-3 (Chuck Berry)	unissued film version
No Particular Place To Go -1 (Chuck Berry)	unissued film version
Too Much Monkey Business -1-3 (Chuck Berry)	■ M.C.A. MCA-6217
Johnny B. Goode -1-5-7 (Chuck Berry)	■ M.C.A. MCA-6217
Almost Grown -1-2-3-5-12 (Chuck Berry)	unissued film version
Little Queenie -1 (Chuck Berry)	■ M.C.A. MCA-6217
Wee Wee Hours -5-8-9 (Chuck Berry)	■ M.C.A. MCA-6217
Back In The USA -2-5-6 (Chuck Berry)	■ M.C.A. MCA-6217
Rock And Roll Music -5-10-11 (Chuck Berry)	unissued
Reelin' And Rockin' -1 -11 (Chuck Berry)	unissued

And so to the 60th birthday celebrations themselves, which consisted of two concerts, the first commencing at 7:30 pm on 18th October — Chuck's birthday — and the second, five hours later at half past midnight on the following day.

The venue was the 'fabulous' Fox Theatre, a wonderfully ornate Victorian pile situated on North Grand Boulevard in downtown St. Louis (the 'Great White Way' as Berry describes it in the film). The self-same place to which he and his daddy were refused entry because of their skin colour when he was taken there as a child to catch some culture in the form of *A Tale Of Two Cities*. The irony and sweet justice of the current situation are not lost on our hero.

The session details shown above and on the next session have been compiled from the film itself, the soundtrack CD, a tape of the second show recorded by a fan in the audience, a bootleg LP and a contemporary report in the local newspaper, the *Riverboat Times*. By comparing the recordings on these sources, the CD and film takes have been attributed to the first or second shows. The tape of the second concert is incomplete, but nevertheless contains more songs than listed in the first, so it could be that these were also performed at the former (which went on for hours, with innumerable breaks in the performance for camera set-up and other adjustments that are necessary when shooting movies). It is assumed that the running order of the songs was similar for both concerts.

The *Riverboat Times* reporter was not kind to those responsible for the concerts, stating that the continuity of the performance was sacrificed to the movie-making. Punters at the first concert were dismayed to learn that a second show had been hastily added and the so-called 'once in a lifetime' concert was to be a warm-up. "Looks like we got tickets to the dress rehearsal" was the cry, and, at twenty bucks a shot, many felt they were subsidising the making of the film, not experiencing a proper gig — which in essence was true. Many people apparently left before the end of the show, feeling ripped off, which must have left those standing in line for the second show feeling somewhat perplexed! Berry himself did not help matters by largely ignoring the audience between takes and only turning it on when the cameras rolled.

Taylor Hackford, a director of considerable standing with the blockbuster *An Officer And A Gentleman* to his credit, made an excellent job of editing over the cracks, and the film comes across as exciting and spontaneous. In fact, the best way to access the performances is to watch the movie rather than listen to the CD.

At the start of the concert, local deejay J.C. Corcoran sets the scene with some introductory remarks and reads good luck messages from Mick Jagger and President Ronald Reagan (the latter roundly booed), then announces that October 8th had been officially declared 'Chuck Berry Day' by the Mayor of St. Louis.

So much for the bullshit, what of the music itself? Well, despite the rehearsals, the build-up, the so called 'all-star' line-up on stage and the best endeavours of Keith Richards, the music is no great shakes even though Richards does manage to get Berry back closer to the classic arrangement of his hits than he has used for many a gig. The problem is that the songs only occasionally catch fire. 'Competent' is probably the kindest description, but since when does competence alone make for good rock and roll? Earlier in the film, Chuck is depicted playing with Johnnie Johnson and a little pick-up band at the Cosmopolitan Club in front of a middle-aged black audience, and these performances have far more feeling and vitality than this prestigious bash. The music may be rough and ready, and the execution isn't perfect, but the *feeling* is right — isn't that the true essence of rock and roll?

Around and Around is unusual in that it appears on the soundtrack CD but doesn't actually feature in the film. It is also a song that is very rarely included in Berry's concerts. Chuck sings it well but there is little evidence of his guitar-playing; he prefers to leave this to Keith Richards who reprises the licks he used twenty-two years earlier on the Rolling Stones' version.

Sweet Little Sixteen fares a little better, with the band hitting a groove and Berry eliciting strong audience reaction with every mention of St. Louis and each time he performs his 'crazy legs' routine. However, at two minutes thirty-eight seconds the number hardly has time to get started before it's finished. In fact, most of the tracks here are shorter than three minutes. Maybe Richards wanted to capture the essence of the original 45s and avoid over-indulgent solos — the curse of many a live concert recording (including his own with Chuck at the Ritz in 1982).

Five songs are featured in the film but do not appear on the soundtrack CD, four of them from the first concert:

The first, **No Money Down**, is preceded by a wonderful sequence where Chuck, like some disillusioned car salesman, displays the old Cadillacs he keeps shrouded in plastic sheeting, like a row of bodies in a morgue. He 's not selling because, as time passes, they are accruing in value. Strangely enough, he doesn't seem to attach the same values to his guitars: "Tools of the trade — tax deductible," he grins... but wouldn't a Gibson as played by Chuck Berry also attract a premium in the auction rooms?

"I'm an all-American boy," is how Berry introduces his best-ever blues composition, and owning a car of his specification is the all-American dream incarnate. This is a strong version with some unusual guitar licks at the close.

Memphis Tennessee, one of Chuck's most-covered and enduring songs, is better yet. He performs the splits while doing all the guitar-work and it's surprising that it doesn't seem to feature in the second show. Then again, neither does **Reelin' And Rockin'** — an inevitable consequence, perhaps, of having such an extensive back catalogue to choose from.

Guest time arrives with the blues's major crossover artist, Robert Cray: the original **Brown Eyed Handsome Man** meets the new Great Brown Hope. "He's right at the age I was when I started out, in fact the dude even looks like me!" Chuck modestly remarks about one of the best-looking bluesmen on the circuit today. They duet on a smooth, relaxed version of the paean to African American masculinity which, although it lacks the urgency of the original, is most acceptable. Cray has no immediate musical connection with Berry, not having recorded any of his songs and favouring a more soul-oriented style. However, after his performance, he settles into the band with no problems.

As with *Brown Eyed Handsome Man*, the tempo of **Too Much Monkey Business** is slowed down, perhaps to allow Chuck to get his chops around the lines, which he manages pretty well. At his instruction "Go, Keith, blow!" Richards strikes out with a sharp solo in the fashion of the master while Berry does a knee-shaking foot-shuffle in the fashion of Jackie Wilson.

Star time again? Well, not really. Julian Lennon gets the star treatment he never deserves. "Don't he look like his pa?" Chuck enthuses. Well, sure, but he don't sing like him. In fact, his singing is dreadful and it's a pity that Berry's prime song **Johnny B. Goode** is squandered on him. Otherwise, the band hit the mark from the note-perfect guitar, the rolling rhythm and the fiery solo shared by Chuck and Keef.

Little Queenie always was a rabble-rouser and it is used to that effect here, Berry punching the air with each "Go!" of the famous refrain. Richards takes the solo again and, for once, overdoes it. I could have sworn there was more than one verse to this classic, but after years of combining it with *Carol*, Chuck seems to have forgotten the words.

Next up is — as Berry puts it — "man of the blues" Eric Clapton with **Wee Wee Hours**. Eric has come a long way since he played *Too Much Monkey Business* with the Yardbirds, and here he plays a most accomplished version of Chuck and Johnnie's earliest blues. Chuck pays rather theatrical homage by kneeling at Clapton's feet, but it is the acknowledgement given by the ex-God to Johnnie Johnson that comes across with more sincerity. Towards the end of the track, Clapton plays a solo on a huge vintage Gibson Byrdland that is as immaculate as his Armani clobber.

Back in 1978, Linda Ronstadt had a huge US hit with **Back In The USA**, so quite naturally she was invited to sing the song at Berry's birthday bash. She makes a pretty decent job of it too, her strong voice belying her small stature. Richards, Spampinato and Jordan provide back-up vocals while Berry hot-legs around her like a dog around a bitch on heat. "Gee, but you're pretty," comments the old wolf. Maybe this was all too much for Ms. Ronstadt, who only showed up at the last minute for rehearsals at the theatre and who had disappeared by the second show. Richards plays the solo, but it is Berry's insistent rhythm that pushes the song along.

Bruce Springsteen's affectionate reminiscences about the trials and tribulations of backing Berry (which are reproduced verbatim in the forward to Chuck's autobiography) precede **Nadine** and her coffee-coloured Cadillac. This reading is taken a shade too fast and has Leavell's organ taking precedence over the sax in the breaks, which is surprising with Bobby Keys on hand. Chuck takes time out to scoot across the stage and before you can say "Southern diplomat" it's all done and dusted.

The incongruity of a sixty year old man singing that he is **Almost Grown** isn't entirely lost, but only someone of the stature of Chuck Berry could pull it off. After all, if the octogenarian Rufus Thomas can still do the *Funky Chicken*, why shouldn't Chuck claim to be "doing all right in school"?

"Got my eye on a little goil/ She's really out of this woild," he declares with a twinkle in that self-same eye while the whole assembly chant "Wah-doo-day!" He fools with Bobby Keys as he blows his sax, grimacing when he hits an off-key riff. Johnnie Johnson hits the solo of the session, and Brother Keith closes the number down with a succinct guitar passage.

During **No Particular Place To Go**, Chuck demonstrates the gentle art of performing the splits whilst playing guitar (at age sixty, remember!) but apart from this highlight, the song goes no particular place. After all these years, he still "can't get the belt a-loose" and therefore, with the stamp of his outstretched left leg and a curt "That's all folks!" he quickly moves on to more profitable activities.

The first birthday show closed in the usual fashion with a rendition of **Reelin And Rockin',** on which Ingrid duetted with her dad. However, this performance wasn't deemed suitable for inclusion either in the film or the CD.

SESSION 88
CHUCK BERRY

Chuck Berry, vocal-1/guitar; Johnnie Johnson, piano; Keith Richards, guitar/backing vocals -2; Joey Spampinato, bass/backing vocals -2; Bobby Keys, tenor saxophone -3; Chuck Leavell, organ; Steve Jordan, drums; Robert Cray, vocal -4/guitar -5; Julian Lennon, vocal -7/backing vocals -8; Eric Clapton, vocal -9/guitar -10; Etta James, vocal -11/backing vocals -8; Ingrid Berry, backing vocals -12

LIVE RECORDINGS
Fox Theatre *(second show)*
527 North Grand Boulevard
St. Louis, Missouri   **17 October 1986**

Maybellene -1 *(Chuck Berry)*	■ M.C.A. MCA-6217
Around And Around -1 *(Chuck Berry)*	unissued
No Money Down -1 *(Chuck Berry)*	unissued
Sweet Little Sixteen -1 *(Chuck Berry)*	unissued
Roll Over Beethoven -1-5 *(Chuck Berry)*	■ M.C.A. MCA-6217
Instrumental -5 *(Chuck Berry)*	unissued
Brown Eyed Handsome Man -1-4-5 *(Chuck Berry)*	unissued
Nadine -1-3 -5 *(Chuck Berry)*	unissued
Too Much Monkey Business -1-3 -5 *(Chuck Berry)*	unissued
Johnny B. Goode -1-5-7 *(Chuck Berry)*	unissued
Instrumental -5 *(Chuck Berry)*	unissued
Almost Grown -1-2-3-5-12 *(Chuck Berry)*	unissued
Little Queenie -1-5 *(Chuck Berry)*	unissued

Instrumental -5 *(Chuck Berry)*	unissued
Wee Wee Hours -5-9-10 *(Chuck Berry)*	unissued
Instrumental -5-10 *(Chuck Berry)*	unissued
Instrumental Blues Jam -5-10 *(Chuck Berry)*	unissued
Havana Moon *[part]* -1-5 -10 *(Chuck Berry)*	unissued
Havana Moon -1-5-10 *(Chuck Berry)*	unissued
Jo Jo Gunne -1-5-10 *(Chuck Berry)*	unissued
Everyday I Have The Blues -1-3-5-10 *(Aaron Sparks)*	■ Diamond Sound 011
Instrumental -5-10 *(Chuck Berry)*	■ Diamond Sound 011
Rock And Roll Music -5-10-11 *(Chuck Berry)*	■ M.C.A. MCA-6217
Hoochie Coochie Man -3-5-10-11 *(Willie Dixon)*	unissued
Instrumental 'Reelin' and Rockin' Jam -1-3-5 *[Berry omitted]* *(Chuck Berry)*	unissued
School Day -1-3-5-8-10-12 *(Chuck Berry)*	unissued film version

The second show, for which the audience had queued outside for hours, commenced at 12:30 am, five long hours after the start of a gig of stops and starts that was more like a recording session than a concert. It's surprising that the oldsters on stage weren't 'too pooped to pop', but **Maybellene** — one of only three songs from the second show that made it onto the album — proves that old rockers never die, they just play another gig.

"I think it is very fitting and proper that we should do for the first number the one that put me on Interstate 70, my first recording, *Maybellene*," is how Chuck makes the introduction and then turns in a performance that captures all the vim and velocity of Chess single 1604. Good vocalisation and guitarisation with a great slap-back bass sound.

As always, Berry's dynamic guitar intro is a great start to **Roll Over Beethoven**, but, when the organ comes in instead of piano, it's like listening to the Mercury remake rather than his immortal Chess waxing. Richards and Cray take turns with the guitar duties while Chuck invites the assembled music lovers to advise Beethoven to rotate — which they do so loudly that he must surely have felt the vibrations by now. It is during this performance that Chuck decides it is all going too smoothly and that he must increase the tension by changing key in mid-song. To his credit, Keith Richards resists this act of musical hari-kari.

After a tentative start, **Everyday I Have The Blues** hits its stride, which on this occasion is a pretty relaxed gait. Apart from the opening couplet, the number is instrumental with Richards and young Bob Cray taking turns to solo. The thing closes with Chuck scatting over Bobby Keys's saxophone: "That's the blues," he states, "the swinging-out blues."

The track entitled **Instrumental** only recently surfaced on the Diamond Sound album and, although it doesn't feature on the tape of the second show, it so seamlessly follows *Everyday I Have The Blues* that there can be little doubt that it emanated from it. It is a long seven-and-a-half minute mid-paced boogie jam with Richards taking the lion's share of the guitar chores. Chuck Leavell gets a chance to shine, taking a couple of impromptu solos, but it is Johnnie Johnson who sparkles on the ivories. Only at about four-and-a-half minutes into the proceedings do we hear the distinctive tones of Berry's Gibson. For a bootleg, the recording quality is reasonable, but the extraneous audience noise indicates that this was surreptitiously captured on a tape recorder secreted somewhere under a seat in the front stalls.

The tape of the remaining titles is so exceedingly lo-fi that it is unfair to comment about the quality of the performance of most of the remaining titles, although it does introduce some songs that are rare fare indeed at the ritual that the Chuck Berry concert has become. Sandwiched between the aimless jams are items such as **Jo Jo Gunne** and **Havana Moon** — very late arrivals indeed at the Berry ball. Maybe it was the lateness of the hour or the influence of the distinguished band members, but this set has a decidedly bluesy feel to it. One segment, however, does merit comment:

"And now, the fantastic, the fabulous, the tremendous, powerful lady of the blues, Miss Etta James. Come here baby. This is *my* girl!" is Chuck's introduction to the *real* star of the night — and he means every word of it. After a lifetime of abuse and misuse, Etta can still blast most female competition within a radius of thirty feet right off the stage. Tonight, she gives it her all, belting out the lyrics of **Rock And Roll Music** for all she's worth at a slower-than-normal tempo with an emphasised back-beat that you just *can't* lose. Chuck shouts encouragement to her in-between phrases, stamping his feet and demonstrating the mambo and tango at the appropriate junctures. The symbolism cannot be misinterpreted when he advances, stage left, with his guitar neck extended in some primordial fertility dance. The pair eagle-rock and Chuck ends up seated on a plynth, legs splayed and grinning from ear to ear.

Etta James, of course, sang back-up vocals on Berry's *Almost Grown* and *Back In The USA* back in the fifties with her boyfriend Harvey Fuqua's group, the Moonglows. Despite of the friendly exuberance exhibited here, in her biography, *Rage To Survive,* she is rather disparaging towards him: 'He was a wiseguy, a cynic and a skinflint,' she states, recounting that, although he advised her to look out for her royalties, when it came to feeding her at the session all he handed out were little yellow peanut butter crackers from the vending machine.

Tonight, however, all this is history and, as Chuck leaves the stage to prepare for the finale, she pays tribute to the "King of Rock and Roll" with a personalised version of **Hoochie Coochie Man** in which Berry is portrayed as the mythical man himself. James sings the song with true conviction and Brothers Richards and Clapton solo in turn. If this performance still exists in some video vault, it should be resurrected as soon as possible!

By now the hour is late, the show is drawing to a close and the audience are in a state of subdued exhaustion. Director Hackford encourages them to cheer for the grand finale, but it only takes Keith Richards to hit a split second of the opening riff of *Start Me Up* to spark them into life. The band play an instrumental based on the changes from **Reelin' And Rockin'** before Chuck reappears, riding in the back of a bright red vintage Cadillac Coupe DeVille with white-walled tyres and wire chromed wheels. Predictably, the final song is **School Day** with its immortal "Hail! Hail! Rock and roll" refrain. The performance is only an approximation of the original, but this matters not — only a scrote could watch it and not wish he'd been there.

In the final analysis, Keith Richards did succeed in serving up Chuck with the best band he's had for years, and I do believe he evened up the score and knocked at least a bit off the chip that Berry carries on his shoulder. The film itself is a lasting tribute to the enigma that is Chuck Berry.

SESSION 89
CHUCK BERRY AND BAND FEATURING JOHNNY JOHNSON
Chuck Berry, vocal/guitar; Johnnie Johnson, piano; Ingrid Berry, vocal -1/ harmonica -2; George French, bass; Herman Jackson, drums

LIVE RECORDINGS
Nyon, Switzerland   **24 July 1987**

Roll Over Beethoven *(Chuck Berry)*	◎ Discurios DIS-124CD
Hail, Hail Rock And Roll [School Day] *(Chuck Berry)*	◎ Discurios DIS-124CD
Sweet Little Sixteen *(Chuck Berry)*	◎ Discurios DIS-124CD
Wee Wee Hours -2 *(Chuck Berry)*	◎ Discurios DIS-124CD
Let It Rock *(E. Anderson)*	◎ Discurios DIS-124CD
Nadine *(Chuck Berry)*	◎ Discurios DIS-124CD
Dust My Broom -2 *(Elmore James)*	◎ Discurios DIS-124CD
Rock And Roll Music -1 *(Chuck Berry)*	◎ Discurios DIS-124CD
Memphis Tennessee *(Chuck Berry)*	◎ Discurios DIS-124CD

Caravan *[instrumental]*
(Duke Ellington, Juan Tizol, Irving Mills)

◉ Discurios DIS-124CD

Johnny B. Goode
(Chuck Berry)

◉ Discurios DIS-124CD

Reelin' And Rockin' -1
(Chuck Berry)

◉ Discurios DIS-124CD

In the mid-sixties, Chuck Berry's stalled career was kick-started by the patronage of the British beat groups, notably the Rolling Stones and the Beatles. In the seventies, Chuck peaked again on the back of his *Ding-A-Ling*, which gave him another ten good years on the concert circuit. In the eighties, the publication of his autobiography and the *Hail! Hail! Rock'n'Roll* film again put him on a desirable high.

However, this time it wasn't only Chuck who benefitted from the exposure: at long last Johnnie Johnson started getting his dues. This is reflected on this bootleg release which is credited to *'Chuck Berry and band Feat. Johnny Johnson'* — albeit that this legend appears only on the back of the case and the bootleggers spelled his name wrong!

Johnson also went on to cut over half-a-dozen legitimate albums of his own during the nineties: 1991's prestigious *Johnnie B. Bad* which reprised the *Hail! Hail!* band with Keith Richards, Eric Clapton, Joey Spampinato and Steve Jordan; 1992's *Rockin' Eighty Eights*, which he shared with fellow St. Louis pianists Clayton Love and Jimmy Vaughan; 1993's *That'll Work* with the Kentucky Headhunters, *Blue Hand Johnnie* and the live *Johnnie B. Back*; and 1998's *J.J. Live In N.Y.* His latest recordings appear on the CD that is included with his snappily-titled biography, *Father Of Rock & Roll: The Story Of Johnnie 'B. Goode' Johnson*, published in 1999. It is a collection of his favourite tunes and includes no fewer than six Chuck Berry songs.

The tour from which the Discurios CD emanates was put together by Chuck's road manager Quint Davis, and was only the second occasion that Berry and Johnson had played together in Europe (the first was a solitary

Sweet, Sweet Rock and Roll

concert in Sweden back in 1984). Also in the band were drummer Herman Jackson from Baton Rouge and veteran bassist George French from New Orleans. Back in the sixties, French played in the Dave Bartholomew Band and the Royal Dukes Of Rhythm in and around New Orleans, and is featured on Crescent City hits by Earl King (*Trick Bag* and *Mama And Papa*), Robert Parker (*Barefootin'*), Willie Tee (*Teasin' You*) and the Deacon John & The Ivories' classic, *I Can't Wait* b/w *When I'm With You*. In more recent times, he had played for tourists in the Storyville Jazz Band.

With a rhythm section like this, Berry was on a roll, but on this recording (and to a greater extent on a Swedish Radio broadcast of a Stockholm concert from the same tour on 3rd July) he gives scant respect to his classic compositions. Thus, the first three selections, **Roll Over Beethoven**, *School Day* (here masquerading under the title, **Hail, Hail Rock And Roll**) and **Sweet Little Sixteen** all come over with a throwaway attitude. All three also feature audience participation in the form of 'sing along with Chuck' which, unfortunately (or fortunately, depending on your preference) is undermiked, making their response sound very distant. This gives the impression that they are indifferent to what was going on, which I'm sure was not the case.

The band seem more comfortable with the blues of **Wee Wee Hours**, and there is some fine interplay between Chuck and Johnnie. Berry instructs the audience in do-it-yourself pyrotechnics before — surprise, surprise — Ingrid Berry pops up to play some rather insipid harmonica.

Let It Rock is one of the better numbers, featuring some fine fiery guitar. George French also turns it on, earning the rare Berry accolade of being acknowledged by name. In fact, all the band get individual name-checks, indicating that Chuck was both pleased and comfortable with them.

Drum and bass are to the fore on **Nadine**, and Johnson takes a hot solo at the instruction to "Play *Nadine*! Go, Johnnie, blow!".

Elmore's trade-lick is dusted off once again as Ingrid contributes more anaemic harp on **Dust My Broom** over a powerful backbeat rhythm.

Rock And Roll Music is a great version, very 'on the edge', with great interplay between guitar and piano, hard-rocking drumming and thumping bass lines. Chuck claims to be singing like Etta James before Ingrid takes control of the vocals and gives it her all, coming over better than ever before.

Sadly, **Memphis** never gets the treatment it deserves: only one verse sung and a short instrumental passage before it is closed down. If Berry is so bored with his songs that he treats them with such contempt, why does he bother performing them at all?

Maybe he just wanted to get into some of that "swinging-out jazz" — something he wouldn't have attempted with a lesser band. His choice is **Caravan**, the exotic 1936 composition by Duke Ellington and Juan Tizol, his Puerto Rican valve-trombonist who also wrote that other jazz evergreen, *Perdido* (Irving Mills, Duke's music publisher, is also sometimes credited, but his contribution was roughly the same as Fratto's and Freed's to *Maybellene*). Ellington's band was the first to record it and it was a pop hit in 1953 for the Ralph Marterie Orchestra. More significantly, perhaps, it was also cut by Nat Cole and one of Johnnie Johnson's favourite pianists, Oscar Peterson.

It is a real pleasure to hear Chuck and Johnnie stretch out on the type of music close to both their hearts. With sympathetic backing from the jazz-based musicians on bass and drums, *Caravan* emerges as the most interesting track of the set. Berry sets the pace like a down-bound train as Johnson picks up the melody, itself superbly underscored by the very busy bass and drums. He then echoes Johnson's playing on his instrument before all too quickly bringing the number to a halt amid tumultuous applause.

Without pausing, Berry strikes up a blues lick that sounds suspiciously like his intro to *Everyday I Have The Blues*, but cuts it off in favour of the perennial diehard, **Johnny B. Goode**. In this instance, the classic doesn't translate well to disc because of the non-existent (or at any rate non-recorded) interaction with the crowd. Capturing the audience participation and reaction — as was so expertly done at Coventry in 1972 — is a prerequisite for any live Berry recording. Here it is simply a non-event.

The closing song is, of course, **Reelin' And Rockin'** with Ingrid — in good voice — joining her poppa again on the bawdy duet. The best parts are the demonstrations of musical telepathy between the guitarist and pianist in the impromptu instrumental passages. "Play it Johnnie, play your piano," Chuck entreats and Johnson obliges while he chomps down on the rhythm. Finally, after several advance notices of "We got to go now, we got to close the show now," one of the greatest rock anthems of the Twentieth Century is brought to an artistic conclusion by three delicate minor key piano chords directly from Count Basie's songbook.

SESSION 90
CHUCK BERRY
Chuck Berry, speech

Unknown location   *Broadcast:* **18 October 1989**

Interview   ■ *Solid Gold Scrapbook* (Unistar
                                       Radio Programming – no number)

Yet more interview material, this time for Unistar Radio Programming's retrospective *Solid Gold Scrapbook* show. In the interview — which again is presented in the form of snippets of dialogue sandwiched between his hits — Berry talks illuminatingly about different aspects of his life and work. Various extracts were used for at least three *Chuck Berry Birthday Salute* programmes in 1989, 1990 and 1991 (and there may well be others). All the interview segments feed from the source interview listed above, though there are slight differences between the selected sound bites.

Chuck reveals the origins of *Roll Over Beethoven* (his sister monopolised the family piano to do her classical practice, so the germ of telling Beethoven to revolve and advise old Peter Ilich was set) and comments on the dichotomy of being twenty-nine plus years old and writing songs for teenagers. He also modestly declines to accept the accolade as the inventor of rock and roll and suggests Louis Jordan as the prime candidate for that honour.

The 1991 birthday tribute features slightly longer snippets of the same segment plus a bit about *Johnny B. Goode* being a fictional composition, not autobiographical. This disc also contains a comment from Johnnie Johnson in which he reveals that *Maybellene* was inspired by the name of a mascara bottle, and that the first Chess session took from 8 am until midnight.

These portions of dialogue crop up time and again on Unistar products from 1989 onwards with various presenters providing the links: Norm N. Nite does the first, then Dave Charity (Nicey's Stateside cousin?) continues the tradition. The whole lot culminates in a four-hour *Rock, Roll And Remember* spectacular on the United Stations Radio Networks hosted by the ever-genial

Dick Clark who pretends that he has just interviewed Berry for the show. This last album was aired on New Year's Eve 1995 and includes the above comments from Chuck plus some interesting new observations on life's little problems. These provide a revealing insight into his personality and are worth noting in full:

On life before music: "Both my sisters were cosmetologists and I knew the route right quick, and I sort-of followed the family tradition. Both my older sisters were cosmetologists and I just followed them."

On taking care of business: "I have lived and learned as I went. Had a manager for about, what, six months, and found out that he wasn't doing anything I couldn't do and was doing things I wouldn't do to a person if I was their manager. So I ridded myself of him and took care of my own business, which isn't really too hard if you have ambition and determination."

On 1950s racism: "She looked about 26 and said she was 21, and I believed her and took her back to Missouri to have her as an escort in a club that we had on Grand Avenue called Club Bandstand. But it was on Grand Avenue in St. Louis, and in '55 Grand Avenue in St. Louis was known as the 'Great White Way'. So, anyway, it wasn't wanted on Grand Avenue. That's my impression of what was going on."

On the effects of rip-offs and racism: "The many things that have been bad in my life have not come as a thing to hate or a thing to be. That would give me a downer because I have tried to train myself not to accept insults and degradation, but at the same time I lost the thrill and gratis of glorification so to speak. My spectrum of emotions is very narrow."

On his favourite compositions: "They don't come in 'favourites'. They come in the amount of success they generate, actually, like other artists copying the songs, or the response from the audience as I do them. Like a father, I love all my songs equally."

On being a rock and roll icon: "I don't ever bother about calling myself. It's other people who call me names, who direct my ability and the extent of my success. I don't register it. I keep track of things that belong to me and I have control of, like my bank account, my character, my health and things like that."

All these exposés, together with perceptive comments from Clark, are woven with consummate ease into the programme between Chuck's Chess hits.

SESSION 91
SHABBA RANKS FEATURING CHUCK BERRY

Shabba Ranks, vocal; Chuck Berry, vocal/guitar; *possibly* Lloyd 'Gitsy' Willis, guitar; *possibly* Homer Harris, piano; *possibly* Robbie Shakespeare, bass; *possibly* Sly Dunbar, drums; unknown, saxophone; *possibly* Goldmine (Brian Thomson, Patrick Morrison, Anthony Hawthorne), backing vocals

New York City?   **1994**

      Go Shabba Go   ◎ Epic EPC-477482-2
      (Rexton Gordon, Chuck Berry, Clifton
      'Specialist' Dillon, Sly Dunbar, Lloyd
      'Gitsy' Willis, Homer Harris)

So to Chuck Berry's last released studio recording, and what a surprise it turns out to be! After three decades of regurgitating the songs that made him rich and famous, one might reasonably have expected that this would also be one of these. But no, his return to the recording studio after a fifteen-year absence is as a subsidiary to one Rexton Rawlston Fernando Gordon, better known as Shabba Ranks. How, when, where, and perhaps most importantly, why this came about is a mystery.

How Chuck hooked up with Ranks, a young Jamaican reggae-cum-rap dancehall deejay king remains to be fully answered, however it is understood

Bradford, 6 March 1995.

that Shabba is a Berry fan and approached him with the idea of doing a duet. Money changed hands, and there you have it! The number was produced by Clifton 'Specialist' Dillon, who also had a hand in writing it.

Chuck always had a soft spot for Caribbean rhythms, hence *Havana Moon* and the other pseudo-calypso songs he cut. The feeling appears to have been mutual with at least some islanders (as evidenced by Eddy Grant's tribute *Chuck Is The King* and Peter Tosh's 1983 reworking of *Johnny B. Goode*) but other than this, there is no direct link between Chuck's brand of rock and roll and Shabba's uptown top rankin' rap.

Ranks came to prominence in the mid-

A nod's as good as a wink, Shabba!

eighties as the most successful of the group of nineties' 'rude boy' Jamaican deejay performers, recording such self-promoting titles as *Mr. Loverman* and *Mr. Maximum*. Even his professional name promotes his superstud status: 'Shabba' meaning an African king (the Queen of Sheba's, no less) and 'Ranks' in Kingston patois being related to rankin' (as in top-man uptown struttin'). He hit the big time after moving from Kingston, Jamaica to Jamaica, New York City and clicked with several top reggae/rap albums including *X-Tra Naked* and two volumes titled *Rough And Ready* before the release of 1994's *A Mi Shabba,* on which **Go Shabba Go** appeared. (Incidentally, the song was only included as a bonus track on the European pressing of the CD, which boasts a sticker on the front proclaiming Chuck Berry's presence — indicating that he still has some sales pulling-power in Europe at least.)

Other than 1994, the date of the recording remains elusive, as does its location though, considering the players, it is likely to be Jamaica. In today's recording melée, however, there is no guarantee that Berry and Ranks ever even met, let alone recorded together in the same building at the same time. Indeed, the album lists no fewer than ten separate studios as being involved in its production — most of them in New York City — so it is probably a reasonable assumption that Chuck cut his contribution here.

The information given against the track is sparse in comparison with the others, but the composer credits read: 'R. Gordon, C. Berry, C. 'Specialist' Dillon, S. Dunbar, L. 'Gitsy' Willis and H. Harris.

Clifton Dillon, the producer, came to prominence in the mid-eighties 'dancehall' boom where DJs supplanted singers, producing artists like Yellowman and Josey Wales as well as Shabba Ranks. In 1988, he was responsible for *Boom Bye Bye*, a major dancehall hit for Buju Banton that is still notorious on account of the storm of media protest it unleashed because of its violently homophobic stance.

'S. Dunbar' is of course Sly Dunbar, the drumming half of Sly & Robbie — the dynamic drums-and-bass duo who have played with everyone from the Upsetters to Chaka Demus & Pliers, Bob Dylan and Britain's own rhythm-poet, Ian Dury. It's a fairly safe assumption that if Sly plays drums, Robbie's also there playing bass.

Lloyd 'Gitsy' Willis is a guitarist of some renown who has worked regularly with Messrs. Dunbar and Shakespeare, while Homer Harris — another producer — may well be the pianist on this track. Similarly, the backing vocals may be provided by 'the Goldmine', a rather ambitious *nom de disque* for three production assistants at the gig.

"Hey, what's up Shabba?" Chuck exclaims in the preamble to *Go Shabba Go*. As the title suggests, the song is an ego-massaging opportunity for both artists, performed to the beat of skanking reggae and swanking rock and roll.

"A mi the unexpected. Give it to I, what they are not expecting," Shabba declares — and he's not wrong!

"Ah, Chuck Berry keep the world merry, ah Shabba keep the girls happy," the ranking one proclaims.

"Hey Shabba, you *are* the king of the dancehalls," Chuck responds with due 'respec'.

"Oh yes, I'm proud of that statement. Yes, father and keeper of the universal language, because it is all we can manage. Chuck Berry give it to dem! Chuck Berry give it to dem!"

To which Chuck sings the title refrain: "Go Shabba go" and "Shabba go, go, go," while Ranks raps his mostly incomprehensible thoughts about rock and reggae music, Chuck Berry ("King of Lyrics") and, of course, himself. Not to be out-egoed, Chuck eventually sums it up by simply chanting "Chuck Berry! Chuck Berry!" Top that, Ranks!

The music itself is a cacophony of styles, Berry's guitar and the baying sax representing US rock and roll, while the drum and bass lay down a pure Trenchtown gangsta reggae beat. Trapped between this rock and a hard place is the persistent, infectious plinking of an electric piano sitting somewhere off the Florida Keys.

Traditional hardcore old-school Berry *aficionados* will hate *Go Shabba Go*; those of a more relaxed inclination will view it as an intriguing experiment: Chuck Berry finally trying something different after years of musical stagnation. If Chuck doesn't enter a recording studio again, it will certainly be a strange swansong to sign off his musical canon, sitting like a full stop at the end of a lengthy sentence — or perhaps more accurately, a huge question mark!

SESSION 92
CHUCK BERRY
Chuck Berry, vocal/guitar; Mark Stevens, piano; Jim Marsala, bass; Jeff Seopardie, drums

LIVE RECORDINGS
Oberhausen Arena
Oberhausen, Germany   **15 July 1998**

Roll Over Beethoven *(Chuck Berry)*	◉ (white label) LGRR01(3)
Sweet Little Sixteen *(Chuck Berry)*	◉ (white label) LGRR01(3)
Let It Rock *(E. Anderson)*	◉ (white label) LGRR01(3)
Memphis *(Chuck Berry)*	◉ (white label) LGRR01(3)
Deep Feeling [Mean Old World] *(Aaron 'T-Bone' Walker)*	◉ (white label) LGRR01(3)
Carol *(Chuck Berry)*	◉ (white label) LGRR01(3)
Little Queenie *(Chuck Berry)*	◉ (white label) LGRR01(3)
Wee Wee Hours [Honest I Do] *(Chuck Berry)*	◉ (white label) LGRR01(3)
Johnny B. Goode *(Chuck Berry)*	◉ (white label) LGRR01(3)
Rock And Roll Music *(Chuck Berry)*	◉ (white label) LGRR01(3)

You Never Can Tell   ◎ (white label) LGRR01(3)
  (Chuck Berry)

Havanna Moon *[sic]*   ◎ (white label) LGRR01(3)
  (Chuck Berry)

Reelin' And Rockin'   ◎ (white label) LGRR01(3)
  (Chuck Berry)

It is a great pity that Chuck Berry's oeuvre didn't end with the quirky Shabba Ranks duet. Unfortunately, this and the following bootleg set have since crawled out of the fretwork.

In 1997, Chuck had toured Europe with Little Richard and Jerry Lee Lewis as *The Legends of Rock 'n' Roll*. The tour was lucrative enough for them to venture out again the following summer as — you guessed it — *The Legends of Rock'n'Roll 1998*.

The itinerary had been planned to start on 14th July in Paris, but lack of interest resulted in the date being cancelled — hardly an auspicious start for the so-called legends. So instead, the geriatric rockers hit the road in Oberhausen, Germany on the 15th, and wended their merry way through Europe for the remainder of the month calling in on the good folks of Rotterdam, Bremen, Brussels, London, Munich, Clam (Austria), Budapest, Zurich, Sunne and Gothenburg (Sweden), and Esbjerg (Denmark) This set was recorded on the first date of the tour in Oberhausen.

For once, Chuck is provided with a halfway decent rhythm section — the same guys who had previously backed him on the 1997 *Legends* jaunt. Pianist Mark Stevens acquits himself well and the drummer, Jeff Seopardie, is a cut above the usual skin-bashers he is saddled with. Bass is by the ever-steady Jim Marsala. It's just a shame that Berry himself isn't up to it anymore. His guitar playing is mediocre, his lungs unable to sustain a complete line of his wonderful lyrics without a break, completely changing the dynamics of his songs, and his overall treatment of his classic repertoire is perfunctory at best.

This lacklustre performance is matched by the production quality of the disc, which is minimalist to say the least. A white label bootleg with no photos, no notes and the almost obligatory mis-titling of the less familiar songs. Worse still is the sound, which is recorded from the stalls with intrusive noise from the audience. The off-beat clapping is bad enough, but worse still, on the slower, quieter songs, we get a Homer Simpson soundalike who persists in reciting the song lyrics (incorrectly in most cases) a few seconds in front of Chuck. I suppose if you were half-drunk this could be mildly amusing.

The performance starts, quite predictably, with **Roll Over Beethoven**. The band try to drive the song forward but Berry's broken phrasing never allows it to get beyond second gear. **Sweet Little Sixteen** gets the 'softly softly' treatment, allowing the audience to do their worst. Mercifully it is very short. **Let It Rock**, which usually comes across pretty well in these latter-day concerts, does so again with at least some sense of urgency to the guitar solo and interplay with the piano.

The polite **Memphis** beat provides scope for some major out-of-time clapping and Homer has a field day anticipating the lines in true moronic fashion.

The inclusion of **Deep Feeling** on the playlist looks intriguing but, alas, it is not Chuck's seminal 1957 instrumental that we get but a mis-titled *Mean Old World*. This does, however, turn out to be one of the better performances of the gig — which isn't saying much.

The usual **Carol/Little Queenie** coupling follows, with *Carol* getting more than her fair share of the time allocation. After a rather long and laborious solo, Chuck forgets what song he's performing (yet again) and sings about people scrambling around trying to get the workers out the way of the train before getting back on track. The spoken passages in *Little Queenie* again provide Homer with ample opportunity to mis-quote, which he unfortunately doesn't squander.

Wee Wee Hours starts off as a half-decent version of *Honest I Do* with an extended piano solo reminiscent of Charlie Rich. As it is only the last verse which is actually from *Wee Wee Hours,* one must presume that the bootlegger was unfamiliar with the Jimmy Reed hit.

There is no mistaking **Johnny B. Goode**, however, which features some strong piano, but again is spoiled by poor guitar with bum notes aplenty. "Go, go, go!" Chuck

Liverpool, 12 July 2000.

sings and, frankly, it is rather a relief when he eventually does.

Suddenly, amongst the dross, a spark of originality breaks through in the form of **Rock And Roll Music** with new lyrics: "Sometimes it's loud and gets out of control/ Can't even understand the story told/ But if you love it, you ain't never too old/ To cut the mustard with rock and roll!" And again later on: "Some people say rock and roll is dead/ It's forty years since that remark was made/ I'm here to show it's live and well/ And all-American like ringing a bell."

You Never Can Tell is a reasonably satisfactory version with fluid guitar–piano passages during which Berry shouts encouragement to his pianist.

In response to "You name it, we'll play it", **Havana Moon** is requested. "We haven't played that in about four years," Chuck admits, then proceeds to turn in the best performance of the concert, even though he does get the words mixed up. The drummer strikes a real cool jazzy rhythm and the band all fall in behind. More's the pity then that he decides to wind it up prematurely to make way for the eight minutes plus of mindless boogie that **Reelin' And Rockin'** has become.

Clearly an amateur production, the CD bears the inscription: *'Any commercial duplication of this CD-R is prohibited'* — which, to say the least, is highly unlikely.

SESSION 93
CHUCK BERRY
Chuck Berry, vocal/guitar; Mark Stevens, piano; Jim Marsala, bass; Jeff Seopardie, drums

LIVE RECORDINGS
Rock Legends i Esbjerg
Cirkuspladsen
Gl. Vardevej
Esbjerg, Denmark   **1 August 1998**

Roll Over Beethoven *(Chuck Berry)*	unissued
School Day *(Chuck Berry)*	unissued
Sweet Little Sixteen *(Chuck Berry)*	unissued
Memphis Tennessee *(Chuck Berry)*	◎ Pyramid 1999-10/11/12
In The Heat Of The Day [Let It Rock] *(E. Anderson)*	◎ Pyramid 1999-10/11/12
Tell Me That I Love You [Honest I Do / Mean Old World] *(Jimmy Reed) / (Aaron 'T-Bone' Walker)*	◎ Pyramid 1999-10/11/12
Carol / Little Queenie *(Chuck Berry)*	◎ Pyramid 1999-10/11/12
Johnny B. Goode *(Chuck Berry)*	unissued
You Never Can Tell *(Chuck Berry)*	◎ Pyramid 1999-10/11/12
Waltz *(Tony Joe White)*	◎ Pyramid 1999-10/11/12
Rock And Roll Music *(Chuck Berry)*	◎ Pyramid 1999-10/11/12
Round And Round *(Chuck Berry)*	◎ Pyramid 1999-10/11/12
Reelin' And Rockin' *(Chuck Berry)*	◎ Pyramid 1999-10/11/12

The last gig of the 1998 *Legends* tour was a twelve-hour rock and roll festival in Esbjerg, Denmark, where this set was recorded. The afternoon's entertainment was provided by the Booze Brothers, the Jeff Healey Band and the Rockabillys; in the early evening, the 'legends' hit the stage.

During the tour, the three protagonists had alternated the order of performance. Perhaps this was to placate inflated egos, or more likely in order to perform first and get back to the hotel for an early bath and a mug of cocoa. On this occasion, Chuck was first on, followed by Jerry Lee, then — surprise, surprise for a rock and roll festival, and for one night only — blues legend B.B. King and his band. Little Richard closed the show.

It is these four who were caught for posterity, digitally recorded on a *'Sony mini-disc and edited in a sound studio'*, as we are so prominently advised on the CD label.   What it unfortunately also fails to advise is that the Sony mini-disc recorder was located somewhere in the auditorium and recorded as much audience babble as the sounds emanating from the stage. And, as far as the editing goes, it is a shambles — particularly the B.B. King tracks, which are hacked about mercilessly for no apparent reason other than the compiler seemed to get bored with the blues.

To justify its bootlegged provenance, the 3-CD set purports to be produced by fans for fans and not for sale. Needless to say, I didn't receive my copy free of charge. It is also clear that the set is aimed at Penniman fanatics, as it is he who gets the lion's share of one and a half discs.

Chuck's contribution is forty-one minutes extracted from his sixty-minute contracted performance. According to an eye-witness report, he looked resplendent in a white sea-captain's cap and a cherry red shirt to match his cherry red Gibson. He was on good form and — probably more importantly — in a good mood, duckwalking with a boy from the audience and allowing a little girl to play his guitar.

Here, the band is stripped down to a basic piano–bass–drums line-up without even a rhythm guitar to help Chuck with the chores. As with the previous session, pianist Stevens and drummer Seopardie together with Jim Marsala on bass provide a semblance of empathy for the 'legend'; it is just a shame that Berry's guitar playing doesn't rise to meet the occasion.

Of course, what is recalled from the heat of the event and what sounds good at the time does not always translate well to disc, and that sadly is the case here. The appalling recording quality doesn't help either, and while the performance may have been a visual treat, aurally it doesn't measure up.

Memphis Tennessee starts reasonably well in a relaxed sort of way.

However, Chuck's guitar sounds decidedly off-centre in the breaks. He seems to find the runs okay, but oh, those wayward chords! At the close, he apologises — not for the rendition, but for the overzealous 'security' who are preventing photographs being taken. "You guys can take a picture of me any time you want, it's all right," he confirms. "I know I ain't purty, but you can take a picture any time you want," he adds, with perhaps just a hint of irony considering his own photographic excesses of recent times.

In The Heat Of The Day is, as any Berry fan would know instantly, *Let It Rock*. Now, what does that tell you about the compiler of the disc? Again, this song fares pretty well in comparison with the other numbers from Chuck's standard repertoire. The piano-man takes the major share of the solos and handles them well: "Can he play the piano? Can he play the piano?" Chuck enthuses. In fact, Mark Stevens's playing is exemplary throughout the set.

Tell Me That I Love You is another spurious title — one which doesn't actually feature in what is in reality a blues medley consisting of *Honest I Do* and *Mean Old World*, again prominently featuring the piano. Audience mutter, from a crowd restless for rock and roll, is at its worst during this quieter interlude.

Halfway through the extended instrumental passage in the **Carol/Little Queenie** coupling, Chuck makes a choice selection from the Book of Bum Chords. He gets so enthralled with the selection that he really does forget what he is performing and returns to *Let It Rock* for a line before recovering (or should that be covering up?) the situation. His guitar-playing on this number just plain sucks. Maybe he was distracted by the female dancers? "Let's give the dancers a hand, especially big mama — she's *my* kind, you know," he leers.

Worse still, he completely eschews the wonderfully descriptive lyrics of **You Never Can Tell**, preferring to wing it instrumentally.

"Just let me play some more **Rock And Roll Music**" is the opening line of this classic. If only he would, instead of churning out these careless renditions!

Round And Round, unfortunately, is simply more of the same. This relatively unusual choice from Berry's back catalogue is treated with the same contempt as its more familiar relatives. After two minutes it ends abruptly with a curt: "That's all!" And it sure is.

In amongst the golden oldies and blues fillers of a typical Chuck Berry concert there are always one or two off-the-wall songs that provide an insight into the man's musical tastes. **Waltz** is one of these, and as such emerges as the most interesting number of the whole set.

"Now here's my impression of the best waltz that was written," is Chuck's introduction to the tune which has been in his concert repertoire for the past few years, and which here is carried as much by the piano as the guitar. Its proper title is *3/4 Time*, penned by Tony Joe White and premiered by Ray Charles on his 1983 Columbia album, *Wish You Were Here Tonight*.

In Brother Ray's hands it is a lilting, country number full of shading and subtleties; in Brother Chuck's hands, in this concert setting, it is a much cruder affair. When Ray sings of finding a woman who likes to make love in 3/4 time, you can believe it; in contrast, Chuck's search is clearly for sex rather than love, as he resorts to a base enticement of the audience to join him in chanting "Ugh!" in waltz time.

Finally, we are subjected to eight minutes of ***Reelin' And Rockin'***, which unfortunately seems a darn sight longer. Two quick throwaway verses, then down to the interminable boogie with the obligatory "We gotta go now. Y'all want us to stay?" routine, then more boogie as Chuck, guitar outstretched, backs off the stage.

This disappointing set brings to a close Chuck Berry's recorded works to date and inevitably begs the question: why does he continue to do it? Seventy-four years old, a rich man, a famous man — does he really need it? Do *we* need it? Presumably he does

Liverpool, 12 July 2000.

still enjoy the venerable adulation he receives, particularly in Europe. His performance schedule has reduced in recent years and he can't make those famous duckwalks and splits as he would like, but his energy levels remain high.

As I write, long distance information has just arrived that Chuck plans to release a new studio album consisting of thirteen new compositions including one tantalisingly called *Lady B. Good* (no prizes for guessing the progenitor of this song!) and another titled *Loco Joe* (said to be *Jo Jo Gunne* with new lyrics) in celebration of his 75th birthday. I for one can hardly wait!

In his 1987 autobiography, Chuck wrote that the entire catalogue of his songs was to follow in a 'Chuck Berry Songbook'. This was to contain full information about the when, where and by whom of his recordings. Until this publication appears, I hope this book will suffice and enhance the enjoyment for those who, like myself, love Chuck Berry's music.

3

Chuck Berry on Record

This section contains chronological listings by format of Chuck Berry's principal/ notable releases and significant reissues. Where only the year of release is known, records are listed in alphabetical order by label, then by catalogue number, within each year.

Releases prefixed with the symbol ▶ appear in the *Sessionography*.

Song titles are shown exactly as listed on each release. The number shown after each song title is a cross-reference to the session at which it was cut.

Where an album was issued on several discs, the titles appearing on each disc are preceded by the disc number thus: ❶ Maybellene (2), Wee Wee Hours (2) .....

SINGLES
US Singles

Label/Cat No	Titles	Released
▶ Ballad AA1008-X45	Oh Maria (1) / I Hope These Words Will Find You Well (1) *(Both sides by Joe Alexander & The Cubans)*	Aug 1954
▶ Chess 1604	Maybellene (2) / Wee Wee Hours (2)	July 1955
▶ Chess 1610	Thirty Days (3) / Together (We Will Always Be) (3)	Sep 1955
▶ Chess 1615	No Money Down (4) / The Down Bound Train (4)	Dec 1955
▶ Chess 1626	Roll Over Beethoven (5) / Drifting Heart (5)	May 1956
▶ Chess 1635	Too Much Monkey Business (5) / Brown Eyed Handsome Man (5)	Sep 1956
▶ Chess 1645	You Can't Catch Me (4) / Havana Moon (6)	Nov 1956
▶ Chess 1653	School Day (9) / Deep Feeling (9)	Mar 1957
▶ Chess 1664	Oh Baby Doll (10) / Lajaunda (9)	June 1957
▶ Chess 1671	Rock And Roll Music (10) / Blue Feeling (9)	Sep 1957
▶ Chess 1683	Sweet Little Sixteen (12) / Reelin' And Rockin' (12)	Feb 1958
▶ Chess 1691	Johnny B. Goode (13) / Around And Around (14)	Apr 1958
▶ Chess 1697	Vacation Time (15) / Beautiful Delilah (15)	July 1958
▶ Chess 1700	Carol (16) / Hey Pedro (16)	Aug 1958
▶ Chess 1709	Sweet Little Rock And Roller (19) / Jo Jo Gunne (18)	Oct 1958
▶ Chess 1714	Run Rudolph Run (20) / Merry Christmas Baby (20)	Dec 1958
▶ Chess 1716	Anthony Boy (19) / That's My Desire (20)	Jan 1959
▶ Chess 1722	Almost Grown (21) / Little Queenie (20)	Mar 1959
▶ Chess 1729	Back In The USA (21) / Memphis Tennessee (18)	Jun 1959
▶ Chess 1737	Broken Arrow (22) / Childhood Sweetheart (22)	Sep 1959
▶ Argo 5353	Say You'll Be Mine (22) / Let Me Sleep Woman (22) *(Both sides by the Ecuadors)*	Nov 1959
▶ Chess 1747	Too Pooped To Pop (22) / Let It Rock (22)	Jan 1960
▶ Chess 1754	Bye Bye Johnny (23) / Worried Life Blues (23)	Aug 1960
▶ Chess 1763	I Got To Find My Baby (23) / Mad Lad (24)	Aug 1960
▶ Chess 1767	Jaguar And Thunderbird (23) / Our Little Rendezvous (23)	Oct 1960
▶ Chess 1779	I'm Talking About You (25) / Little Star (24)	Feb 1961
▶ Chess 1799	Go Go Go (26) / Come On (26)	Oct 1961

►Chess 1853	I'm Talking About You **(25)** / Diploma For Two **(24)**	Apr 1963
►Chess 1866	Sweet Little Sixteen (Surfin' USA) **(12)** /	
	Memphis Tennessee **(18)**	July 1963
	(Both sides with overdubbed audience)	
►Chess 1883	Nadine (Is It You?) **(27)** / O'Rangutang **(27)**	Feb 1964
►Chess 1898	No Particular Place To Go **(29)** / You Two **(29)**	Apr 1964
►Chess 1906	You Never Can Tell **(27)** / Brenda Lee **(28)**	July 1964
►Checker 1089	Chuck's Beat **(30,** *single edit***)** / Bo's Beat **(30,** *single edit***)**	Aug 1964
	(Both sides by Chuck Berry & Bo Diddley)	
►Chess 1912	Little Marie **(32)** / Go, Bobby Soxer **(32)**	Sep 1964
►Chess 1916	Promised Land **(28)** / Things I Used To Do **(27)**	Nov 1964
►Chess 1926	Dear Dad **(33)** / Lonely School Days **(33,** *slow version***)**	Mar 1965
►Chess 1943	It Wasn't Me **(39)** / Welcome Back Pretty Baby **(39)**	Sep 1965
►Chess 1963	Lonely School Days **(40,** *fast version***)** / Ramona, Say Yes **(40)**	Jun 1966
►Chess 1963	Ramona, Say Yes **(40)** / Havana Moon **(6)**	Aug 1966
►YMCA DJS-1/2	Y.M.C.A. DJ Special **(50)** *(33⅓ rpm Various Artists single)*	1967
►Mercury 72643	Club Nitty Gritty **(43)** / Laugh And Cry **(41)**	Jan 1967
►Mercury 72680	Back To Memphis **(45)** / I Do Really Love You **(45)**	May 1967
►Mercury 72748	It Hurts Me Too **(49)** / Feelin' It **(48)**	Nov 1967
►Mercury 72840	Louie To Frisco **(52)** / Ma Dear **(52)**	July 1968
►Mercury 72963	It's Too Dark In There **(53)** / Good Lookin' Woman **(53)**	Aug 1969
►Chess CH-2090	Tulane **(55)** / Have Mercy Judge **(55)**	Aug 1970
►Chess CH-2131	My Ding-A-Ling **(59)** / Johnny B. Goode **(59)**	July 1972
►Chess CH-2136	Reelin' And Rockin' **(59)** / Let's Boogie **(60)**	Nov 1972
►Chess CH-2140	Bio **(66)** / Roll 'Em Pete **(59)**	May 1973
►Chess CH-2169	Shake, Rattle And Roll **(70)** /	
	Baby What You Want To Do **(70)**	Feb 1975
►Atco 7203	Oh What A Thrill **(75)** / California **(75)**	Aug 1979

Notable reissue

►Spindle SPN-2001	Oh Maria **(1)** / I Hope These Words Will Find You Well **(1)**	1995
	(Both sides by Joe Alexander & The Cubans)	

Note: Throughout the 1970's and 1980's Chuck Berry's Chess hits were reissued time and again as the catalogue changed corporate hands: GRT's Chess 'Blue Chip' series (1974-75), All-Platinum's Chess 'Blue Chip' series (1975), Eric 'Oldies But Goodies' (1981), Sugar Hill's Chess label (1983), MCA's Chess label (1984), Replete 'Gold Nuggets' (1985) and Collectables (1987-88). Mercury got in on the reissues act even earlier, recycling his mid-sixties remakes in 1972 via their 'Celebrity' series.

UK Singles

Label/Cat No	Titles	Released
London HLU-8275	No Money Down **(4)** / The Downbound Train **(4)**	May 1956
London HLN-8375	You Can't Catch Me **(4)** / Havana Moon **(6)**	Feb 1957
London HLU-8428	Roll Over Beethoven **(5)** / Drifting Heart **(5)**	May 1957
Columbia DB-3951	School Day **(9)** / Deep Feeling **(9)**	Jun 1957
London HLM-8531	Rock And Roll Music **(10)** / Blue Feeling **(9)**	Dec 1957
London HLM-8585	Sweet Little Sixteen **(12)** / Reelin' And Rockin' **(12)**	Mar 1958
London HLM-8629	Johnny B. Goode **(13)** / Around And Around **(14)**	Jun 1958
London HL-8677	Beautiful Delilah **(15)** / Vacation Time **(15)**	Aug 1958
London HL-8712	Carol **(16)** / Hey Pedro **(16)**	Oct 1958
London HLM-8767	Sweet Little Rock And Roller **(19)** / Joe Joe Gunne **(18)**	Dec 1958
London HLM-8853	Almost Grown **(21)** / Little Queenie **(20)**	Apr 1959
London HLM-8921	Back In The USA **(21)** / Memphis Tennessee **(18)**	July 1989
London HLM-9069	Too Pooped To Pop **(22)** / Let It Rock **(22)**	Mar 1960
London HLM-9159	Bye Bye Johnny **(23)** / Mad Lad **(24)**	July 1960

Pye Int'l. 7N.25100	I'm Talking 'Bout You **(25)** / Little Star **(24)**	Sep 1961
Pye Int'l. 7N.25209	Go Go Go **(26)** / Come On **(26)**	July 1963
Pye Int'l. 7N.25218	Let It Rock **(22)** / Memphis Tennessee **(18)**	Sep 1963
Pye Int'l. 7N.25228	Run Rudolph Run **(20)** / Johnny B. Goode **(13)**	Dec 1963
Pye Int'l. 7N.25236	Nadine **(27)** / O'Rangutang **(27)**	Feb 1964
Pye Int'l. 7N.25242	No Particular Place To Go **(29)** / Liverpool Drive **(29)**	May 1964
Pye Int'l. 7N.25257	You Never Can Tell **(27)** / Brenda Lee **(28)**	Aug 1964
Pye Int'l. 7N.25271	Little Marie **(32)** / Go, Bobby Soxer **(32)**	Oct 1964
Pye Int'l. 7N.25285	The Promised Land **(28)** / Things I Used To Do **(27)**	Jan 1965
Chess CRS-8006	I Got A Booking **(35)** / Lonely School Days **(33**, *slow version*)	Mar 1965
Chess CRS-8012	Dear Dad **(33)** / My Little Love Light **(35)**	Apr 1965
Chess CRS-8022	It Wasn't Me **(39)** / It's My Own Business **(37)**	Oct 1965
Chess CRS-8037	Ramona, Say Yes **(40)**/ Lonely School Days **(40**, *fast version*)	Jun 1966
Chess CRS-8075	Johnny B. Goode **(13)** / Sweet Little Sixteen **(12)**	May 1966
Chess CRS-8089	No Particular Place To Go **(29)** / It Wasn't Me **(39)**	Apr 1966
Mercury MF-958	Club Nitty Gritty **(43)** / Laugh And Cry **(41)**	Dec 1966
Mercury MF-994	Back To Memphis **(45)** / I Do Really Love You **(45)**	July 1967
Mercury MF-1057	St. Louis To Frisco **(52)** / Ma Dear **(52)**	Oct 1968
Mercury MF-1102	Back To Memphis **(45)** / Roll Over Beethoven **(42)**	May 1969
Chess 6078 707	Sweet Little Sixteen **(12)** / Guitar Boogie **(12)**	May 1971
▶ Chess 6145 019	My Ding-A-Ling **(59)** / Let's Boogie **(60)**	Oct 1972
Chess 6145 020	Reelin' And Rockin' **(59)** / I Will Not Let You Go **(60)**	Jan 1973
▶ Chess 6145 027	South Of The Border **(62)** / Bio **(66)**	Nov 1973
Chess 6145 038	Shake Rattle and Roll **(70)** / I'm Just A Name **(67)**	Feb 1975
Atlantic K-11354	Oh What A Thrill **(74)** / California **(74)**	Aug 1979

Foreign Singles

Label/Cat No	Titles	Released
▶ Bellaphon BF-18214	Bio **(66)** / Roll 'Em Pete **(58)**	West Germany, 1973

EPs & MAXISINGLES
US EPs

▶**AFTER SCHOOL SESSION** (Chess EP-5118) *also issued as* **HEAD OVER HEELS**   1957

School Day **(9)**, Wee Wee Hours **(2)**, Too Much Monkey Business **(5)**, Brown Eyed Handsome Man **(5)**

▶**ROCK AND ROLL MUSIC** (Chess EP-5119)   1958

Rock And Roll Music **(10)**, Blue Feeling **(9)**, Oh Baby Doll **(10)**, La Jaunda **(9)**

▶**SWEET LITTLE 16** (Chess EP-5121)   1958

Sweet Little Sixteen **(12)**, Rockin' At The Philharmonic **(12)**, Reelin' And Rockin' **(12)**, Guitar Boogie **(12)**

▶**PICKIN' BERRIES** (Chess EP-5124)   1958

Beautiful Delilah **(15)**, Vacation Time **(15)**, Carol **(16)**, Hey Pedro **(16)**

▶**SWEET LITTLE ROCK AND ROLLER** (Chess EP-5126)   1958

Sweet Little Rock And Roller **(19)**, Jo Jo Gunne **(18)**, Johnny B. Goode **(13)**, Around And Around **(14)**

UK EPs & Maxisingles

RHYTHM AND BLUES WITH CHUCK BERRY (London RE-U-1053)   June 1956

Maybellene **(2)**, Wee Wee Hours **(2)**, Thirty Days **(3)**, Together (We Will Always Be) **(3)**

REELIN' AND ROCKIN' (London RE-M-1188)   March 1959

Reelin' And Rockin' **(12)**, Rock And Roll Music **(10)**, Sweet Little Sixteen **(12)**, Guitar Boogie **(12)**

Chuck Berry / Bo Diddley
CHUCK & BO (Pye International NEP-44009)   September 1963

Roll Over Beethoven **(5)**, Our Little Rendezvous **(23)**. *Chuck Berry does not appear on other tracks.*

CHUCK BERRY (Pye International NEP-44011)   October 1963

Johnny B. Goode **(13)**, Oh Baby Doll **(10)**, School Day **(9)**, Back In The USA **(21)**

Chuck Berry / Bo Diddley
CHUCK & BO (VOLUME 2) (Pye International NEP-44012)   November 1963

You Can't Catch Me **(4)**, No Money Down **(4)**. *Chuck Berry does not appear on other tracks.*

THIS IS CHUCK BERRY (Pye International NEP-44013)   December 1963

Bye Bye Johnny **(23)**, Rock And Roll Music **(10)**, Childhood Sweetheart **(22)**, Broken Arrow **(22)**

Chuck Berry / Bo Diddley
CHUCK & BO (VOLUME 3) (Pye International NEP-44017)   February 1964

Too Pooped To Pop **(22)**, It Don't Take But A Few Minutes **(14)**. *Chuck Berry does not appear on other tracks.*

THE BEST OF CHUCK BERRY (Pye International NEP-44018)   April 1964

Memphis Tennessee **(18)**, Roll Over Beethoven **(5)**, I'm Talking About You **(25)**, Sweet Little Sixteen **(12)**

CHUCK BERRY HITS (Pye International NEP-44028)   October 1964

Johnny B. Goode **(13)**, Nadine **(27)**, No Particular Place To Go **(29)**, Memphis Tennessee **(18)**

▶**BLUE MOOD** (Pye International NEP-44033)   December 1964

Drifting Blues **(23)**, Lonely All The Time **(27)**, Things I Used To Do **(27)**, Fraulein **(27)**

THE PROMISED LAND (Chess CRE-6002)   March 1965

You Never Can Tell **(27)**, Brenda Lee **(28)**, Promised Land **(28)**, Things I Used To Do **(27)**

COME ON (Chess CRE-6005)   October 1965

Come On **(26)**, Reelin' And Rockin' **(12)**, Around And Around **(14)**, Don't You Lie To Me **(23)**

I GOT A BOOKING (Chess CRE-6012)   February 1966

I Want To Be Your Driver **(33)**, St. Louis Blues **(35)**, Dear Dad **(33)**, I Got A Booking **(35)**

YOU CAME A LONG WAY FROM ST. LOUIS (Chess CRE-6016)   May 1966

You Came A Long Way From St. Louis **(34)**, His Daughter Caroline **(33)**, My Little Love Light **(35)**, Jamaica Farewell **(34)**

untitled (Chess 6145 007)   March 1972

Rock And Roll Music **(10)**, Johnny B. Goode **(13)**, School Day **(9)**

Chuck Berry / Bo Diddley
BIG DADDIES (Chess 6145 012)   August 1972

Johnny B. Goode **(13)**, Down The Road Apiece **(24)** *Chuck Berry does not appear on other tracks.*

untitled (Chess 6198 080)   May 1976

Sweet Little Rock And Roller **(19)**, No Particular Place To Go **(29)**, Back In The USA **(21)**

LPs
US LPs

Chuck Berry / Flamingos / Moonglows
▶**ROCK, ROCK, ROCK** (Chess LP-1425) *mono*   November 1956
Maybellene **(2)**, Thirty Days **(3)**, You Can't Catch Me **(4)**, Roll Over Beethoven **(5)**.
Chuck Berry does not appear on other tracks.
*NB Chess also pressed 600 copies of a promotional LP (unnumbered) featuring all twenty songs
from the film for distribution to movie theatre managers.*

▶**AFTER SCHOOL SESSION** (Chess LP-1426) *mono*   May 1957
School Day **(9)**, Deep Feeling **(9)**, Too Much Monkey Business **(5)**, Wee Wee Hours **(2)**, Rolli
Polli **(4)**, No Money Down **(4)**, Brown Eyed Handsome Man **(5)**, Berry Pickin' **(4)**, Together (We Will
Always Be) **(3)**, Havana Moon **(6)**, Downbound Train **(4)**, Drifting Heart **(5)**

▶**ONE DOZEN BERRYS** (Chess LP-1432) *mono*   March 1958
Sweet Little Sixteen **(12)**, Blue Feeling **(9)**, La Jaunda **(9**, *alt. take*), Rockin' At The Philharmonic
(12), Oh, Baby Doll **(10)**, Guitar Boogie **(12)**, Reelin' And Rockin' **(12)**, Ingo **(14)**, Rock And Roll
Music **(10)**, How You've Changed **(10)**, Low Feeling **(9)**, It Don't Take But A Few Minutes **(14)**

▶**CHUCK BERRY IS ON TOP** (Chess LP-1435) *mono*   July 1959
Almost Grown **(21)**, Carol **(16)**, Maybellene **(2)**, Sweet Little Rock And Roller **(19)**, Anthony
Boy **(19)**, Johnny B. Goode **(13)**, Little Queenie **(20)**, Jo Jo Gunne **(18)**, Roll Over Beethoven **(5)**,
Around And Around **(14)**, Hey Pedro **(16)**, Blues For Hawaiians **(14)**

▶**ROCKIN' AT THE HOPS** (Chess LP-1448) *mono*   July 1960
Bye Bye Johnny **(23)**, Worried Life Blues **(23)**, Down The Road Apiece **(24)**, Confessin' The
Blues **(24)**, Too Pooped To Pop **(22)**, Mad Lad **(24)**, I Got To Find My Baby **(23)**, Betty Jean **(22)**,
Childhood Sweetheart **(22)**, Broken Arrow **(22)**, Drifting Blues **(23)**, Let It Rock **(22)**

▶**NEW JUKE BOX HITS** (Chess LP-1456) *mono*   March 1961
I'm Talking About You **(25)**, Diploma For Two **(24)**, Thirteen Question Method **(24)**, Away From
You **(24)**, Don't You Lie To Me **(23)**, The Way It Was Before **(24)**, Little Star **(24)**, Route 66 **(25)**,
Sweet Sixteen **(24)**, Run Around **(23)**, Stop And Listen **(24)**, Rip It Up **(25)**

▶**TWIST** (Chess LP-1465) *mono*   February 1962
reissued as **MORE CHUCK BERRY**   November 1963
Maybellene **(2)**, Roll Over Beethoven **(5)**, Oh, Baby Doll **(10)**, Around And Around **(14)**, Come
On **(26)**, Let It Rock **(22)**, Reelin' And Rockin' **(12)**, School Days **(9)**, Almost Grown **(21)**, Sweet
Little Sixteen **(12)**, Thirty Days **(3)**, Johnny B. Goode **(13)**, Rock And Roll Music **(10)**, Back In The
USA **(21)**

▶**CHUCK BERRY ON STAGE** (Chess LP-1480) *mono*   August 1963
Go, Go, Go **(26)**, Memphis Tennessee **(18)**, Maybelline **(2)**, Surfin' Steel **(24)**, Rocking On The
Railroad **(22)**, Brown Eyed Handsome Man **(26)**, I Still Got The Blues **(24)**, Sweet Little
Sixteen **(12)**, Jaguar And The Thunderbird **(23)**, I Just Want To Make Love To You **(22)**,
All Aboard **(26)**, Trick Or Treat **(26)**, The Man And The Donkey **(26)**, How High The Moon **(10)**
Last title is not listed on the album. All the tracks were overdubbed with audience noise.

▶**CHUCK BERRY'S GREATEST HITS** (Chess LP-1485) *mono*   April 1964
Roll Over Beethoven **(5)**, School Days **(9)**, Rock And Roll Music **(10)**, Too Much Monkey
Business **(5)**, Johnny B. Goode **(13)**, Oh, Baby Doll **(10)**, Nadine **(27)**, Maybellene **(2)**,
Memphis **(18)**, Sweet Little Sixteen **(12)**, Thirty Days **(3)**, Brown Eyed Handsome Man **(5)**

Bo Diddley & Chuck Berry
▶**TWO GREAT GUITARS** (Checker LP-2991/LPS-2991) *mono/stereo*   August 1964
Liverpool Drive **(29)**, Chuck's Beat **(30)**, Bo's Beat **(30)**. *Chuck Berry does not appear on the
remaining track.*

▶**ST. LOUIS TO LIVERPOOL** (Chess LP-1488/LPS-1488) *mono/stereo*   November 1964

Little Marie (32), Our Little Rendezvous (23), No Particular Place To Go (29), You Two (29), Promised Land (28), You Never Can Tell (27), Go, Bobby Soxer (32), The Things I Used To Do (27), Liverpool Drive (29), Night Beat (12), Merry Christmas Baby (20, *alt. take*), Brenda Lee (28). *On LPS-1488 'Our Little Rendezvous', 'Night Beat', 'Merry Christmas Baby' and 'Brenda Lee' are in mono.*

▶**CHUCK BERRY IN LONDON** (Chess LP-1495/LPS-1495) *mono/stereo*   April 1965

My Little Love Light (35), She Once Was Mine (34), After It's Over (34), I Got A Booking (35), Night Beat (12), His Daughter Caroline (33), You Came A Long Way From St. Louis (34), St. Louis Blues (35), Jamaica Farewell (34), Dear Dad (33), Butterscotch (33), The Song Of My Love (33), Why Should We End This Way (34), I Want To Be Your Driver (33). *A longer, unfaded version of 'Jamaica Farewell' appears on the stereo album. 'Night Beat' is in mono, even on the stereo LP.*

▶**FRESH BERRY'S** (Chess LP-1498/LPS-1498) *mono/stereo*   April 1966

It Wasn't Me (39), Run Joe (37), Every Day We Rock & Roll (37), One For My Baby (37), Welcome Back Pretty Baby (39), It's My Own Business (37), Right Off Rampart Street (39), Vaya Con Dios (38), Merrily We Rock & Roll (38), My Mustang Ford (37), Ain't That Just Like A Woman (39), Wee Hour Blues (38)

▶**CHUCK BERRY'S**
   GOLDEN DECADE (Chess LP-1514D/LPS-1514D) *mono/electronic stereo*   January 1967

❶ Maybellene (2), Deep Feeling (9), Johnny B. Goode (13), Wee Wee Hours (2), Nadine (27), Brown Eyed Handsome Man (5), Roll Over Beethoven (5), Thirty Days (3), Havana Moon (6), No Particular Place To Go (29), Memphis Tennessee (18), Almost Grown (21)

❷ School Day (9), Too Much Monkey Business (5), Oh, Baby Doll (10), Reelin' And Rockin' (12), You Can't Catch Me (4), Too Pooped To Pop (22), Bye Bye Johnny (23), Around And Around (14), Sweet Little Sixteen (12), Rock And Roll Music (10), Anthony Boy (19), Back In The USA (21)

▶**CHUCK BERRY'S GOLDEN HITS** (Mercury MG-21103/SR-61103) *mono/stereo*   1967

Sweet Little Sixteen (42), Memphis (42), School Days (42), Maybelline (42), Back In The USA (43), Johnny B. Goode (42), Rock'n'Roll Music (42), Roll Over Beethoven (42), Thirty Days (43), Carol (44), Club Nitty Gritty (43). *NB 'Club Nitty Gritty' was issued in mono only.*

▶**CHUCK BERRY IN MEMPHIS** (Mercury MG-21123/SR-61123) *mono/stereo*   September 1967

Back To Memphis (45), I Do Really Love You (45), Ramblin' Rose (45), Sweet Little Rock'n'Roller (47), My Heart Will Always Belong To You (47), Oh Baby Doll (47), Check Me Out (45), It Hurts Me Too (46), Bring Another Drink (46), So Long (46), Goodnight, Well It's Time To Go (46)

▶ **LIVE AT FILLMORE AUDITORIUM** (Mercury MG-21138/SR-61138) *mono/stereo*   Nov. 1967

Rockin' At The Fillmore/Everyday I Have The Blues (48), C.C. Rider (48), Driftin' Blues (48), Feelin' It (48), Flying Home (48), I'm Your Hoochie Coochie Man (49), It Hurts Me Too (49), Fillmore Blues (49), Wee Baby Blues (49), Johnny B. Goode (49)

From this point all LPs are in stereo only

▶**FROM ST. LOUIE TO FRISCO** (Mercury SR-61176)   November 1968

Louie To Frisco (52), Ma Dear (52), The Love I Lost (52), I Love Her, I Love Her (52), Little Fox (52), Rock Cradle Rock (52), Soul Rockin' (51), I Can't Believe (51), Misery (43), My Tambourine (41), Oh Captain (43), Mum's The Word (41)

▶**CONCERTO IN B GOODE** (Mercury SR-61223)   June 1969

Good Lookin' Woman (53), My Woman (53), It's Too Dark In There (53), Put Her Down (53), Concerto In B Goode (53)

▶**BACK HOME** (Chess LPS-1550)   November 1970

Tulane (55), Have Mercy Judge (55), Instrumental (56), Christmas (56), Gun (56), I'm A Rocker (56), Flyin' Home (56), Fish & Chips (56), Some People (56)

▶**SAN FRANCISCO DUES** (Chess CH-50008)   June 1971

Oh Louisiana **(58)**, Let's Do Our Thing Together **(58)**, Your Lick **(58)**, Festival **(58)**, Bound To Lose **(58)**, Bordeaux In My Pirough **(58)**, San Francisco Dues **(58)**, Viva Rock & Roll **(40)**, My Dream **(58)**, Lonely School Days **(40)**

▶**THE LONDON CHUCK BERRY SESSIONS** (Chess CH-60020)   April 1972

Let's Boogie **(60)**, I Will Not Let You Go **(60)**, Mean Old World **(60)**, I Love You **(60)**, London Berry Blues **(60)**, Reelin' And Rockin' **(59)**, My Ding-A-Ling **(59)**, Johnny B. Goode **(59)**

▶**ST. LOUIE TO FRISCO TO MEMPHIS** (Mercury SRM2-6501)   October 1972

❶ Rockin' At The Fillmore/Everyday I Have The Blues **(48)**, C.C. Rider **(48)**, Driftin' Blues **(48)**, Feelin' It **(48)**, Flying Home **(48)**, I'm Your Hoochie Coochie Man **(49)**, It Hurts Me Too **(49)**, Fillmore Blues **(49)**, Wee Baby Blues **(49)**, Johnny B. Goode **(49)**

❷ St. Louie To Frisco **(52)**, Ma Dear **(52)**, Soul Rockin' **(51)**, Check Me Out **(45)**, Little Fox **(52)**, Back To Memphis **(45)**, My Tambourine **(41)**, Misery **(43)**, It's Too Dark In There **(53)**, I Do Really Love You **(45)**, I Can't Believe **(51)**, My Heart Will Always Belong To You **(47)**, So Long **(46)**

▶**JOHNNY B. GOODE** (Pickwick SPC-3327)   1972

Johnny B. Goode **(42)**, Memphis Tennessee **(42)**, Roll Over Beethoven **(42)**, Sweet Little Sixteen **(42)**, School Days **(42)**, Maybelline **(42)**, Reelin' And Rockin' **(44)**, Rock And Roll Music **(42)**, Back In The USA **(43)**

▶**CHUCK BERRY'S GOLDEN DECADE (VOLUME 2)** (Chess 2CH-60023)   February 1973

❶ Carol **(16)**, You Never Can Tell **(27)**, No Money Down **(4)**, Together (We Will Always Be) **(3)**, Mad Lad **(24)**, Run Rudolph Run **(20)**, Let It Rock **(22**, *alt. mix*), Sweet Little Rock And Roller **(19)**, It Don't Take But A Few Minutes **(14)**, I'm Talking About You **(25)**, Drifting Blues **(23)**, Go Go Go **(26)**

❷ Jaguar And Thunderbird **(23)**, Little Queenie **(20)**, Betty Jean **(22**, *alt. take*), Guitar Boogie **(12)**, Down The Road Apiece **(24)**, Merry Christmas Baby **(20**, *single version*), Promised Land **(28)**, Jo Jo Gunne **(18)**, Don't You Lie To Me **(23)**, Rockin' At The Philharmonic **(12)**, La Jaunda **(9**, *alt. take*), Come On **(26)**

▶**BIO** (Chess CH-50043)   July 1973

Bio **(66)**, Hello Little Girl, Goodbye **(66)**, Woodpecker **(66)**, Rain Eyes **(65)**, Aimlessly Driftin' **(66)**, Got It And Gone **(65)**, Talkin' About My Buddy **(66)**

John Lennon
▶**TELECASTS** (Trade Mark of Quality TMQ-71046) *bootleg*   1973

Memphis Tennessee **(61)**, Johnny B. Goode **(61)**. *Chuck Berry does not appear on other tracks.*

▶**CHUCK BERRY'S GOLDEN DECADE (VOLUME 3)** (Chess 2CH-60028)   April 1974

❶ Beautiful Delilah **(15)**, Go, Bobby Soxer **(32)**, I Got To Find My Baby **(23)**, Worried Life Blues **(23)**, Rolli Polli **(4)**, Downbound Train **(4)**, Broken Arrow **(22)**, Confessin' The Blues **(24)**, Drifting Heart **(5)**, Ingo **(14)**, The Man And the Donkey **(26)**, St. Louis Blues **(35)**

❷ Our Little Rendezvous **(23)**, Childhood Sweetheart **(22)**, Blues For Hawaiians **(14)**, Hey Pedro **(16)**, My Little Love Light **(35)**, Little Marie **(32)**, County Line **(22)**, Viva Viva Rock And Roll **(40)**, House Of Blue Lights **(16)**, Time Was **(16)**, Blue On Blue **(21)**, Oh Yeah **(16)**

▶**CHUCK BERRY** (Chess CH-60032)   February 1975

Swanee River **(69)**, I'm Just A Name **(67)**, I Just Want To Make Love To You **(70)**, Too Late **(67)**, South Of The Border **(68)**, Hi-Heel Sneakers **(68)**, You Are My Sunshine **(69)**, My Babe **(70)**, Baby What You Want Me To Do **(70)**, A Deuce **(65)**, Shake Rattle And Roll **(70)**, Sue Answer **(65)**, Don't You Lie To Me **(69)**

Various Artists
▶**AMERICAN HOT WAX** (A&M SP-6500)   1978

Reelin' And Rockin' **(74)**, Roll Over Beethoven **(74)**, Sweet Little Sixteen **(12)**. *Chuck Berry does not appear on other tracks.*

▶**CHUCK BERRY LIVE IN CONCERT** (Magnum MR-703)   1978

Rock And Roll Music **(54)**, Nadine **(54)**, School Day **(54)**, Wee Wee Hours **(54)**, Johnny B. Goode/Carol/Promised Land **(54)**, Hoochie Coochie Man **(54)**, Sweet Little Sixteen **(54)**, Memphis Tennessee **(54)**, Too Much Monkey Business **(54)**, My Ding-A-Ling **(54)**, Reelin' And Rockin' **(54)**, Johnny B. Goode **(54)**, Maybellene **(54)**

Various Artists
▶**RECORDED LIVE ON STAGE** (WINS 1010) *bootleg*   1978

Maybelline **(7)**, Roll Over Beethoven **(7)**. *Chuck Berry does not appear on other tracks.*

Various Artists
▶**ROCK'N'ROLL RADIO** (Radiola MR-1087) *bootleg*   1978

Maybelline **(7)**, Roll Over Beethoven **(7)**. *Chuck Berry does not appear on other tracks.*

▶**ROCKIT** (Atco SD38-118)   1979

Move It **(74)**, Oh What A Thrill **(74)**, I Need You Baby **(75)**, If I Were **(75)**, House Lights **(75)**, I Never Thought **(75)**, Havana Moon **(75)**, Wuden't Me **(75)**, California **(74)**, Pass Away **(74)**

▶**THE CHUCK BERRY SPECIAL** (NBC Radio Network, 18, 19 or 20 January 1980)   Jan. 1980

❶ Interview **(77)**, Roll Over Beethoven **(5)**, Interview **(77)**, Bio **(66)**, Maybellene **(2)**, Interview **(77)**, In The Wee Wee Hours **(2)**, Interview **(77)**, Too Much Monkey Business **(5)**, Brown Eyed Handsome Man **(5)**, Interview **(77)**, Rock And Roll Music **(10)**, School Day **(9)**, Interview **(77)**, Almost Grown **(21)**, Interview **(77)**, Sweet Little Sixteen **(12)**, Interview **(77)**, Carol **(44)**, Johnny B. Goode **(13)**
❷ Interview **(77)**, Nadine **(27)**, No Particular Place To Go **(29)**, Interview **(77)**, Promised Land **(28)**, Back In The USA **(21)**, Interview with George Thorogood, It Wasn't Me *by George Thorogood*, Memphis Tennessee **(18)**, My Tambourine **(41**, *incomplete)*, My Ding-A-Ling **(59)**, Interview **(77)**, Reelin' and Rockin' **(59)**, Interview **(77)**, Oh What A Thrill **(74)**, Havana Moon **(75)**, Move It **(74)**, Interview with Bo Diddley, Almost Grown **(21)**
NB Only the non-musical tracks are included in the Sessionography.

▶**AMERICA'S HOTTEST WAX** (Reelin' 001) *bootleg*   1980

Rock And Roll Music **(8**, *demo)*, Childhood Sweetheart **(22**, *alt. take)*, 21 **(15)**, Let Me Sleep Woman **(22)**, Do You Love Me **(21**, *alt. take)*, 21 Blues **(15)**, One O'Clock Jump **(22)**, Reelin' And Rockin' **(12**, *alt. take)*, Sweet Little 16 **(11**, *alt. take)*, Brown Eyed Handsome Man **(26**, *stereo)*, Say You'll Be Mine **(22)**, I've Changed **(4)**, 13 Question Method **(10)**, How High The Moon **(10)**

Chuck Berry / George Thorogood
▶**IN CONCERT** (Westwood One/ABC Radio Network 81-1)   April 1981

Maybellene **(78)**, Sweet Little Sixteen **(78)**, Carol/Little Queenie **(78)**. *Chuck Berry does not appear on other tracks.*

▶**THE GREAT TWENTY-EIGHT** (Chess CH2-8201)   September 1982

❶ Maybellene **(2)**, Thirty Days **(3)**, You Can't Catch Me **(4)**, Too Much Monkey Business **(5)**, Brown Eyed Handsome Man **(5)**, Roll Over Beethoven **(5)**, Havana Moon **(6)**, School Day **(9)**, Rock And Roll Music **(10)**, Oh, Baby Doll **(10)**, Reelin' And Rockin' **(12)**, Sweet Little Sixteen **(12)**, Johnny B. Goode **(13)**, Around And Around **(14)**
❷ Carol **(16)**, Beautiful Delilah **(15)**, Memphis **(18)**, Sweet Little Rock And Roller **(19)**, Little Queenie **(20)**, Almost Grown **(21)**, Back In The USA **(21)**, Let It Rock **(22)**, Bye Bye Johnny **(23)**, I'm Talking About You **(25)**, Come On **(26)**, Nadine **(27)**, No Particular Place To Go **(29)**, I Want To Be Your Driver **(33)**

Various Artists
▶ **WEEKLY MUSIC MAGAZINE**
   'POP PIONEERS' (RKO Radio Networks, week of 22 May 1982)   May 1982

Interview **(81)**, Sweet Little Sixteen **(12)** *Chuck Berry does not appear on other tracks.*
NB Only the non-musical track is included in the Sessionography.

Various Artists
THE SOURCE – THE FATHERS OF ROCK (NBC Radio Network, 15, 16 or 17 June 1984)   June 1984

Interview **(77)**, Maybellene **(2)**, Johnny B. Goode **(13)**. *Chuck Berry does not appear on other tracks.*

▶**ROCK'N'ROLL RARITIES** (Chess CH2-92521)   February 1986

❶ No Particular Place To Go **(29**, *stereo*), Rock And Roll Music **(10**, *alt. take*), It Wasn't Me **(39**, *stereo*), Reelin' And Rockin' **(12**, *alt. take*), Come On **(26**, *alt. take*), Little Queenie **(20**, *alt. take*), You Never Can Tell **(27**, *stereo*), Sweet Little Sixteen **(12**, *alt. take*), County Line **(22)**, Run Rudolph Run **(20)**

❷ Nadine **(27**, *stereo*), Betty Jean **(22**, *alt. take*), I Want To Be Your Driver **(33**, *stereo*), Beautiful Delilah **(15**, *alt. takes*), Oh Yeah **(16)**, Johnny B. Goode **(13**, *alt. takes*), Bye Bye Johnny **(23**, *stereo*), Little Marie **(32**, *stereo*), Time Was **(16)**, Promised Land **(28**, *stereo*)

▶**MORE ROCK'N'ROLL RARITIES** (Chess CH-9190)   August 1986

Ain't That Just Like A Woman **(39**, *stereo*), Rock And Roll Music **(8**, *demo*), Down The Road Apiece **(24**, *stereo*), Brown Eyed Handsome Man **(26**, *stereo*), Route 66 **(25**, *alt. take*), Sweet Little Rock And Roller **(19**, *alt. take*), My Mustang Ford **(37**, *stereo*), Sweet Little Sixteen **(11**, *demo*), I Got To Find My Baby **(23**, *stereo*), I'm Talking About You **(25**, *stereo*), House Of Blue Lights **(16)**, Go Go Go Johnny B. Goode *[Go Go Go]* **(26**, *stereo*)

Chuck Berry / Keith Richard / Rolling Stones
▶**LET IT ROCK** (Vinyl Gang Production) *2-LP bootleg*   1986

Roll Over Beethoven **(84)**, Sweet Little Sixteen **(84)**, Schoolday (Ring Ring Goes The Bell) **(84)**, Instrumental **(84)**, Memphis Tennessee **(84)**, Let It Rock **(84)**, Introduction **(84)**, Mean Old World **(84)**, Carol **(84)**, Little Queenie **(84)**, Johnny B. Goode **(84)**, Every Day I Have The Blues **(84)**, Reelin' And Rockin' **(84)**. *Chuck Berry does not appear on other tracks.*

▶**HAIL! HAIL! ROCK'N'ROLL** (M.C.A. MCA-6217)   November 1987

Maybellene **(88)**, Around And Around **(87)**, Sweet Little Sixteen **(87)**, Brown Eyed Handsome Man **(87)**, Memphis Tennessee **(87)**, Too Much Monkey Business **(87)**, Back In The USA **(87)**, Wee Wee Hours **(87)**, Johnny B. Goode **(87)**, Little Queenie **(87)**, Rock And Roll Music **(88)**, Roll Over Beethoven **(88)**, I'm Thru' With Love **(86)**

▶**THE CHESS BOX** (Chess CH6-80001)   December 1988

❶ Maybellene **(2)**, Wee Wee Hours **(2)**, Thirty Days **(3)**, You Can't Catch Me **(4)**, No Money Down **(4)**, Downbound Train **(4)**, Brown Eyed Handsome Man **(5)**, Drifting Heart **(5)**, Roll Over Beethoven **(5)**, Too Much Monkey Business **(5)**, Havana Moon **(6)**, School Day **(9)**

❷ Rock And Roll Music **(10)**, Oh Baby Doll **(10)**, I've Changed **(4)**, Reelin' And Rockin' **(12)**, Rockin' At The Philharmonic **(12)**, Sweet Little Sixteen **(12**, *correct speed*), Johnny B. Goode **(13)**, Time Was **(12)**, Around And Around **(14)**, Beautiful Delilah **(15)**, House Of Blue Lights **(16)**, Carol **(16)**

❸ Memphis **(18)**, Anthony Boy **(19)**, Jo Jo Gunne **(18)**, Sweet Little Rock'n'Roller **(19)**, Merry Christmas Baby **(20**, *single version*), Run Rudolph Run **(20)**, Little Queenie **(20)**, Almost Grown **(21)**, Back In The USA **(21)**, Betty Jean **(22)**, Childhood Sweetheart **(22)**, Let It Rock **(22)**, Too Pooped To Pop **(22)**

❹ Bye Bye Johnny **(23)**, Jaguar And Thunderbird **(23)**, Down The Road Apiece **(24)**, Confessin' The Blues **(24)**, Thirteen Question Method **(24)**, Crying Steel **(24)**, I'm Just A Lucky So And So **(24)**, I'm Talking About You **(25)**, Come On **(26)**, Nadine (Is It You?) **(27)**, Crazy Arms **(27)**, You Never Can Tell **(27)**, The Things I Used To Do **(27)**, Promised Land **(28)**

❺ No Particular Place To Go **(29)**, Liverpool Drive **(29)**, You Two **(29)**, Chuck's Beat **(30)**, Little Marie **(32)**, Dear Dad **(33)**, Sad Day, Long Night **(39)**, It's My Own Business **(37)**, It Wasn't Me **(39)**, Ramona, Say Yes **(40**, *alt. mix*), Viva Viva Rock'n'Roll **(40)**

❻ Tulane **(55)**, Have Mercy Judge **(55)**, My Dream **(58)**, Reelin' And Rockin' **(59)**, My Ding-A-Ling **(59**, *single edit*), Johnny B. Goode **(59)**, A Deuce **(65)**, Woodpecker **(66)**, Bio **(66)**

Keith Richard
▶**STILL ON THE ROAD** (Diamond Sound 011) *bootleg*   1988

Instrumental **(88)**, Everyday I Have The Blues **(88)**. *Chuck Berry does not appear on other tracks.*

▶ **SOLID GOLD SCRAPBOOK:**
A BIRTHDAY SALUTE (Unistar Radio Programming, 18 October 1989)   October 1989

Maybellene **(2)**, Interview **(90)**, Roll Over Beethoven **(5)**, School Days **(9)**, Rock & Roll Music **(10)**, Around And Around **(14)**, Sweet Little Sixteen **(12)**, Johnny B. Goode **(13)**, Interview **(90)**, Carol **(16)**, Reelin' And Rockin' **(12)**, Little Queenie **(20)**, Interview **(90)**, Back In The USA **(21)**, Nadine **(27)**, No Particular Place To Go **(29)**, Interview **(90)**, You Never Can Tell **(27)**, My Ding-A-Ling **(59)**. *NB Only the non-musical tracks are included in the Sessionography.*

▶ **MISSING BERRIES: RARITIES (VOLUME 3)** (Chess CH-9318)   July 1990

Childhood Sweetheart **(22**, *alt. take***)**, Do You Love Me **(21**, *alt. take***)**, Big Ben Blues **(28**, *stereo***)**, The Man And The Donkey **(26)**, One O'Clock Jump **(22)**, Little Girl From Central **(27**, *stereo***)**, Untitled Instrumental **(8)**, Let Me Sleep Woman **(22)**, Vacation Time **(15)**, 21 Blues **(15)**

SOLID GOLD SCRAPBOOK:
A CHUCK BERRY BIRTHDAY SALUTE (Unistar Radio Programming, 18 October 1990)   Oct. 1990

Maybellene **(2)**, Interview **(90)**, Roll Over Beethoven **(5)**, School Days **(9)**, Rock & Roll Music **(10)**, Sweet Little Sixteen **(12)**, Johnny B. Goode **(13)**, Carol **(16)**, Memphis **(18)**, Interview **(90)**, Almost Grown **(21)**, Little Queenie **(20)**, Back In The USA **(21)**, Interview **(90)**, Bye Bye Johnny **(23)**, Nadine **(27)**, No Particular Place To Go **(29)**, You Never Can Tell **(27)**, My Ding-A-Ling **(59)**, Interview **(90)**

SOLID GOLD SCRAPBOOK:
BIRTHDAY SALUTE (Unistar Radio Programming, 18 October 1991)   October 1991

Interview with Johnnie Johnson, Maybellene **(2)**, School Day **(9)**, Interview **(90)**, Roll Over Beethoven **(5)**, Rock & Roll Music **(10)**, Sweet Little Sixteen **(12)**, Interview **(90)**, Johnny B. Goode **(13)**, Carol **(16)**, Almost Grown **(21)**, Nadine (Is It You) **(27)**, Interview **(90)**, No Particular Place To Go **(29)**, You Never Can Tell **(27)**, Memphis *by Johnny Rivers*, Back In The USA *by Linda Ronstadt*, Interview **(90)**, My Ding-A-Ling **(59)**

ROCK, ROLL AND REMEMBER
(United Stations Radio Networks, 30 December 1994 and 1 January 1995) *4-LP*   December 1994

Nadine (Is It You) **(27)**, Roll Over Beethoven **(5)**, Rock & Roll Music **(10)**, Interview **(90)**, Maybellene **(2)**, Interview **(90)**, Johnny B. Goode **(13)**, Interview **(90)**, Sweet Little Sixteen **(12)**, Interview **(90)**, Carol **(16)**, Interview **(90)**, No Particular Place To Go **(29)**, Interview **(90)**, School Day **(9)**, Interview **(90)**. *Chuck Berry does not appear on other tracks.*

UK LPs

ONE DOZEN BERRYS (London HA-M-2132) *mono*   November 1959

Same tracks as US LP Chess LP-1432 (1958).

JUKE BOX HITS (Pye International NPL-28019) *mono*   June 1962

Same tracks as US LP Chess LP-1456 (New Juke Box Hits, 1961).

CHUCK BERRY (Pye International NPL-28024) *mono*   April 1963

Maybellene **(2)**, Down The Road Apiece **(24)**, Mad Lad **(24)**, School Day (Ring, Ring Goes The Bell) **(9)**, Sweet Little Sixteen **(12)**, Confessin' The Blues **(24)**, Back In The USA **(21)**, Johnny B. Goode **(13)**, Oh, Baby Doll **(10)**, Come On **(26)**, I Got To Find My Baby **(23)**, Betty Jean **(22)**, 'Round And 'Round **(14)**, Almost Grown **(21)**

CHUCK BERRY ON STAGE (Pye International NPL-28027) *mono*   September 1963

Same tracks as US LP Chess LP-1480 (1963), but 'How High The Moon' is faded out earlier.

MORE CHUCK BERRY (Pye International NPL-28028) *mono*   November 1963

Sweet Little Rock And Roller **(19)**, Anthony Boy **(19)**, Little Queenie **(20)**, Worried Life Blues **(23)**, Carol **(16)**, Reelin' And Rockin' **(12)**, Thirty Days (To Come Back Home) **(3)**, Brown Eyed Handsome Man **(5)**, Too Much Monkey Business **(5)**, Wee Wee Hours **(2)**, Jo Jo Gunne **(18)**, Beautiful Delilah **(15)**

▶THE LATEST AND THE GREATEST (Pye International NPL-28031) *mono*   June 1964

Nadine **(27)**, Fraulein **(27)**, Guitar Boogie **(12)**, Things I Used To Do **(27)**, Don't You Lie To Me **(23)**, Drifting Blues **(23)**, Liverpool Drive **(29)**, No Particular Place To Go **(29)**, Lonely All The Time **(27)**, Jaguar And The Thunderbird **(23)**, O'Rangutang **(27)**, You Two **(29)**, Deep Feeling **(9)**, Bye Bye Johnny **(23)**

▶YOU NEVER CAN TELL (Pye International NPL-28039) *mono*   October 1964

You Never Can Tell **(27)**, Diploma For Two **(24)**, The Little Girl From Central **(27)**, The Way It Was Before **(24)**, Around And Around **(14)**, Big Ben **(28)**, Promised Land **(28)**, Back In The USA **(21)**, Run Around **(23)**, Brenda Lee **(28)**, Reelin' And Rockin' **(12)**, Come On **(26)**

Chuck Berry & Bo Diddley
TWO GREAT GUITARS (Pye International NPL-28047) *mono*   January 1965

Same tracks as US LP Checker LP-2991 (1964).

CHUCK BERRY IN LONDON (Chess CRL-4005) *mono*   March 1965

Same tracks as US LP Chess LP-1495 (1965), except that 'Jamaica Farewell' has one guitar overdub less than (mono and stereo) US pressings.

▶FRESH BERRY'S (Chess CRL-4506) *mono*   December 1965

It Wasn't Me **(39)**, Run Joe **(37)**, Every Day We Rock & Roll **(37)**, One For My Baby **(37)**, Sad Day, Long Night **(39)**, It's My Own Business **(37)**, Right Off Rampart Street **(39)**, Vaya Con Dios **(38)**, Merrily We Rock & Roll **(38)**, My Mustang Ford **(37)**, Ain't That Just Like A Woman **(39)**, Wee Hour Blues **(38)**

▶YOU NEVER CAN TELL (Marble Arch MAL-702) *mono, 10 tracks*   September 1967

You Never Can Tell **(27)**, Diploma For Two **(24)**, The Little Girl From Central **(27)**, The Way It Was Before **(24)**, Big Ben **(28)**, The Promised Land **(28)**, Back In The USA **(21)**, Run Around **(23)**, Brenda Lee **(28)**, Reelin' And Rockin' **(12)**

▶YOU NEVER CAN TELL (Marble Arch MALS-702) *stereo, 10 tracks*   September 1967

You Never Can Tell **(27)**, Diploma For Two **(24)**, The Little Girl From Central **(27)**, The Way It Was Before **(24)**, Big Ben **(28)**, The Promised Land **(28)**, Back In The USA **(21)**, Run Around **(23)**, Brenda Lee **(28)**, Reelin' And Rockin' **(12)**. *Underlined* tracks are in stereo; others are in mono.

▶YOU NEVER CAN TELL (Marble Arch MALS-702) *stereo, 12 tracks*   September 1967

You Never Can Tell **(27)**, Diploma For Two **(24)**, The Little Girl From Central **(27)**, The Way It Was Before **(24)**, Around And Around **(14**, *alt. take)*, Big Ben **(28)**, The Promised Land **(28)**, Back In The USA **(21)**, Run Around **(23)**, Brenda Lee **(28)**, Reelin' And Rockin' **(12)**, Come On **(26**, *alt. take)* *Underlined* tracks are in stereo; others are in mono. 'Around And Around' and 'Come On' not listed on either the label or the sleeve.

▶SIX TWO FIVE (Driving Wheel LP-1001) *bootleg*   1972

Roll Over Beethoven **(62)**, Sweet Little Sixteen **(62)**, Memphis **(62)**, South Of The Border **(62)**, Beer Drinking Woman **(62)**, Let It Rock **(62)**, Mean Old World **(62)**, Carol **(62)**, Liverpool Drive **(62)**, Nadine **(62)**, Bye Bye Johnny **(62)**, Bonsoir Cherie/Johnny B. Goode **(62)**

▶CHUCK BERRY'S GOLDEN DECADE (VOLUME 3) (Chess 6641 177)   June 1974

Same tracks as US LP Chess 2CH-60028 (1974) except 'Time Was' replaced by the previously unissued 'Do You Love Me **(21)** *and 'Viva Rock'n'Roll' replaced by 'Berry Pickin' '* **(4)**. *Only 'Do You Love Me' is listed in the Sessionography.*

MOTORVATIN' (Chess 9286 690)   January 1977

Johnny B. Goode **(13)**, Roll Over Beethoven **(5)**, School Day **(9)**, Maybellene **(2)**, Rock And Roll Music **(10)**, Oh Baby Doll **(10)**, Too Much Monkey Business **(5)**, Carol **(16)**, Let It Rock **(22**, *alt. mix)*, Sweet Little Rock And Roller **(19)**, Bye Bye Johnny **(23)**, Reelin' And Rockin' **(12)**, No Particular Place To Go **(29)**, Thirty Days **(3)**, Sweet Little Sixteen **(12)**, Little Queenie **(20)**, Memphis Tennessee **(18)**, You Never Can Tell **(27)**, Brown Eyed Handsome Man **(5)**, Promised Land **(28)**, Back In The USA **(21)**

►**CHESS MASTERS** (Chess CXMP-2011)   March 1983

Same tracks as US LP Reelin' 001 (1980).

Chuck Berry & The Flying Saucers
►**CHUCK BERRY'S ROCK'N'ROLL PARTY** (Driving Wheel C-7788) *bootleg*   1989

Roll Over Beethoven **(73)**, School Days **(73)**, Sweet Little Sixteen **(73)**, Let It Rock **(73)**, Maybellene **(73)**, Memphis **(73)**, The Promised Land **(73)**, Nadine **(73)**, Too Much Monkey Business **(73)**, No Money Down **(73)**, Little Queenie **(73)**, Round And Round **(73)**, You Never Can Tell **(73)**, Hamburg Berry Blues **(73)**, Reelin' And Rockin' **(73)**

Foreign LPs

Chuck Berry / Bo Diddley / Jerry Lee Lewis / Carl Perkins
►**ROCK SMUK** (Sun/Chess NQCS-1) *bootleg*   Netherlands, late 1972

Introduktie [Introduction] **(64)**, Maybellene **(2)**, Sweet Little Sixteen **(12)**, School Day **(9)**
Chuck Berry does not appear on other tracks.
NB Only the non-musical track is included in the Sessionography.

Chuck Berry / Bo Diddley / Jerry Lee Lewis / Carl Perkins
►**4 ROCK GIANTS – TALKS & HITS** (Bellaphon BI-15119)   West Germany, 1973

Interview **(64)**, Maybellene **(2)**, Sweet Little Sixteen **(12)**, School Day **(9)**
Chuck Berry does not appear on other tracks.
NB Only the non-musical track is included in the Sessionography.

►**ROCK! ROCK! ROCK'N'ROLL!** (Mercury 6463 044)   West Germany, 1980

Maybelline **(42)**, Back In The USA **(43)**, Johnny B. Goode **(42)**, Rock'n'Roll Music **(42)**, Carol **(44)**, Sweet Little Sixteen **(42)**, Roll Over Beethoven **(42)**, Reelin' And Rockin' **(44)**, Let It Rock **(44)**, Sweet Little Rock'n'Roller **(47)**, Oh Baby Doll **(10)**, Goodnight, Well It's Time To Go **(46)**

►**CHUCK BERRY TOKYO SESSION** (East World WTP-90072)   Japan, 1981

School Day **(79)**, Roll Over Beethoven **(79)**, In The Wee Wee Hours **(79)**, Ding-A-Ling **(79)**, Memphis Tennessee **(79)**, Sweet Little Sixteen **(80)**, Rock And Roll Music **(80)**, Carol/Little Queenie **(80)**, Bio **(80)**, Johnny B. Goode **(80)**

Chuck Berry / Sam Moore and his Sam & Dave Revue / R.C. Succession
►**THE DAY OF R&B** (East World WTP-72403)   Japan, 1983

Bio **(82)**, Johnny B. Goode **(82)**. *Chuck Berry does not appear on other tracks.*

►**LET IT ROCK** (Checkmate LP-1955) *bootleg*   Netherlands, 1986

Let It Rock **(22**, *alt. mix*), Sweet Little Sixteen **(11**, *demo*), Childhood Sweetheart **(22**, *alt. take*), One O'Clock Jump **(22)**, Thirteen Question Method **(10)**, Do You Love Me **(21**, *alt. take*), Big Ben Blues **(28)**, Vacation Time **(15)**, O-Rangutang **(27)**, Ramona, Say Yes **(40)**, Rock And Roll Music **(8**, *demo*), Reelin' And Rockin' **(12**, *alt. take*),The Little Girl From Central High **(27)**, Brown Eyed Handsome Man **(26**, *stereo*), Twenty One Blues **(15)**, I've Changed **(4)**, That's My Desire **(20)**, Lonely Schooldays **(33)**, Interview **(64)**, South Of Her *[sic]* Border **(62)**

Various Artists
►**THE ROCK'N'ROLL RADIO COLLECTION** (Deja Vu DVLP-2130)   Italy, 1988

Maybelline **(7)**, Roll Over Beethoven **(7)**. *Chuck Berry does not appear on other tracks.*
Also issued on CD.

Kingsize Taylor & The Dominoes
►**DOMINOES & KINGSIZE TAYLOR – LIVERPOOL'S FIRST ROCK'N'ROLL BAND**
(Merseyside's Greatest MGBOX-801005-8) *4-LP*   Germany, 1991

Memphis Tennessee **(31**, *incomplete*), Sweet Little Sixteen **(31**, *incomplete*), Interview **(31)**, Nadine **(31**, *incomplete*), Johnny B. Goode **(31)**. *Chuck Berry does not appear on other tracks.*

CDs

There have been literally hundreds of Chuck Berry CD releases throughout the world. This list only contains those CDs considered to be significant.

US CDs

BIO (Chess CHD-91510)   1986
Same tracks as US LP Chess CH-50043 (1973).

THE GREAT TWENTY-EIGHT (Chess CHD-92500)   April 1987
Same tracks as US 2-LP Chess CH2-8201 (1982).

MORE ROCK'N'ROLL RARITIES (Chess CHD-9190)   April 1987
Same tracks as US LP Chess CH-9190 (1986).

HAIL! HAIL! ROCK'N'ROLL (M.C.A. MCAD-6217)   November 1987
Same tracks as US LP M.C.A. MCA-6217 (1987).

ROCK'N'ROLL RARITIES (Chess CHD-92521)   December 1987
Same tracks as US 2-LP Chess CH2-92521 (1986).

CHUCK BERRY IS ON TOP (Chess CHD-31260)   February 1988
Same tracks as US LP Chess LP-1435 (1959).

ST. LOUIS TO LIVERPOOL (Chess CHD-31261)   February 1988
Same tracks as US LP Chess LP(S)-1488 (1964).

Chuck Berry / Flamingos / Moonglows
ROCK, ROCK, ROCK (Chess CHD-31270)   February 1988
Same tracks as US LP Chess LP-1425 (1956).

ROCKIN' AT THE HOPS (Chess CHD-9259)   May 1988
Same tracks as US LP Chess LP-1448 (1960).

THE CHESS BOX (Chess CHD3-80001)   December 1988
Same tracks as US 6-LP box set Chess CH6-80001 (1988).

AFTER SCHOOL SESSION (Chess CHD-9284)   December 1988
Same tracks as US LP Chess LP-1426 (1957).

▶**CHUCK BERRY'S GOLDEN HITS** (Mercury 826 256-2)   June 1989
Sweet Little Sixteen **(42)**, Memphis **(42)** School Days **(42)**, Maybelline **(42)**, Back In The USA **(43)**, Around And Around **(43)**, Brown Eyed Handsome Man **(44)**, Johnny B. Goode **(42)**, Rock'n'Roll Music **(42)**, Roll Over Beethoven **(42)**, Thirty Days **(43)**, Carol **(44)**, Let It Rock **(44)**, Reelin' And Rockin' **(44)**, Club Nitty Gritty **(43)**. *This CD was also released in France and Germany.*

▶**CHUCK BERRY IN MEMPHIS** (Mercury 836 071-2)   June 1989
Back To Memphis **(45)**, I Do Really Love You **(45)**, Ramblin' Rose **(45)**, Sweet Little Rock'n'Roller **(47)**, My Heart Will Always Belong To You **(47)**, Oh Baby Doll **(47)**, Check Me Out **(45)**, It Hurts Me Too **(46)**, Bring Another Drink **(46)**, So Long **(46)**, Goodnight Well It's Time To Go **(46)**, Flying Home **(47)**. *This CD was also released in France and Germany.*

276

▶**LIVE AT FILLMORE AUDITORIUM** (Mercury 836 072-2)　　　　June 1989

Rockin' At The Fillmore/Everyday I Have The Blues **(48)**, C.C. Rider **(48)**, Driftin' Blues **(48)**, Feelin' It **(48)**, Flying Home **(48)**, Hoochi Coochi Man **(49)**, It Hurts Me Too **(49)**, Good Morning Little Schoolgirl **(49)**, Fillmore Blues **(49)**, Wee Baby Blues **(49)**, Bring Another Drink **(49)**, Worried Life Blues **(49)**, Reelin' And Rockin' **(49)**, My Ding-A-Ling **(49)**, Johnny B. Goode **(49)**
This CD was also released in France and Germany.

▶**FROM ST. LOUIE TO FRISCO** (Mercury 836 073-2)　　　　June 1989

Louie To Frisco **(52)**, Ma Dear **(52)** The Love I Lost **(52)**, I Love Her, I Love Her **(52)**, Little Fox **(52)**, Rock Cradle Rock **(52)**, Soul Rockin' **(51)**, I Can't Believe **(51)**, Misery **(43)**, Almost Grown **(44)**, My Tambourine **(41)**, Laugh And Cry **(41)**, Oh Captain **(43)**, Campus Cookie **(41)**, Mum's The Word **(41)**, Song Of My Love **(52)**　　*This CD was also released in France and Germany.*

▶**CONCERTO IN B GOODE** (Mercury 836 074-2)　　　　June 1989

Same tracks as US LP Mercury SR-61223 (1969). This CD was also released in Germany.

THE LONDON CHUCK BERRY SESSIONS (Chess CHD-9295)　　　　June 1989

Same tracks as US LP Chess CH-60020 (1972).

NEW JUKE BOX HITS (Chess CHD-9171)　　　　December 1989

Same tracks as US LP Chess LP-1456 (1961).

▶**MISSING BERRIES: RARITIES (VOLUME 3)** (Chess CHD-9318)　　　　July 1990

Childhood Sweetheart **(22**, *alt. take)*, Do You Love Me **(21**, *alt. take)*, Big Ben Blues **(28**, *stereo)*, The Man And The Donkey **(26)**, One O'Clock Jump **(22)**, Little Girl From Central **(27**, *stereo)*, Untitled Instrumental **(8)**, Let Me Sleep Woman **(22)**, That's My Desire **(20)**, Blue On Blue **(21)**, Vacation Time **(15)**, 21 Blues **(15)**

Bo Diddley & Chuck Berry
▶**TWO GREAT GUITARS** (Chess CHD-9170)　　　　October 1992

Liverpool Drive **(29)**, Chuck's Beat **(30)**, Bo's Beat **(30)**, Chuckwalk **(12)**. *Chuck Berry does not appear on other tracks.*

Various Artists
CHESS RHYTHM & ROLL (Chess CHD4-9354) *4-CD*　　　　July 1995

Maybellene **(2)**, Too Much Monkey Business **(5)**, School Day **(9)**, Johnny B. Goode **(13)**, Do You Love Me **(21**, *alt. take)*, Let It Rock **(22)**, No Particular Place To Go **(29)**. *Chuck Berry does not appear on other tracks.*

AFTER SCHOOL SESSION (M.C.A. MCAD-20873)　　　　1995

Too Much Monkey Business **(5)**, Wee Wee Hours **(2)**, Roly Poly **(4)**, Deep Feeling **(9)**, School Day **(9)**, No Money Down **(4)**, Brown Eyed Handsome Man **(5)**, Havana Moon **(6)**, Berry Pickin' **(4)**, Drifting Heart **(5)**

LET IT ROCK (M.C.A. MCAD-20931)　　　　1996

Let It Rock **(22)**, Back In The USA **(21)**, Oh Baby Doll **(10)**, You Never Can Tell **(27)**, Memphis **(18)**, Too Pooped To Pop **(22)**, Almost Grown **(21)**, Promised Land **(28)**, Sweet Little Rock'n'Roller **(19)**, Little Queenie **(20)**

HIS BEST (VOLUME 1) (Chess CHD-9371)　　　　February 1997

Maybellene **(2)**, Thirty Days **(3)**, You Can't Catch Me **(4)**, Down Bound Train **(4)**, Brown Eyed Handsome Man **(5)**, Roll Over Beethoven **(5)**, Too Much Monkey Business **(5)**, Havana Moon **(6)**, School Day **(9)**, Rock And Roll Music **(10)**, Oh Baby Doll **(10)**, Reelin' And Rockin' **(12)**, Sweet Little Sixteen **(12)**, Johnny B. Goode **(13)**, Around And Around **(14)**, In-Go **(14)**, It Don't Take But A Few Minutes **(14)**, Blues For Hawaiians **(14)**, Beautiful Delilah **(15)**, Carol **(16)**, Anthony Boy **(19)**, Jo Jo Gunne **(18)**, Memphis **(18)**

HIS BEST (VOLUME 2) (Chess CHD-9381)   May 1997

Sweet Little Rock'n'Roller **(19)**, Little Queenie **(20)**, Almost Grown **(21)**, Back In The USA **(21)**, Let It Rock **(22)**, Too Pooped To Pop **(22)**, Bye Bye Johnny **(23)**, Jaguar And Thunderbird **(23)**, Confessin' The Blues **(24)**, Down The Road Apiece **(24)**, I'm Talking About You **(25)**, Come On **(26)**, Nadine (Is It You) **(27)**, You Never Can Tell **(27)**, Promised Land **(28)**, No Particular Place To Go **(29)**, I Want To Be Your Driver **(33)**, Tulane **(55)**, My Ding-A-Ling **(59)**, Reelin' And Rockin' **(59)**

▶ **LIVE** (Columbia River Entertainment Group VMK-1154)   1997

Roll Over Beethoven **(83)**, School Day **(83)**, Sweet Little Sixteen **(83)**, Nadine (Is It You) **(83)**, Let It Rock **(83)**, Promised Land **(83)**, Memphis Tennessee **(83)**, Johnny B. Goode **(83)**, Brown Eyed Handsome Man **(83)**, Too Much Monkey Business **(83)**, Carol/Little Queenie **(83)**, Rock And Roll Music **(83)**, Instrumental **(83)**, Reelin' And Rockin' **(83)**
NB Four of the tracks are not listed on either the disc or the packaging.

ROCKIT (Atlantic 7567-80759-2)   1998

Same tracks as US LP Atco SD38-118 (1979).

20th CENTURY MASTERS – THE MILLENNIUM COLLECTION
THE BEST OF CHUCK BERRY (M.C.A. MCAD-11944)   1999

Maybellene **(2)**, Roll Over Beethoven **(5)**, Brown Eyed Handsome Man **(5)**, School Day **(9)**, Rock And Roll Music **(10)**, Sweet Little Sixteen **(12)**, Johnny B. Goode **(13)**, Carol **(16)**, You Never Can Tell **(27)**, My Ding-A-Ling **(59**, *single edit)*, No Particular Place To Go **(29)**

CLASSIC CHUCK BERRY (M.C.A. 112 172-2)   1999

Johnny B. Goode **(13)**, Roll Over Beethoven **(5)**, Maybellene **(2)**, School Day **(9)**, Rock And Roll Music **(10)**, Oh Baby Doll **(10)**, Too Much Monkey Business **(5)**, Let It Rock **(22)**, Carol **(16)**, Sweet Little Rock And Roller **(19)**, My Ding-A-Ling **(59)**, Reelin' And Rockin' **(12)**, No Particular Place To Go **(29)**, Sweet Little Sixteen **(12)**, Little Queenie **(20)**, Brown Eyed Handsome Man **(5)**, Nadine **(27)**, Too Pooped To Pop **(22)**, Back In The USA **(21)**, Bye Bye Johnny **(23)**

Various Artists
THE CHESS STORY 1947-75 (M.C.A. 380 596-2) *15-CD set*   December 1999

Maybellene **(2)**, Thirty Days **(3)**, No Money Down **(4)**, Roll Over Beethoven **(5)**, Brown Eyed Handsome Man **(5)**, Too Much Monkey Business **(5)**, School Day **(9)**, Rock And Roll Music **(10)**, Sweet Little Sixteen **(12**, *correct speed)*, Carol **(16)**, Sweet Little Rock And Roller **(19)**, Almost Grown **(21)**, Back In The USA **(21)**, Let It Rock **(22)**, Come On **(26)**, Nadine **(27)**, Promised Land **(28)**, My Ding-A-Ling **(59**, *single edit)*, Bio **(66)**
On early pressings of this set, 'Rock And Roll Music' is omitted in error. Disc 14 contains a UK radio interview with Marshall Chess in the course of which he rates the selection of 'Johnny B. Goode' as one of the items sent into space on Voyager 2 as the pinnacle of the Chess label's/his father's achievements. Disc 15 is an interactive disc which contains a US Chess CD catalogue and various film clips including Chuck Berry, introduced by Trini Lopez on the 1965 US TV show 'Hullabaloo!', singing just one minute of 'Johnny B. Goode'.

CHUCK BERRY – THE ANTHOLOGY (M.C.A. 088 112 304-2)   2000

❶ Maybellene **(2)**, Wee Wee Hours **(2)**, Thirty Days **(3)**, You Can't Catch Me **(4)**, Downbound Train **(4)**, No Money Down **(4)**, Brown Eyed Handsome Man **(5)**, Roll Over Beethoven **(5)**, Too Much Monkey Business **(5)**, Havana Moon **(6)**, School Day **(9)**, Rock And Roll Music **(10)**, Oh Baby Doll **(10)**, Sweet Little Sixteen **(12)**, Guitar Boogie **(12)**, Reelin' And Rockin' **(12)**, Johnny B. Goode **(13)**, Around And Around **(14)**, Beautiful Delilah **(15)**, House Of Blue Lights **(16)**, Carol **(16)**, Jo Jo Gunne **(18)**, Memphis Tennessee **(18)**, Sweet Little Rock And Roller **(19)**, Little Queenie **(20)**, Almost Grown **(21)**

❷ Back In The USA **(21)**, Do You Love Me **(21**, *alt. take)*, Betty Jean **(22)**, Childhood Sweetheart **(22)**, Let It Rock **(22)**, Too Pooped To Pop **(22)**, I Got To Find My Baby **(23)**, Jaguar And Thunderbird **(23)**, Down The Road Apiece **(24)**, Confessin' The Blues **(24)**, I'm Talkin' About You **(25)**, Come On **(26)**, Nadine (Is It You) **(27)**, You Never Can Tell **(27)**, Promised Land **(28)**, No Particular Place To Go **(29)**, Dear Dad **(33)**, I Want To Be Your Driver **(33)**, Tulane **(55)**, My Ding-A-Ling **(59**, *single edit)*, Reelin' And Rockin' **(59)**, Bio **(66)**

UK CDs

HAIL! HAIL! ROCK'N'ROLL (M.C.A. DMCF-3411)　　　　　　　February 1988

Equivalent of US M.C.A. MCAD-6217 (1987).

GREATEST HITS (Chess CDCHESS-21)　　　　　　　　　　October 1988

Maybelline **(2)**, Thirty Days **(3)**, Brown Eyed Handsome Man **(5)**, Roll Over Beethoven **(5)**, Too Much Monkey Business **(5)**, Schooldays **(9)**, Rock And Roll Music **(10)**, Sweet Little Sixteen **(12)**, Reeling And Rocking **(12)**, Johnny B. Goode **(13)**, Around And Around **(14)**, Carol **(16)**, Memphis Tennessee **(18)**, Sweet Little Rock And Roller **(19)**, Little Queenie **(20)**, Back In The USA **(21)**, Let It Rock **(22)**, Nadine **(27)**, You Never Can Tell **(27)**, Promised Land **(28)**, No Particular Place To Go **(29)**, Beautiful Delilah **(15)**, Bye Bye Johnny **(23)**

ROCKIT (Magnum Force CDMF-065)　　　　　　　　　　November 1988

Same tracks as US LP Atco SD38-118 (1979).

HAIL! HAIL! ROCK'N'ROLL (Chess CDCHESS-1003)　　　　　October 1989

Maybellene **(2)**, Thirty Days **(3)**, No Money Down **(4)**, Roll Over Beethoven **(5)**, Brown Eyed Handsome Man **(5)**, Too Much Monkey Business **(5)**, You Can't Catch Me **(4)**, School Day (Ring! Ring! Goes The Bell) **(9)**, Rock & Roll Music **(10)**, Sweet Little Sixteen **(12)**, Reelin' And Rockin' **(12)**, Johnny B. Goode **(13)**, Around And Around **(14)**, Beautiful Delilah **(15)**, Carol **(16)**, Sweet Little Rock And Roller **(19)**, Almost Grown **(21)**, Little Queenie **(20)**, Back In The USA **(21)**, Memphis Tennessee **(18)**, Too Pooped To Pop **(22)**, Let It Rock **(22)**, Bye Bye Johnny **(23)**, I'm Talking About You **(25)**, Come On **(26)**, Nadine (Is It You) **(27)**, No Particular Place To Go **(29)**, You Never Can Tell **(27)**, Little Marie **(32)**, Promised Land **(28)**, Tulane **(55)**, My Ding-A-Ling **(59)**

ROCK & ROLL RARITIES (Chess CDCHESS-1005)　　　　　October 1989

Rock And Roll Music **(8**, *demo)*, Rock And Roll Music **(10**, *alt. take)*, Sweet Little Sixteen **(11**, *demo)*, Sweet Little Sixteen **(12**, *alt. take)*, Reelin' And Rockin' **(12**, *alt. take)*, Johnny B. Goode **(13**, *alt. take)*, Beautiful Delilah **(15**, *alt. take)*, Oh Yeah **(16)**, House Of Blue Lights **(16)**, Time Was **(16**, *fast version)*, Sweet Little Rock And Roller **(19**, *alt. take)*, Run Rudolph Run **(20)**, Little Queenie **(20**, *alt. take)*, Betty Jean **(22)**, County Line **(22)**, Bye Bye Johnny **(23**, *stereo)*, I Got To Find My Baby **(23**, *stereo)*, Down The Road Apiece **(24**, *stereo)*, Route 66 **(25**, *alt. take)*, I'm Talking About You **(25**, *stereo)*, Come On **(26**, *alt. take)*, Go Go Go **(26**, *stereo)*, Brown Eyed Handsome Man **(26**, *stereo)*, Nadine (Is That You) **(27**, *stereo)*, You Never Can Tell **(27**, *stereo)*, Promised Land **(28**, *stereo)*, No Particular Place To Go **(29**, *stereo)*

FRUIT OF THE VINE (Chess CDRED-19)　　　　　　　　　April 1990

Downbound Train **(4)**, Wee Wee Hours **(2)**, No Money Down **(4)**, Drifting Heart **(5)**, Brown Eyed Handsome Man **(5)**, Havana Moon **(6)**, Oh Baby Doll **(10)**, Anthony Boy **(19)**, Merry Christmas Baby **(20)**, Jo Jo Gunne **(18)**, Childhood Sweetheart **(22)**, I Got To Find My Baby **(23)**, Worried Life Blues **(23)**, Jaguar And The Thunderbird **(23)**, Confessin' The Blues **(24)**, Thirteen Question Method **(24)**, The Things I Used To Do **(27)**, You Two **(29)**, Little Marie **(32)**, Dear Dad **(33)**, It Wasn't Me **(39)**, Ramona, Say Yes **(40)**, Tulane **(55)**, Have Mercy Judge **(55)**

THE LONDON SESSIONS (Chess CDRED-20)　　　　　　　June 1990

Same tracks as US LP Chess CH-60020 (The London Chuck Berry Sessions, 1972).

Various Artists
▶**ROCK AND ROLL DANCE PARTY** (Magnum Force CDMF-075)　　　1991

Maybellene **(7)**, Roll Over Beethoven **(7)**　*Chuck Berry does not appear on other tracks.*

THE EP COLLECTION (See For Miles SEECD-320)　　　　　May 1991

Reelin' And Rockin' **(12)**, Johnny B. Goode **(13)**, Nadine **(27)**, Don't You Lie To Me **(23)**, Round And Round **(14)**, No Particular Place To Go **(29)**, Childhood Sweetheart **(22)**, My Little Love-Light **(35)**, Maybellene **(2)**, I'm Talking About You **(25)**, Roll Over Beethoven **(5)**, Sweet Little Sixteen **(12)**, You Can't Catch Me **(4)**, Memphis Tennessee **(18)**, I Got A Booking **(35)**, You Never Can Tell **(27)**, The Things I Used To Do **(27)**, Jamaica Farewell **(34)**, Thirty Days **(3)**, Oh, Baby Doll **(10)**, School Day **(9)**, Bye Bye Johnny **(23)**, Back In The USA **(21)**, Rock And Roll Music **(10)**

THE CHESS YEARS (Chess CDREDBOX-2)   November 1991

❶ Maybellene **(2)**, Wee Wee Hours **(2)**, Thirty Days **(3)**, Together (We Will Always Be) **(3)**, You Can't Catch Me **(4)**, Roly Poly **(4)**, Berry Pickin' **(4)**, Down Bound Train **(4)**, No Money Down **(4)**, Drifting Heart **(5)**, Brown Eyed Handsome Man **(5)**, Roll Over Beethoven **(5)**, Too Much Monkey Business **(5)**, Havana Moon **(6)**, Rock And Roll Music **(8**, *demo*), Deep Feelin' **(9)**, School Day **(9)**, La Jaunda **(9)**, Blue Feeling **(9)**, Low Feeling **(9)**, Wee Wee Hours (Blues) **(2)**, How You've Changed **(10)**, Rock And Roll Music **(10)**, Oh Baby Doll **(10)**, Sweet Little Sixteen **(11**, *demo*)

❷ Thirteen Question Method **(10)**, How High The Moon **(10)**, I've Changed **(4)**, Sweet Little Sixteen **(12)**, Rockin' At The Philharmonic **(12)**, Guitar Boogie **(12)**, Night Beat **(12)**, Time Was **(12**, *slow version*), Reelin And Rockin' **(12)**, Johnny B. Goode **(13)**, Around And Around **(14)**, In-Go **(14)**, It Don't Take But A Few Minutes **(14)**, Blues For Hawaiians **(14)**, Beautiful Delilah **(15)**, Vacation Time **(15)**, 21 **(15)**, 21 Blues **(15)**, Carol **(16)**, Oh Yeah **(16)**, Hey Pedro **(16)**, Time Was **(16**, *fast version*), House of Blue Lights **(16)**, Anthony Boy **(19)**, Jo Jo Gunne **(18)**, Sweet Little Rock & Roller **(19)**, Memphis Tennessee **(18)**, Merry Christmas Baby **(20)**, Run Rudolph Run **(20)**, Little Queenie **(20)**

❸ That's My Desire **(20)**, Little Queenie **(20**, *alt. take*), Do You Love Me **(21**, *alt. take*), Almost Grown **(21)**, Back In The USA **(21)**, Blue On Blue **(21)**, Betty Jean **(22)**, County Line **(22)**, Childhood Sweetheart **(22)**, One O'Clock Jump **(22)**, I Just Want To Make Love To You **(22**, *with fake audience*), Broken Arrow **(22)**, Let It Rock **(22)**, Too Pooped To Pop **(22)**, Say You'll Be Mine **(22)**, Let Me Sleep Woman **(22)**, Childhood Sweetheart **(22**, *alt. take*), Drifting Blues **(23)**, I Got To Find My Baby **(23)**, Don't You Lie To Me **(23)**, Worried Life Blues **(23)**, Our Little Rendezvous **(23)**, Bye Bye Johnny **(23)**, Run Around **(23)**, Jaguar And Thunderbird **(23)**, Diploma For Two **(24)**, Little Star **(24)**, The Way It Was Before **(24)**, Away From You **(24)**, Down The Road Apiece **(24)**

❹ Confessin' The Blues **(24)**, Sweet Sixteen **(24)**, Thirteen Question Method **(24)**, Stop And Listen **(24)**, Still Got The Blues **(24**, *with fake audience*), Lucky So And So **(24)**, Mad Lad **(24)**, Cryin' Steel **(24)**, Surfin' Steel **(24**, *with fake audience*), Route 66 **(25)**, I'm Talking About You **(25)**, Rip It Up **(25)**, Come On **(26)**, The Man And The Donkey **(26**, *with fake audience*), Go Go Go **(26**, *with fake audience*), Trick Or Treat **(26**, *with fake audience*), Brown Eyed Handsome Man **(26**, *with fake audience*), All Aboard **(26**, *with fake audience*), How High The Moon **(10**, *with fake audience*), Nadine **(27)**, You Never Can Tell **(27)**, The Girl From Central High **(27)**, Things I Used To Do **(27)**, Fraulein **(27)**, Crazy Arms (Lonely All The Time) **(27)**, Orangutang **(27)**, Big Ben Blues **(28)**, Promised Land **(28)**, Brenda Lee **(28)**

❺ No Particular Place To Go **(29)**, Liverpool Drive **(29)**, You Too **(29)**, Chuck's Beat **(30**, *incomplete*), Bo's Beat **(30**, *incomplete*), Little Marie **(32)**, Go, Bobby Soxer **(32)**, Lonely Schooldays **(33**, *slow version*), His Daughter Caroline **(33)**, Dear Dad **(33)**, I Want To Be Your Driver **(33)**, The Song Of My Love **(33)**, Butterscotch **(33)**, After It's Over **(34)**, Why Should We End This Way **(34)**, You Came A Long Way From St. Louis **(34)**, She Once Was Mine **(34)**, Jamaica Farewell **(34)**, My Little Lovelight **(35)**, I Got A Booking **(35)**, St. Louis Blues **(35)**, Run Joe **(37)**, It's My Own Business **(37)** One For My Baby **(37)**, Everyday We Rock & Roll **(37)**

❻ My Mustang Ford **(37)**, Merrily We Rock & Roll **(38)**, Vaya Con Dios **(38)**, Wee Hours Blues **(38)**, It Wasn't Me **(39)**, Ain't That Just Like A Woman **(39)**, Right Off Rampart Street **(39)**, Welcome Back Pretty Baby **(39)**, Sad Day Long Night **(38)**, Ramona, Say Yes **(40)**, Viva Viva Rock & Roll **(40)**, Lonely Schooldays **(40**, *fast version*), Tulane **(55)**, Have Mercy Judge **(55)**, Instrumental **(56)**, Christmas **(56)**, Gun **(56)**, I'm A Rocker **(56)**, Flyin' Home **(56)**, Fish & Chips **(56)**, Some People **(56)**, Oh Louisiana **(58)**, Festival **(58)**, Let's Do Our Thing Together **(58)**, Your Lick **(58)**, Bound To Lose **(58)**, Bordeaux In My Pirough **(58)**

❼ San Francisco Dues **(58)**, My Dream **(58)**, My Ding-A-Ling **(59)**, Johnny B. Goode **(59)**, Reelin' And Rockin' **(59)**, Let's Boogie **(60)**, Mean Old World **(60)**, I Love You **(60)**, I Will Not Let You Go **(60)**, London Berry Blues **(60)**, Rain Eyes **(65)**, Sue Answer **(65)**, Got It And Gone **(65)**, A Deuce **(65)**

❽ Talkin' About My Buddy **(66)**, Hello Little Girl Goodbye **(66)**, Aimlessly Driftin' **(66)**, Woodpecker **(66)**, Bio **(66)**, I'm Just A Name **(67)**, Too Late **(67)**, Hi-Heel Sneakers **(68)**, South Of The Border **(68)**, Swannee River **(69)**, You Are My Sunshine **(69)**, Don't Lie To Me **(69)**, My Babe **(70)**, I Just Want To Make Love To You **(70)**, Shake Rattle & Roll **(70)**, Baby What You Want Me To Do **(70)**

❾ Rock'n'Roll Music **(10**, *alt. take*), Sweet Little Sixteen **(12**, *alt. take*), Reelin' And Rockin' **(12**, *alt. take*), Johnny B. Goode **(13**, *alt. take*), Beautiful Delilah **(15**, *alt. takes*), Sweet Little Rock & Roller **(19**, *alt. take*), Betty Jean **(22**, *alt. take*), I Got To Find My Baby **(23**, *stereo*), Bye Bye Johnny **(23**, *stereo*), Down The Road Apiece **(24**, *stereo*), Route 66 **(25**, *alt. take*), I'm Talking About You **(25**, *stereo*), Come On **(26**, *alt. take*), Go Go Go **(26**, *stereo*), Brown Eyed Handsome Man **(26**, *stereo*), Nadine **(27**, *stereo*), You Never Can Tell **(27**, *stereo*), Promised Land **(28**, *stereo*), No Particular Place To Go **(29**, *stereo*), Little Marie **(32**, *stereo*), I Want To Be Your Driver **(33**, *stereo*), My Mustang Ford **(37**, *stereo*), It Wasn't Me **(39**, *stereo*), Ain't That Just Like A Woman **(39**, *stereo*)

▶**ON THE BLUES SIDE** (Ace CDCH-397)   September 1993

Confessin The Blues **(24)**, Run Around **(23)**, Worried Life Blues **(23)**, The Things That I Used To Do **(27)**, Blues For Hawaiians **(14)**, Wee Wee Hours **(2)**, I Still Got The Blues **(24**, *alt. take*), Down The Road Apiece **(24)**, No Money Down **(4)**, Stop And Listen **(24)**, Blue On Blue **(21)**, Sweet Sixteen **(24)**, I Got To Find My Baby **(23**, *stereo*), I Just Want To Make Love To You **(22)**, Merry Christmas Baby **(20)**, Deep Feeling **(9)**, Wee Hour Blues **(38)**, Don't You Lie To Me **(23)**, Ain't That Just Like A Woman **(39**, *stereo*), Drifting Blues **(23)**, Blue Feeling **(9)**

POET OF ROCK'N'ROLL (Charly Rock'n'Roll CDDIG-1)   May 1994

❶ Johnny B. Goode **(13)**, Maybellene **(2)**, Roll Over Beethoven **(5)**, Rock & Roll Music **(10)**, Schoolday **(9)**, Sweet Little Sixteen **(12)**, Carol **(16)**, Almost Grown **(21)**, Back In The USA **(21)**, Nadine **(27)**, Too Much Monkey Business **(5)**, Brown-Eyed Handsome Man **(5)**, Oh Baby Doll **(10)**, Promised Land **(28)**, Things I Used To Do **(27)**, Worried Life Blues **(23)**, Run Around **(23)**, Childhood Sweetheart **(22)**, Ingo **(14)**, Drifting Blues **(23)**, Confessin' The Blues **(24)**, Sweet Sixteen **(24)**, Deep Feelin' **(9)**, Bio **(66)**, Lucky So And So **(24)**, Wee Wee Hours **(2)**, After It's Over **(34)**

❷ No Particular Place To Go **(29)**, Reelin' & Rockin' **(12)**, You Never Can Tell **(27)**, Thirty Days **(3)**, No Money Down **(4)**, Little Queenie **(20)**, Memphis Tennessee **(18)**, Sweet Little Rock'n'Roller **(19)**, Let It Rock **(22)**, Come On **(26)**, Go, Bobby Soxer **(32)**, Go Go Go **(26**, *stereo*), Beautiful Delilah **(15**, *alt. takes*), Hello Little Girl Goodbye **(66)**, Blue Feeling **(9)**, Why Should We End This Way **(34)**, Welcome Back Pretty Baby **(39)**, I've Changed **(4)**, Blue On Blue **(21)**, She Once Was Mine **(34)**, Right Off Rampart Street **(39)**, Mean Old World **(60)**, Instrumental **(56)**, I Got A Booking **(35)**, San Francisco Dues **(58)**, I Want To Be Your Driver **(33)**, Merry Christmas Baby **(20)**

❸ You Can't Catch Me **(4)**, I Got To Find My Baby **(23**, *stereo*), Jo Jo Gunne **(18)**, Betty Jean **(22)**, Butterscotch **(33)**, Rip It Up **(25)**, Bye Bye Johnny **(23)**, Don't You Lie To Me **(23)**, Roly Poly **(4)**, Jaguar & The Thunderbird **(23)**, Down The Road Apiece **(24**, *stereo*), Ain't That Just Like A Woman **(39)**, Around & Around **(14)**, It Wasn't Me **(39**, *stereo*), Ramona, Say Yes **(40)**, My Mustang Ford **(37**, *stereo*), Orangutang **(27)**, Sue Answer **(65)**, Tulane **(55)**, Have Mercy Judge **(55)**, Gun **(56)**, I Love You **(60)**, I'm Talking About You **(25**, *stereo*), Oh Yeah **(16)**, Liverpool Drive **(29)**, Little Marie **(32)**

❹ Berry Pickin' **(4)**, Havana Moon **(6)**, La Jaunda **(9)**, Vaya Con Dios **(38)**, I'm Just A Name **(67)**, Crazy Arms (Lonely All The Time) **(27)**, You Two **(29)**, Fraulein **(27)**, Too Late **(67)**, Bound To Lose **(58)**, Lonely Schooldays **(33)**, Bordeaux In My Pirough **(58)**, Oh Louisiana **(58)**, Got It And Gone **(65)**, Guitar Boogie **(12)**, Down Bound Train **(4)**, Route 66 **(25**, *stereo alt. take*), Rockin' At The Philharmonic **(12)**, One For My Baby **(37)**, Away From You **(24)**, Do You Love Me **(21**, *alt. take*), My Dream **(58)**, Wee Hours Blues **(38)**, Anthony Boy **(19)**, Too Pooped To Pop **(22)**

CHUCK BERRY IS ON TOP (Chess CHLD-19250)   September 1994

Almost Grown **(21)**, Carol **(16)**, Maybellene **(2)**, Sweet Little Rock And Roller **(19)**, Anthony Boy **(19)**, Johnny B. Goode **(13)**, Little Queenie **(20)**, Jo Jo Gunne **(18)**, Roll Over Beethoven **(5)**, Around And Around **(14)**, Hey Pedro **(16)**, Blues For Hawaiians **(14)**, Down The Road Apiece **(24)**, No Money Down **(4)**, Downbound Train **(4)**, Jaguar And Thunderbird **(23)**, The Things I Used To Do **(27)**, No Particular Place To Go **(29)**, Fraulein **(27)**, Nadine (Is It You) **(27)**

CHARLY R&B MASTERS (VOLUME 12): OH YEAH (Charly R&B CDRB-12)   October 1994

No Money Down **(4)**, 21 Blues **(15)**, Oh Yeah **(16)**, Do You Love Me **(21**, *alt. take*), Childhood Sweetheart **(22)**, Drifting Blues **(23)**, Got To Find My Baby **(23)**, Jaguar And Thunderbird **(23)**, Down The Road Apiece **(24)**, Confessin The Blues **(24)**, The Things I Used To Do **(27)**, I Want To Be Your Driver **(33)**, She Once Was Mine **(34)**, I Got A Booking **(35)**, Lonely Schooldays **(33)**, Lets Do Our Thing Together **(58)**, Your Lick **(58)**, San Francisco Dues **(58)**, Lets Boogie **(60)**, Bio **(66)**

▶**LIVE ON STAGE** (Magnum Force CDMF-092)   1994

Schooldays **(85)**, Sweet Little Sixteen **(85)**, Roll Over Beethoven **(85)**, Everyday I Have The Blues **(85)**, Bio **(85)**, Maybelline/Mountain Dew **(85)**, Let It Rock **(85)**, Carol/Little Queenie **(85)**, Keys To The Highway **(85)**, Got My Mojo Working **(85)**, Reelin' And Rockin' **(85)**, Johnny B. Goode **(85)**

Shabba Ranks
▶**A MI SHABBA** (Epic EPC-477482-2)   June 1995

Go Shabba Go **(91)**. *Chuck Berry does not appear on other tracks.*

Chuck Berry & Bo Diddley / Howlin' Wolf, Muddy Waters & Bo Diddley
TWO GREAT GUITARS / SUPER SUPER BLUES BAND (Beat Goes On BGOCD-334)   Sept. 1996

Liverpool Drive **(29)**, Chuck's Beat **(30)**, Bo's Beat **(30)**. *Chuck Berry does not appear on other tracks.*

THE BEST OF CHUCK BERRY (M.C.A. MCD-11560)   November 1996

❶ Roll Over Beethoven **(5)**, Sweet Little Sixteen **(12)**, Johnny B. Goode **(13)**, You Never Can Tell **(27)**, Down Bound Train **(4)**, Too Much Monkey Business **(5)**, Havana Moon **(6)**, School Day **(9)**, Oh Baby Doll **(10)**, Beautiful Delilah **(15)**, Sweet Little Rock And Roller **(19)**, Anthony Boy **(19)**, Little Queenie **(20)**, Almost Grown **(21)**, Let It Rock **(22)**, Back In The USA **(21)**, Reelin' And Rockin' **(59)**, Around And Around **(14)**, Brown Eyed Handsome Man **(5)**
❷ Maybellene **(2)**, No Particular Place To Go **(29)**, Rock And Roll Music **(10)**, Run Rudolph Run **(20)**, Jo Jo Gunne **(18)**, Carol **(16)**, Confessin' The Blues **(24)**, Jaguar And Thunderbird **(23)**, Down The Road Apiece **(24)**, Thirty Days **(3)**, Merry Christmas Baby **(20)**, My Ding-A-Ling **(59)**, I'm Talkin' About You **(25)**, Too Pooped To Pop **(22)**, Bye Bye Johnny **(23)**, Promised Land **(28)**, Tulane **(55)**, Come On **(26)**, Nadine (Is It You) **(27)**, Memphis Tennessee **(18)**

▶ **THE ESSENTIAL COLLECTION** (Newsound/Penny PYCD-260)   1996

❶ Roll Over Beethoven **(62)**, Sweet Little Sixteen **(62)**, Memphis Tennessee **(62)**, South Of The Border **(62)**, Beer Drinking Woman **(62)**, Let It Rock **(62)**, Mean Old World **(62)**, Carol **(62)**, Liverpool Drive **(62)**, Nadine **(62)**, Bye Bye Johnny **(62)**, Bonsoir Cherie/Johnny B. Goode **(62)**.
❷ Rock And Roll Music **(54)**, Long Live Rock And Roll *[School Day]* **(54)**, Johnny B. Goode/ Carol **(54)**, Hoochie Coochie Man **(54)**, Maybellene **(54)**, Too Much Monkey Business **(54)**, Reelin' And Rockin' **(54)**, Sweet Little Sixteen **(54)**, In The Wee Wee Hours **(54)**, Promised Land **(83)**, School Days **(83)**, Brown Eyed Handsome Man **(83)**

▶ **FOREVER CLASSIC** (MasterTone 0301)   1997

Schoolday (Ring, Ring, Goes The Bell) **(54)**, Maybellene **(54)**, Reelin' & Rockin' **(54)**, The Wee Wee Hours **(54)**, Sweet Little Sixteen **(83)**, Nadine (Is It You) **(83)**, Promised Land **(83)**, Johnny B. Good **(83)**, Carol/Little Queenie **(83)**, Rock'n'Roll Music **(54)**, Hoochie Coochie Man **(54)**, Too Much Monkey Business **(54)**, Roll Over Beethoven **(83)**, Let It Rock **(83)**, Memphis Tennessee **(83)**, Brown Eyed Handsome Man **(83)**, Mean Old World **(62)**

THE BEST OF CHUCK BERRY (Universal MCBD-19536)   1997

No Particular Place To Go **(29)**, School Day (Ring, Ring Goes The Bell) **(9)**, Sweet Little Sixteen **(12)**, Let It Rock **(22)**, Memphis Tennessee **(18)**, Nadine (Is It You) **(27)**, You Never Can Tell **(27)**, Promised Land **(28)**, Reelin' And Rockin' **(12)**, My Ding-A-Ling **(59)**, Maybellene **(2)**, Roll Over Beethoven **(5)**, Johnny B. Goode **(13)**, Carol **(16)**, Almost Grown **(21)**, Back In The USA **(21)**, Little Queenie **(20)**, Brown Eyed Handsome Man **(5)**, Sweet Little Rock And Roller **(19)**, Rock And Roll Music **(10)**

SWEET LITTLE ROCK'N'ROLLER (Chess MCD-80245)   March 1997

Carol **(16)**, Back In The USA **(21)**, Sweet Little Rock'n'Roller **(19)**, Little Queenie **(20)**, School Days **(9)**, Promised Land **(28)**, Maybelline **(2)**, Nadine **(27)**, Blues For Hawaiians **(14)**, No Money Down **(4)**, Fraulein **(27)**, Roll Over Beethoven **(5)**, Memphis Tennessee **(18)**, Sweet Little Sixteen **(12)**, Johnny B. Goode **(13)**, No Particular Place To Go **(29)**, Down The Road Apiece **(24)**, Let It Rock **(22)**, You Never Can Tell **(27)**, My Ding-A-Ling **(59)**

CHUCK BERRY / MORE CHUCK BERRY (Beat Goes On BGOCD-394)   September 1997

Same tracks as UK LPs Pye International NPL-28024 (1963) and NPL-28028 (1963).

IN LONDON / FRESH BERRY'S (Beat Goes On BGOCD-395)   April 1998

Same tracks as UK LPs Chess CRL-4005 (1965) and CRL-4506 (1965).

▶ **THE LATEST AND THE GREATEST /**
YOU NEVER CAN TELL (Beat Goes On BGOCD-428)   September 1998

Same tracks as UK LPs Pye International NPL-28031 (1964) and NPL-28039 (1964), except that 'O'Rangutang' is an unfaded version and 'The Little Girl From Central' is in stereo.

ONE DOZEN BERRYS / JUKE BOX HITS (Beat Goes On BGOCD-458)   August 1999

Same tracks as UK LPs London HA-M-2132 (1959) and Pye International NPL-28019 (1962).

Foreign CDs

▶ **SIX TWO FIVE** (Archivio ARC CD-001) *bootleg*   Italy, 1991

Roll Over Beethoven **(62)**,Sweet Little Sixteen **(62)**, Memphis **(62)**, South Of The Border **(62)**, Beer Drinking Woman **(62)**, Let It Rock **(62)**, Mean Old World **(62)**, Carol **(62)**, Liverpool Drive **(62)**, Nadine **(62)**, Bye Bye Johnny **(62)**, Bonsoir Cherie/Johnny B. Goode **(62)**

Chuck Berry and Band Feat. Johnny Johnson
▶ **SWEET, SWEET ROCK AND ROLL** (Discurios DIS-124CD)   Switzerland, 1992

Roll Over Beethoven **(89)**, Hail, Hail Rock And Roll *[School Day]* **(89)**, Sweet Little Sixteen **(89)**, Wee Wee Hours **(89)**, Let It Rock **(89)**, Nadine **(89)**, Dust My Broom **(89)**, Rock And Roll Music **(89)**, Memphis Tennessee **(89)**, Caravan **(89)**, Johnny B. Goode **(89)**, Reelin' And Rockin ' **(89)**

Various Artists
▶ **NEWPORT JAZZ FESTIVAL 1958:**
JULY 3RD-6TH, BLUES IN THE NIGHT (Phontastic PHONT NCD-8815)   Sweden, 1992

Introduction **(17)**, Schooldays **(17)**, No Money Down **(17)**, Sweet Little Sixteen **(17)**, Johnny Be Goode **(17)**. *Chuck Berry does not appear on other tracks.*

Chuck Berry & Matchbox
▶ **CHUCK BERRY MEETS MATCHBOX** (white label HRTCD-93003) *bootleg*   Germany, 1994

Liverpool Drive **(72)**, Carol **(72)**, Little Queenie **(72)**, Hail, Hail, Rock'n'Roll *[School Day]* **(72)**, Sweet Little Sixteen **(72)**, Memphis Tennessee **(72)**, Let It Rock **(72)**, Everyday I Have The Blues **(72)**, Wee Wee Hours **(72)**, I Believe **(72)**, Promised Land **(72)**, You Never Can Tell **(72)**, My Ding-A-Ling **(72)**, Johnny Be Goode **(72)**, Reelin' And Rockin' **(72)**
NB The CD tray inlay card bears the inscription 'Promised Land Records PL72 1977', but the disc itself is blank apart from the number shown above. No other issues of this material are known.

Various Artists
ALAN FREED'S ROCK AND ROLL DANCE PARTY (Go Cat Go TECX-20943)   Japan, 1995

Maybellene **(7)**, Roll Over Beethoven **(7)**. *Chuck Berry does not appear on other tracks.*

▶ **ORIGINAL LEGENDS VERSIONS** (Mandarim MR-03978)   Republic of Ireland, 1996

Schoolday **(54)**, Maybelline **(54)**, Reelin' And Rockin' **(54)**, In The Wee Wee Hours **(54)**, Sweet Little Sixteen **(83)**, Nadine (Is It You) **(83)**, Promised Land **(83)**, Memphis Tennessee **(83)**, Rock And Roll Music **(54)**, Too Much Monkey Business **(54)**, Roll Over Beethoven **(83)**, Let It Rock **(83)**

▶ **OUR LITTLE RENDEZ-VOUS** (Wolf 2010CD)   Austria, 1997

Interview **(64)**, Roll Over Beethoven **(62)**, Sweet Little 16 **(62)**, Memphis Tennessee **(62)**, South Of The Border **(62)**, Beer Drinking Woman **(62)**, Let It Rock **(62)**, Mean Old World **(62)**, Carol **(62)**, Liverpool Drive **(62)**, Nadine **(62)**, Bye Bye Johnny **(62)**, Maybelline **(7)**, Roll Over Beethoven **(7)**, Sweet Little Sixteen **(17)**, Night Beat **(12)**, Our Little Rendez-vous **(23)**, How You've Changed **(10)**, Orangutang **(27)**
NB. 'Bonsoir Cherie/Johnny B. Goode' is listed on the CD cover but is not included on the disc.

Various Artists
▶ **CRUISIN' CLASSICS (VOLUME 1)**
LOST ROCK 'N' ROLL TREASURES (Mr. DJ 101) *bootleg*   Netherlands(?), 1998

Oh Maria **(1)** *credited to 'Chuck Berry & The Cubans'. Chuck does not appear on other tracks.*

Chuck Berry / B.B. King / Jerry Lee Lewis / Little Richard
▶ **ROCK LEGENDS** (Pyramid 1999 10/11/12) *3-CD bootleg*   Netherlands, 1999

Memphis Tennessee **(93)**, In The Heat Of The Day *[Let It Rock]* **(93)**, Tell Me That I Love You **(93)**, Carol/Little Queenie **(93)**, You Never Can Tell **(93)**, Waltz **(93)**, Rock'n'Roll Music **(93)**, Round And Round **(93)**, Reelin' And Rockin' **(93)**. *Chuck Berry does not appear on other tracks.*

▶**THE LEGENDS OF ROCK AND ROLL: CHUCK BERRY**
(white label LGRR-01(3)) *bootleg*   Germany, 2000

Roll Over Beethoven **(92)**, Sweet Little Sixteen **(92)**, Let It Rock **(92)**, Memphis **(92)**, Deep Feeling *[Mean Old World]* **(92)**, Carol **(92)**, Little Queenie **(92)**, Wee Wee Hours *[Honest I Do]* **(92)**, Johnny B. Goode **(92)**, Rock And Roll Music **(92)**, You Never Can Tell **(92)**, Havanna Moon **(92)**, Reelin' And Rockin' **(92)**. *Chuck Berry does not appear on other tracks.*

▶**CHUCK BERRY IN LONDON** (Official 4012-FS) *bootleg*   Netherlands, 2000

My Little Love Light **(35)**, She Once Was Mine **(34)**, After It's Over **(34)**, I Got A Booking **(35)**, Night Beat **(12)**, His Daughter Caroline **(33)**, You Came A Long Way From St. Louis **(34)**, St. Louis Blues **(35)**, Jamaica Farewell **(34)**, Dear Dad **(33)**, Butterscotch **(33)**, The Song Of My Love **(33)**, Liverpool Drive **(29)**, Big Ben Blues **(28)**, London Berry Blues **(60)**, Nadine **(36)**, Promised Land **(36)**, No Particular Place To Go **(36)**, Nadine **(36)**, Promised Land **(36)**, No Particular Place To Go **(36)**, School Day **(31)**, Memphis Tennessee **(31)**, Sweet Little Sixteen **(31)**
NB. The date on the disc says 1994, but it was actually released in 2000.

4

Chuck Berry on the Charts

The following survey lists the details of Chuck Berry's chart successes on single, EP and LP in the USA and the UK. Considering his enormous influence on rock and popular music, Berry's success on the charts — particularly the pop charts — has been relatively modest. *Billboard's Hottest 'Hot 100' Hits* by Fred Bronson [Billboard Books, 1995] ranks the following Chuck Berry releases among its *Top 5000 Songs Of The Rock Era* (the strongest *Billboard* 'Hot 100' chart performers 1955–94): *School Day* (890th), *My Ding-A-Ling* (1648th), *Rock And Roll Music* (1985th), *Johnny B. Goode* (2049th), *Sweet Little Sixteen* (2079th), *Maybellene* (2200th) and *No Particular Place To Go* (4371st). 100 points were allocated for each week spent at No. 1, 99 points for each week at No. 2 etc. By this method, *School Day* interestingly emerges as Chuck's all-time hottest (and therefore biggest?) hit.

US CHARTS

Billboard R&B singles

Three separate R&B charts were in existence when Chuck Berry scored his first hit: 'Most Played In Juke Boxes' (inaugurated 8 February 1945), 'Best Sellers In Stores' (inaugurated 22 May 1948) and 'Most Played By Jockeys' (inaugurated 22 January 1955). Chart positions shown below are suffixed JB, BS *and* DJ *respectively to indicate which chart they refer to.*

Size of chart	Date of chart entry	Highest position attained	No. of weeks on chart	Title	Label and catalogue number
9-15 14-15 8-10	6 Aug 55	1 BS 1 DJ 1 JB	16	**Maybellene**	Chess 1604
8-10 14-15	10 Sep 55	10 JB 15 DJ	1	**Wee Wee Hours**	Chess 1604
8-10 14-15 9-15	29 Oct 55	2 JB 6 DJ 8 BS	11	**Thirty Days**	Chess 1610
14-15 9-15	25 Feb 56	8 DJ 11 BS	5	**No Money Down**	Chess 1615
8-10 9-15 14-15	9 Jun 56	2 JB 7 BS 8 DJ	7	**Roll Over Beethoven**	Chess 1626
9-10 14-15 13-15	6 Oct 56	4 JB 7 BS 11 DJ	6	**Too Much Monkey Business**	Chess 1635
13-15	20 Oct 56	5 DJ	8	**Brown Eyed Handsome Man**	Chess 1635
14-15 13-15 9-10	13 Apr 57	1 BS 1 DJ 1 JB	15	**School Day**	Chess 1653
The 'Most Played In Juke Boxes' chart was discontinued after 17 June 1957.					
13-15	22 Jul 57	12 DJ	1	**Oh Baby Doll**	Chess 1664
14-15 13-15	18 Nov 57	6 BS 7 DJ	9	**Rock And Roll Music**	Chess 1671

Size of chart	Date of chart entry	Highest position attained	No. of weeks on chart	Title	Label and catalogue number
20 13-15	24 Feb 58	1 BS 1 DJ	11	Sweet Little Sixteen	Chess 1683
13-15 20	5 May 58	2 DJ 5 BS	12	Johnny B. Goode	Chess 1691
13-15 20	15 Sep 58	9 DJ 12 BS	8	Carol	Chess 1700
	*The 'Best Selling In Stores' and 'Most Played By Disk Jockeys' charts were discontinued after 13 October 1958 and replaced by the 'Hot R&B' chart.*				
30	15 Dec 58	13	3	Sweet Little Rock And Roller	Chess 1709
30	13 Apr 59	3	13	Almost Grown	Chess 1722
30	6 Jul 59	16	8	Back In The USA	Chess 1729
30	4 Apr 60	18	3	Too Pooped To Pop	Chess 1747
	*No R&B charts were published between 30 November 1963 and 30 January 1965. The name of the chart was changed to 'Best Selling Soul Singles' on 23 August 1969.*				
50	30 Sep 72	42	7	My Ding-A-Ling	Chess 2131

Billboard pop singles

As with R&B, three separate pop charts were in existence when Chuck Berry scored his first hit: 'Most Played In Juke Boxes', 'Best Sellers In Stores' and 'Most Played By Jockeys'. Chart positions shown below are suffixed JB, BS and DJ respectively to indicate which chart they refer to.

Size of chart	Date of chart entry	Highest position attained	No. of weeks on chart	Title	Label and catalogue number
20-50	20 Aug 55	5 BS 6 JB 13 DJ	11	Maybellene	Chess 1604
	*The 'Top 100' chart commenced on 12 November 1955.*				
100	30 Jun 56	29	5	Roll Over Beethoven	Chess 1626
100	6 Apr 57	5	26	School Day	Chess 1653
100	29 Jul 57	57	7	Oh Baby Doll	Chess 1664
100	11 Nov 57	8	19	Rock And Roll Music	Chess 1671
100	17 Feb 58	2	16	Sweet Little Sixteen	Chess 1683
100	28 Apr 58	8	15	Johnny B. Goode	Chess 1691
100	28 Jul 58	81	2	Beautiful Delilah	Chess 1697
	*The 'Top 100' chart was renamed the 'Hot 100' on 4 August 1958.*				
100	25 Aug 58	18	10	Carol	Chess 1700
100	10 Nov 58	47	9	Sweet Little Rock And Roller	Chess 1709
100	17 Nov 58	83	5	Jo Jo Gunne	Chess 1709
100	15 Dec 58	69	3	Run Rudolph Run	Chess 1714
100	15 Dec 58	71	3	Merry Christmas Baby	Chess 1714
100	16 Feb 59	60	5	Anthony Boy	Chess 1716
100	30 Mar 59	32	13	Almost Grown	Chess 1722

Size of chart	Date of chart entry	Highest position attained	No. of weeks on chart	Title	Label and catalogue number
100	13 Apr 59	80	4	Little Queenie	Chess 1722
100	22 Jun 59	37	8	Back In The USA	Chess 1729
100	1 Feb 60	42	6	Too Pooped To Pop	Chess 1747
100	1 Feb 60	64	8	Let It Rock	Chess 1747
100	7 Mar 64	23	10	Nadine	Chess 1883
100	23 May 64	10	11	No Particular Place To Go	Chess 1898
100	1 Aug 64	14	9	You Never Can Tell	Chess 1906
100	24 Oct 64	54	6	Little Marie	Chess 1912
100	12 Dec 64	41	7	Promised Land	Chess 1916
100	3 Apr 65	95	4	Dear Dad	Chess 1926
100	5 Aug 72	1	17	My Ding-A-Ling	Chess 2131
100	2 Dec 72	27	13	Reelin' And Rockin'	Chess 2136

Billboard 'Bubbling Under The Hot 100' pop singles

Chart commenced 1 June 1959.

Size of chart	Date of chart entry	Highest position attained	No. of weeks on chart	Title	Label and catalogue number
15	28 Sep 59	108	4	Broken Arrow	Chess 1737
15	7 Nov 60	109	4	Jaguar And Thunderbird	Chess 1767

Billboard pop albums

Chart commenced 8 January 1955 as 'Best Selling Popular Albums' fluctuating in size between 15 and 50 positions up until 9 January 1961. Between 9 January and 3 April 1961, approximately 200 albums were listed each week as 'essential inventory' without being ranked. From 3 April 1961 separate charts were published for mono and stereo albums (150 and 50 positions respectively), finally being combined into one 'Top LPs' chart on 17 August 1963.

Size of chart	Date of chart entry	Highest position attained	No. of weeks on chart	Title	Label and catalogue number
150	24 Aug 63	29	17	Chuck Berry On Stage	Chess LP-1480
150	6 Jun 64	34	21	Chuck Berry's Greatest Hits	Chess LP-1485
150	12 Dec 64	124	7	St. Louis To Liverpool	Chess LP(S)-1488
Chart increased to 175 positions on 1 April 1967, and to 200 on 13 May 1967.					
200	20 May 67	191	3	Chuck Berry's Golden Decade	Chess LP(S)-1514D
200	10 Jun 72	8	47	The London Chuck Berry Sessions	Chess CH-60020
200	21 Oct 72	72	17	Chuck Berry's Golden Decade *re-entry*	Chess LPS-1514D
200	4 Nov 72	185	7	St. Louie To Frisco To Memphis	Mercury SRM2-6501

Size of chart	Date of chart entry	Highest position attained	No. of weeks on chart	Title	Label and catalogue number
200	24 Feb 73	110	8	Chuck Berry's Golden Decade (Volume 2)	Chess 2CH-60023
200	8 Sep 73	175	6	Bio	Chess CH-50043

Billboard R&B albums

Chart commenced 30 January 1965 as 'Hot R&B LPs', was renamed 'Best Selling Soul LPs' 23 August 1969.

Size of chart	Date of chart entry	Highest position attained	No. of weeks on chart	Title	Label and catalogue number
50	1 Jul 72	8	33	The London Chuck Berry Sessions	Chess CH-60020
50	22 Sep 73	58	2	Bio	Chess CH-50043

Cash Box pop singles

Chart commenced 25 March 1950 as 'Nation's Top 10 Juke Box Tunes'.

Size of chart	Date of chart entry	Highest position attained	No. of weeks on chart	Title	Label and catalogue number
10	24 Sep 55	5	5	Maybellene	Chess 1604
'Top 50 Best Selling Records' chart commenced 4 August 1956.					
50	6 Apr 57	3	17	School Day	Chess 1653
'Top 60' chart commenced 13 April 1957.					
60	20 Jul 57	45	5	Oh Baby Doll	Chess 1664
60	9 Nov 57	14	12	Rock And Roll Music	Chess 1671
60	15 Feb 58	2	12	Sweet Little Sixteen	Chess 1683
60	26 Apr 58	11	12	Johnny B. Goode	Chess 1691
'Top 75' chart commenced 21 June 1958.					
75	30 Aug 58	31	10	Carol	Chess 1700
'Top 100' chart commenced 13 September 1958.					
100	15 Nov 58	52	9	Sweet Little Rock And Roller	Chess 1709
100	15 Nov 58	74	7	Jo Jo Gunne	Chess 1709
100	27 Dec 58	97	1	Merry Christmas Baby	Chess 1714
100	7 Feb 59	76	5	Anthony Boy	Chess 1716
100	4 Apr 59	31	10	Almost Grown	Chess 1722
100	4 Apr 59	91	2	Little Queenie	Chess 1722
100	20 Jun 59	49	5	Back In The USA	Chess 1729
100	25 Jul 59	87	5	Memphis Tennessee	Chess 1729
100	6 Feb 60	56	7	Too Pooped To Pop	Chess 1747
100	13 Feb 60	60	5	Let It Rock	Chess 1747

Size of chart	Date of chart entry	Highest position attained	No. of weeks on chart	Title	Label and catalogue number
100	4 Jun 60	64	4	**Bye Bye Johnny**	Chess 1754
100	26 Nov 60	93	3	**Jaguar And Thunderbird**	Chess 1767
100	29 Feb 64	32	14	**Nadine**	Chess 1883
100	30 May 64	9	10	**No Particular Place To Go**	Chess 1898
100	8 Aug 64	15	8	**You Never Can Tell**	Chess 1906
100	24 Oct 64	51	6	**Little Marie**	Chess 1912
100	12 Dec 64	35	8	**Promised Land**	Chess 1916
100	29 Jul 72	1	18	**My Ding-A-Ling**	Chess 2131
100	25 Nov 72	30	13	**Reelin' And Rockin'**	Chess 2136

Cash Box R&B singles

Chart commenced 2 January 1960 as 'Top 50 In R&B Locations'.

Size of chart	Date of chart entry	Highest position attained	No. of weeks on chart	Title	Label and catalogue number
50	30 Jan 60	22	7	**Let It Rock**	Chess 1747
50	6 Feb 60	20	7	**Too Pooped To Pop**	Chess 1747
	No R&B charts were published between 12 March 1960 and 10 December 1960. The chart restarted 17 December 1960.				
50	22 Feb 64	7	18	**Nadine**	Chess 1833
50	30 May 64	2	14	**No Particular Place To Go**	Chess 1898
50	24 Oct 64	30	6	**Little Marie**	Chess 1912
50	12 Dec 64	16	10	**Promised Land**	Chess 1916
50	27 Mar 65	29	5	**Dear Dad**	Chess 1926
50	18 Jun 66	7	11	**Havana Moon**	Chess 1963
	The chart was renamed 'Top 60 In R&B Locations' on 8 August 1970, although a 'Top 60' was also listed under 25 July's 'Top 50' chart heading.				
60	22 Jul 72	2	18	**My Ding-A-Ling**	Chess 2131
60	2 Dec 72	19	8	**Reelin' And Rockin'**	Chess 2136

Billboard chart information courtesy of Billboard Publications Inc. and Record Research Inc.
Cash Box chart information courtesy of
Cash Box and George Albert, Pat Downey and Frank Hoffman.

UK CHARTS
Record Mirror/Record Retailer/Music Week 'Top Singles'

The following data is taken from the Record Mirror's singles chart (January 1955 to 5 March 1960) and the Record Retailer chart (12 March 1960 onwards). Record Retailer was renamed 'Music Week' on 18 March 1972.

Size of chart	Date of chart entry	Highest position attained	No. of weeks on chart	Title	Label and catalogue number
20	29 Jun 57	20	1	School Day	Columbia DB-3951
20	19 Apr 58	11	6	Sweet Little Sixteen	London HLM-8585
20	7 Jun 58	17	1	Johnny B. Goode	London HLM-8629
Record Retailer launched their 'Top 50' singles chart on 12 March 1960.					
50	13 Jul 63	38	6	Go Go Go	Pye Int'l. 7N.25209
50	12 Oct 63	6	13	Let It Rock / Memphis Tennessee	Pye Int'l. 7N.25218
50	22 Dec 63	36	6	Run Rudolph Run	Pye Int'l. 7N.25228
50	15 Feb 64	27	6	Nadine	Pye Int'l. 7N.25236
50	4 Apr 64	43	1	Nadine *re-entry*	Pye Int'l. 7N.25236
50	9 May 64	3	12	No Particular Place To Go	Pye Int'l. 7N.25242
50	22 Aug 64	23	8	You Never Can Tell	Pye Int'l. 7N.25257
50	16 Jan 65	26	6	Promised Land	Pye Int'l. 7N.25285
50	4 Nov 72	1	17	My Ding-A-Ling	Chess 6145 019
50	3 Feb 73	18	7	Reelin' And Rockin'	Chess 6145 020

Record Retailer 'Top EPs'

Chart commenced 12 March 1960 and ran until 16 December 1967.

Size of chart	Date of chart entry	Highest position attained	No. of weeks on chart	Title	Label and catalogue number
20	5 Oct 63	6	15	Chuck & Bo	Pye Int'l. NEP-44009
20	5 Oct 63	7	10	Chuck Berry	Pye Int'l. NEP-44011
20	30 Nov 63	15	2	Chuck & Bo (Volume 2)	Pye Int'l. NEP-44012
20	21 Dec 63	15	3	Chuck Berry *1st re-entry*	Pye Int'l. NEP-44011
20	18 Jan 64	20	1	Chuck Berry *2nd re-entry*	Pye Int'l. NEP-44011
20	25 Jan 64	17	4	Chuck & Bo *1st re-entry*	Pye Int'l. NEP-44009
20	8 Feb 64	10	6	The Best Of Chuck Berry	Pye Int'l. NEP-44018

Size of chart	Date of chart entry	Highest position attained	No. of weeks on chart	Title	Label and catalogue number
20	15 Feb 64	12	5	**Chuck & Bo (Volume 3)**	Pye Int'l. NEP-44017
20	28 Mar 64	15	3	**The Best Of Chuck Berry** *1st re-entry*	Pye Int'l. NEP-44018
20	2 May 64	18	3	**Chuck & Bo** *2nd re-entry*	Pye Int'l. NEP-44009
20	23 May 64	5	12	**The Best Of Chuck Berry** *2nd re-entry*	Pye Int'l. NEP-44018
20	29 Aug 64	13	4	**The Best Of Chuck Berry** *3rd re-entry*	Pye Int'l. NEP-44018

Record Retailer/Music Week 'Top LPs'

Chart commenced 26 March 1960. Record Retailer was renamed 'Music Week' on 18 March 1972.

Size of chart	Date of chart entry	Highest position attained	No. of weeks on chart	Title	Label and catalogue number
20	25 May 63	12	16	**Chuck Berry**	Pye Int'l. NPL-28024
20	5 Oct 63	6	11	**Chuck Berry On Stage**	Pye Int'l. NPL-28027
20	7 Dec 63	9	8	**More Chuck Berry**	Pye Int'l. NPL-28028
20	30 May 64	8	7	**The Latest & The Greatest**	Pye Int'l. NPL-28037
20	3 Oct 64	18	2	**You Never Can Tell**	Pye Int'l. NPL-28039
Between 14 April 1966 and 9 January 1971, the chart varied in size between 15 and 77. It stabilised at 50 positions from 16 January 1971, increasing to 60 from 5 July 1975.					
60	12 Feb 77	7	9	**Motorvatin'**	Chess 9286 690

Chart information courtesy of BMRB, CIN, Gallup, Music Week,
Tony Jasper, George R. White and Grrr Books Ltd.

5

Chuck Berry on TV, Film & Video

The following is a survey of Chuck Berry's notable TV and film appearances and their availability — in whole or in part — on VHS videotape (▢) and DVD (◈). Where performances have been released on record, the relevant session number is given in parentheses after the title of each song.

FILMS

ROCK, ROCK, ROCK
Distributor Corp. of America (85 min) ▢◈   1956

Directed by Will Price, featuring Tuesday Weld in her first film (her singing parts overdubbed by Connie Francis), Alan Freed, Teddy Randazzo, the Moonglows, Frankie Lymon & The Teenagers, the Flamingos, the Johnny Burnette Trio, LaVern Baker, Jimmy Cavello & The House Rockers, the Three Chuckles, Cirino & The Bowties and six year old prodigy Ivy Shulman. A quickie black-and-white rocksploitation movie with little plot (Tuesday Weld has to raise $30 to buy a dress for a high school dance) which only comes alive when Berry and his cohorts perform. Chuck mimes to *You Can't Catch Me* **(4)**.

MISTER ROCK AND ROLL
Paramount Pictures (86 min)   1957

Directed by Charles Dubin, featuring Alan Freed, Little Richard, Clyde McPhatter, LaVern Baker, Lionel Hampton, Teddy Randazzo, Frankie Lymon & The Teenagers, the Moonglows, Brook Benton, Ferlin Husky, Shaye Cogan, Fisher & Marks, Rocky Graziano and Lois O'Brien. Another monochrome quickie in which we find out that rock and roll was invented by Alan Freed, and if you believe that you'll probably like the movie. Again the film is saved by the musical interludes including the tremendous performance by Little Richard and his band (with no fewer than four saxophones) doing *Lucille*, his best song ever. Chuck mimes to *Oh Baby Doll* **(10)**.

JAZZ ON A SUMMER'S DAY
Galaxy/Raven (85 min) ▢◈   1958

An atmospheric full-colour documentary record of the 1958 *Newport Jazz Festival* directed by Bert Stern, featuring Louis Armstrong, Big Maybelle, Dinah

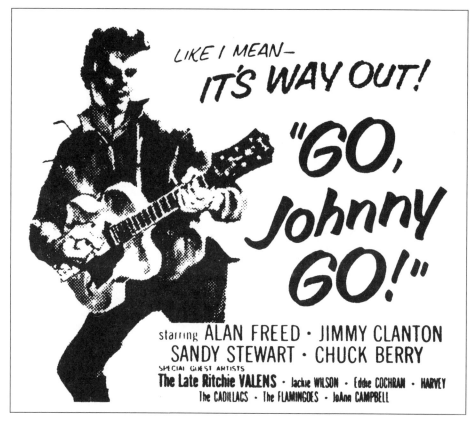

LIKE I MEAN—
ITS WAY OUT!
"GO, Johnny GO!"

starring ALAN FREED · JIMMY CLANTON
SANDY STEWART · CHUCK BERRY
SPECIAL GUEST ARTISTS
The Late Ritchie VALENS · Jackie WILSON · Eddie COCHRAN · HARVEY
The CADILLACS · The FLAMINGOES · JoAnn CAMPBELL

Washington, Gerry Mulligan, Thelonious Monk, Anita O'Day, Sonny Stitt, the Jimmy Guiffre Trio, the Chico Hamilton Quintet, Eli's Chosen Six, Nathan Gersham, the George Shearing Quintet, Mahalia Jackson and Jack Teagarden. Just a shame Ray Charles and Big Joe Turner, both of whom played the gig, were not included. Chuck performs *Sweet Little Sixteen* **(17)**.

GO, JOHNNY, GO! *Hal Roach Distribution Corporation (75 min)* ☐ 1959

The opening titles are accompanied by a heavily-doctored version of *Johnny B. Goode* which is overdubbed by a brass section and retitled *Go Johnny Go* in the publicity blurb. This doctored version is not on the promo LP issued when the film was released but is replaced with the plain and wholesome *Johnny B. Goode* we all know and love. Directed by Paul Landres, featuring Jimmy Clanton, Alan Freed, Sandy Stewart, Jo-Ann Campbell, the Cadillacs, Ritchie Valens, Eddie Cochran, Harvey Fuqua, the Flamingos and Jackie Wilson. The third and final fifties Berry monochrome movie in which Chuck acts a little as well as doing some singing. The plot is a little thicker, but again it's the music that makes it worthwhile sitting through the film. Chuck mimes to *Memphis Tennessee* **(18)** and *Little Queenie* **(20)**.

THE T.A.M.I. SHOW *American International Pictures (114 min)* ☐ 1965

Directed by Steve Binder, featuring James Brown, the Rolling Stones, the Supremes, Jan & Dean, the Beach Boys, the Barbarians, Gerry & The Pacemakers, the Miracles and Lesley Gore. Black and white recording (in more senses than one) of the *Teenage Awards Music International* show staged at the Santa Monica Civic Auditorium on 29th October 1964. Chuck performs *Johnny B. Goode*, *Sweet Little Sixteen*, *Maybellene* and *Nadine*.

GATHER NO MOSS *(85 min)*   1965

The UK version of **THE T.A.M.I. SHOW** with the emphasis on the Rolling Stones, hence the change of title.

TEENAGE COMMAND PERFORMANCE *(85 min)*   1965

Gather No Moss under a different title.

THE BIG BEAT *American International Pictures (74 min)*   1966

This is a compilation of the black acts from **THE T.A.M.I. SHOW** combined with three black acts (Bo Diddley, Ike & Tina Turner and the Ronettes) from **THE BIG T.N.T. SHOW** *(American International Pictures, 1966)*, the follow-up to the **T.A.M.I.** movie. Chuck's performances of *Johnny B. Goode*, *Sweet Little Sixteen*, *Maybellene* and *Nadine* are included.

THIS COULD BE THE NIGHT   1966

The Big Beat under a new title.

SWEET TORONTO *Leacock–Pennebaker Inc. (135 min)* ☐◈   1970

Technicolor highlights from the outdoor *Toronto Rock'n'Roll Revival*, staged at the Varsity Stadium in front of an audience of 25,000 on 13th September 1969. Directed by D.A. Pennebaker, featuring the Plastic Ono Band, Bo Diddley, Jerry Lee Lewis, Little Richard and Chuck Berry, who performs *Rock And Roll Music* **(54)**, *School Day* **(54)**, *Johnny B. Goode/Carol/Promised Land* **(54)**, *Hoochie Coochie Man* **(54)**, *Sweet Little Sixteen* **(54)**, *Reelin' And Rockin'* **(54)** and *Johnny B. Goode (Encore)* **(54)**. [See also **ALICE IN THE CITIES** *(1974)* below.]

TORONTO POP *Leacock–Pennebaker Inc. (min)*   1970

Edited version of *Sweet Toronto* including Chuck's performances of *Sweet Little Sixteen* **(54)** and *Johnny B. Goode* **(54)**.

KEEP ON ROCKIN' *Leacock–Pennebaker Inc. (102 min)*   1972

A further re-edit of *Sweet Toronto* featuring the rockers from the festival — Berry, Richard, Lewis and Diddley. Includes Chuck's performances of *Rock And Roll Music* **(54)**, *School Day* **(54)**, *Johnny B. Goode/Carol/Promised Land* **(54)**, *Hoochie Coochie Man* **(54)**, *Sweet Little Sixteen* **(54)**, *Reelin' And Rockin'* **(54)** and *Johnny B. Goode (Encore)* **(54)**.

LET THE GOOD TIMES ROLL *Columbia Pictures (98 min)* ☐   1973

A good documentary film intersersing fifties' black and white footage with colour footage of a May 1972 *Rock & Roll Revival* concert staged at the Nassau Coliseum, Uniondale, Long Island. Directed by Sid Levin and Bob Abel, featuring Bo Diddley, Chubby Checker, Little Richard, the Coasters, Bill Haley & His Comets, the Five Satins, Fats Domino, Danny & The Juniors and the Shirelles. Chuck performs *School Day*, *Reelin' And Rockin'*, *Sweet Little Sixteen*, *Bonsoir Cherie/Johnny B. Goode* and an instrumental jam with Bo Diddley. *Maybellene* **(2)** is also heard on the soundtrack played over a montage of vintage fifties' cars.

THE LONDON ROCK'N'ROLL SHOW *Notting Hill Studios (84 min)* ☐   1973

Directed by Peter Clifton, and first shown on European TV in 1973 and then on general release in 1978, this is a decent record of a concert staged on 5th August 1972 at the Empire Stadium, Wembley (the first of many similar events to be staged there). The show was witnessed by 35,000 people, started at 12.30 pm and lasted eleven hours. And what a line-up! The artists included the Houseshakers, Billy Fury, Screaming Lord

Sutch, Roy Wood & Wizzard, the MC5, Gary Glitter, Emile Ford, Heinz, Bo Diddley, Jerry Lee Lewis, Bill Haley, Little Richard and, top of the bill, Chuck Berry. All for the princely sum of £1.20 to £2.80! Chuck performs *School Day, Memphis Tennessee, Sweet Little Sixteen/Mean Ol' Frisco, Beer Drinkin' Woman, Wee Wee Hours/Let It Rock/Roll 'Em Pete/Carol/Little Queenie* and *Reelin' And Rockin'*.

ALICE IN DEN STÄDTEN
(ALICE IN THE CITIES) *Filmverlag der Autoren (110 min)* ▢◈   1974

A pretentious black and white 'art' short directed by Wim Wenders featuring Rüdiger Vogler, Yella Röttlander, Lisa Kreuzer and Edda Köchl, in which the hero stumbles into a Chuck Berry gig which purports to be in an Amsterdam club. *Memphis Tennessee* is, in fact, an out-take from the Toronto Festival not available elsewhere! Chuck performs *Memphis Tennessee* **(54)**, and *Johnny B. Goode* **(12)** is heard on the soundtrack.

1959. New York City. The battleground was Rock and Roll. It was the beginning of an era.

You shoulda been there.

"AMERICAN HOT WAX"
Starring TIM McINTIRE · LARAINE NEWMAN
JOHN LEHNE · JAY LENO
CHUCK BERRY · JERRY LEE LEWIS
Screenplay by JOHN KAYE
Story by JOHN KAYE and ART LINSON
Produced by ART LINSON
Directed by FLOYD MUTRUX

AMERICAN HOT WAX *Paramount Picture Corporation (91 min)* ▢   1978

Directed by Floyd Mutrux and featuring Tim McIntire (as Alan Freed), Fran Drescher, Jay Leno, John Lehne, Laraine Newman, Jeff Altman, Frankie Ford, Jerry Lee Lewis and Screaming Jay Hawkins, who is seen arriving at the theatre but whose performance was not included in the film (just as with the *Mister Rock And Roll* movie from the fifties, it seems that Jay's act was still considered degrading to African Americans by the politically-correct movie moguls). Anyway, it's the Alan Freed story again, in which we learn Freed invented rock and roll, and in which Chuck plays for free at a rock and roll concert at the Brooklyn Paramount — what!?!? Obviously a totally fictitious script! Chuck performs *Reelin And Rockin'* **(74)** and *Johnny B. Goode* **(74)** and also has a minor acting role in the film.

NATIONAL LAMPOON'S CLASS REUNION *Fox/ABC (84 min)* ☐◈   1982

Directed by Michael Miller and featuring Gerrit Graham, Michael Lerner, Fred McCarren, Miriam Flynn, Stephen Furst, Marya Small, Shelley Smith, Zane Busby and Anne Ramsey. A desperately unfunny follow-up to *National Lampoon's Animal House* in which a class reunion at Lizzie Borden High is stalked by a psycho-killer. Chuck plays *Festival*, *It Wasn't Me* and *My Ding-A-Ling* live at the fraternity house hop, but we only get to see snatches of his performance.

HAIL! HAIL! ROCK'N'ROLL *Universal Pictures (116 min)* ☐◈   1987

Directed by Taylor Hackford and featuring star guests Robert Cray, Eric Clapton, Linda Ronstadt, Julian Lennon and Etta James, plus Keith Richards, Bruce Springsteen, Bo Diddley, Little Richard, Jerry Lee Lewis, Ingrid Berry and Johnnie Johnson, this is a first class documentary which gets as close as anyone is likely to get to the enigma that is Chuck Berry. The film culminates in the show of a lifetime, recorded in a theatre that barred the young Chuck from its doors because of his skin colour — an irony that is not lost on the astute Mr. Berry. However, in spite of the all-star show, the most abiding sequences are the electrifying clash between Berry and Richards at the Berry Park rehearsal and the haunting scene at the close of the film where the camera floats through Berry Park, finally coming to rest on Chuck, immersed in the blues he is playing on his steel guitar.

Chuck performs *Maybellene*, two instrumentals (the second on the theme of *Honest I Do*) and *Bio* at the Cosmopolitan Club, St. Louis; *Carol*, *It Don't Take But A Few Minutes* (duet with Eric Clapton), *I'm Thru' With Love* **(86)** and *A Cottage For Sale* **(86)** at rehearsals at the Berry Park Club (*Come On* is also featured, performed by Robert Cray and Ingrid Berry); *Roll Over Beethoven* **(88)**, *Almost Grown* **(87)**, *Back In The USA* (duet with Linda Ronstadt) **(87)**, *Sweet Little Sixteen* **(87)**, *No Money Down* **(87)**, *Nadine* **(87)**, *Johnny B. Goode* (duet with Julian Lennon) **(87)**, *Memphis Tennessee* **(87)**, *Little Queenie* **(87)**, *Brown Eyed Handsome Man* (duet with Robert Cray) **(87)**, *Too Much Monkey Business* **(87)**, *No Particular Place To Go* **(87)**, *Wee Wee Hours* (duet with Eric Clapton) **(87)**, *Rock And Roll Music* (duet with Etta James) **(86)** and *School Day* **(88)** at the Fox Theatre, St. Louis; and finally *Deep Feeling* at Berry Park.

FILM SOUNDTRACKS

The following movies, listed in chronological order, all feature Chuck Berry recordings on their soundtracks. However, where soundtrack albums have been released, not all necessarily include Chuck's contribution.

SUMMER IN THE CITY (1970) .... unknown song(s)
FRITZ THE CAT (1972) .... *Johnny B. Goode*
UNHOLY ROLLERS (1972) .... *Johnny B. Goode, Sweet Little Sixteen, Memphis Tennessee, Reelin' And Rockin' and Rock And Roll Music*
AMERICAN GRAFFITI (1973) .... *Johnny B. Goode* and *Almost Grown*
HEAVY TRAFFIC (1973) .... *Maybellene*
RETURN TO MACON COUNTY (1974) ... *Johnny B. Goode*
ROCK 'N' ROLL HIGH SCHOOL (1979) . *School Day*
CRUISIN' (1980) .... *No Particular Place To Go*
PORKY'S (1981) .... *Maybellene*
MISSING (1982) .... *My Ding-A-Ling*
LA BAMBA (1987) .... *Betty Jean*

CONCRETE ANGELS (1987) .... unknown song(s)
JOHNNY BE GOOD (1988) .... *Johnny B. Goode*
THE RESCUE (1988) .... *Sweet Little Sixteen*
BOOK OF LOVE (1990)........................... *School Day*
HOME ALONE (1990) .... *Run Rudolph Run*
A RAGE IN HARLEM (1991) .... *Brown Eyed Handsome Man*
PULP FICTION (1994) .... *You Never Can Tell*
LAST DAYS OF FRANKIE THE FLY (1996) *No Particular Place To Go*
SGT. BILKO (1996) .... *No Particular Place To Go*
SPY HARD (1996) .... *You Never Can Tell*
HOME ALONE 3 (1997) .... *Almost Grown* and *School Day*

And finally, the next time **THE BONNIE PARKER STORY** (1958) is shown as a late night movie on TV, listen to the incidental music used in the opening titles and in the bedroom seduction scene. Is this Mr. Berry? I think not, but it's mighty close!

NOTABLE TV APPEARANCES

The following is a survey of notable TV shows on which Chuck Berry appeared, some of which have been released on video/DVD. In many instances it is not known whether Chuck mimed or performed live, or if the footage still exists.

ALAN FREED'S BIG BEAT *(WABC-TV)*   USA, 19 July 1957

AMERICAN BANDSTAND *(WFIL-TV, networked on ABC)*   USA, 8 November 1957
Chuck mimes to *Rock And Roll Music* **(10)**.

AMERICAN BANDSTAND *(WFIL-TV, networked on ABC)*   USA, 1958
Chuck mimes to *Sweet Little Sixteen* **(12)**.

AMERICAN BANDSTAND *(WFIL-TV, networked on ABC)*   USA, 5 March 1959
Chuck mimes to *Anthony Boy* **(19)** and *Almost Grown* **(21)**.

DICK CLARK'S SATURDAY NIGHT BEECHNUT SHOW *(ABC-TV)*   USA, 1959?

TONIGHT *(BBC1)*   UK, January 1965

TIENERKLANKEN *(BRT)*   Belgium, 12 April 1965
Interview and possibly one song leased from *Face Au Public* — see below.

HULLABALOO! *(NBC-TV)* ▢◆   USA, 4 May 1965
Chuck performs *Johnny B. Goode* and duets with Trini Lopez on *Memphis*.

FACE AU PUBLIC *(RTB)* ▢   Belgium, 11 May 1965
Live show filmed on 6th February 1965 at Universal Studios, Waterloo, Belgium. Chuck plays a storming set with a jazz group consisting of Willy Albimoor, piano; Ed Rogers *[Roger van Haverbeke]*, double bass; Willie Donni, guitar and Eddie Hunton, drums. The songs performed are *Maybellene, The Things I Used To Do, Roll Over Beethoven, Memphis Tennessee, No Particular Place To Go, Promised Land* and *Johnny B. Goode*. This recording captures Berry at his very best — great singing, tremendous guitar playing and a performance where man and guitar become as one.

CHUCK BERRY ZINGT *(NTS2)*   Netherlands, 3 June 1965

25-minute live show in a similar style to *Face Au Public* [above], with backing provided Dutch jazz musicians Wim Jongbloed, piano; Eddy Essen, guitar; Dub Dubois, bass and Gerard van Bezey, drums. Included in the performance are *Roll Over Beethoven*, *Memphis* and *You Never Can Tell*. Other titles unknown. Directed by Nico Hiltrop.

SHINDIG! *(ABC-TV)* ▢   USA, 1965

Chuck performs *Back In The USA*.

HOLLYWOOD A-GO-GO *(syndicated)*   USA, 1965

Chuck performs *Roll Over Beethoven*.

FROM THE BITTER END *(WOR-TV)*   USA, 1968

Chuck performs *Roll Over Beethoven* and *Maybellene*.

UPBEAT *(WNEW-TV, syndicated)*   USA, 1968

THE DICK CAVETT SHOW *(ABC-TV)*   USA, 1970

DISCO 2 *(BBC2)*   UK, 3 June 1971

THE MIKE DOUGLAS SHOW *(CBS-TV)* ▢   USA, 16 February 1972

Chuck is inteviewed by Mike Douglas, takes part in a macrobiotic cookery session and, standing nose-to-nose, duets with John Lennon on *Memphis Tennessee* **(61)** and *Johnny B. Goode* **(61)**.

OLD GREY WHISTLE TEST *(BBC2)*   UK, 28 March 1972

UNKNOWN TITLE *(unknown TV station)*   France, 1972

Live show from the Paris Olympia featuring *Memphis Tennessee, Rock And Roll Music, Sweet Little Sixteen, Carol, Let It Rock, Roll Over Beethoven, Maybellene, School Day* and *Johnny B. Goode*.

JAZZ MONTREUX *(TV-SSR)*   Switzerland, June 1972

Eighteen minute segment of Chuck's performance on 16th June 1972 at the *Montreux Jazz Festival* including *Roll Over Beethoven* **(63)**, *Sweet Little Sixteen* **(63)**, *Memphis Tennessee* **(63)** and *Nadine* **(63)**.

JAZZ MONTREUX *(TV-SSR)*   Switzerland, June 1972

Another chunk of Chuck's performance at the 1972 *Montreux Jazz Festival* featuring *Maybellene* **(63)**, *Wee Wee Hours* **(63)**, *Rock And Roll Music* **(63)**, one unknown title **(63)** and T-Bone Walker's guest appearance on *Everyday I Have The Blues* **(63)**.

SOUNDS FOR SATURDAY *(BBC2)*   UK, 22 July 1972

Dynamic live concert filmed on 29th March 1972 at the BBC Television Theatre, London. Backed by Rockin' Horse, Chuck performs: *Roll Over Beethoven* **(62)**, *Sweet Little Sixteen* **(62)**, *Memphis* **(62)**, *South Of The Border* **(62)**, *Beer Drinking Woman* **(62)**, *Let It Rock* **(62)**, *Mean Old World* **(62)**, *Carol* **(62)**, *Liverpool Drive* **(62)**, *My Ding-A-Ling* **(62)**, *Nadine* **(62)**, *School Day* **(62)**, *Too Much Monkey Business* **(62)**, *Rock And Roll Music* **(62)**, *Promised Land* **(62)**, *Reelin' And Rockin'* **(62)**, *Bye Bye Johnny* **(62)** and *Bonsoir Cherie/Johnny B. Goode* **(62)**.

SOUL TRAIN *(WNEW-TV, syndicated)*   USA, 1973

Chuck is interviewed by Don Cornelius and performs *Reelin' & Rockin', Wee Wee Hours, Roll 'Em Pete* and *Johnny B. Goode* backed by Junior Lace.

DICK CLARK PRESENTS THE ROCK & ROLL YEARS *(ABC-TV)*   USA, 1973

THE SONNY AND CHER COMEDY HOUR *(CBS-TV)* ☐   USA, 16 or 17 August 1973

Chuck performs *Johnny B. Goode, Rock And Roll Music, School Day* and, with Sonny & Cher and Jerry Lee Lewis in support, *Reelin' And Rockin'*.

THE HELEN REDDY SHOW *(NBC-TV)*   USA, August 1973

Chuck performs *Johnny B. Goode* and *Reelin' And Rockin'*.

CHUCK BERRY & FRIENDS IN CONCERT *(ABC-TV)*   USA, 1974

TV special recorded at the Aquarius Theatre in Hollywood on 18th March 1974 in which Chuck performs *School Day, Sweet Little Sixteen, My Ding-A-Ling, Roll Over Beethoven, Memphis Tennessee* (with Johnny Rivers) and *Song Of My Love* (with Ingrid Berry). He plays guitar with Bo Diddley on *Bo Diddley-itis* and *Bo Diddley* and conducts a question-and-answer session between himself, Bo and the audience. The finale is the usual jam with all the guests joining in. The backing band on this occasion was Spoon River, Ingrid's regular band which also included Chuck's younger daughter Melody's husband on drums. Berry rehearsed the band all day and by showtime he was just too pooped to pop. I'm afraid it shows on the recording.

THE TOM JONES SHOW *(syndicated)*   USA, 1974(?)

Featuring Paul Anka, Kiki Dee and Chuck Berry, who performs *Johnny B. Goode* and duets with the show's host on *School Day*.

SALUTE TO THE BEATLES *(ABC-TV)*   USA, 1975

MIDNIGHT SPECIAL *(NBC-TV)*   USA, 1975

Chuck is introduced by Paul Anka and performs *Sweet Little Sixteen* and *Maybellene*.

DON KIRSHNER'S ROCK CONCERT *(WNEW-TV, syndicated)*   USA, 1975

SAMMY AND COMPANY *(NBC-TV)*   USA, 1975

BST [Blood, Sweat & Tears Special] *(CBC)*   Canada, 1975

Backed by Blood, Sweat & Tears, Chuck performs *Maybellene* and joins the group's vocalist, David Clayton-Thomas, Chubby Checker, Bo Diddley and Carl Perkins for the grand finale, *What'd I Say*.

OMNIBUS: THE FRIENDLY INVASION *(BBC1)*   UK, 30 November 1975

Documentary about American influence on European music. Features a mid-seventies performance by Chuck of *Johnny B. Goode* [source unconfirmed].

DINAH AND HER BEST FRIENDS *(CBS-TV)*   USA, 1976

DONNY & MARIE *(ABC-TV)*   USA, 1977

SATURDAY NIGHT *(NBC-TV)*   USA, 1977

ALL YOU NEED IS LOVE: HAIL! HAIL! ROCK'N'ROLL *(ITV/LWT)* UK, 7 May 1977

Chuck performs *School Day.*

AMERICAN BANDSTAND'S 25TH ANNIVERSARY *(ABC-TV)* USA, 1977

Show from Los Angeles including clips of Chuck performing *Sweet Little Sixteen* and *Johnny B. Good*e, and a grand finale with him leading an all-star band including Booker T, Donald Byrd, Charlie Daniels, Les McCain, Walter Murphy, Nigel Olsson, the Pointer Sisters, Johnny Rivers, Bobby Rydell, Nino Tempo, Junior Walker and others in a rousing version of *Roll Over Beethoven.*

THE MERV GRIFFIN SHOW *(WNEW-TV, syndicated)* USA, 1977

DON KIRSHNER'S ROCK CONCERT *(WNEW-TV, syndicated)* USA, 1977

SHA NA NA *(NBC-TV)* USA, 1977

Chuck does a comedy sketch and performs *Roll Over Beethoven* with Sha Na Na.

AMERICAN MUSIC AWARDS *(ABC-TV)* USA, 1978

THE CHUCK BARRIS RAH RAH SHOW *(NBC-TV)* USA, February-April 1978

THE TODAY SHOW *(NBC-TV)* USA, 1978

THE MIKE DOUGLAS SHOW *(CBS-TV)* USA, 1978

THE MERV GRIFFIN SHOW *(WNEW-TV, syndicated)* USA, 1978

DICK CLARK'S LIVE WEDNESDAY *(NBC-TV)* USA, 1978

OMNIBUS: JOHNNY BE GOOD *(BBC1)* UK, 1979

Documentary filmed in the Bandstand Club in St. Louis, Berry Park, the White House, Washington, DC and other locations, featuring a mixture of live and recorded Chuck Berry music. Chuck performs *Johnny B. Goode, Reelin' And Rockin', Baby What You Want Me To Do, Maybellene, Too Much Monkey Business, Nadine* and *Everyday I Have The Blues* at a concert. He also recites his poem, *Pass Away,* in the Berry Park studio and sings along with Johnnie Johnson and Ebby Hardy at the Club Bandstand to his latest recording, *Oh What A Thrill* **(74)**. *Bio* **(66)**, *No Money Down* **(4)**, *Promised Land* **(28)** and *School Day* **(9)** are heard on the soundtrack. He also performs *Roll Over Beethoven* for President Carter on the White House lawn. The programme also includes a riveting piece where Chuck stonewalls the interviewer who has the temerity to ask him about Officer Medley, who supposedly arrested him on one occasion. The interview is abruptly terminated when the words 'Indian girl' are mentioned.

UNKNOWN TITLE *(unknown TV station)* West Germany, 1979

Live show from Munich Olympiahalle or Cirkus Krone featuring *Roll Over Beethoven, School Days, Sweet Little Sixteen, Memphis Tennessee, Rock And Roll Music, Carol, Maybellene, Baby What You Want Me To Do, Promised Land, My Ding-A-Ling, Johnny B. Goode, Let It Rock, Reelin' And Rockin'* and the customary "Goodbye, it's time for us to go" routine.

LA GRANDE PARADE DU JAZZ *(unknown TV station)* France, 1980

Film of a live show at Arènes de Cimiez, Nice on 13th July 1979 in which Chuck performs *Roll Over Beethoven, School Day, Sweet Little Sixteen, Maybellene, Nadine, Let It Rock,*

Memphis Tennessee, Bio, Baby What You Want Me To Do and *Wee Wee Hours.* Directed by Jean-Christophe Averty.

THE SAMMY DAVIS JR. SHOW *(NBC-TV?)*   USA, 1980

Chuck performs *Promised Land* and *Reelin' And Rockin'* .

ROOTS OF ROCK'N'ROLL
PART 1: THE EARLY YEARS 1955-58 *(unknown TV station)*   USA, 1981

Includes Chuck's performance of *Little Queenie* from the *Go, Johnny, Go!* film.

CHUCK BERRY SHOW *(unknown TV station)*   Italy, 1983

Live show from Covo di Nord Est, S. Margherita Ligure in which Chuck performs *Let It Rock, Wee Wee Hours, Brown Eyed Handsome Man, Jamaica Farewell, Ramblin' Rose, Nadine, Everyday I Have The Blues, Johnny B. Goode, Key To The Highway* (duet with Ingrid Berry), *Going Down* (duet with Ingrid Berry) and *Reelin' And Rockin'* (duet with Ingrid Berry).

CHUCK BERRY LIVE AT THE ROXY *(BBC1)* ☐   UK, 1984

Directed by Scott Sternberg, this is a record of a typical, none-too-exciting gig shot at the Roxy Theatre, Hollywood in 1982. Features Tina Turner, who at the time was struggling to make it on her own having finally split with Ike, and who was no doubt glad of any exposure, even with an old-time rocker like Berry. Chuck performs *Roll Over Beethoven* **(83)**, *School Day* **(83)**, *Sweet Little Sixteen* **(83)**, *Nadine* **(83)**, *Let It Rock* **(83)**, *Promised Land* **(83)**, *Memphis Tennessee* **(83)**, *Johnny B. Goode* **(83)**, *Brown Eyed Handsome Man* **(83)**, *Too Much Monkey Business* **(83)**, *Carol/Little Queenie* **(83)**, *Rock And Roll Music* (duet with Tina Turner) **(83)**, *Instrumental* **(83)** and *Reelin' And Rockin'* (duet with Ingrid Berry) **(83)**.

THE ROCK ROLLS ON *(unknown TV station)*   USA, 1984

Chuck co-hosts and performs *Johnny B. Goode* and *Roll Over Beethoven.*

SUPER NIGHT OF ROCK'N'ROLL *(unknown TV station)*   USA, 1984

50s and 60s clips of performances by various artists interspersed with concert footage from the Hollywood Palladium shot on 13th January 1984. Chuck performs *Roll Over Beethoven* and *Johnny B. Goode*, and leads the all-star finale: *Rock And Roll Music.*

ROCK AROUND THE CLOCK *(Vara TV)*   Netherlands, 1985

Chuck performs *Johnny B. Goode* dressed in a cowboy outfit.

CHUCK & RICHARD IN ITALY *(RAI-TV)*   Italy, 5 December 1987

Chuck performs *Memphis Tennessee* and *Let It Rock* before a studio audience.

THE TONIGHT SHOW STARRING JOHNNY CARSON *(NBC-TV)*   USA ,1987

Chuck is interviewed by Johnny Carson and performs one song [title unknown] with the Doc Severinson Orchestra.

ETAD DE ONO *(unknown TV station)*   Spain, 17 October 1987

ASPEL AND COMPANY *(ITV)*   UK, 1988

Chuck is interviewed by Michael Aspel and performs *Memphis Tennesse*e.

HAIL! HAIL! ROCK'N'ROLL:
CHUCK BERRY IN DEN MEDIEN *(unknown TV station)*   West Germany, 1988

Includes live footage from a Cannes (MIDEM) concert (January 1988?), a Berlin concert on 14th February 1988, clips from the *Hail! Hail! Rock'n'Roll* movie, and a review of the UK TV show, *Aspel And Company* [see above].

NIGHT NETWORK *(unknown TV station)*   USA(?), 1988

SID & MARTY KROFT'S REDEYE EXPRESS *(CBS-TV)*   USA, 9 March 1988

THE LEGENDS OF ROCK'N'ROLL—
ONCE MORE WITH FEELING *(Network 7)*   Australia, 1989
Toyota Tour show from Melbourne in which Chuck performs *Let It Rock, Nadine, School Day* and *Sweet Little Sixteen.*

THE SALLY JESSIE RAPHAEL SHOW *(MTV)*   USA, 1991
Chuck performs *Johnny B. Goode, Memphis Tennessee* and *Carol.*

MOJO WORKING *(Channel 4)*   UK, 15 July 1992

THE DIAMOND AWARDS SHOW *(BRT)*   Belgium, 28 November 1992
Chuck performs *Roll Over Beethoven* and *School Day.*

THE ATHLETICS WORLD CHAMPIONSHIP
OPENING CEREMONY *(unknown TV station)*   Germany, 13 August 1993
Live broadcast from Stuttgart. Chuck performs *Rock And Roll Music, Memphis Tennessee* and *Let It Rock.*

OMNIBUS: SWEET HOME CHICAGO *(BBC1)* ▢   UK, 19 October 1993
Excellent documentary about Chicago blues and Chess Records which includes a portion of *Promised Land* **(54)** from the 1969 Toronto gig and *No Particular Place To Go* **(29)** as background music. Also includes Johnnie Johnson discussing his musical relationship with Chuck, and Mick Jagger recalling Chuck's comments on hearing the playback of *Around And Around* by the Stones at the Chess studios: "You've nearly got it" — with the emphasis on the 'nearly'!

APOLLO HALL OF FAME *(unknown TV station)*   USA, 1994
Introduced by Ingrid Berry, Chuck performs *Johnny B. Goode* backed by Vernon Reid.

LETTERMAN IN LONDON *(BBC2)*   UK, 23 May 1995

ROCK AND ROLL HALL OF FAME CONCERT *(HBO)*   USA, 2 Sept. 1995
Show from Cleveland, Ohio in which Chuck performs *Johnny B. Goode* with Bruce Springsteen and the reformed E Street Band.

BILLY CONNOLLY'S WORLD TOUR OF MUSIC *(BBC1)*   UK, 27 May 1996

THE LATE SHOW WITH DAVID LETTERMAN *(CBS-TV)*   USA, 1997
Chuck performs *Let It Rock.*

LE SECRET *(unknown TV station)*   France, 2000

CHRISTMAS IN WASHINGTON *(unknown TV station)*   USA, 17 December 2000
Seasonal show featuring Chuck, Marc Anthony, the Corrs, Billy Gilman and Jessica Simpson.

VIDEO/DVD ONLY RELEASES

CHUCK BERRY & BO DIDDLEY'S ROCK'N'ROLL ALL-STAR JAM *(55 min)* ◈

This concert, filmed 25th October 1985 at the Irvine Meadows Amphitheatre, Los Angeles, was televised in 1986 and has been available on several VHS video releases since 1989. However, until this DVD release it only featured Bo Diddley, backed an assorted array of the great and good (and not so great or good) from the world of rock. Now, however, it includes three songs by Chuck Berry — well, two and a bit really. Chuck performs *My Ding-A-Ling* and *Bio* (here retitled *Destination*) and joins in the *Rock And Roll Music* finale by asking the crowd: "Do you want us to stop or do you want us to stay and boogie?" etc, etc, etc.

... and, last but by no means least:

SWEET LITTLE SEXTEEN *(80 min)* ▭

This is a German bootleg of Chuck's home videoing efforts in which he 'performs' for eighty minutes! To paraphrase the man: "There's nothing wrong with sex — it's just the way that you handle it!"

6

Influences on the Music of Chuck Berry

In 1973, Chuck modestly confided to one interviewer: "I've never really created anything. I just re-expose what I hear." Though the reality is somewhat more complicated, the recordings listed in this section all influenced him to a greater or lesser degree. There is some great music here and, for those interested in hearing the originals, much of it is now available on CD. However, the vagaries of the CD market, are such that some may not now be readily available.

(va) *after CD title indicates 'various artists'.*

Roy Acuff - *Wabash Cannonball* **[Vocalion 4466] 1938**
CD: *The King Of Country Music* [A.S.V. AJA-5244] UK, 1998

Albert Ammons - *Swanee River Boogie* **[Mercury 8022] 1946**
7-CD: *Blues, Boogie And Bop - The 1940's Mercury Sessions* **(va)**
[Polygram/Verve 525-609-2 BK01] USA, 1995

Gene Autry - *South Of The Border (Down Mexico Way)* **[Columbia 37185] 1946**
3-CD: *Sing, Cowboy, Sing* [Rhino R2-72630] USA, 1997

Mildred Bailey - *I'm Through With Love*
Note: Although Mildred Bailey is credited with 'introducing' this song, it has proved impossible to trace any recording of it by her.

Dave Bartholomew - *Little Girl Sing Ding-A-Ling* **[Imperial 5210] 1952**
2-CD: *The Genius Of Dave Bartholomew* **(va)** [E.M.I. 0777-7-80184-2] USA, 1992

Dave Bartholemew - *My Ding-A-Ling* **[King 4544] 1952**
CD: *In The Alley* [Charly CD-273] UK, 1991

Count Basie (Vocal: Joe Williams) - *Every Day (Parts 1 & 2)* **[Clef 89149] 1955**
CD: *Blues Masters (Volume 13: New York City Blues)* **(va)** [Rhino R2-71131] USA,1993
See also Joe Williams

Count Basie - *One O'Clock Jump* **[Decca 1363] 1937**
3-CD: *The Complete American Decca Recordings* [M.C.A. GRP-36112] Germany, 1993

Count Basie - *St. Louis Blues* **[Columbia 36711] 1942**
CD: *Compact Jazz: Count Basie* [Verve 2312-132] UK, 1994

Bob Beckham - *Crazy Arms* **[Decca 31029] 1959**
CD: No known reissue

Bees - *Toy Bell* **[Imperial 5314] 1954**
2-CD: *The Genius Of Dave Bartholomew* **(va)** [E.M.I. 0777-7-80184-2] USA, 1992

Harry Belafonte - *Banana Boat (Day-O)* **[RCA-Victor 6771] 1957**
CD: *All Time Greatest Hits* [R.C.A. ND-90366] UK, 1989

Harry Belafonte - *Jamaica Farewell* **[RCA-Victor 6663] 1956**
CD: *All Time Greatest Hits* [R.C.A. ND-90366] UK, 1989

Big Maceo - *Worried Life Blues* **[Bluebird B-8827] 1941**
   CD: *The Bluebird Recordings (1941-42)* [R.C.A. 07863-66715-2] USA, 1995

Big Three Trio - *Big Three Stomp* **[Columbia 30166] 1949**
   CD: *Willie Dixon/ The Big Three Trio* [C.B.S. 467248-2] USA, 1990

Big Three Trio - *Signifying Monkey* **[Columbia 37358] 1946**
   CD: *Willie Dixon / The Big Three Trio* [C.B.S. 467248-2] USA, 1990

Big Thee Trio - *You Sure Look Good To Me* **[Columbia 38093] 1948**
   CD: *I Feel Like Steppin' Out* [Dr. Horse RBD-804] Sweden, 1986

Big Vernon *[Joe Turner]* - *Around The Clock Blues (Parts 1 & 2)* **[Stag 508] 1947**
   CD: *Tell Me Pretty Baby* [Arhoolie ARHCD-333] USA, 1993

Big Vernon – See also Joe Turner

Wee Bea Booze - *See See Rider* **[20th Century 20-48, Harlem 1003] 1946**
   2-CD: *1942-45: The R&B Hits* **(va)** [Indigo IGODCD-100] UK, 1997

Will Bradley Trio featuring Freddie Slack and Ray McKinley -
                              Down The Road Apiece **[Columbia 35707] 1940**
   CD: *Juke Joint Jump-A Boogie Woogie Celebration* **(va)**
                              [Columbia Legacy CK-64988] USA, 1997

Big Bill Broonzy - *Key To The Highway* **[OKeh 06242] 1941**
   CD: *I Feel So Good* [Indigo IGOCD-2006] UK, 1994

Ruth Brown - *So Long* **[Atlantic 879] 1949**
   2-CD: *Miss Rhythm - Greatest Hits And More* [Sequel RSDCD-816] UK, 1994

Walter Brown with the Jay McShann Orch. - *Confessin' The Blues* **[Decca 8559] 1941**
   CD: *Trouble In Mind* **(va)** [Indigo IGOCD-2079Z] UK, 1998

Willie Bryant - *Around The Clock Blues (Parts 1 & 2)* **[Apollo 364] 1945**
   CD: *Blues Around the Clock* [Delmark DE-685] USA, 1996

Bumble Bee Slim - *Ida Red* **[Fidelity 3004] 1952**
   CD: *Jumpin' And Jivin'* **(va)** [Ace CDCHD-654] UK, 1997

Cadets - *Stranded In The Jungle* **[Modern 994] 1956**
   CD: *Modern Vocal Groups* **(va)** [Ace CDCHD-764] UK, 2000

Cab Calloway - *The Jungle King* **[Columbia 37500] 1947**
   CD: *Minnie The Moocher* [Tring CDGRF-077] UK, 1993

Leroy Carr - *Midnight Hour Blues* **[Vocalion 1703] 1932**
   CD: *Hurry Down Sunshine* [Indigo IGOCD-2016] UK, 1995

Goree Carter & His Hepcats - *Rock Awhile* **[Freedom 1506] 1949**
   CD: *The Rocking 40's* **(va)** [Hoy Hoy 40-S-01] USA, 1992

Ray Charles - *3/4 Time* **[LP: Columbia FC-38293, Wish You Were Here Tonight] 1983**
   4-CD: *The Complete Country & Western Recordings (1959-86)* [Rhino R2-75328] USA, 1999

Ray Charles - *Lonely Avenue* **[Atlantic 1108] 1956**
   3-CD: *The Birth Of Soul* [Atlantic 7-82310-2] USA, 1991

Ray Charles - *Swanee River Rock* **[Atlantic 1154] 1957**
   3-CD: *The Birth Of Soul* [Atlantic 7-82310-2] USA, 1991

Ray Charles - *This Little Girl Of Mine* **[Atlantic 1063] 1955**
   3-CD: *The Birth Of Soul* [Atlantic 7-82310-2] USA, 1991

Ray Charles - *You Are My Sunshine* **[A.B.C.-Paramount 10375] 1963**
   3-CD: *The Classic Years* [Castle Communications ESBCD-144] UK, 1991

Charlie Christian - *Air Mail Special* **[Columbia CL-652] 1941**
   CD: *The Genius Of The Electric Guitar* [C.B.S. CK-40846] USA, 1987

Eugene Church - *Good News* [Rendezvous 132] 1960
CD: *The Class & Rendezvous Story* (va) [Ace CDCHD-461] UK, 1993

Rosemary Clooney & Bing Crosby - *You Came A Long Way From St. Louis*
[LP: R.C.A.-Victor LPM-1854, *Fancy Meeting You Here*] 1958
CD: *Clap Hands, Here Comes Rosie* (Rosemary Clooney) [Taragon TARCD-1060] USA, 2000

Ann Cole & The Suburbans - *Got My Mojo Working* [Baton 237] 1957
CD: *Sol's Story* (va) [Ace CDCHD-505] UK, 1998

Nat 'King' Cole - *A Cottage For Sale* [LP: Capitol W-1031, *Cole Espanol*] 1958
5-CD: *The Collection* [Music For Pleasure CDMFBOX-5] UK,1992

Nat 'King' Cole - *Bring Another Drink* [Capitol 192] 1945
3-CD: *Capitol Blues Collection 20: The Cocktail Combos* (va) [Capitol CDP-52042-2] USA, 1997

Nat 'King' Cole - *Calypso Blues* [Capitol 915] 1950
CD: *The Nat 'King' Cole Story* [Capitol CDS-7951292] UK, 1991

Nat 'King' Cole - *The Frim Fram Sauce* [Capitol 224] 1945
3-CD: *Capitol Blues Collection 20: The Cocktail Combos* (va) [Capitol CDP-52042-2] USA, 1997

Nat 'King' Cole - *Get Your Kicks On Route 66* [Capitol 256] 1946
3-CD: *Capitol Blues Collection 20: The Cocktail Combos* (va) [Capitol CDP-52042-2] USA, 1997

Nat 'King' Cole - *I'm Through With Love* [Capitol 20064] 1945
3-CD: *Capitol Blues Collection 20: The Cocktail Combos* (va) [Capitol CDP-52042-2] USA, 1997

Nat 'King' Cole - *Little Joe From Chicago* [radio broadcast] 1944
CD: *Nat 'King' Cole* [T.K.O. UAE-30132] UK, 1996

Nat 'King' Cole - *Ramblin' Rose* [Capitol 4804] 1962
CD: *Capitol Collector Series* [Capitol CDCZ-303] UK, 1990

Nat 'King' Cole - *St. Louis Blues* [LP: Capitol W-993, *St. Louis Blues*] 1958
CD: *At The Movies* [Capitol CDP-7993732] UK, 1992

Nat 'King' Cole - *Straighten Up And Fly Right* [Capitol 154] 1943
3-CD: *Capitol Blues Collection 20: The Cocktail Combos* (va) [Capitol CDP-52042-2] USA, 1997

Nat 'King' Cole - *See also* Jazz At The Philharmonic

Pee Wee Crayton - *Blues After Hours* [Modern 20-624] 1948
CD: *The Modern Legacy (Volume 1)* [Ace CDCHD-632] UK, 1996

Jimmie Davis - *You Are My Sunshine* [Decca 5813] 1940
5-CD: *You Are My Sunshine (1937-46)* [Bear Family BCD-16216EI] Germany, 1998

Fats Domino - *Don't Lie To Me* [Imperial 5123] 1951
4-CD: *They Call Me The Fat Man - The Legendary Imperial Recordings*
[E.M.I. E2-7-96784-2] USA, 1991

Don & Dewey - *Ko Ko Joe* [Specialty 639] 1958
5-CD: *The Specialty Story* [Specialty 5SPCD-4412-2] USA, 1994

Jimmy Dorsey & His Orchestra (Vocal: Bob Eberley) - *Time Was* [Decca 3859] 1941
CD: *I Remember You* [Empress RAJCD-852] UK, 1995

Tommy Dorsey & His Orchestra - *Boogie Woogie* [Victor 26054] 1938
CD: *Boogie Woogie - Great Original Performances (1928-41)* (va)
[Robert Parker Jazz Classics RPCD-601] Australia, 1992

Billy Eckstine - *A Cottage For Sale* [National 9014] 1945
CD: *Mr. B. And The Blues* [Savoy Jazz SV-0264] Japan, 1995

Duke Ellington - *Caravan* [Mas 131, Columbia 36120] 1936
CD: *16 Most Requested Songs* [Columbia Legacy CK-57901] USA,1994

Duke Ellington (Vocal: Al Hibbler) - *I'm Just A Lucky So And So* [Victor 20-1799] **1945**
CD: *The Best Of The Complete RCA-Victor Mid-Forties Recordings (1944-46)*
[B.M.G. 09026-63462-2] UK, 2000

Shep Fields & His Rippling Rhythm (Vocal: Hal Derwin) -
South Of The Border (Down Mexico Way) [Bluebird B-10376] **1939**
CD: No known reissue

Lowell Fulson - *Everyday I Have The Blues [Lonely Heart Blues]*
[Swing-Time 196, Elko 254, Hollywood 1029] **1949**
2-CD: *The Swing-Time Records Story* (va) [Capricorn 9-42024] USA, 1994

Clarence 'Bon Ton' Garlow - *Route 90* [Flair 1021] **1954**
CD: *Long Gone Daddies* (va) [Ace CDCHD-768] UK, 2000

Rev. J.M. Gates - *Death's Black Train Is Coming* [Victor 20211, Bluebird B-7758] **1926**
CD: *Rev. J.M. Gates' Complete Recorded Works In Chronological Order (Volume 1: 1926)*
[Document DOCD-5414] Austria, 1995

Jazz Gillum - *Key To The Highway* [Bluebird B-8529, Victor 20-2160] **1940**
CD: *Harmonica Chicago Blues (1937-47)* [Fremeaux FA-260] France, 1998

Benny Goodman - *Flyin' Home* [Columbia 35254] **1939**
CD: *The Essential Benny Goodman* [Columbia 467151-2] UK, 1993

Benny Goodman - *St. Louis Blues* [Victor 24511] **1936**
3-CD: *The Birth Of Swing (1935-36)* [B.M.G. (R.C.A.) ND-90601] USA, 1991

Benny Goodman (Guitar: Charlie Christian) - *Seven Come Eleven* [Columbia 35349] **1940**
CD: *Charlie Christian, The Genius Of The Electric Guitar* [C.B.S. CK-40846] USA, 1987

Benny Goodman (Guitar: Charlie Christian) - *Solo Flight* [Columbia 36684] **1941**
CD: *Charlie Christian, The Genius Of The Electric Guitar* [C.B.S. CK-40846] USA, 1987

Guitar Slim - *The Things That I Used To Do* [Specialty 482] **1953**
CD: *The Things That I Used To Do* [Ace CDCHD-318] UK, 1991

Lionel Hampton & His Orch. featuring Illinois Jacquet - *Flying Home* [Decca 18394] **1942**
CD: *Classic Big Band Jazz* [Avid CDAVC-540] UK, 1994

Wynonie Harris - *Around The Clock Blues (Parts 1 & 2)* [Philo 103, Aladdin 103] **1945**
2-CD: *Bootin' The Boogie - The Birth Of Rock And Roll (Volume 2)* (va)
[Charly CPCD 8300-2] UK, 1998

Erskine Hawkins - *After Hours* [Bluebird B-10879] **1940**
2-CD: *Roots Of Rhythm & Blues (1939-45)* (va) [Fremeaux FA-050] France, 1998

Bobby Helms - *Fraulein* [Decca 30194] **1957**
2-CD: *Fraulein - His Decca Recordings* [Bear Family BCD-15594] Germany, 1992

Howlin' Wolf - *Killing Floor* [Chess 1923] **1964**
3-CD: *The Chess Box* [Chess CHD3-9332] USA, 1991

Helen Humes & The Bill Doggett Octet - *Be-Baba-Leba* [Philo PV-106, Aladdin AV-106] **1945**
2-CD: *The Aladdin Records Story* (va) [E.M.I. E2-30882] UK, 1994

Elmore James - *Baby What's Wrong* [Meteor 5003] **1953**
3-CD: *The Classic Early Recordings (1951-56)* [Ace ABOXCD-4] UK, 1993

Elmore James - *Dust My Broom* [Trumpet 146] **1951**
3-CD: *The Classic Early Recordings (1951-56)* [Ace ABOXCD-4] UK, 1993

Elmore James - *I Believe* [Meteor 5000] **1952**
3-CD: *The Classic Early Recordings (1951-56)* [Ace ABOXCD-4] UK, 1993

Elmore James - *It Hurts Me Too* [Chief 7004] **1957**
4-CD: *King Of The Slide Guitar* [Charly R&B CDREDBOX-4] UK, 1992

Elmore James - *It Hurts Me Too* [Enjoy 2015] **1965**
4-CD: *King Of The Slide Guitar* [Charly R&B CDREDBOX-4] UK, 1992

Harry James & His Orch. (Vocal: Dick Haymes) - *You've Changed* [Columbia 36412] 1941
    CD: *Dick Haymes, Legendary Song Stylist* [Pulse PLSCD-307] UK 1999

Illinois Jacquet & His All Stars - *Flying Home (Parts 1 & 2)*
                                             [Philo P-101, Aladdin A-101] 1945
    CD: *The Aladdin Records Story* (va) [E.M.I. E2-30882] UK, 1994

Illinois Jacquet - *See also* Jazz At The Philharmonic

Jazz At The Philharmonic featuring Nat Cole, Les Paul and Illinois Jacquet - *Blues*
    [78 rpm album: Disc 6024 and 6025, *Jazz At The Philharmonic (Volume 4)*] 1948
    CD: *Jazz At The Philharmonic - The Beginning* [Charly Le Jazz CD-41] UK, 1995

Bill Jennings & His Orch. - *You Came A Long Way From St. Louis* [Gotham 232] 1951
    CD: *Stomping With Bill* [Collectables CD-5338] USA, 1990

Johnnie Johnson - *Johnnie's Boogie* [1999 recording of a 1950s composition]
    CD accompanying Johnnie Johnson's biography, *Father Of Rock & Roll* by Travis Fitzpatrick
        [Published by Thomas, Cooke & Co, Houston, Texas] USA, 1999

Luke Jones & His Orch. (Vocal: Red Mack) - *Disc Jockey Blues* [Atlas 144] 1947
    CD: *Luke Jones (1946-49) / Doc Sausage (1940)* [Blue Moon BMCD-6012] Spain, 1996

Louis Jordan - *Ain't That Just Like A Woman* [Decca 23669] 1946
    8-CD: *Let The Good Times Roll - The Complete Decca Recordings (1938-54)*
                        [Bear Family BCD-15557] Germany, 1990

Louis Jordan - *Choo Choo Ch' Boogie* [Decca 23610] 1946
    8-CD: *Let The Good Times Roll - The Complete Decca Recordings (1938-54)*
                        [Bear Family BCD-15557] Germany, 1990

Louis Jordan - *Ration Blues* [Decca 8654] 1943
    8-CD: *Let The Good Times Roll - The Complete Decca Recordings (1938-54)*
                        [Bear Family BCD-15557] Germany, 1990

Louis Jordan - *Reconversion Blues* [Decca 18762] 1945
    8-CD: *Let The Good Times Roll - The Complete Decca Recordings (1938-54)*
                        [Bear Family BCD-15557] Germany, 1990

Louis Jordan - *Run Joe* [Decca 24448] 1947
    8-CD: *Let The Good Times Roll - The Complete Decca Recordings (1938-54)*
                        [Bear Family BCD-15557] Germany, 1990

Louis Jordan - *Saturday Night Fish Fry (Parts 1 & 2)* [Decca 24725] 1949
    8-CD: *Let The Good Times Roll - The Complete Decca Recordings (1938-54)*
                        [Bear Family BCD-15557] Germany, 1990

Chris Kenner - *Something You Got* [Instant 3237] 1961
    2-CD: *The Minit & Instant Story* (va) [Charly LAB-101] UK, 1995

B.B. King - *Every Day I Have The Blues* [R.P.M. 421] 1955
    4-CD: *King Of The Blues* [M.C.A. MCAD4-10677] USA, 1992

B.B. King - *Sweet Sixteen (Parts 1 & 2)* [Kent 330] 1959
    CD: *King Of The Blues* [Pickwick PWKS-4211] UK, 1994

Andy Kirk & His Twelve Clouds Of Joy - *Floyd's Guitar Blues* [Decca 2483] 1939
    CD: *Andy Kirk & His Twelve Clouds Of Joy 1939-40* [Classics 640] France, 1996

Andy Kirk & His Twelve Clouds Of Joy - *Little Joe From Chicago* [Decca 1710] 1938
    CD: *Andy Kirk & His Twelve Clouds Of Joy 1937-38* [Classics 581] France, 1996

Frankie Laine - *That's My Desire* [Mercury 5007] 1947
    CD: *Memories In Gold (20 Greatest Hits)* [Prestige CDPC-5004] UK, 1992

Meade Lux Lewis - *Honky Tonk Train Blues* [Paramount 12896] 1928
    CD: *Shake Your Wicked Knees* (va) [Yazoo 2035] USA, 1998

Little Miss Cornshucks with Marl Young's Orchestra - *So Long*
[Sunbeam 104, Old Swing-Master 26] 1947
CD: No known reissue.

Little Richard - *Rip It Up* **[Specialty 579] 1956**
3-CD: *The Specialty Sessions* [Specialty/Ace SPCD-8508] USA/UK, 1989

Little Walter - *I Got To Find My Baby* **[Checker 1013] 1954**
CD: *Confessin' The Blues* [Chess CHD-9344] USA, 1996

Little Walter - *Key To The Highway* **[Checker 904] 1958**
CD: *His Best* [Chess CHD-9384] USA, 1997

Little Walter - *Last Night* **[Checker 805] 1954**
CD: *His Best* [Chess CHD-9384] USA, 1997

Little Walter - *Mean Old World* **[Checker 764] 1952**
CD: *His Best* [Chess CHD-9384] USA, 1997

Little Walter - *My Babe* **[Checker 811] 1955**
CD: *His Best* [Chess CHD-9384] USA, 1997

Louvin Brothers - *Too Late* **[LP: Capitol T-910,** *Ira & Charlie***] 1957**
8-CD: *Close Harmony* [Bear Family BCD-15561] Germany, 1992

Jimmy McCracklin - *Rockin' All Day* *[Reelin' And Rockin']* **[Modern 20-762] 1950**
CD: *The Modern Recordings (1948-50)* [Ace CDCHD-720] UK, 1999

Ray McKinley & His Orchestra (Vocal: Ray McKinley) -
You Came A Long Way From St. Louis **[Victor 20-2913] 1948**
CD: No known reissue.

Memphis Minnie - *I'm Talkin' 'Bout You* **[Vocalion 1476] 1930**
CD: *Memphis Minnie & Kansas Joe - Complete Recorded Works 1929-34 In Chronological Order
(Volume 1: 1929-30)* [Document DOCD-5028] Austria, 1991

Memphis Minnie - *Me And My Chauffeur Blues* **[OKeh 06288] 1941**
CD: *Memphis Minnie & Kansas Joe - Complete Recorded Works 1929-34 In Chronological Order
(Volume 1: 1929-30)* [Document DOCD-5028] Austria, 1991

Memphis Slim - *Beer Drinking Woman* **[Bluebird B-8584] 1940**
CD: *The Bluebird Recordings (1940-41)* [R.C.A. 07863- 66720-2] USA ,1997

Memphis Slim - *Nobody Loves Me* *[Every Day I Have The Blues]* **[Miracle 145] 1948**
CD: *Life Is Like That* [Charly CD-249] UK, 1991

Johnny Moore's Three Blazers (Vocal: Charles Brown) - *Drifting Blues*
[Philo P-112, Aladdin A-112] 1945
2-CD: *The Aladdin Records Story* **(va)** [E.M.I. E2-30882] UK, 1994

Johnny Moore's Three Blazers (Vocal: Charles Brown) - *Merry Christmas Baby*
[Exclusive 63] 1947
CD: *The Rhythm & Blues Hits 1947* **(va)** [Indigo IGOCD-2081] UK, 1998

Russ Morgan & His Orch. (Vocal: Russ Morgan) - *So Long* **[Decca 25080] 1940**
CD: *The Best Of Russ Morgan* [M.C.A. Jazz 4036] USA, 1987

Ella Mae Morse with Don Raye and the Freddie Slack Trio –
The House Of Blue Lights **[Capitol 251] 1946**
2-CD: *Capitol Blues Collection 19: Jumpin' Like Mad - Cool Cats And Hip Chicks* **(va)**
[Capitol 7243-8-52051-2-5] USA, 1996

Muddy Waters - *Got My Mojo Working* **[Chess 1652] 1957**
3-CD: *The Chess Box* [Chess CHD3-80002] USA, 1989

Muddy Waters - *I'm Your Hoochie Coochie Man* **[Chess 1560] 1954**
CD: *His Best (1947-55)* [Chess CHD-9370] USA, 1997

Muddy Waters - *Just Make Love To Me* *[I Just Want To Make Love To You]*
[Chess 1571] 1954
CD: *His Best (1947-55)* [Chess CHD-9370] USA, 1997

Muddy Waters - *Long Distance Call* [Chess 1452] 1951
3-CD: *The Chess Box* [Chess CHD3-80002] USA, 1989

Willie Nelson - *Mountain Dew* [R.C.A. 12328] 1981
CD: *The Best Of Willie Nelson* [R.C.A. 66406] USA, 1994

Les Paul & Mary Ford - *How High The Moon* [Capitol 1451] 1951
CD: *The Capitol Years - The Best Of Les Paul & Mary Ford*
[Capitol/E.M.I. CDP-791-299-2] UK, 1989

Les Paul & Mary Ford - *St. Louis Blues* [Capitol 15932] 1950
4-CD: *The Legend And The Legacy* [Capitol CDS-797654-2] USA, 1991

Les Paul & Mary Ford - *Vaya Con Dios* [Capitol 2486] 1953
CD: *The Capitol Years - The Best Of Les Paul & Mary Ford*
[Capitol/E.M.I. CDP-791-299-2] UK, 1989

Les Paul - *See also* Jazz At The Philharmonic

Pilgrim Travelers - *How Jesus Died* [Specialty 889] 1955
CD: No known reissue.

Lloyd Price - *Lawdy Miss Clawdy* [Specialty 428] 1952
5-CD: *The Specialty Story* **(va)** [Specialty 5SPCD-4412-2] USA, 1994

Ray Price - *Crazy Arms* [Columbia 21510] 1957
CD: *The Essential Ray Price 1951-62* [Columbia CK-48532] USA, 1991

Gertrude 'Ma' Rainey - *C.C. Rider* [Paramount 12252] 1924
CD: *The Blues Ladies* **(va)** [Indigo IGOCD-2042] UK, 1996

Jimmy Reed - *Baby What You Want Me To Do* [Vee-Jay 333] 1959
CD: *Bright Lights, Big City - His Greatest Hits* [Charly CDBM-17] UK, 1992

Jimmy Reed - *Big Boss Man* [Vee-Jay 380] 1960
CD: *Bright Lights, Big City - His Greatest Hits* [Charly CDBM-17] UK, 1992

Jimmy Reed - *Honest I Do* [Vee-Jay 253] 1957
CD: *Bright Lights, Big City - His Greatest Hits* [Charly CDBM-17] UK, 1992

Jimmy Reed - *You Don't Have To Go* [Vee-Jay 119] 1954
CD: *Bright Lights, Big City - His Greatest Hits* [Charly CDBM-17] UK, 1992

Willard Robison & His Deep River Orchestra - *A Cottage For Sale*
Note: Although Robison is credited with 'introducing' this song, which he co-wrote in 1930 with Larry Conley, it has proved impossible to trace any recording of it by him.

Charlie Segar - *Key To The Highway* [Vocalion 05441] 1940
CD: *Chicago Blues 1940-47* **(va)** [Fremeaux FA-150] France, 1998

Arkie Shibley & His Mountain Dew Boys - *Hot Rod Race* [Gilt-Edge 5021] 1950
CD: *Arkie Shibley & His Mountain Dew Boys* [Collector Records CLCD-2856] Netherlands, 1997

Frank Sinatra - *A Cottage For Sale* [LP: Capitol W-1221, *No One Cares*] 1959
CD: *No-One Cares* [Capitol CZ-392] UK, 1991

Frank Sinatra - *In The Wee Small Hours Of The Morning* [Capitol 14360] 1955
CD: *In The Wee Small Hours* [Capitol CDP7-96826] USA, 1991

Frank Sinatra - *One For My Baby (And One More For The Road)* [Capitol 15258] 1947
CD: *Sings For Only The Lonely* [Capitol ED-2601392] UK, 1988

Frank Sinatra - *South Of The Border* [Capitol 2638] 1954
CD: *The Best Of The Capitol Years* [Capitol/E.M.I. 99225] USA, 1992

Sir Douglas Quintet - *Mendocino* **[Smash 2191] 1969**
CD: *The Sir Douglas Quintet Collection* [Castle CCSCD-133] UK, 1986

Freddie Slack & His Orchestra featuring T-Bone Walker - *Riffette* **[Capitol 129] 1942**
2-CD: *1942-45: The R&B Hits* **(va)** [Indigo IGODCD-100] UK, 1997

Bessie Smith - *St. Louis Blues* **[Columbia 14064-D] 1925**
CD: *The Complete Recordings (Volume 2)* [Sony/Columbia 468767-2] USA, 1991

Sons of the Pioneers - *Riders In The Sky* **[R.C.A.-Victor 48-0060] 1950**
4-CD: *Wagons West* [Bear Family BCD-15640] Germany, 1993

Spaniels - *Goodnite, Sweetheart, Goodnite* **[Vee-Jay 107] 1954**
2-CD: *The Vee-Jay Story* **(va)** [Charly CD LAB-104] UK, 1996

Aaron 'Pinetop' Sparks - *Every Day I Have The Blues* **[Bluebird B-6125] 1935**
CD: *The Sparks Brothers - Complete Recorded Works In Chronological Order (1932-35)*
[Document DOCD-5315] Austria, 1994

Arbee Stidham - *My Heart Belongs To You* **[Victor 20-2572] 1947**
CD: No known reissue.

Tampa Red - *Don't You Lie To Me* **[Bluebird B-8654] 1940**
CD: *It Hurts Me Too* [Indigo IGOCD-2004] UK, 1994

Tampa Red - *It Hurts Me Too* **[Bluebird B-8635] 1940**
CD: *It Hurts Me Too* [Indigo IGOCD-2004] UK, 1994

Sister Rosetta Tharpe - *This Train* **[Decca 2558] 1939**
CD: *The Complete Sister Rosetta Tharpe (Volume One: 1938-43)*
[Fremeaux FA-1301] France, 1998

Tommy Tucker - *Hi-Heel Sneakers* **[Checker 1067] 1963**
CD: *Hi-Heel Sneakers* [Chess MCD-32644] UK, 1995

Big Joe Turner - *Feeling Happy* **[Atlantic 1122] 1957**
CD: *Greatest Hits* [Atlantic Jazz 7-81752-2] USA, 1989

Big Joe Turner - *Roll 'Em Pete* **[Vocalion 4607] 1939**
CD: *Juke Joint Jump - A Boogie Woogie Celebration* **(va)**
[Columbia Legacy CK-64988] USA, 1997

Big Joe Turner - *St. Louis Blues* **[LP: Atlantic SD-1234, *Boss Of The Blues*] 1956**
CD: *Boss Of The Blues* [Atlantic 8812-2] USA, 1988

Big Joe Turner - *Shake Rattle And Roll* **[Atlantic 1026] 1954**
CD: *Greatest Hits* [Atlantic Jazz 7-81752-2] USA, 1989

Big Joe Turner - *Sweet Sixteen* **[Atlantic 960] 1952**
CD: *Greatest Hits* [Atlantic Jazz 7-81752-2] USA, 1989

Big Joe Turner - *TV Mama* **[Atlantic 1016] 1953**
CD: *The Rhythm & Blues Years* [Atlantic 781663-2] USA, 1986

Big Joe Turner - *Wee Baby Blues* **[Decca 8526] 1941**
CD: *The Boss Of The Blues (1939-47)* [E.P.M. 159112] USA, 1998

Big Joe Turner - *See also* Big Vernon

Unknown - *The Signifying Monkey*
[LP: Rounder 2014, *Get Your Ass In The Water And Swim Like Me*] 1968
CD: *Get Your Ass In The Water And Swim Like Me* **(va)** [Rounder CDROU-2014] USA, 1998

Jimmy Wakely - *Too Late* **[Decca 5909] 1941**
CD: *The Very Best Of Jimmy Wakely* [Varese Sarabande 5928] USA, 1998

T-Bone Walker - *Bobby Sox Blues* **[Black & White 110] 1946**
3-CD: *The Complete Capitol/Black & White Recordings* [Capitol 7243-8-29379-2-0] USA, 1995

T-Bone Walker - *Call It Stormy Monday* **[Black & White 122] 1947**
  3-CD: *The Complete Capitol/Black & White Recordings* [Capitol 7243-8-29379-2-0] USA, 1995

T-Bone Walker - *The Hustle Is On* **[Imperial 5081] 1950**
  2-CD: *The Complete Imperial Recordings (1950-55)* [E.M.I. CDP-7-96737-2] USA, 1991

T-Bone Walker - *I'm Gonna Find My Baby* **[Black & White 110] 1946**
  3-CD: *The Complete Capitol/Black & White Recordings* [Capitol 7243-8-29379-2-0] USA, 1995

T-Bone Walker - *Mean Old World* **[Capitol 10033] 1942**
  3-CD: *The Complete Capitol/Black & White Recordings* [Capitol 7243-8-29379-2-0] USA, 1995

T-Bone Walker - *Strollin' With Bones* **[Imperial 5071] 1950**
  2-CD: *The Complete Imperial Recordings (1950-55)* [E.M.I. CDP-7-96737-2] USA, 1991

T-Bone Walker - *T-Bone Jumps Again* **[Black & White 125] 1947**
  3-CD: *The Complete Capitol/Black & White Recordings* [Capitol 7243-8-29379-2-0] USA, 1995

T-Bone Walker - *T-Bone Shuffle* **[Comet 53] 1948**
  3-CD: *The Complete Capitol/Black & White Recordings* [Capitol 7243-8-29379-2-0] USA, 1995

T-Bone Walker - *That's Better For Me* **[Black & White 126] 1948**
  3-CD: *The Complete Capitol/Black & White Recordings* [Capitol 7243-8-29379-2-0] USA, 1995

T-Bone Walker - *Too Much Trouble Blues* **[Capitol 944] 1947**
  3-CD: *The Complete Capitol/Black & White Recordings* [Capitol 7243-8-29379-2-0] USA, 1995

T-Bone Walker - *See also* Freddie Slack & His Orchestra featuring T-Bone Walker

Clara Ward & Her Famous Ward Singers - *This Little Light Of Mine* **[Savoy 4038] 1952**
  CD: *Savoy Gospel Greats* [Savgos PCD-4901] Japan, 1997

James Wayne - *Junco Partner* **[Sittin' In With 607] 1951**
  CD: *Bluestream -The Best Of Mainstream Blues* **(va)** [Mainstream MDCD-904] UK, 1990

Hank Williams - *Jambalaya (On The Bayou)* **[M-G-M 11283] 1952**
  2-CD: *40 Greatest Hits* [Polydor 8212332] UK, 1989

Hank Williams - *Mind Your Own Business* **[M-G-M 10461] 1949**
  2-CD: *40 Greatest Hits* [Polydor 8212332] UK, 1989

Joe Williams & The King Kolax Orch. - *Everyday I Have The Blues* **[Checker 762] 1952**
  15-CD: *The Chess Story 1947-75* **(va)** [M.C.A. 380596-2] USA, 1999
                See also Count Basie

Sonny Boy Williamson - *Good Morning Schoolgirl* **[Bluebird B-7059] 1937**
  CD: *The Bluebird Recordings (1940-41)* [R.C.A. 07863-66723-2] USA, 1997

Bob Wills & His Texas Playboys - *Ida Red* **[M-G-M 10570] 1950**
  CD: *Greatest Hits* [Curb CRBD-77389] USA, 1990

7

Cover Versions of Chuck Berry's Songs

A clear indication of Chuck Berry's influence on popular music is the enduring popularity of his songs. Set out below are Chuck's compositions ranked by the number of times they have been recorded by other artists, together with details of time-span and geographical spread. Watch out for the forthcoming fully detailed listing of every Berry cover recording by Morten Reff, from which this list has been compiled.

JOHNNY B. GOODE *originally recorded 1957, released 1958*

358 recordings from 1958 to 1999 made in the USA, UK, Austria, Australia, Canada, Czechoslovakia, Denmark, Finland, France, Germany, Italy, Jamaica, Japan, Mexico, the Netherlands, New Zealand, Norway, Poland, Russia, Sweden, Thailand and Yugoslavia, including five versions in Danish, three in Swedish, two each in Norwegian and Finnish, one each in French and German, and eleven instrumentals.

MEMPHIS TENNESSEE *originally recorded 1958, released 1959*

290 recordings from 1963 to 1999 made in the USA, UK, Australia, Canada, Czechoslovakia, Denmark, Finland, France, Germany, the Netherlands, Norway, Spain, Sweden, Thailand and Yugoslavia, including three versions in German, two each in Danish and Finnish, one each in Norwegian and Swedish, and no fewer than forty-two instrumentals!

ROLL OVER BEETHOVEN *originally recorded 1956, released 1956*

222 recordings from 1956 to 2000 made in the USA, UK, Australia, Canada, Czechoslovakia, Denmark, Germany, Ireland, Italy, Mexico, the Netherlands, Norway, Sweden and Yugoslavia, including two versions in French, one each in Spanish, Swedish and Norwegian, and six instrumentals.

SWEET LITTLE SIXTEEN *originally recorded 1957, released 1958*

217 recordings from 1957 to 2000 made in the USA, UK, Australia, Canada, Denmark, Finland, France, Germany, Italy, Japan, Mexico, the Netherlands, Norway, Sweden, Switzerland, Yugoslavia and... the Faeroe Islands(!), including four versions in German, two each in Finnish and Swedish, one each in Danish, French, Norwegian and Spanish, and eight instrumentals. Many are versions of *Surfin' USA*, after the Beach Boys' reworking of the Berry classic.

MAYBELLENE *originally recorded 1955, released 1955*

132 recordings from 1955 to 2000 made in the USA, UK, Australia, Canada, Denmark, Finland, France, Germany, Latvia, Mexico, the Netherlands, Norway, Sweden and Switzerland, including two versions in Swedish, one each in Danish, Finnish and German, and four instrumentals.

ROCK AND ROLL MUSIC *originally recorded 1956, released 1957*

117 recordings from 1958 to 1999 made in the USA, UK, Australia, Canada, Czechoslovakia, Denmark, Finland, Germany, Hungary, Ireland, Israel, Malta, the Netherlands, Norway, Sweden and Yugoslavia, including one version each in Norwegian and Finnish, and six instrumentals.

PROMISED LAND *originally recorded 1964, released 1964*

112 recordings from 1965 to 1998 made in the USA, UK, Australia, Austria, Canada, Denmark, Finland, France, Germany, Norway, Spain, Sweden and Switzerland, including three versions in French and one each in Danish, Finnish and Swedish.

LITTLE QUEENIE *originally recorded 1958, released 1959*

101 recordings from 1964 to 2000 made in the USA, UK, Australia, Belgium, Denmark, Finland, France, Germany, Greece, the Netherlands, Norway and Sweden, including one instrumental.

AROUND & AROUND *originally recorded 1958, released 1958*

81 recordings from 1964 to 2000 made in the USA, UK, Canada, Finland, France, Germany, Ireland, Japan, the Netherlands, Norway, and Sweden, including one version each in Finnish, French and Norwegian, and three instrumentals.

YOU NEVER CAN TELL *originally recorded 1963, released 1964*

76 recordings from 1965 to 1999 made in the USA, UK, Austria, Denmark, Finland, France, Germany, the Netherlands, Norway, Sweden and Switzerland, including four versions in Swedish, two in Danish, one in Norwegian, and one instrumental.

TOO MUCH MONKEY BUSINESS *originally recorded 1956, released 1956*

75 recordings from 1956 to 2000 made in the USA, UK, Canada, Denmark, Finland, Germany, the Netherlands, Portugal and Sweden, including one instrumental.

BROWN EYED HANDSOME MAN *originally recorded 1956, released 1956*

73 recordings from 1956 to 2000 made in the USA, UK, Australia, Canada, Finland, Germany and the Netherlands, including one instrumental.

SCHOOL DAY *originally recorded 1957, released 1957*

71 recordings from 1957 to 2000 made in the USA, UK, Austria, Australia, Finland, France, Germany, Mexico, the Netherlands, Norway, Sweden and Switzerland, including one version each in Finnish, Norwegian and Spanish, and three instrumentals.

LET IT ROCK *originally recorded 1959, released 1960*

66 recordings from 1963 to 1997 made in the USA, UK, Canada, Germany, Italy Norway and Sweden.

NO PARTICULAR PLACE TO GO *originally recorded 1964, released 1964*

64 recordings from 1964 to 1997 made in the USA, UK, Austria, Denmark, France, Germany, the Netherlands, Norway and Sweden, including four versions in Swedish, three versions in Norwegian, one version each in Danish and Finnish, and two instrumentals.

BYE BYE JOHNNY *originally recorded 1960, released 1960*

61 recordings from 1964 to 1999 made in the USA, UK, Australia, Austria, Belgium, Denmark, France, Germany, the Netherlands and Sweden, including two versions in German, one in French, and one instrumental.

CAROL *originally recorded 1958, released 1958*

59 recordings from 1958 to 2000 made in the USA, UK, Australia, Belgium, Denmark, France, Germany, Norway and Sweden, including two versions in French, one in German, and one instrumental.

THIRTY DAYS *originally recorded 1955, released 1955*

59 recordings from 1956 to 2000 made in the USA, UK, Canada, Denmark, Finland, France, Germany, the Netherlands, Norway and Sweden, including two versions in French, and one instrumental. Many are versions of *Forty Days*, after Ronnie Hawkins's reworking of the Berry classic.

NADINE *originally recorded 1963, released 1964*

52 recordings from 1965 to 2000 made in the USA, UK, Austria, Canada, Finland, France, Germany, the Netherlands, Norway and Sweden, including one instrumental.

REELIN' AND ROCKIN' *originally recorded 1957, released 1958*

52 recordings from 1964 to 1998 made in the USA, UK, Denmark, Finland, Germany, the Netherlands, Sweden and Switzerland, including one version each in Finnish and Swedish, and four instrumentals.

I'M TALKING ABOUT YOU *originally recorded 1961, released 1963*

49 recordings from 1963 to 1999 made in the USA, UK, Australia, Denmark, Finland, Germany, Italy, the Netherlands, Norway and Sweden, including one version in Finnish.

BACK IN THE USA *originally recorded 1959, released 1959*

39 recordings from 1965 to 2000 made in the USA, UK, Denmark, the Netherlands and Sweden.

SWEET LITTLE ROCK AND ROLLER *originally recorded 1958, released 1958*

37 recordings from 1964 to 2000 made in the USA, UK, Denmark, Finland, France, Germany, Norway, Sweden, including one version in Finnish.

RUN RUDOLPH RUN *originally recorded 1958, released 1958*

35 recordings from 1975 to 1998 made in the USA, UK, Australia, Canada, the Netherlands, Norway and Sweden.

NO MONEY DOWN *originally recorded 1955, released 1955*

27 recordings from 1957 to 1998 made in the USA, UK, Germany, Italy and Sweden.

ALMOST GROWN *originally recorded 1959, released 1959*

23 recordings from 1959 to 2000 made in the USA, UK, Belgium, France, Germany, Norway and Sweden, including one instrumental.

YOU CAN'T CATCH ME *originally recorded 1955, released 1956*

23 recordings from 1963 to 2000 made in the USA, UK, Finland, Germany and Sweden, including one version each in Finnish and German, and one instrumental.

BEAUTIFUL DELILAH *originally recorded 1958, released 1958*

22 recordings from 1964 to 2000 made in the USA, UK, Denmark, Germany, Italy, Norway and Sweden.

WEE WEE HOURS *originally recorded 1955, released 1955*

21 recordings from 1965 to 2000 made in the USA, UK, Denmark and Sweden, including one instrumental.

COME ON *originally recorded 1961, released 1961*

17 recordings from 1963 to 2000 made in the USA, UK, Australia, Canada, Denmark, France, the Netherlands, Norway and Sweden.

TULANE *originally recorded 1969, released 1970*

12 recordings from 1976 to 1998 made in the USA, UK and Finland.

DOWNBOUND TRAIN *originally recorded 1955, released 1955*

10 recordings from 1956 to 1996 made in the USA, UK and Sweden.

GUITAR BOOGIE *instrumental originally recorded 1957, released (on EP and LP) 1958*

10 recordings from 1965 to 1999 made in the USA, UK and Norway.

HAVANA MOON *originally recorded 1956, released 1956*

10 recordings from 1977 to 1997 made in the USA, UK, Canada and Denmark.

DEAR DAD *originally recorded 1964, released 1965*

7 recordings from 1977 to 1999 made in the USA, UK and Sweden.

JAGUAR AND THUNDERBIRD *originally recorded 1960, released 1960*

7 recordings from 1966 to 1993 made in the USA, UK and Denmark.

BACK TO MEMPHIS *originally recorded 1967, released 1967*

6 recordings from 1966 to 2000 made in the USA, Germany and Sweden, including one instrumental.

317

OH BABY DOLL *originally recorded 1957, released 1957*

6 recordings from 1964 to 1997 made in the USA, UK, Germany and the Netherlands.

ALL ABOARD *originally recorded 1961, released (on LP) 1963*

5 recordings from 1966 to 1986 made in the USA and UK.

GO GO GO *originally recorded 1961, released 1961*

5 recordings from 1964 to 1986 made in the USA, UK and Norway.

IT DON'T TAKE BUT A FEW MINUTES *originally recorded 1958, released (on LP) 1958*

5 recordings from 1976 to 1994 made in the USA, UK and Sweden.

IT'S MY OWN BUSINESS *originally recorded 1965, released (on LP) 1966*

5 recordings from 1977 to 1988 made in the USA and UK.

I WANT TO BE YOUR DRIVER *originally recorded 1964, released (on LP) 1965*

5 recordings from 1966 and 1996 made in the USA.

OH WHAT A THRILL *originally recorded 1979, released 1979*

5 recordings from 1980 to 1996 made in the UK and Sweden, including two versions in Swedish.

I'M A ROCKER *originally recorded 1967, released (on LP) 1970*

4 recordings from 1974 and 1975 made in the USA, UK, Denmark and France.

IT WASN'T ME *originally recorded 1965, released 1965*

4 recordings from 1978 to 1986 made in the USA and UK.

OUR LITTLE RENDEZVOUS *originally recorded 1960, released 1960*

4 recordings from 1964 to 1987 made in the USA , UK and Denmark.

BETTY JEAN *originally recorded 1959, released (on LP) 1960*

3 recordings from 1964 to 1997 made in the USA, Germany and Sweden.

JO JO GUNNE *originally recorded 1958, released 1958*

3 recordings from 1966 to 1985 made in the USA and UK.

THIRTEEN QUESTION METHOD *originally recorded 1957, recut 1960 and released (on LP) 1961*

3 recordings from 1987 to 1999 made in the USA , UK and Norway.

BROKEN ARROW *originally recorded 1959, released 1959*

2 recordings, both from 1964, made in the USA and UK.

COUNTY LINE *originally recorded 1959, released 1974*

2 recordings from 1993 and 1997 made in the USA and UK respectively.

I GOT A BOOKING *originally recorded 1965, released (on LP) 1965*

2 recordings from 1967 and 1992 made in the USA and Denmark respectively.

ROCK AT THE PHILHARMONIC *instrumental orig. recorded 1957, released (on EP and LP) 1957*

2 recordings, both from 1961, made in the USA and UK.

THE MAN AND THE DONKEY *originally recorded 1961, released (on LP) in 1963*

2 recordings from 1992 and 1999 made in the UK and Finland respectively.

ANTHONY BOY *originally recorded 1958, released 1959*

1 recording from 1981 made in the UK.

BLUE FEELING *instrumental originally recorded 1957, released 1957*

1 recording from 1966 made in the USA.

BLUES FOR HAWAIIANS *instrumental originally recorded 1958, released (on LP) 1959*

1 recording from 1989 made in the USA.

CHILDHOOD SWEETHEART *originally recorded 1959, released 1959*

1 recording from 2000 made in Sweden.

DEEP FEELING *instrumental originally recorded 1957, released 1957*

1 recording from 1996 made in the USA.

DRIFTING HEART *originally recorded 1956, released 1956*

1 recording from 1988 made in the USA.

HAVE MERCY JUDGE *originally recorded 1969, released 1970*

1 recording from 1971 made in the USA.

HELLO LITTLE GIRL, GOODBYE *originally recorded 1973, released (on LP) 1973*

1 recording from 1991 made in the USA.

HOW YOU'VE CHANGED *originally recorded 1957, released (on LP) 1958*

1 recording from 1965 made in the UK.

LITTLE MARIE *originally recorded 1964, released 1964*

1 recording from 1986 made in the USA (in medley with *Memphis*).

LOUIE TO FRISCO *originally recorded 1968, released 1968*

1 recording from 1982 made in the USA.

VACATION TIME *originally recorded 1958, released 1958*

1 recording from the 1990s made in Finland.

WUDEN'T ME *originally recorded 1979, released (on LP) 1979*

1 recording from 1982 made in Denmark (in Danish).

Finally, Chuck Berry's most (in)famous composition, which isn't totally his composition after all. Chuck took the basic concept from — and retained the refrain of — Dave Bartholomew's original, added his own lyrics and developed the song into the one we all love to hate: *My Ding-A-Ling.* It's true to say, however, the twenty covers would never have happened had Chuck not had the international success with his naughty little ditty.

MY DING-A-LING, *originally recorded and released in 1967, but most famously in 1972*

20 recordings from 1972 to 1998 made in the USA, UK, Finland, France, Germany, Norway and Sweden, including two versions in Swedish and one each in Finnish and French.

8

Bibliography

The following sources were consulted during the preparation of this book:

BOOKS

Aeppli, Felix - *The Rolling Stones (1962-95): The Ultimate Guide*
 (Record Information Services, London) 1996
Albert, George, & Frank Hoffman - *The Cash Box Black Contemporary Singles Charts (1960-84)*
 (Scarecrow Press, Metuchen, New Jersey) 1986
Badman, Keith - *The Beatles After The Break-Up (1970-2000)* (Omnibus Press, London) 1999
Bacon, Tony - *The Ultimate Guitar Book* (Dorling Kindersley, London) 1991
Basie, Count, as told to Albert Murray - *Good Morning Blues: The Autobiography Of Count Basie*
 (Paladin, London) 1987
Bayles, Martha - *Hole In My Soul* (Maxwell Macmillan, London) 1994
Bernard, Shane - *Swamp Pop* (University Of Mississippi, Oxford, Mississippi) 1996
Berry, Chuck - *Chuck Berry: The Autobiography* (Faber & Faber, London) 1987
Bocock, Mike, Paul Roberton & Mike Leadbitter - *Collectors Classics Booklet No. B3*
 (Blues Unlimited, Bexhill-On-Sea, Sussex) 1964
Bokris, Victor - *Keith Richards: The Biography* (Hutchinson, London) 1992
Booth, Stanley - *Rythm Oil* (Jonathan Cape, London) 1991
Booth, Stanley - *Till I Roll Over Dead* (Headline, London) 1994
Bowker, R.R. – *Bowker's Complete Video Directory 2000* (R.R. Bowker, New Providence, NJ) 2000
Brady, Barry - *Reelin' And Rockin': The Golden Age Of Rock And Roll Movies*
 (Schwarze & Brady Graphics, Australia) 1982
Bronson, Fred - *Billboard's Hottest 'Hot 100' Hits* (Billboard Books, New York) 1995
Chilton, John - *Let The Good Times Roll: The Story Of Louis Jordan And His Music*
 (Quartet Books, London) 1992
Chilton, John - *Who's Who Of Jazz* (Papermac, London) 1989
Cimino, Al - *Great Record Labels* (Apple, London) 1992
Cohn, Lawrence *(ed)* - *Nothing But The Blues* (Abbeville Press, New York) 1993
Cohodas, Nadine - *Spinning Blues Into Gold: The Chess Brothers and the Legendary Chess*
 Records (St. Martin's Press, New York) 2000
Collier, James Lincoln - *Duke Ellington* (Pan, London) 1989
Collins, Tony - *Rock Mr. Blues: The Life And Music Of Wynonie Harris*
 (Big Nickel, Milford, New Hampshire) 1995
Colman, Stuart - *They Kept On Rockin'* (Blandford Press, London) 1982
Crenshaw, Marshall - *Hollywood Rock* (Plexus, London) 1994
Dance, Helen Oakley - *Stormy Monday: The T-Bone Walker Story* (Da Capo, New York) 1987
Daniels, William R. - *The American 45 & 78 rpm Record Dating Guide (1940-59)*
 (Greenwood Press, Westport, Connecticut) 1985
Davison, Jim, & Dave Marsh - *What Was The First Rock And Roll Record?*
 (Faber & Faber, London) 1992
Dellar, Fred - *Frank Sinatra: His Life And Times* (Omnibus, London) 1995
DeWitt, Howard, & Morten Reff - *Chuck Berry: Rock'n'Roll Music (second edition)*
 (Pierian Press, Ann Arbor, Michigan) 1985
Dixon, R.M.W., & J. Godrich - *Blues and Gospel Records 1902-1943*
 (Storyville, Chigwell, Essex) 1982
Downey, Pat, George Albert & Frank Hoffman – *Cash Box Pop Singles Charts 1950-1993*
 (Libraries Unlimited, Englewood, Colorado) 1994
Elliot, Martin - *The Rolling Stones Complete Recording Sessions* (Blandford Press, London) 1990
Engelhardt, Kristofer - *Beatles Undercover* (Collector's Guide Publishing, Toronto) 1998

Escott, Colin, with George Merritt and William McEwen - *Hank Williams: The Biography*
    (Little Brown, Boston/New York) 1994

Escott, Colin, & Martin Hawkins - *Good Rockin' Tonight: Sun Records and the Birth Of Rock'n' Roll*
    (Virgin, London) 1991

Ewan, David *(ed)* - *American Songwriters* (Robert Hale, London) 1987

Fancourt, Leslie - *British Blues On Record* (self-published, Faversham, Kent) 1989

Fancourt, Leslie - *Chess Blues Discography* (self-published, Faversham, Kent) 1983

Fancourt, Leslie - *Chess R&B Discography* (self-published, Faversham, Kent) 1984

Fitzpatrick, Travis - *The Father Of Rock & Roll: The Story Of Johnnie 'B. Goode' Johnson*
    (Thomas, Cooke & Co, Houston, Texas) 1999

Flanagan, Bill - *Written On My Soul* (Omnibus, London) 1990

Gambaccini, Paul, Tim Rice & Jonathan Rice - *Top 40 Charts* (Guinness, Enfield, Middlesex) 1992

Gambaccini, Paul, Tim Rice & Jonathan Rice - *British Hit Singles (8th edition)*
    (Guinness, Enfield, Middlesex) 1991

Garon, Paul & Beth - *Woman With Guitar: Memphis Minnie's Blues* (Da Capo, New York) 1992

Gart, Galen - *First Pressings: The History Of Rythm & Blues (Volume 4: 1954)*
    (Big Nickel, Milford, New Hampshire) 1990

Gart, Galen - *First Pressings: The History Of Rythm & Blues (Volume 5: 1955)*
    (Big Nickel, Milford, New Hampshire) 1990

Gart, Galen - *First Pressings, The History Of Rythm & Blues (Volume 6: 1956)*
    (Big Nickel, Milford, New Hampshire) 1991

Gart, Galen - *First Pressings, The History Of Rythm & Blues (Volume 7: 1957)*
    (Big Nickel, Milford, New Hampshire) 1993

Gart, Galen - *First Pressings: The History Of Rythm & Blues (Volume 8: 1958)*
    (Big Nickel, Milford, New Hampshire) 1995

Gordon, Robert - *It Came From Memphis* (Secker & Warburg, London) 1995

Gregory, Hugh Gregory - *Who's Who In Country Music* (Weidenfeld & Nicholson, London) 1993

Halliwell, Leslie / John Walker *(ed)* - *Halliwell's Film & Video Guide 2000*
    (Harper Collins Entertainment, London) 1999

Harris, Sheldon - *Blues Who's Who* (Da Capo, New York) 1987

Haskins, James, & Kathleen Benson - *Nat 'King' Cole: Man And His Music*
    (Robson Books, London) 1991

Hayes, Cedric, & Robert Laughton - *Gospel Records (1943-69) 2 volumes*
    (Record Information Services, London) 1992

Hoskyns, Barney - *Across the Great Divide: The Band and America* (Viking, London) 1993

Hounsome, Terry - *Rock Record 7* (self-published, Llandysul, Dyfed) 1997

Hounsome, Terry - *Single File* (self-published, Rosemarket, Dyfed) 1990

Humphries, John (ed) - *Music Master Tracks Catalogue*
    (John Humphries Publishing, Hastings, Sussex) 1989

Jackson, John A. - *Big Beat Heat: Alan Freed And The Early Years Of Rock & Roll*
    (Schirmer Books, New York) 1991

James, Etta, & David Ritz - *Rage To Survive* (Villard Books, New York) 1995

Jasper, Tony - *The Top Twenty Book* (Blandford, London) 1991

Joynson, Vernon - *A Tapestry Of Delights (third edition)*
    (Borderline Productions, Wolverhampton) 1995

Kinkle, Roger D. - *The Complete Encyclopedia of Popular Music and Jazz 1900-1950*
    (Arlington House, New Rochelle, NY) 1974 *4 volumes*

Langley, Graham *(ed)* - *Music Master Jazz & Blues Catalogue* (second edition)
    (Retail Entertainment Data Publishing Ltd, London) 1994

Larkin, Colin (ed) – *The Guinness Who's Who Of Country Music*
    (Guinness, Enfield, Middlesex) 1995

Larkin, Colin (ed) – *The Guinness Who's Who Of Sixties Music*
    (Guinness, Enfield, Middlesex) 1995

Larkin, Colin (ed) – The Guinness *Who's Who Of Reggae Music*
    (Guinness, Enfield, Middlesex) 1994

Leadbitter, Mike, & Neil Slaven - *Blues Records A-K (1943-70)*
    (Record Information Services, London) 1987

Leadbitter, Mike, Leslie Fancourt & Paul Pelletier - *Blues Records L-Z (1943-70)*
    (Record Information Services, London) 1994

Lewisohn, Mark - *The Complete Beatles Chronicle* (Hamlyn, London) 1995

Maltin, Leonard - *TV Movies & Video Guide* (Signet, New York) 1989

Lord, Tom - *The Jazz Discography* (Lord Music Reference Inc, West Vancouver) 1998
    (multiple volumes)

Lowe, Leslie *(ed)* - *Music Master Directory Of Popular Music* (Waterlow, London) 1992

Marsh, Dave - *The Heart Of Rock And Soul* (Plume, New York) 1989

McAleer, Dave - *Hit Parade Heroes: British Beat Before The Beatles* (Hamlyn, London) 1993

Jim Miller *(ed)* - *The Rolling Stone Illustrated History of Rock And Roll*
(Picador/Pan, London) 1981   [Chuck Berry chapter by Robert Christgau]

Murray, Charles Shaar - *Boogie Man* (Viking, Harmondsworth, Middlesex) 2000

Murray, Charles Shaar, & Neil Spencer - *Shots From The Hip*
(Penguin, Harmondsworth, Middlesex) 1991

Nichols, Richard - *American Sports Cars* (New Burlington, London) 1988

Norman, Philip - *Buddy: The Biography* (MacMillan, London) 1996

Parth, Johnny - *Document Records CD Catalogue* (self-published, Vienna, Austria) 1996

Pruter, Robert - *Doowop—The Chicago Scene*
(University of Illinois Press, Urbana & Chicago, Illinois) 1996

Pruter, Robert (ed) - *The Blackwell Guide To Soul Recordings* (Blackwell, Oxford) 1993

Reese, Krista - *Chuck Berry: Mr. Rock'n'Roll* (Proteus, New York) 1982

Rice, Jo and Tim, Paul Gambaccini & Mike Read - *The Guinness Book of British Hit Albums*
(Guinness Books, Enfield, Middlesex) 1983

Ruppli, Michel - *The Chess Labels [2 volumes]* (Greenwood Press, Westport, CT) 1983

Ruppli, Michel, & Ed Novitsky - *The Mercury Labels (Volume 3)*
(Greenwood Press, Westport, CT) 1993

Rust, Brian - *The American Dance Band Discography 1917-1942 [2 volumes]*
(Arlington House, New Rochelle, NY) 1975

Rust, Brian - *Jazz Records 1897-1942 [2 volumes]* (Storyville, London) 1969

Rust, Brian with Allen G. Debus - *The Complete Entertainment Discography mid-1890s to 1942*
(Arlington House, New Rochelle, NY) 1973

Sandahl, Linda J. - *Encylopedia Of Rock Music On Film* (Blandford Press, London) 1987

Shapiro, Nat, & Bruce Pollock *(eds)* - *Popular Music (1920-79): A Revised Cumulation*
(Gale, Detroit, Michigan) 1985

Shaw, Arnold - *The Rockin' 50s* (Da Capo, New York) 1987

Shaw, Shaw - *Honkers And Shouters* (Collier Books, New York) 1978

Shore, Michael, with Dick Clark - *The History of American Bandstand*
(Ballantine Books, New York) 1985

Sokolow, Fred - *Chuck Berry: Recorded Guitar Versions* (Goodman Group, New York)

Smith, Steve - *Rock Day By Day* (Guinness, Enfield, Middlesex) 1987

Snowden, Don - *I Am The Blues: The Willie Dixon Story* (Da Capo, New York) 1990

Stacy, Jan, & Ryder Syvertsen - *Rockin' Reels* (Contemporary Books Inc, Chicago) 1984

Tooze, Sandra B. - *Muddy Waters: The Mojo Man* (E.C.W. Press, Toronto) 1997

Tosches, Nick - *Unsung Heroes Of Rock'n'Roll* (Secker & Warburg, London) 1991

Topping, Ray - *New Orleans R&B Record Label Listing*
(Flyright Records, Bexhill-On-Sea, Sussex) 1978

Townley, Eric - *Tell Your Story* (Storyville, Chigwell, Essex) 1976

Vernon, Paul - *African-American Blues, Rhythm & Blues, Gospel and Zydeco on Film and Video,*
1925-97 (Ashgate Publishing Company, Aldershot, Hants) 1999

Welding, Pete, & Toby Byron *(eds)* - *Bluesland: Portraits Of Twelve Major American Blues Masters*
(Dutton/Penguin, Harmondsworth, Middlesex) 1991
[*Berryland* chapter by Bob Blumenthal]

Whitburn, Joel - *Bubbling Under The Hot 100 (1959-81)*
(Record Research, Menomonee Falls, WI) 1982

Whitburn, Joel - *Top Pop (1955-82)* (Record Research, Menomonee Falls, WI) 1983

Whitburn, Joel - *Top Pop Albums (1955-92)* (Record Research, Menomonee Falls, WI) 1993

Whitburn, Joel - *Top R&B Singles (1942-88)* (Record Research, Menomonee Falls, WI) 1988

Whitburn, Joel - *Top R&B Albums (1965-98)* (Record Research, Menomonee Falls, WI) 1999

White, George R. - *The Complete Bo Diddley Sessions* (self-published, Bradford, W Yorks) 1993

White, George R. - *Bo Diddley: Living Legend* (Castle Communications, Chessington, Surrey) 1995

White, George R. - *(35 Years Of) British Hit EPs* (Music Mentor Books, York) 2001

White, Timothy - *Rock Lives* (Omnibus, London) 1991

Wight, Phil, & Fred Rothwell - *The Complete Muddy Waters Discography*
(Blues & Rhythm, Cheadle, Cheshire) 1990

Wyman, Bill, with Ray Coleman - *Stone Alone: The Story Of A Rock'n'Roll Band*
(Penguin, Harmondsworth, Middlesex) 1991

PERIODICALS

American Music [Sweden] - various issues
The Big Beat [Australia] No. 37 *Roll Over Beethoven, Dig These Rhythm And Blues* (unknown)
Billboard [USA] various 1998 issues
Boppin' News [UK] No. 4 (Spring 1965) *The Quiet Man's Corner—News From Chuck Berry* (unk)
Black Echoes [UK] 29 April 1977 (unknown)
Block [Netherlands] No. 15 - July/August 1977 *Chuck In Lochem* (unknown)
Blues Bag [UK] No. 1 (September 1989), No. 2 (December 1989) and No. 3 (March 1990)
        Chuck Berry—In Retrospect (three parts) (Pete O'Gorman)
Blues & Rhythm [UK] various issues, mainly record and concert reviews.
Blue Suede News [USA] No. 53 (Winter 2000/01) *Forty-Seven Miles Of Barbed Wire: The Story*
        Of Boogie Bob (Dennis A. Blackledge)
Blues Unlimited [UK] various issues including No. 142 *Marshall Chess Shoots The Breeze*
        (Ray Topping and George White)
Cream [UK] March 1972 *Big Red Cars, Little White Chicks And The Chuck Berry Lick*
        (Charles Shaar Murray)
Daily Telegraph [UK] 2 December 1991 *Chucking It In* (David Cheal)
Disc Weekly [UK] 16 January 1965 *Chuck Berry Getting To Old?* (Rod Harrod)
DISCoveries [USA] December 1988 *Walking Down Broadway* (George A. Moonoogian)
Filofax [UK] various issues *Record Reviews* (Pete O'Gorman)
Goldmine [USA] November 1979 *Chuck Berry—An Exclusive Goldmine Interview* (Dan Fries)
      November 1983 *Chuck Berry—A Conversation With Mr. Rock'n'Roll*
        (John Etheredge)
      13 December 1991 *Chuck Berry—And The Joint Was Rockin'* (Cub Koda)
Guitar Player [USA] February 1971 *Exclusive: Chuck Berry* (Fred Stuckley)
       June 1984 *The Chuck Berry Style—A Modern Rocker Pays Tribute To*
        The Master' (Rick Vito)
       March 1988 *Chuck Berry—The Story—The Interview—The Guitar That Shook*
        The World—The Records (Tom Wheeler)
Jazz Beat [UK] No. 4 (April 1964) *A Chuck Berry Recording Session* (Guy Stevens)
Jefferson [Sweden] No. 63 (1983) *Scandinavian Blues Discography* (Tommy Holmström)
Let It Rock [UK] 1973 *Cruisin' And Playin' The Radio* (Ian Hoare)
       The Dark Ages 5–10 BC (Charlie Gillett)
       Records—The Classic Years (Malcolm Jones)
       Records—The Later Years (Philip Parr)
       Back In The UK (John Pidgeon)
       Bootleg Basement (Tony Martin)
Little Richard News [Germany] Nos. 20-21 (July 1999) *Tour Review* (John Garodkin)
Living Blues [USA] various issues, mainly record reviews
Melody Maker [UK] 16 December 1972 *Chuck Berry Speaks* (Patrick William Salvo)
       28 July 1979 *I Looked At My Watch...* (Michael Watts)
       23 June 1979 *Echoes Column—Blue Suede News* (Stuart Colman)
       28 July 1979 *Echoes Column—Blue Suede News* (Stuart Colman)
Music Collector [UK] May 1991 *Chuck Berry's Golden Decade* (Derek Bull)
Music Now [UK] 6 December 1969 *The Plastic Ono Band Live! In Concert In Toronto* (Roy Carr)
Musician [Canada] October 1988 *Keith Richards Takes Unlimited Action* (Charles M. Young)
New Musical Express [UK] 11 October 1969 *Canada's Toronto Turns On Rock* (Roy Carr)
       12 February 1972 *Berry Magic* (Tony Stewart)
       17 and 24 February 1973 *Go, Chuck, Go—We Just Can't Keep Up*
        With You (Charlie Gillett)
       24 February 1974 *How Many Comebacks* (Charlie Gillett)
       29 April 1977 *Chuck Berry—New Victoria Gig* (Paul Rambali)
       28 July 1979 *Woke Up This Morning.... Reelin 'n' Rockin 'n' Jazzin 'n'*
        A-Bluesin' (Nick Kent)
Now Dig This [UK] various issues including a two-part 65th birthday tribute to Chuck (*Y'know, I'm*
      Almost Grown by Pete O'Gorman) and *The Films Of Chuck Berry* (Trevor
      Cajiao) - September 1983
Peterborough Local Press [UK] September 1983 *The Legend Lives On* (Sandra Dane)
Pickin' The Blues [UK] various issues

Q Magazine [UK] 1997 *The Life Of A Ladies Man* (Paul Du Noyer)
Record Collector [UK] various issues
Record Mirror [UK] 16 January 1965 *Chuck Berry Goes Down A Bomb On R&B Tour* (unknown)
30 January 1965 *Berry Favourites* (Peter Meaden)
2 July 1965 *When Chuck Snubbed The Rolling Stones* (James Craig)
4 March 1967 *Rock Lives!* (Norman Jopling)
15 April 1972 *You Rock And Roll Chauffeur* (Rob Mackie)
The Riverfront Times [St. Louis, USA] 22-28 October 1986 *The Hottest Ticket In Town, To The Worst Show Of The Year* (Susan Hegger)
Rolling Stone [USA] 14 June 1969 *Roll Over, Chuck Berry* (Greil Marcus)
23 November 1972 (Patrick William Salvo)
3 December 1987 *Chuck Berry Tells All* (Vince Aletti)
Soul [UK] No. 3 (1966) *The Pride & Joy Of Chuck Berry — This Is Berry Park* (unknown)
Sounds [UK] 15 April 1972 *Faithful To Rock And Roll* (Martin Hayman)
17 February 1973 *Chuck Berry Interview* (Martin Hayman)
St. Louis Post-Dispatch [USA] 26 March 1989 *Blaze Destroys Chuck Berry's Studio* (Carolyn Bower)
13 January 1994 *The Joint Jumpers: Veteran Musicians Still Rocking The Blues* (Paul Hampel)
31 May 1996 *Chuck Berry Rocks Rally In Czech Republic* (Jeffrey Brown)
15 October 1996 *Chuck Berry Will Perform At Blueberry Hill For His Birthday* (unknown)
20 October 1996 *Still Rockin' — Chuck Berry Packs House On 70th Birthday* (Chris Dickinson)
18 May 1998 *Walk Of Fame Inductees Include Schoendienst, Gass* (Marianna Riley)
Tour programme [UK] 1965 (unknown)
Unknown newspaper [UK] June 1973 *This Is America—Elephants Behind Berry* (Linda Solomon)
Zig-Zag [UK] Winter 1970 *I May Go Down Sometime But I Come Back To Rock'n'Roll* (unknown)

RECORDS & CDs

Colin Escott - unpublished essay for aborted Bear Family box set (what a shame!)
Andy McKaie & Billy Altman - *The Chess Box* booklet [Chess/MCA CHD3-80002] USA, 1989
Adam Komorowski - *The Chess Years* booklet [Charly CDREDBOX-2] UK ,1992
... plus dozens of other LP covers and CD inserts

WEBSITES

Chess Catalog: Blues, Rhythm And Roll
http://www.mca.com.mcarecords/library/chesscatalog.html

Chuck Berry Biography (Webmaster: Bruce Pegg)
http://www2.colgate.edu/diw/pegg/CBDiscography.html

Chuck Berry US Discography (Webmaster: Bruce Pegg)
http://departments.colgate.edu/pegg/CBDiscography.html

A Collector's Guide To The Music Of Chuck Berry (Webmaster: Dietmar Rudolph)
http://www.crlf.de/ChuckBerry

Chuck Berry News (Webmaster: Johan Hasselberg)
http://www.geocities.com/allaboard70

9

Indexes to the Sessionography

INDEX OF PEOPLE'S NAMES

Excluding Chuck Berry who is, of course, omnipresent.
Numbers refer to sessions.
Emboldened numbers indicate that the artist played on the session.

INDEX OF SONGS AND ALBUM TITLES

Numbers refer to sessions.
Emboldened number indicates that the song was recorded at the session.
For ease of reference, album titles are prefixed with ◻ (EPs), ◼ (LPs) or ◉ (CDs).

INDEX OF RECORD LABELS AND MUSIC PUBLISHING COMPANIES

Numbers refer to sessions.
Emboldened number indicates the original release label of songs cut at the session.

INDEX OF RECORDING LOCATIONS

Numbers refer to sessions.
Emboldened number indicates that the session was cut at this location.

INDEX OF OTHER LOCATIONS

Numbers refer to sessions.

INDEX OF FILMS AND SHOWS

Names of films, festivals, tours and TV and radio shows.
Numbers refer to sessions.

INDEX OF PEOPLE'S NAMES

INDEX OF SONGS AND ALBUM TITLES

338

INDEX OF RECORD LABELS
AND MUSIC PUBLISHING COMPANIES

INDEX OF RECORDING LOCATIONS

Oberhausen, Germany
Oberhausen Arena *(concert venue)* **92**
Okemos, Michigan
Lansing Sound Studio *(recording studio)* **58**
Peterborough, England
Wirrina Sports Stadium *(concert venue)* **85**
Philadelphia, Pennsylvania
WBC-TV *(TV studio)* **61**
Reseda, California
Wolf & Rismiller's Country Club *(concert venue)* **78**
St. Louis, Missouri
4221 W. Easton Avenue *(Chuck Berry's office)* **18**
CBC *[Chuck Berry Communications] (recording studio)* **71**
Fox Theatre *(concert venue)* **87, 88**
Premier Studio *(recording studio)* **1**
San Francisco, California
916 Kearny Street *(recording studio)* **51, 52**
Fillmore Auditorium *(concert venue)* 2, 44, **48, 49,** 58
Tokyo, Japan
Onkyo Haus No. 3 Studio *(recording studio)* **82**
Shibuya Kokaido *(concert venue)* **80**
Shinjuku Koseinenkin Hall *(concert venue)* **79**
Toronto, Canada
Varsity Stadium *(concert venue)* **54**
Wentzville, Missouri
Berry Park clubhouse *(rehearsal venue)* **86**
Berry Park studio *(recording studio)* 9, 27, 43, **53,** 58, **71, 75, 76,** 86
Yokohama, Japan
Yokohama Stadium *(concert venue)* **82**

INDEX OF OTHER LOCATIONS

INDEX OF FILMS AND SHOWS

ILLUSTRATIONS AND PHOTO CREDITS

Ad on page 20 courtesy of Galen Gart's *First Pressings 1954*; ad on page 24 courtesy of Galen Gart's *First Pressings 1955*; ads on pages 27, 55, 69, 71, 78 and 85 courtesy of George R. White; ads on pages 29, 41, 77, 82, 90, 104, 111, 126, 129, 293, 294 and 304 courtesy of Bill Millar; ads on pages 30 and 34 courtesy of Galen Gart's *First Pressings 1956*; ad on page 44 courtesy of Galen Gart's *First Pressings 1957*; ads on pages 48, 59 and 62 courtesy of Galen Gart's *First Pressings 1958*; ad on page 296 courtesy of Paramount Pictures/George R. White.

Album cover shots on pages 83, 150, 168, 191, 206, 231 and 235 courtesy of Dietmar Rudolph; album cover shot on page 181 courtesy of George R. White; album cover shots on pages 134, 156, 165, 185, 194, 203, 215, 218, 221, 228, 238, 240, 250, 255 and 260 from author's collection.

Label shots on pages 21, 97, 116, 118, 127, 148, 175 and 195 from author's collection; label shots on pages 31 and 160 courtesy of Dietmar Rudolph; label shot on page 75 and picture sleeve on page 114 courtesy of Keith Tillman; label shot on page 142 courtesy of Steve Armitage; label shot on page 162 courtesy of Morten Reff.

Photos on front cover, back cover and pages 32, 120, 122, 123, 138, 143, 153, 254, 258 and 262 by Brian Smith (Courtesy of Brian Smith); photo on page 21 by unknown photographer (Courtesy of Chess Records); photo on page 65 by Chuck Stewart (Courtesy of Colin Escott/Showtime Archives (Toronto)); photo on page 72 by unknown photographer (Courtesy of Hal Roach Distribution Corp/Showtime Archives (Toronto)); photo on page 94 by unknown photographer (Courtesy of Hal Roach Distribution Corp/Raven Design); photos on pages 106, 108 and 109 by unknown photographer (Courtesy of Chess Records/John Garodkin); photo on page 119 by unknown photographer (Courtesy of Chess Records); photo on page 131 by unknown photographer (Courtesy of Pye Records/Bill Millar); photo on page 166 by Robert Altman (Courtesy of Mercury Records); photo on page 173 by unknown photographer (Courtesy of Chess Records); photo on page 178 by unknown photographer (Courtesy of Chess Records/Showtime Archives (Toronto)); photo on page 188 by unknown photographer (Courtesy of Columbia Pictures/John Beecher/Now Dig This); photos on pages 213 and 222 by Paul Harris (Courtesy of Paul Harris).

Sheet music covers on pages 23, 35, 40, 49 and 67 courtesy of Arc Music Corporation/ Showtime Archives (Toronto).

OTHER TITLES FROM MUSIC MENTOR BOOKS

IN CATALOGUE

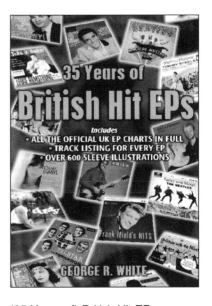

The Complete Bo Diddley Sessions
George R. White
ISBN 0 9519888 0 8

(35 Years of) British Hit EPs
George R. White
ISBN 0 9519888 1 6

FORTHCOMING PUBLICATIONS

The Complete Bo Diddley Sessions (1993-99 Supplement)
George R. White
ISBN 0 9519888 3 2

Available from all good bookshops or by mail order from:

Music Mentor Books
69 Station Road
Upper Poppleton
YORK YO26 6PZ
England

Telephone/Fax: 01904 330308
International Telephone/Fax: +44 1904 330308
email: musicmentor@bun.com

Visit our website for more details plus latest news:
http://www.go.to/musicmentor